D1004200

A CENTURY OF

GEORGE ELIOT

CRITICISM

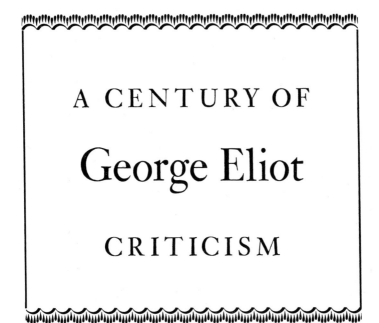

A CENTURY OF

George Eliot

CRITICISM

EDITED BY

GORDON S. HAIGHT

Yale University

HOUGHTON MIFFLIN COMPANY

Boston

Contents

Introduction

Sir Edmund Gosse in his centenary article on George Eliot (1919) declares that all her rivals — the Brontës, Mrs. Gaskell, Dickens, Thackeray, Kingsley, Reade — had died off before she began to publish. "Hence the field was left free for George Eliot, who, without haste or hesitation, built up slowly such a reputation as no one in her own time approached." Gosse's statements are almost always inaccurate, and this is no exception. Of the novelists he lists, only the Brontës had died before her first novel appeared. Her reputation was not "built up slowly," but established overnight by *Adam Bede*, which *The Times* called "a first-rate novel," adding that "its author takes rank at once among the masters of the art" — high praise from *The Thunderer*. The long review filling three whole columns ended with some speculation of who the unknown Mr. George Eliot might be. "Is all this mature thought, finished portraiture, and crowd of characters the product of a 'prentice hand and of callow genius? If it is, the hand must have an extraordinary cunning, and the genius must be of the highest order."

There were cogent reasons for George Eliot's anonymity in the condescension Victorian reviewers habitually assumed towards women authors and in her ambiguous position as "Mrs. Lewes." But her place as a serious artist was firmly established at the start. In reviewing *The Mill on the Floss*, her second novel, *The Times* drew the distinction that George Eliot was "attempting not merely to amuse us, as a novelist, but, as a preacher, to make us think and feel," thus early striking the moral note which was used to condemn her novels at the turn of the century and, fifty years later, to raise them to the peak of the Great Tradition. The praise continued without faltering over *Silas Marner*. That an author "should be able to produce a series of works so good in so very peculiar a style," said the *Saturday Review*, "is as remarkable as anything that has occurred in the history of English literature in this century."

But with *Romola*, which had appeared serially in the *Cornhill Magazine*, there were reservations, many of which are still heard today. It was felt that "sometimes the antiquarian quite drowns the novelist," and that the morality, particularly with regard to sexual relations, was more typical of the nineteenth century than the fifteenth. To most historical novels of the time — *Westward Ho!*, *The Cloister and the Hearth*, or *A Tale of Two Cities* — the same objections might have been made; but they were drawn with stronger contrasts and more generous mixtures of melodrama, and were rarely scrutinized in the cold critical light that was turned on *Romola*. The sharp division of George Eliot's novels into those that are praised for their "charm" and those that appeal to the intellect began with *Romola*. Praise for it came from those who were looking for more than entertainment in fiction. "It cannot be denied that *Romola* is less popular than its predecessors," began the *Westminster Review*, "but we do not hesitate to say that it is its author's greatest work." Yet even the staunch defenders were pleased when in *Felix Holt* George Eliot returned to "the charm of the old touch." *The Times* reviewer, E. S. Dallas, spoke with satisfaction of the "depth and range of George Eliot's sympathies" and the "wondrous charm of her style. . . . We don't know any Englishman who can be placed near her as a writer of prose."

Perhaps the most exacting critic of the book was Henry James, who with the confident rigor of an anonymous twenty-three-year-old reviewed it for the New York *Nation*. He could praise George Eliot's firm delineation of character, her extensive human sympathy, her humor, her morality, and her exquisite rhetoric based on ample and active knowledge. But as a story he found *Felix Holt* "singularly inartistic." Mrs. Transome, one of the book's creative triumphs, seemed to James "an unnatural, or rather we should say, a superfluous figure." Here as in all his comments on George Eliot's novels, James objected to "that disproportion between the meagre effect of the whole and the vigorous character of the different parts, which stamp them as the works of a secondary thinker and an incomplete artist." He was inclined in his reviews to rewrite every one of George Eliot's works to secure the single unified theme that was to distinguish his own. That she should be "offered a higher place than she has earned is easily explained by the charm which such gifts as hers in such abundance are sure to exercise," he concluded, ranking her with Maria Edgeworth and Jane Austen, "though stronger in degree" than either of them. She has "the microscopic observation," but not the "great synthetic guesses with which a real master attacks the truth" — a judgment somewhat vitiated by his example: Charles Reade, "to our mind the most readable of living English novelists" and "a distant kinsman of Shakespeare." In the *Atlantic* two months later in a signed article on "The Novels of George Eliot" James spoke more discriminatingly. *Silas Marner* he pronounced "more nearly a masterpiece" than any of the others because "it has more of that simple, rounded, consummate aspect, that absence of loose ends and gaping issues, which marks a classical work." He recognized George Eliot as "a humorist and something of a satirist"; though she is neither Dickens nor Thackeray, she "has over them the great advantage that she is also a good deal of a philosopher."

Another young critic, Edward Dowden, was less constrained than James by preconceived ideas of what a novel should be. He was the first, I believe, to discuss the important part that the author's voice plays in the novels; he saw it adding to the power with which they grasp the heart and conscience of the reader, but not interfering with the dramatic truthfulness. It is the voice, not of the "real George Eliot," but of a persona, "that 'second self' who writes her books and lives and speaks through them." Defending her against the charge of excessive didacticism, he treated her novels as works of art in which the moral significance coalesces with the narrative. In a second article Dowden treated *Middlemarch* and *Daniel Deronda*.

George Eliot's reputation reached its peak with *Middlemarch*. Edith Simcox justly declared in the *Academy* that it "marks an epoch in the history of fiction in so far as its incidents are taken from the inner life" and "as giving a background of perfect realistic truth to a profoundly imaginative psychological study." James, though disappointed again that the story was not "the organized, moulded, balanced composition" that he would have made it, praised the "constant presence of thought, of generalizing instinct, of *brain*, in a word, behind her observation," denoting "a mind in which imagination is illumined by faculties rarely found in fellowship with it. . . . George Eliot seems to us among English romancers to stand alone. Fielding approaches her, but to our mind she surpasses Fielding. Fielding was didactic — the author of *Middlemarch* is really philosophical." But his praise is not unmingled with strictures. He adds ominously that her style, rich and flexible as it is, is apt to betray her when she tries to say things "to recommend herself to a scientific audience," and we read with amusement that the author of *The Wings of the Dove* and *The Sacred Fount* marked a dozen passages in *Middlemarch* "obscure." His final judgment of the novel was high: "It sets a limit, we think, to the development of the old-fashioned English novel."

With *Daniel Deronda* the tide of acclaim began to turn, and there was a good deal of outspoken disapproval of the Jewish part of the story. Some of the more perceptive critics saw its power: Hutton predicted that it might one day be regarded as George Eliot's greatest work, and Dowden defended her against the silly objection that had been taken to her use of "scientific" words like *dynamic* and *natural selection*. (Samuel Butler's friend Eliza Savage quipped that she had bought a dictionary because "I wished to read *Daniel Deronda* in the original.") Henry James, who had looked forward eagerly to the book, concealed the sharpest edge of his disapproval in the clever dialogue "*Daniel Deronda*: A Conversation," where behind the thin disguise of Constantius he pronounced it the weakest of George Eliot's books, "very sensibly inferior to *Middlemarch*." There were, of course, good things in it; James found Gwendolen and Grandcourt admirable — Gwendolen "a masterpiece"; but Deronda, Mordecai, and Mirah "are hardly more than shadows." Occasionally Constantius fathers an epigram that foreshadows Oscar Wilde, but the brightest and most damaging criticisms of the book he puts into the mouth of Pulcheria, who, he adds apologetically, is "sadly aesthetic."

An undercurrent of detraction had been heard privately in aesthetic circles for a long time. Butler wrote Miss Savage when the praise of *Middlemarch* was at its height: "I call it bad, and not interesting: there is no sweetness in the whole book," while to his sister he complained that the characters "are not lovable" — curious remarks from a man just then beginning to sketch the Pontifex family. Stopford Brooke told his wife that *Middlemarch* was "inferior to any other of George Eliot's works." Anthony Trollope confided to his *Autobiography* a doubt "whether any young person can read with pleasure either *Felix Holt*, *Middlemarch*, or *Daniel Deronda*. I know that they are very difficult to many that are not young." Some sentences he was compelled to read three times before understanding them. After George Eliot's death in 1880 such negative opinions came into the open. In a commemorative article for the *Cornhill* Leslie Stephen set the conventional view: the novels before *Romola* "have the unmistakable mark of high genius"; the later ones suffer increasingly from the "tendency to substitute elaborate analysis for direct presentation, failure of imagination, and lack of charm." Even in *Middlemarch* Stephen did not think she had regained "the old magic." And of *Daniel Deronda* he found it kinder to say little; he omits the title from the list of works by which George Eliot would be remembered. Cross's life of George Eliot in 1885 seemed to confirm the image of the portentous Victorian moralist. Cross had known her only in her most sibylline years, and sought out the sententious passages in her letters for publication, omitting the natural, humorous touches that would have relieved his somber portrait. Most of his readers were disappointed at the absence of personal "revelations" about her private life, and repelled by the marmoreal image of the learned writer presented in Cross's volumes. Of the many reviews Lord Acton's carefully composed essay, combining lofty admiration with profound criticism, was the most discriminating. But it did nothing to change the downward course of George Eliot's reputation.

A new generation had taken over, living for the moment, "curiously testing new opinions and courting new impressions," as Pater put it, "never acquiescing in a facile orthodoxy," which belief in George Eliot had become. "Ah! if she had been less purposeful!" exclaimed George

Moore. The iconoclastic Henley, puffing *Prince Otto* and *Kidnapped*, reacted excessively to the supposed lack of masculinity in George Eliot's "heroes of the divided skirt" and professed himself uncertain whether she wrote "novels disguised as treatises or treatises disguised as novels." Comments on George Eliot from this circle, few of whom had ever seen her, tended towards personal allusions to her supposed plainness, her horse face, and her grotesque dress; their knowledge of her novels grew dimmer with the years. Moore, who to keep up with the fashion removed the warm praise of George Eliot from his *Confessions of a Young Man* (1888) when he reprinted it in 1904, tells of Silas Marner's going with a lantern to find the child — was it a boy or a girl? — at his door. Oliver Elton similarly mentions a melodramatic scene "where Eppie chances on the discovery of the long-murdered body" of Dunstan Cass. In 1896 Arnold Bennett "dipped into *Adam Bede*, and my impression that George Eliot will never be among the classical writers was made a certainty."

Though her novels were out of fashion they were never entirely neglected. Countless children continued to weep over Maggie Tulliver, and *Silas Marner* was always prescribed reading in school. No decade passed without critical studies of George Eliot. Mathilde Blind and George Willis Cooke had anticipated Cross with biographies in 1883; Oscar Browning followed in 1890. Clara Thomson in 1901 and Leslie Stephen in 1902 were paralleled by the long critical studies of W. C. Brownell and H. H. Bonnell in the same years. Saintsbury, Frederic Harrison, Howells, and a dozen others made contributions. Anyone who wishes to see the extent of writing about her must consult the valuable supplementary bibliography compiled by Professor James Donald Barry,[1] which lists hundreds of articles. The centenary in 1919 brought Virginia Woolf's essay in the *Times Literary Supplement*, articles by H. C. Minchin and E. A. Parry in the *Fortnightly*, by Wilbur Cross in the *Yale Review*, and a series of articles by May Tomlinson in the *Sewanee Review*. During the 1920s, when other Victorians were rediscovered, George Eliot remained in eclipse. Her insistence on moral principles bored a generation that had done with morality. The new materialism denied the inevitable consequences her novels insist upon: modern technology seemed fairly bent to control man's destiny. The height of this confidence marked the low ebb of her reputation.

The tradition that George Eliot was unreadable and unread lived on till after the Second World War. Lord David Cecil says in his

---

[1] "The Literary Reputation of George Eliot's Fiction," *Bulletin of Bibliography*, 22 (1959), 176–182. A judicious survey of George Eliot scholarship by W. J. Harvey is found in *Victorian Fiction* (1964), edited by Professor Lionel Stevenson.

Early Victorian Novelists (1934), "It is not just that she is not read, that her books stand on the shelves unopened. If people do read her, they do not enjoy her." He attributed this to her moral point of view. "The virtues of her admiration, industry, self-restraint, conscientious-ness, are drab, negative sort of virtues; they are school-teachers' vir-tues"; and to see her confronting human nature with them made him feel rebellious and resentful. Ten years later when Dr. F. R. Leavis be-gan his revaluation of George Eliot, he saw the moral element as the essence of her superiority. Her reputation has now risen to the point where many authorities place her again in the very top rank of Eng-lish novelists. All her novels except *Felix Holt* have become available in numerous inexpensive editions, and one seldom hears that they are unreadable or unread. Critical and biographical studies have pro-liferated. In 1959 alone there were three volumes of criticism, two dissertations, and more than a dozen articles about her works, and the interest shows little sign of subsiding.

With this wealth of material and the limited space available it has been difficult to make selections for this volume, especially from the more recent work. Though I had the advice of several of the fore-most scholars in the field, I do not mean to suggest that these neces-sarily comprise "the best of George Eliot criticism." Some of the ex-tracts are obviously bad, but are included to show the fluctuation of her reputation. One or two rather technical articles like Axon's on George Eliot's use of dialects and Rendall's on her knowledge of the classics I have reprinted because they are inaccessible and deserve to be better known. I hope that the authors will forgive the editorial lib-erties taken to normalize the use of quotation marks, italics, and ref-erences. A few typographical errors, chiefly in the spelling of the names of characters, have been silently corrected. But all other edi-torial alterations except the points indicating ellipses are enclosed in square brackets. For example, on page 83 where James describes Mr. Casaubon as sinning by "lack of order," I have ventured to emend the text (of which James never saw a proof) to "lack of [ardor]." Few of the extracts are printed complete. Of the long review of *Adam Bede* in *The Times* less than a fifth is given here. To save space I have omitted most of the footnotes and many of the long illustrative quota-tions from George Eliot's works when the thread of argument could be followed clearly without them. If this sometimes seems unfair to the authors, I would plead that my aim is not to supersede the original critiques but to guide readers back to the complete text by setting the extracts in the perspective of the century.

Pierson College   GORDON S. HAIGHT
Yale University

[Samuel Lucas]

Scenes of Clerical Life

... Of the other recent fiction we have been most impressed with the series of *Scenes of Clerical Life*, which have been just reprinted from *Blackwood's Magazine*, and which are now claimed by Mr. George Eliot – a name unknown to us. It is quite possible that this may be a mere *nom de plume*, and we are not curious to inquire at all upon this point. But we should be greatly surprised to hear that the real writer was previously known under any other appelation, for, like others who have speculated on his identity while these tales were publishing, we cannot assign his peculiarities to any living novelist. Were these the early days of Galt or Lockhart, or could even Crabbe come back from the grave in a softer mood and with a resolve to discard versification for prose, we should have some basis for conjecture; but now we have none. We lay no particular stress on the parochial limits of the scene and the parochial relations of its occupants. We observe only that the sources of interest are chiefly domestic and homely and that there is a careful study of familiar types and an absence of exaggeration in their treatment which recall the productions of a school of fiction akin to that of Wilkie in pictorial art. A sobriety which is shown to be compatible with strength, clear and simple descriptions, and a combination of humour with pathos in depicting ordinary situations, are characteristics of this school, and are evinced by Mr. Eliot.

Of the three stories comprised in these clerical scenes, we prefer the "Rev. Mr. Gilfil's Love Story" to "The Sad Fortunes of the Rev. Amos Barton," or to "Janet's Repentance." It has the peculiarity of being a retrospect commencing from Mr. Gilfil's death, and we are drawn into it from an intimation of what the hero became in the decline of life, when his wound was cicatrized and love had given place to softened regret. The picture of Mr. Gilfil at this latter stage is charmingly painted with firm and effective touches, and, as Sir Walter Scott said of the Wakefield Vicar, though each touch serves to show that he is made of mortal mould and is full of human frailties, the effect of the whole is to reconcile us to human nature. The charm, too, is sustained by an adherence to probability and by the allowance

Reprinted from *The Times*, 2 January 1858, p. 9.

1

for influences which the incidents alone do not involve, but which we know to make up a large proportion of every man's life. The artificial elements of the story are thus kept within bounds, the tendency to sacrifice to their exigencies is compensated by a reference to the actual results of experience, and a closer resemblance than usual is thus established between the conceptions of fiction and the realities of the world. . . .

[Summaries of the three stories with long excerpts fill nearly two columns.]

The opening chapter gives the portrait which we so much admire of Mr. Gilfil towards the close of his long widowhood. Here the author rejects the conventional usage of representing a bereaved hero as unhappy ever after. There is a closed chamber at the vicarage into which as the sanctuary of his dearest recollections Mr. Gilfil occasionally enters, but apart from which he takes an interest not only in the duties but in the pleasures of life which still remain to him. In his parish he is rather exemplary than over-zealous; he is social and pleasant with the farmers, acceptable to the gentry, considerate to the poor, and an especial favourite with children, which latter peculiarity, with his liking for a pipe and gin-and-water, more particularly distinguish him from the ordinary heroes of romance in similar circumstances. We take our leave, therefore, of this worthy pastor with the sincerest respect even for the artifices by which he obtains favours with the juveniles, which was, indeed, only a part of "that good understanding which the Vicar had always enjoyed with the rest of his parishioners, from the generation whose children he had christened a quarter of a century before down to that hopeful generation represented by little Tommy Bond. . . ." A writer who can work out his simple theme thus quietly and effectively needs no further commendation or exhibition on our part.

[Eneas Sweetland Dallas]

Adam Bede

There can be no mistake about *Adam Bede*. It is a first-rate novel, and its author takes rank at once among the masters of the art.

Reprinted from *The Times*, 12 April 1859, p. 5.

Hitherto known but as the writer of certain tales to which he gave
the modest title of *Scenes,* and which displayed only the buds of what
we have here in full blossom, he has produced a work which, after
making every allowance for certain crudities of execution, impresses
us with a sense of the novelist's maturity of thought and feeling. Very
seldom are so much freshness of style and warmth of emotion seen
combined with so much solid sense and ripened observation. We
have a pleasant feeling of security in either laughing or crying
with such a companion. Our laughter shall not be trifling, and
our tears shall not be maudlin. We need not fear to yield ourselves entirely to all the enchantments of the wizard whose first
article of belief is the truism which very few of us comprehend until
it has been knocked into us by years of experience — that we are all
alike — that the human heart is one. All the novelists and all the
dramatists that have ever lived have set themselves to exhibit the
differences between man and man. Here, they seem to say, are circumstances precisely similar, and yet mark how various are the characters which grow out of these circumstances. . . . It is in the
enunciation of this difficult truism that Mr. Thackeray differs from
all previous novelists. It is the supreme motive of all that he has
written, and the key to all the criticism that has been poured upon
him. . . . A novelist, writing in accordance with this philosophy, has
a most difficult task to perform. It is comparatively easy to draw a
character so long as we dwell mainly on points of difference and
contrast. But when the object is to touch lightly on mere peculiarities, and to dwell mainly on those traits which we have all in common,
and, which, therefore, are anything but salient, the difficulty of the
task is enormously increased.

We do not mean for one moment to detract from Mr. George
Eliot's originality when we say that after his own fashion he follows
this difficult path in which Mr. Thackeray leads the way. He has
fully reached that idea which it is so easy to confess in words, but so
hard to admit into the secret heart, that we are all alike, that our
natures are the same, and that there is not the mighty difference
which is usually assumed between high and low, rich and poor, the
fool and the sage, the best of us and the worst of us. In general, it is
only matured minds that reach this state of feeling — minds that have
gone through a good deal and seen through a good deal; and our
author has precisely this broad sympathy and large tolerance combined with ripe reflection and finished style, which we admire in Mr.
Thackeray. Here the comparison ends. Mr. Eliot differs so widely
from Mr. Thackeray in his mode of working out the philosophy
which is common to both that some of our readers may wonder how
we could ever see a resemblance between him and the great painter

of human vanities and weakness. Whereas Mr. Thackeray is, to the great disgust of many young ladies, continually asserting that we have all got an evil corner in our hearts, and little deceitful ways of working, Mr. Eliot is good enough to tell us that we have all a remnant of Eden in us, that people are not so bad as is commonly supposed, and that every one has affectionate fibres in his nature — fine, loveable traits, in his character. . . . But, although tending to such opposite results, the principle upon which both novelists work is the same. . . .

The story is simple enough, and as far as the mere skeleton is concerned, soon told. For the sake of introducing a fair young Methodist who has the gift of preaching, the date of the incidents is thrown to the end of last century, but the time is not strictly observed, and we are not very much surprised to be informed that Bartle Massey "lighted a match furiously on the hob," which is far from being the only anachronism in the tale. Mrs. Poyser, the chatty wife of a well-to-do farmer, is the pivot on which the plot revolves. She is the chorus who is continually intervening with her opinions.

[A long summary of the plot follows.]

There is not much of a story it will be seen. The great charm of the novel is rather in the characters introduced than in the action which they carry on. All the characters are so true, and so natural, and so racy that we love to hear them talk for the sake of talking. They are so full of strange humours and funny pretty sayings that we entirely overlook the want of movement in the story. Besides which, when the dialogue ceases, the author's reflections are so pointed, and his descriptions are so vivid, that we naturally think more of what we have than of what we have not. There is not a character in the novel which is not well drawn, and even if the portrait is but a sketch still it is a true one. We have not mentioned the name of Mr. Irwine, the parson, who is very carefully drawn, nor of his mother, who is touched off in a more rapid manner; and yet the former is a very important personage in the dialogue, and is a fine moral influence throughout the tale. He is a very favourable specimen of the moral preachers of the close of last century, and the author has placed him in contrast to the more Scriptural style of which Dinah Morris, the young Methodist, is the representative. He sympathizes strongly with both, but leans most to the side of those moral teachers who have been somewhat harshly judged, he thinks. Comparing Mr. Irwine with the curate of an "evangelical" turn who succeeded him, he makes Mrs. Poyser pronounce this judgment: — "Mr. Irwine was like a good meal o' victual; *you are the better for him without thinking on it;* but Mr. Ryde is like a dose o' physic; he gripes you and worrets you, and after all he leaves you much the same." Irwine is a noble man, with a fine presence and a kindly catholic nature. He was a silent influence, who did not trouble his parish much with theological "notions," but gave them the example of a kind heart, and demanded from them the reward of honest lives. "It's summat like to see such a man as that i' the desk of a Sunday," says that rattling Mrs. Poyser. "As I say to Poyser, it's like looking at a full crop o' wheat, or a pasture with a fine dairy o' cows in it; it makes you think the world's comfortable-like." The tolerance with which an author who is able to conceive the character of Dinah Morris, and to sympathize with her religious views, is thus pleased to regard a very opposite type of the religious character — a type which many worthy people, no doubt, would be disposed to brand as utterly irreligious, is one of the finest things in the novel, and affords a very good illustration of the tendency of the author to beat down all external differences, and bring into the light the grand points of genuine resemblance. . . .

It will be evident that in order to establish the identity of man with man an author must travel a good deal into the region of latent thoughts, and unconscious or but semi-conscious feelings. There is infinite variety in what we express; there is a wonderful monotony in that great world of life which never comes into the light, but moves within us like the beating of the heart and the breathing of the lungs — a constant, though unobserved influence. It is in this twilight of the human soul that our novelist most delights to make his observations. . . . Like Mr. Thackeray, he takes a peculiar pleasure in showing the contrariety between thought and speech, the heart within and the mask without, which we call a face. He is always showing that we are better than we seem, greater than we know, nearer to each other than, perhaps, we would wish. It is a fertile theme of immense interest, and through the three volumes the author has handled it with rare skill. His dissection of all the motives at work in Arthur Donnithorne's mind when he is pleased to trifle with the affections of Hetty is very masterly — how he was tempted, how he struggled with the temptation, and what a strange under-current of feeling was carrying him on to his purpose, while he took note only of the feeble ripple on the surface. In the case of poor Hetty we have a similar analysis, but one still more difficult, owing to the utterly thoughtless character of the girl. She, perhaps, might be accepted as a fair example of the truth of Pope's very unjust saying, "Most women have no characters at all." Not that she is unreal — she is drawn to the life; but she is one of those who are so much less than they seem to be, whose most significant acts mean so little, that it is not easy to fix upon any central principle in their nature, any strong point of thought, or word, or act which belongs to them. "Hetty's face had a language that transcended her feelings," says the novelist. . . .

All through the work the same train of thought runs, and at the very opening of the novel we have a curious illustration of it in a remark uttered by Joshua Rann, the parish clerk, . . . on the occasion of a crowd collecting on the village-green to hear the young Methodist preach. Many were the comments more or less appropriate, of the village worthies on the audacious act which Dinah Morris was about to commit, but, surely, if there was one comment more unmeaning than another, it was that of old Joshway, who in a resounding voice exclaimed, "Sehon, king of the Amorites; for His mercy endureth for ever; and Og, the king of Basan, for His mercy endureth for ever." Mr. George Eliot points out, with great gusto, the unconscious associations which led to this extraordinary speech — how Mr. Rann felt the necessity of maintaining the dignity of the Church, how, further, he felt that this dignity was bound up with his own sonorous utterances of the responses, and how, in accordance with this theory, he volleyed forth a quotation from the Psalm of the previous Sunday, in order to give a practical illustration of the Church's dignity.

The gem of the novel is Mrs. Poyser, who, for that combination of shrewd remark and homely wit with genuine kindliness and racy style which is so taking in Mr. Samuel Weller, is likely to outvie all the characters of recent fiction, with the single exception of the hero we have named. Mrs. Poyser, in her way, is as amusing as Mrs. Gamp or Mrs. Nickleby, and much more sensible. Wife of a rough and ready farmer, she is a great woman. She is the firstling of the author's mind, which he is not likely to surpass, even as that glorious Sam Weller, the firstling of Mr. Dickens's pen, has not been outshone by any successor. Mrs. Poyser pervades the novel. Her wisdom is always coming out, either spoken by herself, or quoted by somebody else, or mentioned by the author. On one occasion, the author, unable to express himself in his own words, introduces Adam Bede to express the thought in his words, and Adam Bede, finding his own language inadequate, is obliged to fall back upon the expressions used by Mrs. Poyser, whom accordingly he quotes. "You're mighty fond o' Craig," says Mrs. Poyser to her husband, speaking of a certain Scotch gardener; "but for my part, I think he's welly like a cock as thinks the sun's rose o' purpose to hear him crow." This is the Poyser style, a good pungent style, remarkably effective when it is necessary to scold her husband, to subdue her nieces, or to lash the maids. It is a fine thing to hear her out of the goodness of her heart and the fullness of her wisdom abuse her household. . . . Her style runs into proverbs. "Folks must put up wi' their own kin, as they put up with their own noses—it's their own flesh and blood"—she says. "If the chaffcutter had the making of us, we should all be straw, I reckon," she says again. "I'm not one o' those as can see the cat i' the dairy an' wonder what she's come after" is another of her sayings. . . . Of mankind she says, "The men are mostly so slow, their thoughts overrun 'em, an' they can only catch 'em by the tail. Howiver, I'm not denyin' the women are foolish; God Almighty made 'em to match the men." She adds a little further on, "Some folks' tongues are like the clocks as run on strikin', not to tell you the time o' the day, but because there's summat wrong i' their own inside." A good homely woman, it will be observed, who knows how to keep her own, and doing her duty well, has a wonderful supply of self-complacency. . . . In some respects, also, Mrs. Poyser is repeated in another good lady with a querulous twist in her,—old Lisbeth Bede, mother of Adam. When her husband is dead, Adam proposes to go to the village to have the coffin made, fearing that if he worked at it himself it would pain his mother. "Nay, my lad, nay," Lisbeth cries out in a wailing tone, "thee wotna let nobody make thy feyther's coffin but thysen? Who'd make it so well? *An' him, as know'd what good work war,* an's got a son as is th' head o' the village, an' all Treddles'on too, for cleverness." . . .

We might go on quoting these speeches until at last we transfer half the novel to our columns. The hero of the work, Adam Bede, is not so remarkable for his speeches as for what he does. He speaks out in a strong, manly way, but not very often with that sharp epigrammatic force which is so characteristic of Mrs. Poyser, Lisbeth Bede, and the schoolmaster, Bartle Massey. . . . The speeches of Seth Bede and of Dinah Morris, though excellent as illustrations of character, are, like those of Adam, not of the epigrammatic sort. Dinah's sermon is very fine, and she herself is a most beautiful piece of portraiture—a perfect chrysolite. The minor sketches are superabundant; they crowd the canvass. We have not here one great and real character in the midst of a mob of lay figures. The subordinate personages are in their way quite as well pictured as the leading one. The whole work, indeed, leaves upon us the impression of something highly finished and well matured, and we close the volumes wondering whether the author is to do better in his next novel,—curious, also, to know who the author really is. Nobody seems to know who is Mr. George Eliot, and when his previous work appeared it was even surmised that he must be a lady, since none but a woman's hand could have painted those touching scenes of clerical life. Now, the question will be raised, can this be a young author? Is all this mature thought, finished portraiture, and crowd of characters the product of a 'prentice hand and of callow genius? If it is, the hand must have

an extraordinary cunning, and the genius must be of the highest
order.

[Eneas Sweetland Dallas]

The Mill on the Floss

"George Eliot" is as great as ever. She has produced a second
novel, equal to her first in power, although not in interest. As far
as interest is concerned, indeed, it would have been exceedingly difficult to repeat the triumph of *Adam Bede*, in which the author contrived to paint the lily and to gild refined gold by adding the charm
of a delightful philosophy to the pleasure of a good story. The
reader will at once remember that he could not help liking all the
characters in that history. The general influence of the book was
to reconcile us to human nature, to make us think better of our
fellow men, to make us feel that in the weakest there is something
to be admired, in the worst something to be loved, to draw us nearer
to each other by showing how completely we are one, and so to give
us not only the temporary delight of listening to a pleasant tale, but
also the permanent good of an increased sympathy with our kind. It
was comparatively easy to excite our interest in the doings of persons
towards whom we were led to entertain such friendly feelings. We
treasured all their sayings, we watched eagerly all their movements,
we were curious as to all their thoughts. The author, apparently
afraid of repeating herself, and determined to avoid the imputation of
representing the world as too good and sugary, now introduces us
to a very different set of personages. A majority of the characters
brought together in these three volumes are unpleasant companions —
prosaic, selfish, nasty. We are launched into a world of pride, vain-
glory, and hypocrisy, envy, hatred and malice, and all uncharitable-
ness. Everybody is quarreling with everybody in a small mean way;
and we have the petty gossip and malignant slander of village worthies
painted to the life. These are not promising materials, but the
authoress has impressed her genius on them, and, relying on her
marvellous powers of delineation, has felt that by the mere force of

Reprinted from *The Times*, 19 May 1860, pp. 10–11.

truth she could command our attention and compel applause. We doubt, indeed, whether Miss Lydia Languish will care much for this novel, and we are almost afraid to dwell on the nature of the theme which "George Eliot" has chosen, lest the timid reader should be repulsed, and we should suggest an allusion to the supposed impossibility of making a silk purse out of a sow's ear. As to the fact that here we have the silk purse there can be no mistake, but it would require the genius of "George Eliot" to describe by what magic it is produced out of materials that appear to be singularly barren of silk.

We can only indicate what lies on the surface, and we must attribute a great part of "George Eliot's" triumph to the charm of her style. She plays with her subject; there is no appearance of effort; even when she is most serious she is half-sportive; even when she has reached her climaxes she is entirely at her ease. This pervading humour is very pleasant, and takes the reader unawares. It does not much matter what is the subject with which such a mind as "George Eliot's plays; the result is sure to be amusing. One of our poets has declared, that in the meanest flowers he found thoughts that were too deep for tears; he might have added, too deep for anybody to care about them. It is not every topic that spontaneously yields the elements of tears and tragedy. The elements of comedy are much more universal, and "George Eliot" manages to make us smile through her novel, and to be tickled by incongruities that in less skilful hands would be as thorns and briars to vex the reader. In the three volumes there is not a dull page. The style is singularly apt and rich, and its felicities are not the result of tricks. Onward it flows and bears us along with a resistless force, and before we can get tired of the sometimes prosy interlocutors of the drama, the author steps in and rouses our attention with a wise remark or a pleasant reflection that shows the wideness of her reading, the closeness of her observation, and the maturity of her thought. It seems, too, not less easy for her to make her characters speak than to speak herself. As if her descriptions were not vivid enough, she prefers to make her characters speak for themselves and the dialogue is sustained with marvellous ability — the slightest shades of difference between the personages being rendered with great subtlety. This is remarkably displayed in the representation of the odious Dodson family, in which the family likeness is strictly preserved, while the individual traits are not lost. Relying on her imitative power in this respect, and on the fascination which a truthful picture exerts over every mind, "George Eliot" has invited our attention to the hard realities of a life in which none but a true genius could find the elements of a successful novel.

The two leading characteristics of almost all the personages to

whom we are introduced are honesty and pugnacity, and these flow
from one and the same source. A strong character, such as is here
described, that feels its own strength, delights in it, and is proud of
it — is honest, because dishonesty is a weakness, not because it is an
injury to others. The Dodson family are stingy, selfish wretches,
who give no sympathy and require none, who would let a neighbour
starve and let a brother be bankrupt when a very little assistance
would save him from the disgrace; but they would not touch a penny
that is not theirs, there is no legal obligation which they would not
discharge, they would scorn the approach of a lie. They would be
truthful and honest, not as a social duty, but as a personal pride —
because nobody should have it in his or her power to say that they
were weak enough to neglect a manifest obligation. From the same
source of self-satisfied strength comes pugnacity in all its forms of
rivalry and contradiction, jealousies and criticisms, lawsuits, and
slanders, and blows. Everybody in this tale is repelling everybody,
and life is in the strictest sense a battle. Even the good angel of the
story, that little Maggie, who is full of affection, and whose affection
is continually leading her into blunders and misfortunes, is first of all
introduced to us while she is indulging an unnatural ferocity towards
her doll, whose head she is punching — driving a nail into it as Jael
drove one into the temples of Sisera. Her brother Tom, who is the
next important personage in the little community, is chiefly remarkable for self-assertion and hard-headed resistance of fate — his strong
wrestling with adversity, and his anxiety to punish the slightest
offence. Her father, Mr. Tulliver, is the incarnation of pugnacity. . . .
   This life of proud self-assertion that on the bad side presents itself
in an incessant bickering, and on the best side appears as a devotion to
justice and truth for selfish ends, may become interesting by being
made heroic. The Brontes — both Charlotte and Emily — were fond
of depicting this character, and by their account, by the account of
Mrs. Gaskell, and by that of "George Eliot," it is a character that
abounds in the northern counties. But when Charlotte or Emily
Bronte dealt with such a nature, they ennobled or at least magnified it.
In their pages we looked on men essentially selfish and unsociable —
men encased in armour of proof against all encroachment — men who
wronged nobody, and who vowed that nobody should wrong them.
But the selfish isolation of such characters was lit up with passion,
was justified or expiated by long suffering from some overwhelming
wrong, was idealized by being joined to the possession of great intellectual powers. "George Eliot" has attempted a more difficult task.
She takes these characters as we find them in real life — in all their
intrinsic littleness. She paints them as she finds them — snapping at
each other over the tea-table; eyeing each other enviously at church;

privately plotting how to astonish each other by some extraordinary display; putting the worst construction on every word and act; officiously proffering advice and predicting calamity; living with perfect content their sordid life of vulgar respectability. The first half of the novel is devoted to the exhibition of this degraded species of existence, which is dissected with a masterly hand. Although it is the least exciting part of the work, it is the part of which the reader will carry away the most vivid recollection. The Dodson family will live for ever, and they inspire the work. With a self-denial which we cannot but admire, the author has resolutely set herself the task of delineating without exaggeration, without extenuation, with minute accuracy, the sort of life which thousands upon thousands of our countrymen lead. . . .

When "George Eliot" got exactly half through her work she foresaw the criticisms which a novel based on such a foundation would certainly provoke, and she commenced her fourth book by uttering against her story all that the most savage critic can have it in his heart to say. . . . We commend these half-dozen pages, in which the author, midway in her work, has stopped to criticize it and to explain her intention to the notice of all who wish to understand, as well as to enjoy what a writer of undoubted genius has invited us to read. . . . The object which the author has set herself of painting in all its nakedness, hideousness, and littleness the life of respectable brutishness which so many persons lead, illumined by not one ray of spiritual influence, by no suspicion of a higher life, of another world, of a surrounding divinity, — lifts the present work out of the category of ordinary novels. The author is attempting not merely to amuse us, as a novelist, but, as a preacher, to make us think and feel. The riddle of life as it is here expounded is more like a Greek tragedy than a modern novel. . . . In the highest sense we might call this a religious novel, only that description is liable to be misunderstood, and especially as religion is chiefly "conspicuous by its absence." We read on, wondering what is the meaning of the story, wondering why these mean, prosaic people, the Dodsons ever live; wondering why a brilliant novelist asks us to make their acquaintance and to become interested in their paltry existence, when suddenly the author breaks in upon us with the criticism to which we have already referred, and which we have partly quoted. She says in effect: — "You, reader, are oppressed by all this meanness — disgusted at all this hardness — perplexed that I should think it worthy of your notice. I perfectly agree with you; but such is life, and it is in the midst of such a life, the most marked quality of which is the utter absence of poetry or religion, that many of us grow up — it was in the midst of such a desert that my little heroine, Maggie, bloomed into beauty. It is well that these things should be impressed upon us, and that we should lay them to heart."

In fulfilling this portion of her task, which occupies exactly the first half of the novel, the author has very cleverly helped herself out of a difficulty. It is difficult to describe adults leading a purely bestial life of vulgar respectability without rendering the picture simply repulsive. But the life of children is essentially an animal life. . . . "George Eliot" relieves the repulsiveness of the insect life which she has exhibited in the Dodson family by making her bigger insects all revolve around these two little creatures, Maggie and Tom Tulliver. Her description of the child life is unique. No one has yet ventured to paint the child life in all its prosaic reality. It is true that we have long since got out of the Mrs. Barbauld and Miss Edgeworth groove, in which we had contrasted pictures of the good boy and the bad boy, the girl who was lazy and the girl who was active. Then succeeded more careful studies of the child nature, and we do not know that in this respect the productions of Mr. Disraeli, both in *Venetia*, where he gives the youth of Lord Byron, and in *Coningsby*, have ever been surpassed. But in his writings and those of other novelists there is not a little of that poetical colouring which is natural to us in looking back on our childhood. "George Eliot," in approaching the subject, determined, as best agreeing with the general scope of her novel, to paint reality; and she has pictured the boy and girl life with the most amusing fidelity. We see all the little squabbling and domineering that goes on among children; we see them disgracefully intent on raspberry tart; we see the boy, after he has eaten up his share, mysteriously surveying his sister's, and wondering whether she will spare him a bit; we see the pleasure which they take in first tickling a toad, and then smashing it with a stone; we see all the envies, and cruelties, and gluttonies that in men would be revolting, but are only grotesque in these funny little animals.

The light of the story is Maggie, who has a warm heart, abounding in sympathy and longing for a return of her affection. Unfortunately, none of the personages by whom she is surrounded is capable of returning it, and "the little wench" finds herself at sixes and sevens with her family circle and with all the world.

[A long summary of Maggie's career follows.]

In the latter half of the novel it is that Maggie and Tom cease to be children; and here, also, we cease to be oppressed as before with that intolerable Dodson family, who are likely to have a proud preeminence in fiction as the most thorny set of people ever introduced into a tale. Other personages are introduced, and especially the character of Bob Jakin, the pedlar, is developed into something very entertaining. The incidents are nothing. "George Eliot" is not very strong in her incidents, and there are several points in the plot about which questions might be raised. It is in the description of character that she chiefly excels, and in the art of making the characters exhibit themselves. Her analysis of what is passing in the mind is very fine, and "George Eliot" takes her place as not one whit behind the greatest of our lady novelists, if she is not, indeed, before them all. . . . Err as she may, sin as she may, the very faults of Maggie are more to be respected and loved than the hard consistency of her brother Tom and the Pharisaical rigidity of the Dodson family. One must not press the maxim too far, and we protest by anticipation against the novels that are sure to be written on the model of the present one, showing that it is a grand thing to lead a Bohemian life, and that respectability and the payment of one's debts is necessarily mean and uninteresting. In its own place, however, it contains a truth which ought to be attended to, and which a writer so sober as "George Eliot" is not likely to overstrain.

The Saturday Review

Silas Marner

The highest tribute that can be paid to this book may be paid it very readily. It is as good as *Adam Bede*, except that it is shorter. And that an author should be able to produce a series of works so good in so very peculiar a style, is as remarkable as anything that has occurred in the history of English literature in this century. The plot of *Silas Marner* is good, and the delineation of character is excellent. But other writers who have the power of story-telling compose plots as interesting, and perhaps sketch characters as well. It is in the portraiture of the poor, and of what it is now fashionable to call "the lower middle class," that this writer is without a rival, and no phase of life could be harder to draw. A person with observation and humour might give a sketch of one or two sets of poor people, and of village farmers and carpenters, but the sketches he could give would be limited by his personal observation. George Eliot alone moves among this unknown, and to most people unknowable, section

Reprinted from the *Saturday Review*, 11 (13 April 1861), 369–370.

of society as if quite at home there, and can let imagination run loose
and disport itself in a field that, we think, has been only very partially opened even to the best writers. Sir Walter Scott drew a few
pictures of humble Scotch life, and none of his creations won him
more deserved reputation than the characters of Andrew Fairservice
and Caleb Balderstone, and the scenes among the poor fishing popula-
tion in *The Antiquary*. But, good as these sketches were, they were
very limited. We soon got to an end of them; but in *Silas Marner*,
the whole book, or nearly the whole book, is made up of such scenes.
The writer can picture what uneducated villagers think and say, and
can reproduce on paper the picture which imagination has suggested.
The gift is so special, the difficulty is so great, the success is so complete, that the works of George Eliot come on us as a new revelation
of what society in quiet English parishes really is and has been. How
hard it is to draw the poor may easily be seen if we turn to the
ordinary tales of country life that are written in such abundance by
ladies. There the poor are always looked at from the point of view
of the rich. They are so many subjects for experimenting on, for
reclaiming, improving, being anxious about, and relieving. They have
no existence apart from the presence of a curate and a district
visitor. They live in order to take tracts and broth. This is a very
natural, and in some degree a very proper view for the well-intentioned rich to take of the poor. It is right that those who have
spiritual and temporal blessings should care for the souls and bodies
of those around them. But the poor remain, during the process and
in its description, as a distinct race. What they think of and do
when they are not being improved and helped, remains a blank.
Those, too, who are above the reach of occasional destitution are
entirely omitted from these portraitures of village life. Everyone is
agreed that it would be impertinent to improve a man who gets anything like a pound a week. When, therefore, George Eliot describes
the whole of a village, from the simple squire down to the wheelwright and his wife, the ground thus occupied is virgin soil.

   There are two chapters in *Silas Marner* describing the conversation
of a coterie at a public-house, and what they did and said on a man
appearing before them to announce a robbery, which are perfectly
wonderful. It is not, perhaps, saying much to say that an intelligent
reader who knew beforehand that such a scene was to be described
would be utterly puzzled to think of any one thing that such people
could satisfactorily be represented as remarking or doing. But some
notion of what George Eliot can do may be obtained by comparing
what the best writers of the day are in the habit of doing when they
attempt scenes of this sort. Sir Edward Lytton and Mr. Dickens
would venture to try such a scene if it came in their way. Sir Edward

Lytton would only go so far as to put some very marked character or some very important personage of the story in the centre of the group, and put everything into relation and connexion with him. This is really the good ladies' novel view of the poor in another shape. The poor cluster round some one superior to them, and the only reason of the superiority which Sir Edward Lytton can claim, so far as he can claim any at all, arises from the poor being supposed to be in a position of greater naturalness and simplicity. They are represented as taking their ease in their inn, and not as being talked to by their anxious-minded betters. Mr. Dickens sets himself to draw the poor and the uneducated much more thoroughly, but his mode is to invest each person with one distinguishing peculiarity. This gives a distinctness to each picture, but it makes the whole group artificial and mechanical. He always, or almost always, keeps us in the region of external peculiarities. We are made to notice the teeth, the hair, the noses, the buttons of the people described, or some oddity of manner that marks them. The sentiment of the poor is often caught in Mr. Dickens's works with great happiness, and the chance observations that they might make under particular circumstances are well conceived; but George Eliot goes far beyond this. The people in the public-house in *Silas Marner* proclaim in a few words each a distinct and probable character, and sustain it. The things they say are perfectly natural, and yet show at once what the sayers are like. We know that these poor are like real poor people, just as we know that the characters in Shakspeare are like real men and women. The humour of the author, of course, pervades the representation, just as it does in the comic parts of Shakspeare. Our enjoyment in a large measure depends on the enjoyment of the writer; nor is it probable that any group at a pothouse would really say so many things on any one evening that, if recorded, would amuse us so much. But this is one of the exigencies of art. In order not to waste space, that which is characteristic must be placed closely together. Were it not for this absence of dilution, the history of the village group of Raveloe, the village in which the scenes of *Silas Marner* are laid, might be a mere record of an actual evening passed at a country public. It is a kind of unpermissible audacity in England to say that anything is as good as Shakspeare, and we will not therefore say that this public-house scene is worthy of the hand that drew Falstaff and Poins; but we may safely say that, however much less in degree, the humour of George Eliot in such passages is of the same kind as that displayed in the comic passages of Shakspeare's historical plays. . . .

Dolly Winthrop, with her quaint kindness, her simple piety, and her good sense, is as touching and at the same time as amusing a character as George Eliot has drawn. She comes in with her little boy, and brings some cakes which she thinks will give a little pleasure to Silas in his affliction. "There's letters pricked on 'em," said Dolly. "I can't read 'em myself, and there's nobody rightly knows what they mean; but they've a good meaning, for they're the same as is on the pulpit-cloth at church. . . ." The difference, so far as truthfulness of description and insight into the poor go, between George Eliot and the usual lady-novelist, cannot be better estimated than by contrast-ing Dolly and her I.H.S. cakes, her reverent belief in "Them," and her views of this world and the next, with the model cottager's wife of domestic fiction. The one is a living woman, the other is an improveable puppet.

We wish to avoid telling the story of Silas Marner to those who have not read the book, and it fortunately happens that there is nothing in the story that calls for observation. There does not appear to us to be a fault in the plot or in the working of it out. The errors that marred *The Mill on the Floss* have been entirely avoided. The classes which the author can draw, and those alone, have been drawn. There is nothing like the inanity of Stephen Guest or the spiritual conflicts of Maggie. On the other hand, the plot secures the writer from the danger of trespassing on unknown ground which was the origin of some weaknesses in *Adam Bede*. The trial and the reprieve of Hetty were incomparably the worst parts of the story, for the simple reason that the writer evidently knew nothing about trials and reprieves. There is, again, nothing painful in *Silas Marner*. The secret is one that it is not distressing either to have concealed or to find out, and the misery of those who are miserable is not of a very intense kind. We are left unembarrassed to enjoy those pictures of humble life which have constituted the great merit of George Eliot's works, and which appear in this new volume with as much freshness, novelty, and humour as ever. All that can be said against *Silas Marner*, as compared with its predecessors, is that it is shorter, and therefore slighter. The author has less ground to cover, and has not been obliged to fill up space with improbable incidents or painful scenes. The work has therefore been easier. The characters have had to be sustained for a shorter time, and the delineation of mental conflicts and emotions has been more in outline. If we take into consideration all the difficulties encountered and surmounted, *Adam Bede* still remains perhaps the author's greatest production. But, within its limits, *Silas Marner* is quite equal to either of its predecessors, and, in combining the display of the author's characteristic excellences with freedom from blemishes and defects, is perhaps superior.

[Eneas Sweetland Dallas]

Silas Marner

To George Eliot belongs this praise — that not only is every one of her tales a masterpiece, but also they may be opened at almost any page, and the eye is certain to light upon something worth reading — some curious dialogue or vivid description, some pregnant thought or happy phrase. *Silas Marner* is, like the rest of her fictions, full of matter and delightful in manner. It is a picture of secluded village life in the midland counties in the early part of the present century, and we owe not a little gratitude to the author for the good which she has done, as well as for the amusement which she has imparted by means of such pictures. She has given dignity to the life of boors and peasants in some of our bucolic districts, and this not by any concealment of their ignorance, follies, and frailties, nor by false colouring, bombastic sentiment, and exceptional events, but by a plain statement of the everyday life of the people. The charm of George Eliot's novels lies in their truthfulness. . . . We see the people amid all their grovelling cares, with all their coarseness, ignorance, and prejudice — poor, paltry, stupid, wretched, well-nigh despicable. This mean existence George Eliot raises into dignity by endowing it with conscience and with kindliness. There is nothing glittering about it. Here we have no mock heroics. . . . Such a novelist, while she amuses, teaches us. We open her volumes confident of most brilliant entertainment, and we close them wondering at the art of a writer who manages to reverse a time-honoured phrase and to render us, not sadder and better, but merrier and better.

While this is the general effect of all George Eliot's tales, it is most marked in what is still her greatest work — *Adam Bede*. The present tale, which is complete in one volume, has for its hero a sort of Seth Bede, and this statement will indicate to most persons the excellences and defects of the novel. A novel of which a Seth Bede is the hero must, of necessity, be less absorbing and ought to be shorter, than one which could boast such a hero as Adam.

[A long summary of the plot follows.]

The first part, forming more than two-thirds of the volume, is thus a magnificent portico to the second part, which is a pretty little

Reprinted from *The Times*, 29 April 1861, p. 12.

cottage, hidden behind a mass of more stately architecture. There are
critics who will regard this objection to the story more seriously than
we can. It amounts to this, that George Eliot laid out the plan of a
great epic, found that she was overstepping the limits of a novel, and
ruthlessly curtailed her design. The result is, that here we have, it
is true, a fragment, but it is a fragment of George Eliot's most ambitious work. It is not finished like *Adam Bede*, but in passages it is
grander and deeper.

That George Eliot should have shrunk from the completion of
her task as she appears to have at first planned it is not surprising.
Her efforts as a writer were strained to the uttermost, but for many
reasons the increase of effort on her part could not be followed by
any increase of effect on the reader. Here we might repeat a good
deal of the criticism suggested by *The Mill on the Floss*, in which
the writer employed her great powers on materials so unpromising
that none but a novelist of the highest class could have turned them
to account. It was strange to see how, by the force of her genius,
George Eliot made a brilliant story out of the little sayings and doings
of the mean, prosaic, odious Dodson family. In her new novel she
has undertaken a task still more difficult, for the centre of interest in
it is a half-witted man. . . . But the pleasure of fiction depends mainly
on our being able to count upon the elements of human character and
calculate results. . . . In all such cases of imbecility, whether it is
natural and permanent or superinduced for the moment, we are out
of our reckoning, we know not what to anticipate, and we are robbed
of that expectancy which enters so largely into the pleasure afforded
by fiction. . . . Mean as the Dodson family are, yet, having the elements of their character before us, we see that they are calculable
elements, and we can forecast their legitimate results. But what can
we anticipate in the play of events for a man who, whatever be his
moral elevation, is of weak mind and is subject to fits which for the
time render his existence a blank? There are novels in which such
a character might not be out of place even as the leading personage
of the tale. In Mr. Wilkie Collins's last novel [*The Woman in White*]
the chief interest centres around two half-witted women in succession.
Events occur which by no possibility could have happened had these
women been in full possession of their senses. But in a novel which
claims our attention chiefly for the intricacy of its plot, . . . we almost
forget the blank unsatisfactory nature of the leading personages in
thinking of the startling incidents that crowd upon our notice. The
interest of George Eliot's tales resting upon a different foundation,
does not admit of such handling. In her stories, the characters are
all in all; the incidents are of secondary importance, and grow out
of the characters; a hero whose mind is nearly a blank and whose

life is represented as the sport of chance, is at variance with the spirit of her books. . . . As in one fit of unconsciousness he lost his all, so in another he obtained a recompense. In either case he was helpless, had nothing to do with his own fate, and was a mere feather in the wind of chance. From this point forward in the tale, however, there is no more chance — all is work and reward, cause and effect, the intelligent mind shaping its own destiny. The honest man bestows kindness upon the child and reaps the benefit of it in his own increasing happiness, quickened intelligence, and social position. Only this is but a very small portion of the tale, so small that, seeing the importance of it, remembering the prominence which is given to it by means of the motto on the title-page, and knowing that the spirit of it more accords with George Eliot's artistic genius than that portion of the volume which occupies the greater number of pages, we have been forced to the conjecture that the story is not what the author originally intended it to be, but is huddled up at the end.

It is one of the evils of criticism that we cannot take any exception to a great work of art without suggesting that it is a failure. But to associate *Silas Marner* with any idea of failure is the very opposite of our intention. Criticize it as we may, the worst we can have to say of it is, that in aim it transcends the field of ordinary novels, and that in accomplished result it suggests too high a standard of measurement. Taking it as it is, and with all its faults, we really could not name another woman capable of producing a greater work, and it may be doubted whether, with the same materials, any man could have done better. As for the writing, it contains some of George Eliot's best composition, though at the same time it should be added that, as there is less of dialogue and more of narrative in the present work than is usual in the novels of this author, she appears to have felt the necessity of elaborating her own remarks to the uttermost. What her sentences in this way gain in force they lose in freedom; but with her rich vein of humour it will readily be understood that even when her writing is most laboured, the loss of freedom is not considerable. Her vein of humour, combined as it is with a peculiar seriousness and sense of the mystery of human life, is very fine, and gives an inexpressible charm to her descriptions of stupid, poverty-stricken boors. An author who manages to make us laugh at them and with them has gone far to make us forget the repulsiveness of their habits, and to prepare us for real sympathy in their struggles. The volume before us is full of those little touches which give vividness and humour to the most homely pictures. We open it at random and come upon a scene in the village public-house where the parochial worthies are drinking their beer, smoking their long pipes, and discussing their little affairs. They are startled by the sudden appear-

ance of Silas Marner who rushes in upon them like a ghost. "The
long pipes," we are told, "gave a simultaneous movement, *like the
antennae of startled insects,* and every man present, not excepting
even the sceptical farrier, had an impression that he saw, not Silas
Marner in the flesh, but an apparition." Few similes could be more
graphic or more amusing than this. . . . The most remarkable combination, however, of humour with seriousness in the present volume
is in the conception of Mrs. Winthrop's character — a good woman
who utters the most profound truths in the most confused comical
fashion. . . .

The weaver of Raveloe is very much in the position of the man
of Uz. He is surrounded with comforters, most of whom are even
less sympathizing than the comforters of Job, and he sinks into a
deeper despair than that of the most patient of men, for, as we have
said, he cursed and denied God in his affliction. The picture of his
misery and the discipline of his repentance are but a homely, human
version of the older and diviner drama. Instead of supernatural incidents and divine colloquies, we have ordinary accidents and village
prattle. Instead of the Deity coming forth to justify his afflicted
creature and to teach him better, a little child proves to the world
the good qualities of his heart, and gives light and liberty to his understanding. It is a noble lesson, beautifully taught, though in saying
thus much we run a risk of conveying the impression that George
Eliot belongs to the class of religious or moralizing novelists who
have rendered hateful the very idea of serious purpose in a novel.
This is not the case, however. Hers is a very spiritual nature, and
she cannot choose but regard life from a very lofty point of view.
But her novels are true novels, not sermons done into dialogue. The
moral purpose which is evident in her writing is mostly an unconscious purpose. It is that sort of moral meaning which belongs to
every great work of art, and which no elevated mind can get rid of.
She tells a simple story without the least idea of inculcating any
copy-book lesson, but by merely elevating the reader to her mount
of observation she cannot fail to suggest to the mind some profound
reflections.

The Saturday Review

Romola

No reader of *Romola* will lay it down without admiration, and few without regret. Great as is the power displayed in it, and varied as is the interest awakened in it, there is still the general impression produced by it that the authoress has been tempted into a field where, indeed, she is not less than she has been, but where her merits are obscured, and their effect impaired. She has left the description and study of English life, and has attempted to overcome the difficulties of the historical novel. Nothing can exceed the diligence with which she has applied herself to her task. She has set herself to paint Florence at the end of the fifteenth century and to present the chief scenes of a decade of Florentine history. And if a sketch of Florence were her main object, she has selected a good time, and has mastered every detail that could give reality and picturesqueness to her representation. The period she has chosen enables her to bring on the canvas Macchiavelli and Savonarola, the exile of the Medici, the triumphant entry of Charles VIII of France, and countless intrigues of one Florentine party against another. It enables her to depict the popular feeling about the Church, the wavering of opinion that preceded the Reformation, and the scholarly quarrels of the literary heroes of the *Renaissance*. Florentine life, also, both in the past and the present, is full of salient curiosities which catch and delight a studious English eye. To note these and to understand them, and to store them up and bring them out at last as children bring out of their baskets the shells and stones they have worked hard to collect, is a great pleasure. But it seems a pity that these things should be done by the authoress of *Adam Bede*. A lesser hand might have been employed to collect these simple treasures. However instructive it may be, it is not without a tax on our patience that we read long accounts of Florentine antiquities, and translations of sermons by Savonarola, and extracts from chronicles of processions. Sometimes the antiquarian quite drowns the novelist, and we are startled at lighting on one of those artless contrivances by which, in Becker's *Charicles* or *Gallus*, a casual remark or passing fancy of the hero introduces a description that admirably illustrates all the hard bits

Reprinted from the *Saturday Review*, 16 (25 July 1863), 124–125.

in a satire of Horace or Juvenal. It is not without a pang that we come to passages in *Romola* such as that where an authoress known and respected as one of the first living writers of fiction actually goes off like Becker, or G. P. R. James, on the *Wars of the Jews,* and having first thrown out a preliminary " 'Fediddio,' exclaimed Francesco Cei, 'that is a well-tanned [San] Giovanni,' " proceeds to say that "to make clear this exclamation of Cei, it must be understood that the car of the Zecca or Mint was originally," &c. &c., and so on for two pages of cram. Nor is this instructive antiquarianism relieved by any success of historical portraiture. Most of the Italians introduced are mere names to us — some few of them, like Politian, old names, but most of them new names — the names of men about whom we know nothing and care nothing, even when the most indefatigable and ingenious antiquarian has tried to teach us and to interest us. Macchiavelli is, indeed, a man whose fame, and opinions, and influence are familiar to us. But historical accuracy forbids the novelist to make Macchiavelli act in the period selected. He is merely a young man allowed occasionally to talk in as smart and cynical a manner as the skill of the authoress can manage. Savonarola alone affords scope for effective historical painting. The conception of the character of Savonarola which is here given is profound, subtle, and probably true. It would be difficult to convey more vividly the strange union of deception and noble truthfulness which was prominent in him. But there is little life in the scenes where he is introduced. He is merely a study, clever, original, and faithful. He does not fascinate and engross us with that semblance of a real man which, with so much less apparent effort of thought and art, Scott knew how to give to those creations of his imagination to which he attached great historical names.

But it must be remembered that readers can only have what authors can give them, and that authors cannot always give what readers would most like. The authoress of *Romola* has already published four tales of English life, and four tales of English life are quite enough to use up the experience and exhaust the reflections even of a mind so acute, so observant, and so meditative. She has only to look at her contemporaries and notice with dismay the effects of continuing to write after the well of thought has run dry, and when the same water has to be pumped backwards and forwards if the fountain is to play at the bidding of publishers. The minds of men gifted with great creative power can, indeed, turn from one set of subjects and one set of characters to another. Shakspeare, and Scott, and Goethe are, within certain limits, inexhaustible. But there is another order of minds, which is really creative and original, but which is always driven into the same groove, and works within

bounds which have been probably assigned by the actual experience
of life. The authoress of *Adam Bede* has a mind of this sort. With
all its humour, and feeling, and philosophical and pictorial power, it
is centred upon a few elements of character, and is controlled as if
by the inevitable presence of certain familiar incidents. Stripped of
their Florentine covering, and divested of those touches of variety
which the genius of the writer imparts to them, several of the characters of *Romola*, and some of the chief events, are old — not in the
sense that they are mere repetitions, or that the authoress ever shows
poverty of invention, but that they involve the same moral problems,
and cause or encounter the same difficulties in life. Especially the
authoress seems to be haunted with the consequences that flow from
the weakness of men. It is not because men are bad, or cruel, or
lustful, so much as because they are weak, and get into little scrapes,
which make them lie, that women are miserable. These weak men,
liking comfort, prone to lie, hoping in a foolish sanguine way for
the best, go tottering to their ruin, and drag down women with
them. They drag down the pretty childish ones with babyish ways
and a thirst for innocent animal delight, and if they do not quite drag
down the nobler natures, the proud, and unselfish, and highminded,
they make their lives a weariness and a bitterness, and rob them of
the high joys for which heaven fitted them. This is the sight in
human life which has wrung the soul and stirred the spirit of the
authoress of *Romola;* and it is this that has supplied her with a base
for that kind of philosophical meditation which derives its strength
from indignation, and its subtlety from the analysis of weak no less
than of powerful characters.

In *Romola*, this weak, wavering man, his own victim and the
victim of the circumstances he creates, assumes a shape which affords
room for so elaborate a delineation as almost to conceal his similarity
to the types of the same character in the earlier works of the authoress.
If she has got nothing else out of her Florentine researches, and out
of her selection of an historical, remote, and uninteresting period, she
has at least got the possibility of drawing such a character as Tito —
a Greek and an Italian at once, beautiful, refined, flexible, mean,
cowardly, and yet charming and kind, and not very bad. In the
latter part of the tale the subtle drawing of his character is swallowed
up by the sad necessities of the Florentine story. His personal history
and his personal character are lost in a dreary network of Medicean
and anti-Medicean intrigues. We know that he is somehow very
cunning, but what he wants, or how he hopes to get it, and why he
should or should not get it, is a mystery. At last he is killed, but the
tragedy of his death is impaired by our anxiety to get him out of
the embroglio of Piagnoni, and Compagnacci, and Arrabbiati some-

how or other — if in no other way, by being flung into the Arno and
then strangled by a private enemy — but, at any rate, somehow. But
in the earlier part of the story his character is worked out with an
infinite vividness, and among much simpler elements. He burns to
get on in the world; he sincerely loves Romola; he likes to play and
trifle with the rural Tessa; and he is haunted day and night by the
fear of Baldassarre, the old man who has been a father to him, but
whom he has deserted, and robbed, and denied. In the midst of these
conflicting feelings and circumstances of his life he moves, instinct
with life and beauty, and so profoundly averse to pain that he wishes
to spare pain to others no less than to himself. It would be impossible to conceive the weak man, doomed to ruin himself and his at-
tendant women, noble and simple, under conditions demanding more
skill to depict and to control them. The authoress has been equal
to the task she has set herself; and if at last all these Medicean intrigues make him flit before us like a wicked bloodless ghost shrouded
in a veil, he leaves behind him the memory of the powerful pictures
which the authoress has associated with him. There is, first, the
picture of a man falling into falsehood, and made positively, though
gradually, worse, not only by the contact with evil, but by the companionship of unrelenting truth and purity, which perpetually reminds him of the barrier between himself and innocence which he
has built up. And there is the picture of a life passed in perpetual
fear, and of the terrible burden which the undying vengeance of
the half-witted old man he has wronged imposes on him in his
greatest prosperity.

Romola, however, is the central character of the work which bears
her name, and the interest attaching to her increases as the book
goes on. Fortunately, as she is a woman, and a good woman, she is
not thought suited to the Medicean intrigues, and only suffers in a
remote and readable way from them. At first, she seems cut on a
bigger scale than there is any occasion for. She is too much of a
goddess to make it fair play for such a weak mortal as Tito to have
to love her. It is only when she discovers his baseness, and gets into
great moral difficulties, and has to settle how to deal with many
conflicting claims of duty, that we see she was not shaped as a goddess
for nothing. Then all the nobleness of her character, and all the
originality and skill of the authoress who created her, begin to appear.
Nothing in her behaviour seems to us more admirably conceived
than her conduct to Tessa. The grateful, meek earnestness with
which she takes up the task imposed on her, and uses it as an escape
from her own feelings, gives her character that air of softness which
it would otherwise want.

Romola is saved by Savonarola from despair, and thenceforth is thrown into close relations with him. It is through Romola that the authoress gives her judgment on Savonarola, and all that is effective in the description of this unsuccessful reformer is connected with Romola's history. We cannot, therefore, separate the relations of Romola and Savonarola from the general mode in which the authoress deals with the questions which Savonarola raised, and with the nature and value of a religious enthusiasm like his. It is here that the peculiar power of her mind shows itself. Nothing in the mere portraiture of character, or in the contrivance of incident, equals the general impression of greatness of mind which her mode of treating such subjects awakens. She makes us feel that we are in the hands of a thinker who has thought far down into the depths of the religious mind, and who has seriously and anxiously desired to ascertain what is the place of religious thought in the facts of life. Romola, at the end, stands aloof from Savonarola, loving him, burning with the recollections of his nobleness and zeal, well aware that enthusiasm does not alter the iron course of things, alive to the deceptions in which the desire for the religious improvement of the world involved him, determined herself not to pretend to be more certain of religious truths than she is, and concentrated in the discharge of daily duty and the offices of love. This is the character which the authoress depicts as surviving in a noble soul the contact with a pure and visionary enthusiasm. It would be difficult to say that, under such circumstances, there is any wisdom wiser than that which Romola displays, and which the authoress has the strength and courage to depict.

The Westminster Review

Romola

It cannot be denied that *Romola* is less popular than its predecessors, but we do not hesitate to say that it is its author's greatest work. We hope we shall be able, in the course of the following observations, in some degree to explain this apparent contradiction. In the minds of a great majority of her readers George Eliot's name is indissolubly connected with the remembrance of Mrs. Poyser, the Dodsons, and

Reprinted from the *Westminster Review*, 80 (October 1863), 344–351.

Dolly Winthrop, and they cannot dispense with the pleasure they have heretofore derived from such quaint and original humour; it is not sufficient that there are passages in *Romola* full of refined wit and as deeply humorous as any to be found in *Adam Bede, The Mill on the Floss*, or in *Silas Marner;* they are not, indeed, set in a homely *entourage* which demands no thought, but rather call for habits of reflection but little cultivated by most novel-readers. Indeed, we have seen it insinuated that the circle of the author's powers had been already filled, and that the recourse to a foreign background for her fable was a sign of weakness and exhaustion. This is an inexcusable criticism; the critic must be himself weak indeed who fancies he can discern any sign of failing powers in *Romola.* It is quite another question whether the selection of a foreign and historical background was judicious. This point is doubtless open to debate, and in our opinion is the only one worth discussion. The strong hold which George Eliot lays on the intellectual and ethical side of all that comes before her mind, and the predominant critical tendency of her mode of thought, make it more necessary with her than with other authors that she should have the direct support of personal experience for the external circumstances in which she places her characters. Her imagination has a strong bias towards moral conceptions rather than towards sensuous, much less passionate ones; with her passion and direct action lie strangled in thought, and deeds present themselves to her rather as problems than as facts. In those dramatic conceptions which give force, unity, and rapid action to a tale she is comparatively deficient. The keenness of her mind urges her on to results, and thought and feeling have so much the upper hand that the lower and more picturesque qualities of our nature have but little attraction for her. The moral progress of mankind is a far higher thing to her than the finest poetry, which is but an instrument in that progress. This bias leads her to treat the events by which she develops the characters of her stories with too great an arbitrariness, and to disregard their natural sequence in a manner which strongly contrasts with the inexorable consecutiveness of every step in the development of the characters themselves. In the minute analysis of moral growth she has no equal; no one has so fully seized the great truth that we can none of us escape the consequences of our conduct, that each action has not only a character of its own, but also an influence on the character of the actor from which there is no escape; "our deeds are like children that are born to us; they live and act apart from our own will. Nay, children may be strangled, but deeds never: they have an indestructible life, both in and out of our consciousness." The strength with which this truth is here expressed shows the deep feeling from which it arises. To this deep moral maxim

George Eliot constantly recurs, not in *Romola* only, but in *Romola* it forms the central idea to which all else is made subservient; the external machinery of the tale is but the means by which it shall be set in an adequate light, considerations of probability are comparatively small matters, and the most fortuitous coincidences are accepted without a pang so that they do but aid in the display of that which is of more importance to the author than any superficial likelihood. If it were possible for her to consider the external circumstances in which she places her hero, apart from the influence those circumstances are intended to exercise on him, and as governed by laws of their own, she would be the first to recognize how remarkable an accumulation of improbable coincidences she heaps on Tito's head. But this is the greatness of George Eliot, that where others are feeble, she is strong, and it is only to be regretted that she is too regardless of that much less difficult accomplishment which is within the reach of any one with one tenth of her genius. On this account, we think it is to be regretted that *Romola* is an Italian story, and a story of the fifteenth century. By departing so far from the life around her she enters into a more full command of her whole material, which forces her to rely upon her imagination for those parts of her fable which the character of her mind strongly leads her to neglect. It would have been more difficult had Romola lived among us to arrange with such facile opportuneness the incidents of Tito's downward course. It is true the remembrance of similar features in *Silas Marner* forces us to allow that even in that case they might have had much of this character, but the greater familiarity of the incidents would have afforded some disguise. The beneficial influence of such a direct study from nature is manifest in the first two volumes of the *Mill on the Floss,* the complete harmony between the Tullivers and Dodsons and the external circumstances in which they are placed, affords the best illustration of our meaning, unless, indeed, that wonderful scene at the Rainbow, in *Silas Marner* be not a more striking example. No care and labour have been spared to give an objective character to the portraiture of ancient Florence, but this care has resulted only in an accumulation of details. The three great parties which divided the state at the close of the fifteenth century are displayed rather in their thoughts than in their actions, their violent passions and unscrupulous deeds are so treated in the light of their results that they are sicklied over with the pale cast of thought, and lose a great part of their local colour. All the minute details of Florentine life with which the canvas is crowded do not produce a lasting and enduring impression. The picture contains too much of the substance of the author's studies, and is brightened rather by the deep and profound general views which they suggested to her than by those living characteristic touches which make a departed age to live before the reader. There is to our feeling a most characteristic difference between the impression produced by the pictures of Italian life and by those which she draws of the personal conflicts in the minds of the characters which are really hers; in these her reflections drop from her like ripe fruit come to its fullest maturity, there is a spontaneousness about them that has an irresistible charm, but in all that concerns the surroundings of her characters there is an evi- dent sign of labour, not indeed upon the surface, but at too short a distance beneath it. The fullest knowledge is insufficient where the mind resists, or does not go forward without effort. This difference is difficult to seize and perhaps impossible fully to analyse; but it resembles that which is always found between a fine original picture and a copy by another artist, however able. The two shall be iden- tical, line for line, and yet no one is deceived by the copy; there is a something wanting, which can only be described as the result of perfect freedom of movement.

Again we do not recognize the truth of detail in a description of public life so remote from us as we should the features of our own time, and the author has not the power to carry us away from the description she gives. The historical background, too, somewhat op- presses the human interest of the tale, and in its ultimate impression affects us like a mediaeval painted window, in which the action has to be disentangled from the blaze of colour and overwhelming ac- cessories. To this source may be traced much of that want of appre- ciation with which the book has met. The general novel-reader is impatient at such details as those of the entry of Charles VIII, and of the Auto-da-fé of Vanities, and longs to hear more of that struggle between Romola and her husband which comes home to his business and bosom. There is another reason why *Romola* is not popular with the crowd. George Eliot's deep insight into the self-questioning human mind places her among those "neutrals who alone can see the finer shades of fact which soften the antithesis of virtue and vice, who are not distressed to discern some folly in martyrs and some judiciousness in those who burn them." The lofty superiority from which she draws the inspiration of that neutrality meets with no an- swering voice in the souls of the multitude. How few in these ques- tions are not in some sense partisans, and where will they find a weapon to their hands in the pages of *Romola?* There is another result of this scientific insight, which, from the point of view of art, exercises a hostile influence over the power of the author's best scenes: they are so philosophically treated, and so full of the subtlest analysis of the varying motives which struggle for the mastery in the actors, that we are in constant danger of being more attracted by the treatment of the moral question than interested by its bearing on the fate of those whom it affects. We have heard many say that they cannot interest themselves in Tito and Romola, but we never heard any one who was capable of entering into the special purpose of this history who thought himself fully able to express his admiration either of the deep insight displayed in it or of the delicate beauty of the distinctions and qualifications by which it is preserved from any excess or exaggeration. If it is said of any book that it offers in every page some food for thought or some rare beauty of expression, it is not generally found to conduce to its immediate perusal. Festus' 1 more convenient season is time enough for such things. How then shall a book which touches on the finest chords of the human heart with a delicacy that proclaims the last results of modern culture be heard among the coarse appeals to curiosity or passion which occupy the public ear?

We cannot but think, however, that this long and elaborate disquisition on the relations between the sexes as a moral question is set forth by George Eliot too much in the colours of the nineteenth century. The conception of the marriage tie which underlies the whole story seems to us antedated by the interval which separates the age of Alexander VI from our own. We think it would be very difficult to produce any evidence of claims to the kind of union to which Romola aspired as existing in the minds of the women of the fifteenth century, much more to prove them so universal as to be within the immediate appreciation of a man merely clever and self-seeking like Tito; and here again we find another reason for wishing that Romola had been a modern Englishwoman, she having so much more the character of one than that of an Italian lady of four centuries since. It is an insufficient excuse to plead that the great features of human life and character are determined by conditions too permanent to offer any radical distinctions between their manifestations from century to century. The hills indeed are, as George Eliot says, where they were of old, and the rivers flow in their accustomed beds; but many and great are the changes which four hundred years produce in these great features of physical nature, and greater far the differences which such a lapse of time brings with it in the form of the moral questions which are offered to each generation of mankind. We cannot escape from the feeling that the chief interest of *Romola* reposes on ideas of moral duty and of right which are of very modern growth and that they would have been more appropriately displayed on a modern stage. The lovely and noble Romola would even now be more admired than loved, and surely we have not retrograded in devotion to all that is good and beautiful.

1 I.e. Felix's; see Acts 24:25. — Ed.

It is not yet given to every one to love a Romola. Tito, too, seems to us to smack more of the intellectual strength and moral weakness of the nineteenth century than of the strong faith and equally strong passions of the age of Caesar Borgia and Machiavelli. Nothing can surpass the skill with which he is displayed, gradually entangled in the web of his own subtleties; but he would have cut short his trials with steel or poison in the age in which he is represented as enduring them. Instead of being content with frightening a wife he no longer loved when she threatened him with exposure and ruin, he would have relieved himself from that fear in a very different way within twenty-four hours. But he is a child of the nineteenth century, and shrinks from the more practical procedure of the fifteenth. He is Hetty, but a man, and not a fool. Indeed, the deepest and most powerful conception of the whole book is this of Tito — amiable, with great abilities and no vices, but living in other men's regards, and shunning every form of personal discomfort; weak, but not naturally wicked. How sad the view of life which at last leads such a man to commit some of the basest deeds, and yet who can say one feature of this wonderful portrait is at all exaggerated? Where was there ever a moral more forcibly set forth? Let no man sport with his existence. *Ernst ist das Leben.* No wonder a doctrine that calls on every one to take heed unto his ways is not universally popular. The novel-reader who takes up a volume to escape from or fill up the void of thought, may well exclaim when he meets with such a lion in his path, that he does not find in *Romola* the amusement of which he was in search; the terrible earnestness of what really comes home to him, is as little welcome as the learning which he either does not appreciate or prefers to seek elsewhere. No! *Romola* is not likely to be generally popular; it is too great both in mind and heart.

There are few things requiring a more delicate touch than such stories as that of Tessa and her little ones; yet what an air of idyllic beauty is thrown over the whole episode by her ignorance and their innocence. George Eliot is always charming in her treatment of children; they have not yet become the theatre of those conflicts which she hates, and she loves them without distrust or remorse. How admirably this episode is made to show that a man may be a villain and yet have soft affections, and a noble woman be jealous of something higher than mere personal fidelity to herself. In her treatment of Baldassarre the author displays all the qualities on which we have remarked. His remorseless vindictiveness and thirst for blood seems to her so near an approach to lunacy, that she makes him mad whenever he has a chance of action. It might be insinuated that this is done in order that the avenging sword may hang a little longer over Tito's head, and that it is but an artifice to prolong the effect of the hovering Nemesis of his hate. But there are no artifices in George Eliot's art. The true reason is, that she does not sufficiently sympathize with such depths of passion to give them adequate expression; they are so repugnant to her that she hardly compassionates the wronged old man, and certainly does not sufficiently display these features of his character which caused him to be successively forsaken by the woman he loved and by the boy he had adopted and tenderly cared for. How was it that he who so longed to be loved was denied all answer to his yearnings where he had set his heart? It can only be because his vindictive hate had so debased him, even in the mind that conceived his character, that no room was left for sympathy; and the savage animalism of his passions lowering him to the brutes made George Eliot less humane to one who had put off what alone interests her as distinctively human. This concentration of self in the reckless pursuit of a personal gratification is the strongest expression of that tendency in our race which is uniformly decried throughout *Romola*, whether it shows itself in the luxurious self-indulgence of Tito or in the noble Romola when she essays to throw off the trammels of a life that no longer answers to her ideal. The same idea is prolonged into the treatment of Savonarola, whose personal aims and longings for the glory that he thought his due are made to be his ruin, and to furnish the road to his defeat and death. That this is a true view of his character is in accordance with all we know of him, and connects him in a peculiar way with the ethical basis of the tale. His influence on its progress is but slight; the power which he exerted for a time over the imagination of Romola was not so much personal as the effect of the new views of duty which he brought before her; Christian morality could have found its way to an intellect like hers without the necessity of an intermediate human idol, and would not then have so failed her when she could no longer lean on his character for support. We do not mean that there is not much profound psychological insight displayed in the treatment of their mutual relations, but that all else in the story which is concerned with Savonarola leaves the reader but slightly moved and but feebly interested; it sinks down into that picture of ancient Florence which is so full of learned detail, and which stands in such grievous need of a central light which shall harmonize the whole.

The conclusion of the story is its weakest part, because here, if anywhere, there was need of action. Few, we think, can be fully satisfied with the manner of Tito's death. It may be said that he fell a victim to a popular tumult which had been indirectly brought about by his own treachery; that he was swept from the scene of his plottings by a side wind of the storm he had called forth by his betrayal of Savonarola; but this conclusion is hardly led up to with sufficient clearness. Rather does it seem to us that the author wishes to indicate how impossible it is for the cleverest schemer to be prepared for every contingency to which his wiles expose him; that all his ingenuity was insufficient to guard him against the low cunning of a Ceccone and a chance opportunity. That he should escape the infuriated mob to fall helpless into the hands of his powerless enemy is so painfully improbable that few have read it without some shock to their feelings. Here again, we may observe the tendency in George Eliot to avoid all violent action; Tito is too exhausted to resist his murderer, and has only strength enough to recognise the retributive avenger before he dies. Romola's history after her second flight is strangely disconnected with the rest of the tale. The pestilential village and its call upon her sympathies is another of those extravagantly fortuitous circumstances of which the author makes such free use. All sense of probability is here sacrificed for a moral effect, which yet jars upon us like an isolated light that does not harmonize with the rest of the picture. But any road is welcome that leads us to the lovely Epilogue, and to that eloquent summary of the whole purpose of the book with which Romola warns her husband's son against the faults of him he knew not was his father. . . .

[John Morley]

Felix Holt, the Radical

The opening lines of *Felix Holt* affect the reader like the first notes of the prelude to an old familiar melody. We find ourselves once more among the Midland homesteads, the hedgerows. . . . Everybody recognises the charm of the old touch in the picture. . . . There was a great deal of nonsense talked about *Romola*, and foolish persons kept on cavilling at that wonderful book, because the authoress had left what they styled her own ground. As if she had not made Florence in the fifteenth century as much her own ground as Loamshire in the nineteenth, and as if, moreover, a writer of genius could always be ready to give the public just what it happens to want, instead of what she happens to be able to give. . . . But though it was

Reprinted from the *Saturday Review*, 21 (16 June 1866), 722–724.

extremely absurd to persist in disliking Romola because she was not a Warwickshire dairymaid, and still more absurd to persist that the authoress had no business to shift her scenes or change her characters, we may still rejoice that she has again come back to those studies of English life, so humorous, so picturesque, and so philosophical, which at once raised her into the very first rank among English novelists.

The popular notion about the excellence and brilliancy of the style of George Eliot's novels is that it is simply the excellence of a painter like Teniers. People talk of *Silas Marner* as if there were nothing in it except Nancy Lammeter and the famous meeting in the parlour of the inn; of *The Mill on the Floss*, as if it were only a rural chronicle of Gleggs and Dodsons and Tullivers; of *Adam Bede*, as if it contained no more than a photographic reproduction of the life of midland dairies and farm-houses and apple-orchards. No doubt the same kind of remarks will be made about the latest, and in some points the best, of the writer's stories. And there is no lack of material even for the limited appreciation involved in such criticism as this. The talk of the miners over their ale; of the respectable farmers and shopkeepers over their three-and-sixpenny ordinary in the country market-town; of the upper servants in the butler's pantry of an old manor-house, is as witty and as truthful, and in its own way as artistically admirable, as anything that the writer has ever done. And the variety is much greater among these quaint-speaking souls, with narrow slow-moving lives, and only the dimmest and haziest outlook, and the most heavily-clogged sensibilities. Instead of the one or two who have hitherto sufficed to furnish a background for the graver and more tragic action of the story, in *Felix Holt* there are a dozen . . . all fully and clearly drawn, and each thoroughly different from the other, except in the one point of leading a dull uncultured life. For though they all say good things, what they say is not all good in the same way, but because it is in each case the natural style of a distinct character which has been keenly observed and fully conceived. But to see nothing in this or any other novel by the same writer but these droll, stupid, quaint beings, with their odd humours and rude conceits, is as bad as to see nothing in *Hamlet* except the gravediggers, nothing in *Romeo and Juliet* except the nurse and the friar and the apothecary, nothing in the *Midsummer Night's Dream* but Bottom and Snug, Snout and Quince. It is natural that George Eliot's brilliant comedy should be most talked about, because everybody in the world feels bound to like humour, and no man does not think he understands it. And, besides, the authoress's view of life is always brought out with so much mellowness, with such artistic delicacy and finish, with an air of such even tranquillity, that the incautious reader commonly overlooks the profound pathos which lies under the surface of nearly every book she has written. If she allowed herself to take the reader aside and pour deliberately into his ear a stream of general moralizing, or if she borrowed an artificial impressiveness from an abrupt *staccato* style as so many French writers, even writers of eminence, are fond of doing, the half-tragic moral and point of almost all her work would be forced upon the least reflective kind of reader. But her sense of what is due to art, or, in other words, her fine and comprehensive discernment of the proportion between the different elements of human life, and her consciousness of the unnumbered tints and shades which colour its various faces, are enough to prevent her from narrowing and concentrating all her strength upon a single effect, or throwing over her whole picture one single overwhelming colour or light. One living novelist, and an accurate observer of life too, feels only the superficial joys, the fainter pains, by which mortals are affected. Another, who has watched the doings and sufferings of men from loftier and more poetic heights, is roused to declaim like Prometheus against the selfish malignity or cold indifference with which the gods regard the sons of men. In the hands of the first, we are entertained, but we never rise from the ground. In the hands of the other, life is no longer the life of men, but of furious Titans and beneficent demigods. The authoress of *Felix Holt* and of *Romola* is wider and maturer in her philosophy than either. She looks out upon the world with the most entire enjoyment of all the good that there is in it to enjoy, and with an enlarged compassion for all the ill that there is in it to pity. But she never either whimpers over the sorrowful lot of man, or snarls and chuckles over his follies and littlenesses and impotence. . . . If life in her books is never made too small by comparing it with some imaginary standard fit for gods and giants, neither is all excluded that cannot be satisfactorily measured by the stupid little two-inch rule of those who have become optimists with shut-up minds, either out of sheer self-conceit and vanity, or else because a too narrow religion or philosophy has made them so.

One of these puzzles, which runs pathetically through *Felix Holt* as through *Romola* and *The Mill on the Floss*, is the evil usage which women receive at the hands of men. Mrs. Transome, in the novel before us, is perhaps a stronger illustration than either Maggie Tulliver or Romola of the curse which a man can be to a woman. And it is not designed for a mere outburst of impotent anger and misery when she exclaims, partly crushed, partly defiant, that "God was cruel when he made women." She gives a reason for her seemingly impious accusation, and her own history and position supplied an extenuating condition, or else an argument in its support. "A woman's love," she said, "is always freezing into fear; she wants everything, she is secure of nothing. . . ." Mrs. Transome has other causes than a rather cold and self-reliant son to exclaim, "I would not lose the misery of being a woman, now I see what can be the baseness of a man." "One must be a man — first to tell a woman that her love has made her your debtor, and then ask her to pay you by breaking the last poor threads between her and her son." The whole chapter descriptive of the interview in which a man tries to save himself from disagreeable things by inducing a woman whom he has once loved to confess her past degradation to her own son, is a painful though unsurpassedly vigorous delineation of the ugliness to which anybody can stoop when "led on through years by the gradual demands of a selfishness which has spread its fibres far and wide through the intricate vanities and sordid cares of an everyday existence." This is the old strain of *Romola* taken up again. Mr. Jermyn, like Tito, is guilty of a hateful baseness, not because he is a wicked ravening fiend, but because he is weak and mean, and has got to think honour and pity and affection and every other virtue in his relations to another cheaply sacrificed at the price of some gain to himself. "To such uses may tender relations come when they have ceased to be tender."

Yet this strong and repeated conviction of how hard or mean or cruel men are to women has not prevented the authoress, here as in other books, from making a man the effective stirrer-up of a pure and lofty enthusiasm in the mind of her heroine. What Savonarola was to Romola, Felix Holt is to Esther. Only the first had the simpler and stronger lever of religion, while Felix Holt elevates Esther to a height as lofty as his own by the subtle force of his own character. It need scarcely be said that the task which the authoress has set herself in the later case is by much the more difficult, and demands a new delicacy and ingenuity. Religious enthusiasm is full of infection, and might have easily grown up under the teaching of Savonarola in a much less noble and less bitterly tried person than Romola was. But enthusiasm for a teacher who brings no pietistic exaltation to his work, and only preaches the doctrine of self-denial from the social point of view and in its least attractive shape, implies a curious and subtle affinity between the teacher and the proselyte. This affinity and its development are very finely brought out. . . .

The suppleness with which Esther is developed is more than matched in the strong-handed consistency with which the authoress has drawn her hero. It is a pity that the plot of the story, which runs upon the gradual disclosure of a claim to some property, happens to flow from utterly remote and far-off incidents, instead of flowing from the mental movement of the principal actors. Until Esther is

taken away in her carriage by Mrs. Transome, the movement of the
plot and the movement of character rather jar and clang together.
It is true that in the end the possible possession of the property becomes a hinge in the play of character, but meanwhile it has thrown
a considerable artificialness over portions of the story. This, however,
is only a slight drawback in what is essentially a novel of character,
and the figure of Felix Holt stands out with such size and strength,
and almost incisive freshness, as to overshadow any minor defect of
construction. Behind him there are the other two most conspicuous
persons in the book – the sorrowful woman, whose life has been
robbed of all its savour and with a terrible secret crushing her heart,
and, in effective relief with her, the gentle, ripe-minded, fervent old
Dissenting minister, whose views about salvation were barely high
enough to please his flock. The authoress's creative energy has never,
we think, been so exuberantly exercised before. One group succeeds
another, and not a single figure appears in any of them, though it be
ever so far in the background, which is not perfectly drawn and
perfectly coloured. When the young ladies at the Manor, who only
ask when Dissent began, why Government didn't put a stop to it,
and so on, illustrate the intense finish which this accomplished and
profound writer puts on every part of her work. Of her exquisite
humour, her subtlety and delicacy of analysis, the wide suggestive-
ness of her bits of "aside," and her style which is so fascinating because it is so exact an outward expression of the deep and mellow
power with which her mind works and by which it is coloured –
of all these we need not speak. They are as perfect and as delightful
as they ever were.

[Eneas Sweetland Dallas]

Felix Holt, the Radical

   Hitherto Miss Austen has had the honour of the first place among
our lady novelists, but a greater than she has now arisen – a lady who
in grasp of thought, in loftiness of feeling, in subtlety of expression,
in fineness of humour, in reach of passion, and in all those sympathies

Reprinted from *The Times*, 26 June 1866, p. 6.

which go to form the true artist has never been excelled. In the art of weaving a narrative Miss Austen is still pre-eminent among women. Nothing can be more natural than the way in which she evolves an event, leading up to it with the clearest motives and the most likely accidents, never saying too much, never too little, nothing too soon, nothing too late; sparing of reflection, and letting her characters speak for themselves. George Eliot has not attained this ease of story-telling because she has to deal with subjects far more difficult than Miss Austen ever attempted, with wilder passions, with stronger situations, with higher thoughts. Miss Austen scarcely ever gets out of the humdrum of easy-going respectable life; she can therefore well afford to be calm and neat in arranging every thread of the narrative she has to weave. George Eliot undertakes to set forth the issues of a more tumultuous life, to work out deeper problems, and to play with torrents where Miss Austen played with rills. But if thus dealing with stronger forces she has been as a rule unable to give to her plots the finished ease of movement for which her predecessor is famous, she on the other hand succeeds in veiling any deficiency of story by the wondrous charm of her style. We don't know any Englishwoman who can be placed near her as a writer of prose. There is such a pith in her thinking, such a charm in her writing, such a fresh vigour in the combination of both, that — begin where we will in her volumes — we go on reading, now startled by some strange suggestive thought, now tickled by her humour, now touched by her pathos, and ever fascinated by the results of delicate observation and fine literary polish. Her style is very rich, and not only rich with the palpable meaning which in each individual sentence she has to express, but rich also in those swift, indescribable associations which well chosen words recall, allusions to past reading, the reflected sparkle of past thinking, the fragrance of past feeling.

But, great as the charm of her style is, it is not her most attractive quality. Style will go far to cloak the deficiencies of a story, but it will not account for the strong interest which George Eliot always contrives to awaken. The secret of her power is to be found in the depth and the range of her sympathies. She gets to the heart of her characters, and makes us feel with them, care for them, like to know about them. Even if they are stupid people who lead dull lives, she has the happy art of making us take an interest in their story and wish to hear it out. When we come to care for people — men or women — it really does not much matter what their story is: it fixes our attention. And for the most part we care or don't care for people according as we understand them or not. . . . And this is George Eliot's great gift that she sees and makes her readers see the personages of her tale; and we cannot truly see them, with all the stern conflict of their lives and with all the skeletons which they keep in their closets, without sharing in their hopes and fears, mixing in their griefs, and tasting of their joys. Be the man ever so dull, we become part of him and have a personal interest in his story the moment we can see him and understand him as George Eliot enables us to do. Great is Miss Austen's art of weaving a plot, and great is George Eliot's charm of style; but grandest of all as a means of exciting interest is that sympathy which sets a living character before us, and enables us not merely to see it, but also to feel it.

Felix Holt is certainly a work of rare genius, and worthy of the pen that produced in succession *Adam Bede, The Mill on the Floss,* and *Romola.* A critic, if he is in a nibbling mood, may easily pick flaws in it; but what would be the use of such trifling? We could easily show that, according to the approved methods of handling a plot, George Eliot has made several mistakes, that in some parts of her work there is not sufficient movement, and that in others where the movement is quite sufficient it lacks continuity. But it is to be hoped that true criticism will one day get beyond such cavilling, which reminds one rather vividly of the old paltry squabbles about the unities. Critics have been too much in the habit of insisting that if an author is to please us he shall follow certain rules, and that if he pleases us without following these rules he shall be condemned as an artist. . . . If George Eliot had the power of inventing situations and of constructing a story as she has that of brilliant writing and of clear and tender characterization, it would be difficult to name any novelist that could be placed before her. And if we were now to complain that some parts of her story are wanting in form, she would have a right to reply that she fulfils every requirement when she has succeeded, as we admit, in thoroughly awakening an interest in her tale. She enlists our sympathies in the lives of her characters — good and bad — with a heartiness which few other living writers can even rival; we care for them as if they were our intimate friends; and we long to know their story. . . .

[Henry James]

Felix Holt, the Radical

Better, perhaps, than any of George Eliot's novels does *Felix Holt* illustrate her closely wedded talent and foibles. Her plots have always been artificial — clumsily artificial — the conduct of her story slow, and her style diffuse. Her conclusions have been signally weak, as the reader will admit who recalls Hetty's reprieve in *Adam Bede,* the inundation of the Floss, and, worse than either, the comfortable reconciliation of Romola and Tessa. The plot of *Felix Holt* is essentially made up, and its development is forced. The style is the same lingering, slow-moving, expanding instrument which we already know. The termination is hasty, inconsiderate, and unsatisfactory — is, in fact, almost an anti-climax. It is a good instance of a certain sagacious tendency to compromise which pervades the author's spirit, and to which her novels owe that disproportion between the meagre effect of the whole and the vigorous character of the different parts, which stamp them as the works of a secondary thinker and an incomplete artist. But if such are the faults of *Felix Holt*, or some of them, we hasten to add that its merits are immense, and that the critic finds it no easy task to disengage himself from the spell of so much power, so much brilliancy, and so much discretion. In what other writer than George Eliot could we forgive so rusty a plot, and such *langueurs* of exposition, such a disparity of outline and detail? or, we may even say, of outline and outline — of general outline and of particular? so much drawing and so little composition?

In compensation for these defects we have the broad array of those rich accomplishments to which we owe *Adam Bede* and *Romola.* First in order comes the firm and elaborate delineation of individual character, of which Tito, in *Romola*, is a better example than the present work affords us. Then comes that extensive human sympathy, that easy understanding of character at large, that familiarity with man, from which a novelist draws his real inspiration, from which he borrows all his ideal lines and hues, to which he appeals for a blessing on his fictitious process, and to which he owes it that, firm locked in the tissue of the most rigid prose, he is still more or less of a poet. George Eliot's humanity colors all her other gifts — her

Reprinted from the *Nation*, 3 (16 August 1866), 127–128.

humor, her morality, and her exquisite rhetoric. Of all her qualities her humor is apparently most generally relished. Its popularity may, perhaps, be partially accounted for by a natural reaction against the dogma, so long maintained, that a woman has no humor. Still, there is no doubt that what passes for such among the admirers of Mrs. Poyser and Mrs. Glegg really rests upon a much broader perception of human incongruities than belongs to many a masculine humorist. As for our author's morality, each of our readers has felt its influence for himself. We hardly know how to qualify it. It is not bold, nor passionate, nor aggressive, nor uncompromising — it is constant, genial, and discreet. It is apparently the fruit of a great deal of culture, experience, and resignation. It carries with it that charm and that authority which will always attend the assertions of a mind enriched by researches, when it declares that wisdom and affection are better than science. We speak of the author's intellectual culture of course only as we see it reflected in her style — a style the secret of whose force is in the union of the tenderest and most abundant sympathies with a body of knowledge so ample and so active as to be absolutely free from pedantry.

As a story *Felix Holt* is singularly inartistic. The promise of the title is only half kept. The history of the hero's opinions is made subordinate to so many other considerations, to so many sketches of secondary figures, to so many discursive amplifications of incidental points, to so much that is clear and brilliant and entertaining, but that, compared with this central object, is not serious, that when the reader finds the book drawing to a close without having, as it were, brought Felix Holt's passions to a head, he feels tempted to pronounce it a failure and a mistake. As a novel with a hero there is no doubt that it *is* a failure. Felix is a fragment. We find him a Radical and we leave him what? — only "utterly married"; which is all very well in its place, but which by itself makes no conclusion. He tells his mistress at the outset that he was "converted by six weeks' debauchery." These very dramatic antecedents demanded somehow a group of consequents equally dramatic. But that quality of discretion which we have mentioned as belonging to the author, that tendency to avoid extreme deductions which has in some way muffled the crisis in each of her novels, and which, reflected in her style, always mitigates the generosity of her eloquence — these things appear to have shackled the freedom of her hand in drawing a figure which she wished and yet feared to make consistently heroic. It is not that Felix acts at variance with his high principles, but that, considering their importance, he and his principles play so brief a part and are so often absent from the scene. He is distinguished for his excellent good sense. He is uncompromising yet moderate, eager yet patient, earnest yet unimpassioned. He is indeed a thorough young Englishman, and, in spite of his sincerity, his integrity, his intelligence, and his broad shoulders, there is nothing in his figure to *thrill* the reader. There is another great novelist who has often dealt with men and women moved by exceptional opinions. Whatever these opinions may be, the reader shares them for the time with the writer; he is thrilled by the contact of her passionate earnestness, and he is borne rapidly along upon the floods of feeling which rush through her pages. The Radicalism of *Felix Holt* is strangely remote from the reader; we do not say as Radicalism, which we may have overtopped or undermined, but simply as a feeling entertained. In fact, after the singular eclipse or extinction which it appears to undergo on the occasion of his marriage, the reader feels tempted to rejoice that he, personally, has not worked himself nearer to it. There is, to our perception, but little genuine *passion* in George Eliot's men and women. With the exception of Maggie Tulliver in *The Mill on the Floss,* her heroines are all marked by a singular spiritual tenuity. In two of her novels she has introduced seductions; but in both these cases the heroines — Hetty, in *Adam Bede,* and Tessa, in *Romola* — are of so light a character as to reduce to a *minimum* the dramatic interest of the episode. We nevertheless think Hetty the best drawn of her young women. Esther Lyon, the heroine of the present tale, has great merits of intention, but the action subsides without having given her a "chance."

It is as a broad picture of midland country life in England, thirty years ago, that *Felix Holt* is, to our taste, most interesting. On this subject the author writes from a full mind, with a wealth of fancy, of suggestion, of illustration, at the command of no other English writer, bearing you along on the broad and placid rises of her speech, with a kind of retarding persuasiveness which allows her conjured images to sink slowly into your very brain. She has written no pages of this kind of discursive, comprehensive, sympathetic description more powerful or more exquisite than the introductory chapter of the present work. Against the solid and deep-colored background offered by this chapter, in connection with a hundred other passages and touches, she has placed a vast number of rustic figures. We have no space to discriminate them; we can only say that in their aggregate they leave a vivid sense of that multiplicity of eccentricities, and humors, and quaintnesses, and simple *bizarreries,* which appears to belong of right to old English villages. There are particular scenes here — scenes among common people — miners, tinkers, butchers, saddlers, and undertakers — as good as anything that the author has written. Nothing can be better than the scene in which Felix interrupts Johnson's canvass in the tavern, or that of the speech-making at Duffield. In general, we prefer George Eliot's low-life to her high-life. She seems carefully to have studied the one from without, and the other she seems merely to have glanced at from the midst of it. Mrs. Transome seems to us an unnatural, or rather, we should say, a superfluous figure. Her sorrows and trials occupy a space disproportionate to any part that she plays. She is intensely drawn, and yet dramatically she stands idle. She is, nevertheless, made the occasion, like all of her fellow-actors, however shadowy they may be, of a number of deep and brilliant touches. The character of her son, the well-born, cold-blooded, and moneyed Liberal, who divides the heroship with Felix, is delicately and firmly conceived; but like the great Tito even, like Mr. Lyon, the Dissenting preacher in the present work, like Esther Lyon herself, he is too long-drawn, too placid; he lacks dramatic compactness and rapidity. Tito is presented to us with some degree of completeness, only because *Romola* is very long, and because, for his sake, the reader is very patient.

A great deal of high praise has been given to *Felix Holt*, and a great deal more will be given still; a great many strong words will be used about the author. But we think it of considerable importance that these should at least go no further than they have already gone. It is so new a phenomenon for an English novelist to exhibit mental resources which may avail him in other walks of literature; to have powers of thought at all commensurate with his powers of imagination, that when a writer unites these conditions he is likely to receive excessive homage. There is in George Eliot's writings a tone of sagacity, of easy penetration, which leads us to believe that she would be the last to form a false estimate of her works, together with a serious respect for truth which convinces us that she would lament the publication of such an estimate. In our opinion, then, neither *Felix Holt*, nor *Adam Bede*, nor *Romola*, is a master-piece. They have none of the inspiration, the heat, nor the essential simplicity of such a work. They belong to a kind of writing in which the English tongue has the good fortune to abound — that clever, voluble, bright-colored novel of manners which began with the present century under the auspices of Miss Edgeworth and Miss Austen. George Eliot is stronger in degree than either of these writers, but she is not different in kind. She brings to her task a richer mind, but she uses it in very much the same way. With a certain masculine comprehensiveness which they lack, she is eventually a feminine — a delightfully feminine — writer. She has the microscopic observation, not a myriad of whose keen notations are worth a single one of those great synthetic guesses with which a real master attacks the truth, and which, by their occasional occurrence in the stories of

Mr. Charles Reade (the much abused *Griffith Gaunt* included), make him, to our mind, the most readable of living English novelists, and prove him a distant kinsman of Shakespeare. George Eliot has the exquisitely good taste on a small scale, the absence of taste on a large (the vulgar plot of *Felix Holt* exemplifies this deficiency), the un-broken current of feeling and, we may add, of expression, which distinguish the feminine mind. That she should be offered a higher place than she has earned, is easily explained by the charm which such gifts as hers in such abundance are sure to exercise.

Henry James

The Novels of George Eliot

The critic's first duty in the presence of an author's collective works is to seek out some key to his method, some utterance of his literary convictions, some indication of his ruling theory. The amount of labor involved in an inquiry of this kind will depend very much upon the author. In some cases the critic will find express declarations; in other cases he will have to content himself with con-scientious inductions. In a writer so fond of digressions as George Eliot, he has reason to expect that broad evidences of artistic faith will not be wanting. He finds in *Adam Bede* the following passage:

> Paint us an angel, if you can, with a floating violet robe, and a face paled by the celestial light; paint us yet oftener a Madonna, turning her mild face upward and opening her arms to welcome the divine glory; but do not impose on us any aesthetic rules which shall banish from the region of Art those old women scraping carrots with their work-worn hands, those heavy clowns taking holiday in a dingy pot-house, those rounded backs and stupid weatherbeaten faces that have bent over the spade and done the rough work of the world — those homes with their tin pans, their brown pitchers, their rough curs, and their clusters of onions. In this world there are so many of these common coarse people, who have no picturesque sentimental wretchedness! It is so needful we should remember their existence, else we may happen to leave them

Reprinted from the *Atlantic Monthly*, 18 (October 1866), 479–492.

quite out of our religion and philosophy, and frame lofty theories which only fit a world of extremes. Therefore let Art always remind us of them; therefore let us always have men ready to give the loving pains of a life to the faithful representing of commonplace things — men who see beauty in these commonplace things, and delight in showing how the kindly light of heaven falls on them.

But even in the absence of any such avowed predilections as these, a brief glance over the principal figures of her different works would assure us that our author's sympathies are with common people. Silas Marner is a linen-weaver, Adam Bede is a carpenter, Maggie Tulliver is a miller's daughter, Felix Holt is a watchmaker, Dinah Morris works in a factory, and Hetty Sorrel is a dairymaid. Esther Lyon, indeed, is a daily governess; but Tito Melema alone is a scholar. In the *Scenes of Clerical Life* the author is constantly slipping down from the clergymen, her heroes, to the most ignorant and obscure of their parishioners. Even in *Romola* she consecrates page after page to the conversation of the Florentine populace. She is as unmistakably a painter of *bourgeois* life as Thackeray was a painter of life of drawing-rooms.

Her opportunities for the study of the manners of the solid lower classes have evidently been very great. We have her word for it that she has lived much among the farmers, mechanics, and small traders of that central region of England which she has made known to us under the name of Loamshire. The conditions of the popular life in this district in that already distant period to which she refers the action of most of her stories — the end of the last century and the beginning of the present — were so different from any that have been seen in America, that an American, in treating of her books, must be satisfied not to touch upon the question of their accuracy and fidelity as pictures of manners and customs. He can only say that they bear strong internal evidence of truthfulness. If he is a great admirer of George Eliot, he will indeed be tempted to affirm that they *must* be true. They offer a completeness, a rich density of detail, which could be the fruit only of a long term of conscious contact, — such as would make it much more difficult for the author to fall into the perversion and suppression of facts, than to set them down literally. It is very probable that her colors are a little too bright, and her shadows of too mild a gray, that the sky of her landscapes is too sunny, and their atmosphere too redolent of peace and abundance. Local affection may be accountable for half of this excess of brilliancy; the author's native optimism is accountable for the other half. I do not remember, in all her novels, an instance of gross misery of any kind not directly caused by the folly of the sufferer. There are no

pictures of vice or poverty or squalor. There are no rags, no gin,
no brutal passions. That average humanity which she favors is very
borné in intellect, but very genial in heart, as a glance at its representatives in her pages will convince us. In *Adam Bede*, there is
Mr. Irwine, the vicar, with avowedly no qualification for his profession, placidly playing chess with his mother, stroking his dogs,
and dipping into Greek tragedies; there is the excellent Martin Poyser
at the Farm, good-natured and rubicund; there is his wife, somewhat
too sharply voluble, but only in behalf of cleanliness and honesty and
order; there is Captain Donnithorne at the Hall, who does a poor
girl a mortal wrong, but who is, after all, such a nice, good-looking
fellow; there are Adam and Seth Bede, the carpenter's sons, the
strongest, purest, most discreet of young rustics. The same broad
felicity prevails in *The Mill on the Floss*. Mr. Tulliver, indeed, fails
in business; but his failure only serves as an offset to the general integrity and prosperity. His son is obstinate and wilful; but it is all
on the side of virtue. His daughter is somewhat sentimental and
erratic; but she is more conscientious yet. Conscience, in the classes
from which George Eliot recruits her figures, is a universal gift.
Decency and plenty and good-humor follow contentedly in its train.
The word which sums up the common traits of our author's various
groups is the word *respectable*. Adam Bede is pre-eminently a
respectable young man; so is Arthur Donnithorne; so, although he
will persist in going without a cravat, is Felix Holt. So, with perhaps
the exception of Maggie Tulliver and Stephen Guest, is every important character to be found in our author's writings. They all
share this fundamental trait, — that in each of them passion proves
itself feebler than conscience.

The first work which made the name of George Eliot generally
known, contains, to my perception, only a small number of the
germs of her future power. From the *Scenes of Clerical Life* to
Adam Bede she made not so much a step as a leap. Of the three
tales contained in the former work, I think the first is much the best.
It is short, broadly descriptive, humorous, and exceedingly pathetic.
"The Sad Fortunes of the Reverend Amos Barton" are fortunes
which clever story-tellers with a turn for pathos, from Oliver
Goldsmith downward, have found of very good account, — the fortunes of a hapless clergyman of the Church of England in daily
contention with the problem how upon eighty pounds a year to
support a wife and six children in all due ecclesiastical gentility.
"Mr. Gilfil's Love-Story," the second of the tales in question, I
cannot hesitate to pronounce a failure. George Eliot's pictures of
drawing room life are only interesting when they are linked or related
to scenes in the tavern parlor, the dairy, and the cottage. Mr. Gilfil's

love-story is enacted entirely in the drawing-room, and in consequence it is singularly deficient in force and reality. Not that it is
vulgar, — for our author's good taste never forsakes her, — but it is
thin, flat, and trivial. But for a certain family likeness in the use
of language and the rhythm of style, it would be hard to believe that
these pages are by the same hand as *Silas Marner*. In "Janet's Repentance," the last and longest of the three clerical stories, we return
to middle life, — the life represented by the Dodsons in *The Mill on
the Floss*. The subject of this tale might almost be qualified by the
French epithet *scabreux*. It would be difficult for what is called
realism to go further than in the adoption of a heroine stained with
the vice of intemperance. The theme is unpleasant; the author chose
it at her peril. It must be added, however, that Janet Dempster has
many provocations. Married to a brutal drunkard, she takes refuge
in drink against his ill-usage; and the story deals less with her lapse
into disgrace than with her redemption, through the kind offices of
the Reverend Edgar Tryan, — by virtue of which, indeed, it takes its
place in the clerical series. I cannot help thinking that the stern and
tragical character of the subject has been enfeebled by the over-
diffuseness of the narrative and the excess of local touches. The
abundance of the author's recollections and observations of village
life clogs the dramatic movement, over which she has as yet a comparatively slight control. In her subsequent works the stouter fabric
of the story is better able to support this heavy drapery of humor
and digression.

To a certain extent, I think *Silas Marner* holds a higher place than
any of the author's works. It is more nearly a masterpiece; it has
more of that simple, rounded, consummate aspect, that absence of
loose ends and gaping issues, which marks a classical work. What was
attempted in it, indeed, was within more immediate reach than the
heart-trials of Adam Bede and Maggie Tulliver. A poor, dull-witted,
disappointed Methodist cloth-weaver; a little golden-haired foundling
child; a well-meaning, irresolute country squire, and his patient,
childless wife; — these, with a chorus of simple, beer-loving villagers,
make up the *dramatis personae*. More than any of its brother-works,
Silas Marner, I think, leaves upon the mind a deep impression of the
grossly material life of agricultural England in the last days of the
old *régime*, — the days of full-orbed Toryism, of Trafalgar and of
Waterloo, when the invasive spirit of French domination threw
England back upon a sense of her own insular solidity, and made
her for the time doubly, brutally, morbidly English. Perhaps the
best pages in the work are Marner's disappointments in friendship
and in love, his unmerited disgrace, and his long, lonely twilight-life
at Raveloe, with the sole companionship of his loom, in which his

muscles moved "with such even repetition, that their pause seemed almost as much a constraint as the holding of his breath." Here, as in all George Eliot's books, there is a middle life and a low life; and here, as usual, I prefer the low life. In *Silas Marner*, in my opinion, she has come nearest the mildly rich tints of brown and gray, the mellow lights and the undreadful corner-shadows of the Dutch masters whom she emulates. One of the chapters contains a scene in a pothouse, which frequent reference has made famous. Never was a group of honest, garrulous village simpletons more kindly and humanely handled. . . . The best drawn of the village worthies in *Silas Marner* are Mr. Macey, of the scene just quoted, and good Dolly Winthrop, Marner's kindly patroness. . . . Mrs. Winthrop, the wheelwright's wife who, out of the fulness of her charity, comes to comfort Silas in the season of his distress, is in her way one of the most truthfully sketched of the author's figures. . . . I imagine that there is in no other English novel a figure so simple in its elements as this of Dolly Winthrop, which is so real without being contemptible, and so quaint without being ridiculous.

In all those of our author's books which have borne the name of the hero or heroine, — *Adam Bede, Silas Marner, Romola,* and *Felix Holt,* — the person so put forward has really played a subordinate part. The author may have set out with the intention of maintaining him supreme; but her material has become rebellious in her hands, and the technical hero has been eclipsed by the real one. Tito is the leading figure in *Romola.* The story deals predominantly, not with Romola as affected by Tito's faults, but with Tito's faults as affecting first himself, and incidentally his wife. Godfrey Cass, with his life-long secret, is by right the hero of *Silas Marner.* Felix Holt, in the work which bears his name, is little more than an occasional apparition; and indeed the novel has no hero, but only a heroine. The same remark applies to *Adam Bede*, as the work stands. The central figure of the book, by virtue of her great misfortune, is Hetty Sorrel. In the presence of that misfortune no one else, assuredly, has a right to claim dramatic pre-eminence. The one person for whom an approach to equality may be claimed is, not Adam Bede, but Arthur Donnithorne. If the story had ended, as I should have infinitely preferred to see it end, with Hetty's execution, or even with her reprieve, and if Adam had been left to his grief, and Dinah Morris to the enjoyment of that distinguished celibacy for which she was so well suited, then I think Adam might have shared the honors of pre-eminence with his hapless sweetheart. But as it is, the continuance of the book in his interest is fatal to him. His sorrow at Hetty's misfortune is not a *sufficient* sorrow for the situation. That

his marriage at some future time was quite possible, and even natural,
I readily admit; but that was matter for a new story. This point
illustrates, I think, the great advantage of the much-censured method,
introduced by Balzac, of continuing his heroes' adventures from tale
to tale. Or, admitting that the author was indisposed to undertake,
or even to conceive, in its completeness, a new tale, in which Adam,
healed of his wound by time, should address himself to another
woman, I yet hold that it would be possible tacitly to foreshadow
some such event at the close of the tale which we are supposing to
end with Hetty's death, — to make it the logical consequence of
Adam's final state of mind. Of course circumstances would have
much to do with bringing it to pass, and these circumstances could
not be foreshadowed; but apart from the action of circumstances
would stand the fact that, to begin with, the event was *possible*. The
assurance of this possibility is what I should have desired the author
to place the sympathetic reader at a standpoint to deduce for himself.
In every novel the work is divided between the writer and the reader;
but the writer makes the reader very much as he makes his characters. When he makes him ill, that is, makes him indifferent, he
does no work; the writer does all. When he makes him well, that is,
makes him interested, then the reader does quite half the labor. In
making such a deduction as I have just indicated, the reader would
be doing but his share of the task; the grand point is to get him to
make it. I hold that there is a way. It is perhaps a secret; but until
it is found out, I think that the art of story-telling cannot be said
to have approached perfection.

When you re-read coldly and critically a book which in former
years you have read warmly and carelessly, you are surprised to
see how it changes its proportions. It falls away in those parts which
have been pre-eminent in your memory, and it increases in the
small portions. Until I lately read *Adam Bede* for a second time,
Mrs. Poyser was in my mind its representative figure; for I remembered a number of her epigrammatic sallies. But now, after a
second reading, Mrs. Poyser is the last figure I think of, and a fresh
perusal of her witticisms has considerably diminished their classical
flavor. And if I must tell the truth, Adam himself is next to the
last, and sweet Dinah Morris third from the last. The person immediately evoked by the title of the work is poor Hetty Sorrel.
Mrs. Poyser is *too* epigrammatic; her wisdom smells of the lamp.
I do not mean to say that she is not natural, and that women of her
class are not often gifted with her homely fluency, her penetration,
and her turn for forcible analogies. But she is too sustained; her
morality is too shrill, — too much in *staccato;* she too seldom subsides
into the commonplace. Yet it cannot be denied that she puts things

very happily. . . . Mrs. Poyser has something almost of Yankee shrewdness and angularity; but the figure of a New England rural housewife would lack a whole range of Mrs. Poyser's feelings, which, whatever may be its effect in real life, gives its subject in a novel at least a very picturesque richness of color; the constant sense, namely, of a superincumbent layer of "gentlefolks," whom she and her companions can never raise their heads unduly without hitting.

My chief complaint with Adam Bede himself is that he is too good. He is meant, I conceive, to be every inch a man; but, to my mind, there are several inches wanting. He lacks spontaneity and sensibility, he is too stiff-backed. He lacks that supreme quality without which a man can never be interesting to men, — the capacity to be tempted. His nature is without richness or responsiveness. I doubt not that such men as he exist, especially in the author's thrice-English Loamshire; she has partially described them as a class, with a felicity which carries conviction. She claims for her hero that, although a plain man, he was as little an ordinary man as he was a genius. . . .

If she is not a great dramatist, she is at least an exquisite describer. But one can as little help feeling that it is no more than a strictly logical retribution, that in her hour of need (dramatically speaking) she should find them indifferent to their duties as heroes. I profoundly doubt whether the central object of a novel may successfully be a passionless creature. The ultimate eclipse, both of Adam Bede and of Felix Holt would seem to justify my question. Tom Tulliver is passionless, and Tom Tulliver lives gratefully in the memory; but this, I take it, is because he is strictly a subordinate figure, and awakens no reaction of feeling on the reader's part by usurping a position which he is not the man to fill.

Dinah Morris is apparently a study from life; and it is warm praise to say, that, in spite of the high key in which she is conceived, morally, she retains many of the warm colors of life. But I confess that it is hard to conceive of a woman so exalted by religious fervor remaining so cool-headed and so temperate. There is in Dinah Morris too close an agreement between her distinguished natural disposition and the action of her religious faith. If by nature she had been passionate, rebellious, selfish, I could better understand her actual self-abnegation. I would look upon it as the logical fruit of a profound religious experience. But as she stands, heart and soul go easily hand in hand. I believe it to be very uncommon for what is called a religious conversion merely to intensify and consecrate pre-existing inclinations. It is usually a change, a wrench; and the new life is apt to be the more sincere as the old one had less in common with it. But, as I have said, Dinah Morris bears so many indications of being a reflection of facts well known to the author,

— and the phenomena of Methodism, from the frequency with which
their existence is referred to in her pages, appear to be so familiar
to her, — that I hesitate to do anything but thankfully accept her
portrait. About Hetty Sorrel I shall have no hesitation whatever:
I accept her with all my heart. Of all George Eliot's female figures
she is the least ambitious, and on the whole, I think, the most successful. The part of the story which concerns her is much the most
forcible; and there is something infinitely tragic in the reader's sense
of the contrast between the sternly prosaic life of the good people
about her, their wholesome decency and their noonday probity, and
the dusky sylvan path along which poor Hetty is tripping, light-
footed, to her ruin. Hetty's conduct throughout seems to me to be
thoroughly consistent. The author has escaped the easy error of
representing her as in any degree made serious by suffering. She is
vain and superficial by nature; and she remains so to the end. As for
Arthur Donnithorne, I would rather have had him either better or
worse. I would rather have had a little more premeditation before
his fault, or a little more repentance after it; that is, while repentance
could still be of use. Not that, all things considered, he is not a very
fair image of a frank-hearted, well-meaning, careless, self-indulgent
young gentleman; but the author has in his case committed the error
which in Hetty's she avoided, — the error of showing him as redeemed
by suffering. I cannot but think that he was as weak as she. A weak
woman, indeed, is weaker than a weak man; but Arthur Donnithorne
was a superficial fellow, a person emphatically not to be moved by
a shock of conscience into a really interesting and dignified attitude,
such as he is made to assume at the close of the book. Why not
see things in their nakedness? the impatient reader is tempted to ask.
Why not let passions and foibles play themselves out?

It is as a picture, or rather as a series of pictures, that I find *Adam
Bede* most valuable. The author succeeds better in drawing attitudes
of feeling than in drawing movements of feeling. Indeed, the only
attempt at development of character or of purpose in the book
occurs in the case of Arthur Donnithorne, where the materials are
of the simplest kind. Hetty's lapse into disgrace is not gradual, it
is immediate: it is without struggle and without passion. Adam
himself has arrived at perfect righteousness when the book opens;
and it is impossible to go beyond that. In his case too, therefore,
there is no dramatic progression. The same remark applies to Dinah
Morris. It is not in her conceptions nor her composition that
George Eliot is strongest: it is in her *touches*. In these she is quite
original. She is a good deal of a humorist, and something of a
satirist; but she is neither Dickens nor Thackeray. She has over them
the great advantage that she is also a good deal of a philosopher;

and it is to this union of the keenest observation with the ripest reflection, that her style owes its essential force. She is a thinker, — not, perhaps, a passionate thinker, but at least a serious one; and the term can be applied with either adjective neither to Dickens nor Thackeray. The constant play of lively and vigorous thought about the objects furnished by her observation animates these latter with a surprising richness of color and a truly human interest. It gives to the author's style, moreover, that lingering, affectionate, comprehensive quality which is its chief distinction; and perhaps occasionally it makes her tedious. George Eliot is so little tedious, however, because, if, on the one hand, her reflection never flags, so, on the other, her observation never ceases to supply it with material. Her observation, I think, is decidedly of the feminine kind: it deals, in preference, with small things. This fact may be held to explain the excellence of what I have called her pictures, and the comparative feebleness of her dramatic movement. The contrast here indicated, strong in *Adam Bede*, is most striking in *Felix Holt, the Radical*. The latter work is an admirable tissue of details; but it seems to me quite without character as a composition. It leaves upon the mind no single impression. Felix Holt's radicalism, the pretended motive of the story, is utterly choked amidst a mass of subordinate interests. No representation is attempted of the growth of his opinions, or of their action upon his character: he is marked by the same singular rigidity of outline and fixedness of posture which characterized Adam Bede, — except, perhaps, that there is a certain inclination towards poetry in Holt's attitude. But if the general outline is timid and undecided in *Felix Holt*, the different parts are even richer than in former works. There is no person in the book who attains to triumphant vitality; but there is not a single figure, of however little importance, that has not caught from without a certain reflection of life. There is a little old waiting-woman to a great lady, — Mrs. Denner by name, — who does not occupy five pages in the story, but who leaves upon the mind a most vivid impression of decent, contented, intelligent, half-stoical servility. . . .

Of the four English stories, *The Mill on the Floss* seems to me to have most dramatic continuity, in distinction from that descriptive, discursive method of narration which I have attempted to indicate. After Hetty Sorrel, I think Maggie Tulliver the most successful of the author's young women, and after Tito Melema, Tom Tulliver the best of her young men. English novels abound in pictures of childhood; but I know of none more truthful and touching than the early pages of this work. Poor erratic Maggie is worth a hundred of her positive brother, and yet on the very threshold of life she is compelled to accept him as her master. He falls naturally

into the man's privilege of always being in the right. . . . The
portions of the story which bear upon the Dodson family are in
their way not unworthy of Balzac; only that, while our author has
treated its peculiarities humorously, Balzac would have treated them
seriously, almost solemnly. We are reminded of him by the attempt
to classify the Dodsons socially in a scientific manner, and to ac-
cumulate small examples of their idiosyncrasies. I do not mean to
say that the resemblance is very deep. The chief defect – indeed,
the only serious one – in *The Mill on the Floss* is its conclusion.
Such a conclusion is in itself assuredly not illegitimate, and there is
nothing in the fact of the flood, to my knowledge, essentially unnatural: what I object to is its relation to the preceding part of the
story. The story is told as if it were destined to have, if not a
strictly happy termination, at least one within ordinary probabilities.
As it stands, the *dénouement* shocks the reader most painfully.
Nothing has prepared him for it; the story does not move towards
it; it casts no shadow before it. Did such a *dénouement* lie within
the author's intentions from the first, or was it a tardy expedient for
the solution of Maggie's difficulties? This question the reader asks
himself, but of course he asks it in vain. For my part, although, as
long as humanity is subject to floods and earthquakes, I have no
objection to see them made use of in novels, I would in this particular
case have infinitely preferred that Maggie should have been left to
her own devices. I understand the author's scruples, and to a certain
degree I respect them. A lonely spinsterhood seemed but a dismal
consummation of her generous life; and yet, as the author conceives,
it was unlikely that she would return to Stephen Guest. I respect
Maggie profoundly; but nevertheless I ask, Was this after all so
unlikely? I will not try to answer the question. I have shown
enough courage in asking it. But one thing is certain: a *dénouement*
by which Maggie should have called Stephen back would have been
extremely interesting, and would have had far more in its favor than
can be put to confusion by a mere exclamation of horror.

I have come to the end of my space without speaking of *Romola*,
which, as the most important of George Eliot's works, I had kept
in reserve. I have only room to say that on the whole I think it *is*
decidedly the most important, – not the most entertaining nor the
most readable, but the one in which the largest things are attempted
and grasped. The figure of Savonarola, subordinate though it is, is a
figure on a larger scale than any which George Eliot has elsewhere
undertaken; and in the career of Tito Melema there is a fuller representation of the development of a character. Considerable as are our
author's qualities as an artist, and largely as they are displayed in
Romola, the book strikes me less as a work of art than as a work

of morals. Like all of George Eliot's works, its dramatic construction is feeble; the story drags and halts, — the setting is too large for the picture; but I remember that, the first time I read it, I declared to myself that much should be forgiven it for the sake of its generous feeling and its elevated morality. I still recognize this latter fact, but I think I find it more on a level than I at first found it with the artistic conditions of the book. "Our deeds determine us," George Eliot says somewhere in *Adam Bede*, "as much as we determine our deeds." This is the moral lesson of *Romola*. A man has no associate so intimate as his own character, his own career, — his present and his past; and if he builds up his career of timid and base actions, they cling to him like evil companions, to sophisticate, to corrupt, and to damn him. As in Maggie Tulliver we had a picture of the elevation of the moral tone by honesty and generosity, so that when the mind found itself face to face with the need for a strong muscular effort, it was competent to perform it; so in Tito we have a picture of that depression of the moral tone by falsity and self-indulgence, which gradually evokes on every side of the subject some implacable claim, to be avoided or propitiated. At last all his unpaid debts join issue before him, and he finds the path of life a hideous blind alley. Can any argument be more plain? Can any lesson be more salutary? "Under every guilty secret," writes the author, with her usual felicity, "there is a hidden brood of guilty wishes, whose unwholesome, infecting life is cherished by the darkness. The contaminating effect of deeds often lies less in the commission than in the consequent adjustment of our desires, — the enlistment of self-interest on the side of falsity; as, on the other hand, the purifying influence of public confession springs from the fact, that by it the hope in lies is forever swept away, *and the soul recovers the noble attitude of simplicity*." And again: "Tito was experiencing that inexorable law of human souls, that we prepare ourselves for sudden deeds by the reiterated choice of good or evil that gradually determines character." Somewhere else I think she says, in purport, that our deeds are like our children; we beget them, and rear them and cherish them, and they grow up and turn against us and misuse us. The fact that has led me to a belief in the fundamental equality between the worth of *Romola* as a moral argument and its value as a work of art, is the fact that in each character it seems to me essentially prosaic. The excellence both of the spirit and of the execution of the book is emphatically an obvious excellence. They make no demand upon the imagination of the reader. It is true of both of them that he who runs may read them. It may excite surprise that I should intimate that George Eliot is deficient in imagination; but I believe that I am right in so doing. Very readable novels have been written without imagination; and as compared with writers who, like Mr. Trollope, are totally destitute of the faculty, George Eliot may be said to be richly endowed with it. But as compared with writers whom we are tempted to call decidedly imaginative, she must, in my opinion, content herself with the very solid distinction of being exclusively an observer. In confirmation of this I would suggest a comparison of those chapters in *Adam Bede* which treat of Hetty's flight and wanderings, and those of Miss Brontë's *Jane Eyre* which describe the heroine's escape from Rochester's house and subsequent perambulations. The former are throughout admirable prose; the latter are in portions very good poetry.

One word more. Of all the impressions — and they are numerous — which a reperusal of George Eliot's writings has given me, I find the strongest to be this: that (with all deference to *Felix Holt, the Radical*) the author is in morals and aesthetics essentially a conservative. In morals her problems are still the old, passive problems. I use the word "old" with all respect. What moves her most is the idea of a conscience harassed by the memory of slighted obligations. Unless in the case of Savonarola, she has made no attempt to depict a conscience taking upon itself great and novel responsibilities. In her last work, assuredly such an attempt was — considering the title — conspicuous by its absence. Of a corresponding tendency in the second department of her literary character, — or perhaps I should say in a certain middle field where morals and aesthetics move in concert, — it is very difficult to give an example. A tolerably good one is furnished by her inclination to compromise with the old tradition — and here I use the word "old" *without* respect — which exacts that a serious story of manners shall close with the factitious happiness of a fairy-tale. I know few things more irritating in a literary way than each of her final chapters, — for even in *The Mill on the Floss* there is a fatal "Conclusion." Both as an artist and a thinker, in other words, our author is an optimist; and although a conservative is not necessarily an optimist, I think an optimist is pretty likely to be a conservative.

Henry James

The Spanish Gypsy

I know not whether George Eliot has any enemies, nor why she should have any; but if perchance she has, I can imagine them to have hailed the announcement of a poem from her pen as a piece of particularly good news. "Now, finally," I fancy them saying, "this sadly overrated author will exhibit all the weakness that is in her; now she will prove herself what we have all along affirmed her to be, — not a serene, self-directing genius of the first order, knowing her powers and respecting them, and content to leave well enough alone, but a mere showy rhetorician, possessed and prompted, not by the humble spirit of truth, but by an insatiable longing for applause." Suppose Mr. Tennyson were to come out with a novel, or Madame George Sand were to produce a tragedy in French alexandrines. The reader will agree with me, that these are hard suppositions; yet the world has seen stranger things, and been reconciled to them. Nevertheless, with the best possible will toward our illustrious novelist, it is easy to put ourselves in the shoes of these hypothetical detractors. No one, assuredly, but George Eliot could mar George Eliot's reputation; but there was room for the fear that she might do it. This reputation was essentially prose-built, and in the attempt to insert a figment of verse of the magnitude of *The Spanish Gypsy*, it was quite possible that she might injure its fair proportions.

In consulting her past works, for approval of their hopes and their fears, I think both her friends and her foes would have found sufficient ground for their arguments. Of all our English prose-writers of the present day I think I may say, that, as a writer simply, a mistress of style, I have been very near preferring the author of *Silas Marner* and of *Romola*, — the author, too, of *Felix Holt*. The motive of my great regard for her style I take to have been that I fancied it such perfect solid prose. Brilliant and lax as it was in tissue, it seemed to contain very few of the silken threads of poetry; it lay on the ground like a carpet, instead of floating in the air like a banner. If my impression was correct, *The Spanish Gypsy* is not a genuine poem. And yet, looking over the author's novels in memory,

Reprinted from the *North American Review*, 107 (October 1868), 620–635.

looking over them in the light of her unexpected assumption of
the poetical function, I find it hard at times not to mistrust my
impression. I like George Eliot well enough, in fact, to admit, for
the time, that I might have been in the wrong. If I had liked her
less, if I had rated lower the quality of her prose, I should have
estimated coldly the possibilities of her verse. Of course, therefore,
if, as I am told many persons do in England, who consider carpenters
and weavers and millers' daughters no legitimate subject for reputable
fiction, I had denied her novels any qualities at all, I should have
made haste, on reading the announcement of her poem, to speak of
her as the world speaks of a lady, who, having reached a comfortable
middle age, with her shoulders decently covered, "for reasons deep
below the reach of thought," (to quote our author,) begins to go
out to dinner in a low-necked dress "of the period," and say in fine,
in three words, that she was going to make a fool of herself.

But here, meanwhile, is the book before me, to arrest all this *a
priori* argumentation. Time enough has elapsed since its appearance
for most readers to have uttered their opinons, and for the general
verdict of criticism to have been formed. In looking over several
of the published reviews, I am struck with the fact that those immediately issued are full of the warmest delight and approval, and
that, as the work ceases to be a novelty, objections, exceptions, and
protests multiply. This is quite logical. Not only does it take a
much longer time than the reviewer on a weekly journal has at his
command to properly appreciate a work of the importance of *The
Spanish Gypsy*, but the poem was actually much more of a poem
than was to be expected. The foremost feeling of many readers
must have been — it was certainly my own — that we had hitherto
only half known George Eliot. Adding this dazzling new half to
the old one, readers constructed for the moment a really splendid
literary figure. But gradually the old half began to absorb the new,
and to assimilate its virtues and failings, and critics finally remembered that the cleverest writer in the world is after all nothing
and no one but himself.

The most striking quality in *The Spanish Gypsy*, on a first reading,
I think, is its extraordinary rhetorical energy and elegance. The
richness of the author's style in her novels gives but an inadequate
idea of the splendid generosity of diction displayed in the poem. She
is so much of a thinker and an observer that she draws very heavily
on her powers of expression, and one may certainly say that they
not only never fail her, but that verbal utterance almost always bestows upon her ideas a peculiar beauty and fulness, apart from their
significance. The result produced in this manner, the reader will
see, may come very near being poetry; it is assuredly eloquence.

The faults in the present work are very seldom faults of weakness, except in so far as it is weak to lack an absolute mastery of one's powers: they arise rather from an excess of rhetorical energy, from a desire to attain to perfect fulness and roundness of utterance; they are faults of overstatement. . . .

I may say in general, that the author's admirers must have found in *The Spanish Gypsy* a presentment of her various special gifts stronger and fuller, on the whole, than any to be found in her novels. Those who valued her chiefly for her humor — the gentle humor which provokes a smile, but deprecates a laugh — will recognize that delightful gift in Blasco, and Lorenzo, and Roldan, and Juan, — slighter in quantity than in her prose-writings, but quite equal, I think, in quality. Those who prize most her descriptive powers will see them wondrously well embodied in these pages. As for those who have felt compelled to declare that she possesses the Shakespearian touch, they must consent, with what grace they may, to be disappointed. I have never thought our author a great dramatist, nor even a particularly dramatic writer. A real dramatist, I imagine, could never have reconciled himself to the odd mixture of the narrative and dramatic forms by which the present work is distinguished; and that George Eliot's genius should have needed to work under these conditions seems to me strong evidence of the partial and incomplete character of her dramatic instincts. An English critic lately described her, with much correctness, as a critic rather than a creator of characters. She puts her figures into action very successfully, but on the whole she thinks for them more than they think for themselves. She thinks, however, to wonderfully good purpose. In none of her works, are there two more distinctly human representations than the characters of Silva and Juan. The latter, indeed, if I am not mistaken, ranks with Tito Melema and Hetty Sorrel, as one of her very best conceptions. . . .

But now to reach the real substance of the poem, and to allow the reader to appreciate the author's treatment of human character and passion, I must speak briefly of the story. I shall hardly misrepresent it, when I say that it is a very old one, and that it illustrates that very common occurrence in human affairs, — the conflict of love and duty. Such, at least, is the general impression made by the poem as it stands. It is very possible that the author's primary intention may have had a breadth which has been curtailed in the execution of the work, — that it was her wish to present a struggle between nature and culture, between education and the instinct of race. You can detect in such a theme the stuff of a very good drama, — a somewhat stouter stuff, however, than *The Spanish Gypsy* is made of. George Eliot, true to that didactic tendency for which she has hitherto been remarkable, has preferred to make her heroine's predicament a problem in morals, and has thereby, I think, given herself hard work to reach a satisfactory solution. She has, indeed, committed herself to a signal error, in a psychological sense, — that of making a Gypsy girl with a conscience. Either Fedalma was a perfect Zincala in temper and instinct, — in which case her adhesion to her father and her race was a blind, passionate, sensuous movement which is almost expressly contradicted, — or else she was a pure and intelligent Catholic, in which case nothing in the nature of a struggle can be predicted. The character of Fedalma, I may say, comes very near being a failure, — a very beautiful one; but in point of fact it misses it.

It misses it, I think, thanks to that circumstance which in reading and criticising *The Spanish Gypsy* we must not cease to bear in mind, the fact that the work is emphatically a *romance*. We may contest its being a poem, but we must admit that it is a romance in the fullest sense of the word. Whether the term may be absolutely defined I know not; but we may say of it, comparing it with the novel, that it carries much farther that compromise with reality which is the basis of all imaginative writing. In the romance this principle of compromise pervades the superstructure as well as the basis. The most that we exact is that the fable be consistent with itself. Fedalma is not a real Gypsy maiden. The conviction is strong in the reader's mind that a genuine Spanish Zincala would have somehow contrived both to follow her tribe and to keep her lover. If Fedalma is not real, Zarca is even less so. He is interesting, imposing, picturesque; but he is very far, I take it, from being a genuine *Gypsy* chieftain. They are both ideal figures, — the offspring of a strong mental desire for creatures well rounded in their elevation and heroism, — creatures who should illustrate the nobleness of human nature divorced from its smallness. Don Silva has decidedly more of the common stuff of human feeling, more charming natural passion and weakness. But he, too, is largely a vision of the intellect; his constitution is adapted to the atmosphere and the climate of romance. Juan, indeed, has one foot well planted on the lower earth; but Juan is only an accessory figure. I have said enough to lead the reader to perceive that the poem should not be regarded as a rigid transcript of actual or possible fact, — that the action goes on in an artificial world, and that properly to comprehend it he must regard it with a generous mind.

Viewed in this manner, as efficient figures in an essentially ideal and romantic drama, Fedalma and Zarca seem to gain vastly, and to shine with a brilliant radiance. If we reduce Fedalma to the level of the heroines of our modern novels, in which the interest aroused by a young girl is in proportion to the similarity of her circumstances to those of the reader, and in which none but the commonest feelings

are required, provided they be expressed with energy, we shall be
tempted to call her a solemn and cold-blooded jilt. In a novel it would
have been next to impossible for the author to make the heroine renounce her lover. In novels we not only forgive that weakness which
is common and familiar and human, but we actually demand it. But
in poetry, although we are compelled to adhere to the few elementary
passions of our nature, we do our best to dress them in a new and
exquisite garb. Men and women in a poetical drama are nothing, if
not distinguished.

> Our dear young love, — its breath was happiness!
> But it had grown upon a larger life,
> Which tore its roots asunder.

These words are uttered by Fedalma at the close of the poem, and
in them she emphatically claims the distinction of having her own
private interests invaded by those of a people. The manner of her
kinship with the Zincali is in fact very much "larger life" than her
marriage with Don Silva. We may, indeed, challenge the probability
of her relationship to her tribe impressing her mind with a force
equal to that of her love, — her "dear young love." We may declare
that this is an unnatural and violent result. For my part, I think it
is very far from violent; I think the author has employed art in reducing the apparently arbitrary quality of her preference for her
tribe. I say reducing; I do not say effacing; because it seems to me, as
I have intimated, that just at this point her art has been wanting, and
we are not sufficiently prepared for Fedalma's movement by a sense
of her Gypsy temper and instincts. Still, we are in some degree
prepared for it by various passages in the opening scenes of the book,
— by all the magnificent description of her dance in the Plaza. . . .
    We are better prepared for it, however, than by anything else, by
the whole impression we receive of the exquisite refinement and
elevation of the young girl's mind, — by all that makes her so bad a
Gypsy. She possesses evidently a very high-strung intellect, and her
whole conduct is in a higher key, as I may say, than that of ordinary
women, or even ordinary heroines. She is natural, I think, in a
poetical sense. She is consistent with her own prodigiously superfine
character. From a lower point of view than that of the author, she
lacks several of the desirable feminine qualities, — a certain womanly
warmth and petulance, a graceful irrationality. Her mind is very
much too lucid, and her aspirations too lofty. Her conscience, especially, is decidedly over-active. But this is a distinction which she
shares with all the author's heroines, — Dinah Morris, Maggie Tulliver, Romola, and Esther Lyon, — a distinction, moreover, for which

I should be very sorry to hold George Eliot to account. There are
most assuredly women and women. While Messrs. Charles Reade and
Wilkie Collins, and Miss Braddon and her school, tell one half the
story, it is no more than fair that the author of *The Spanish Gypsy*
should, all unassisted attempt to relate the other.

Whenever a story really interests one, he is very fond of paying
it the compliment of imagining it otherwise constructed, and of cap-
ping it with a different termination. In the present case, one is irresistibly tempted to fancy *The Spanish Gypsy* in prose, — a compact,
regular drama: not George Eliot's prose, however: in a diction much
more nervous and heated and rapid, written with short speeches as
well as long. (The reader will have observed the want of brevity,
retort, interruption, rapid alternation, in the dialogue of the poem.
The characters all talk, as it were, standing still.) In such a play as
the one indicated one imagines a truly dramatic Fedalma, — a passionate, sensuous, irrational Bohemian, as elegant as good breeding
and native good taste could make her, and as pure as her actual sister
in the poem, — but rushing into her father's arms with a cry of joy,
and losing the sense of her lover's sorrow in what the author has
elsewhere described as "the hurrying ardor of action." Or in the
way of a different termination, suppose that Fedalma should for the
time value at once her own love and her lover's enough to make her
prefer the latter's destiny to that represented by her father. Imagine,
then, that, after marriage, the Gypsy blood and nature should begin
to flow and throb in quicker pulsations, — and that the poor girl
should sadly contrast the sunny freedom and lawless joy of her
people's lot with the splendid rigidity and formalism of her own.
You may conceive at this point that she should pass from sadness to
despair, and from despair to revolt. Here the catastrophe may occur
in a dozen different ways. Fedalma may die before her husband's
eyes, of unsatisfied longing for the fate she has rejected; or she may
make an attempt actually to recover her fate, by wandering off and
seeking out her people. The cultivated mind, however, it seems to
me, imperiously demands that, on finally overtaking them, she shall
die of mingled weariness and shame, as neither a good Gypsy nor
a good Christian, but simply a good figure for a tragedy. But there
is a degree of levity which almost amounts to irreverence in fancying
this admirable performance as anything other than it is.

After Fedalma comes Zarca, and here our imagination flags. Not
so George Eliot's: for as simple imagination, I think that in the conception of this impressive and unreal figure it appears decidedly at
its strongest. With Zarca, we stand at the very heart of the realm
of romance. There is truly a grand simplicity, to my mind, in the
outline of his character, and a remarkable air of majesty in his poise

and attitude. He is a *père noble* in perfection. His speeches have an exquisite eloquence. In strictness, he is to the last degree unreal, illogical, and rhetorical; but a certain dramatic unity is diffused through his character by the depth and energy of the colors in which he is painted. With a little less simplicity, his figure would be decidedly modern. As it stands, it is neither modern nor mediaeval; it belongs to the world of intellectual dreams and visions. The reader will admit that it is a vision of no small beauty, the conception of a stalwart chieftain who distils the cold exaltation of his purpose from the utter loneliness and obloquy of his race. . . .

Better than Fedalma or than Zarca is the remarkably beautiful and elaborate portrait of Don Silva, in whom the author has wished to present a young nobleman as splendid in person and in soul as the dawning splendor of his native country. In the composition of his figure, the real and the romantic, brilliancy and pathos, are equally commingled. He cannot be said to stand out in vivid relief. As a piece of painting, there is nothing commanding, aggressive, brutal, as I may say, in his lineaments. But they will bear close scrutiny. Place yourself within the circumscription of the work, breathe its atmosphere, and you will see that Don Silva is portrayed with a delicacy to which English story-tellers, whether in prose or verse, have not accustomed us. There are better portraits in Browning, but there are also worse; in Tennyson there are none as good; and in the other great poets of the present century there are no attempts, that I can remember, to which we may compare it. In spite of the poem being called in honor of his mistress, Don Silva is in fact the central figure in the work. Much more than Fedalma, he is the passive object of the converging blows of Fate. The young girl, after all, did what was easiest; but he is entangled in a network of agony, without choice or compliance of his own. It is an admirable subject admirably treated. I may describe it by saying that it exhibits a perfect aristocratic nature, (born and bred at a time when democratic aspirations were quite irrelevant to happiness), dragged down by no fault of its own into the vulgar mire of error and expiation. The interest which attaches to Don Silva's character revolves about its exquisite human weakness, its manly scepticism, its antipathy to the trenchant, the absolute, and arbitrary. . . . Throughout the poem, we are conscious, during the evolution of his character, of the presence of these high mystical influences, which, combined with his personal pride, his knightly temper, his delicate culture, form a splendid background for passionate dramatic action. The finest pages in the book, to my taste, are those which describe his lonely vigil in the Gypsy camp, after he has failed in winning back Fedalma, and has pledged his faith to Zarca. Placed under guard, and left to his own stern thoughts, his

soul begins to react against the hideous disorder to which he has
committed it, to proclaim its kinship with "customs and bonds and
laws," and its sacred need of the light of human esteem. . . . To be
appreciated at their worth, these pages should be attentively read.
Nowhere has the author's marvellous power of expression, the mingled
dignity and pliancy of her style, obtained a greater triumph. She has
reproduced the expression of a mind with the same vigorous distinctness as that with which a great painter represents the expression of
a countenance.

The character which accords best with my own taste is that of the
minstrel Juan, an extremely generous conception. He fills no great
part in the drama; he is by nature the reverse of a man of action; and,
strictly, the story could very well dispense with him. Yet, for all
that, I should be sorry to lose him, and lose thereby the various excellent things which are said of him and by him. I do not include
his songs among the latter. Only two of the lyrics in the work strike
me as good: the song of Pablo, "The world is great: the birds all fly
from me"; and, in a lower degree, the chant of the Zincali, in the
fourth book. . . .

When Juan talks at his ease, he strikes the note of poetry much
more surely than when he lifts his voice in song: —

> Yet if your graciousness will not disdain
> A poor plucked songster, shall he sing to you?
> *Some lay of afternoons, — some ballad strain*
> *Of those who ached once, but are sleeping now*
> *Under the sun-warmed flowers?*

Juan's link of connection with the story is, in the first place, that he
is in love with Fedalma, and, in the second, as a piece of local color. . . .

In every human imbroglio, be it of a comic or a tragic nature, it is
good to think of an observer standing aloof, the critic, the idle com-
mentator of it all, taking notes, as we may say, in the interest of
truth. The exercise of this function is the chief ground of our interest in Juan. Yet as a man of action, too, he once appeals most
irresistibly to our sympathies: I mean in the admirable scene with
Hinda, in which he wins back his stolen finery by his lute-playing.
This scene, which is written in prose, has a simple, realistic power
which renders it a truly remarkable composition.

Of the different parts of *The Spanish Gypsy* I have spoken with
such fulness as my space allows: it remains to add a few remarks
upon the work as a whole. Its great fault is simply that it is not a
genuine poem. It lacks the hurrying quickness, the palpitating warmth,
the bursting melody of such a creation. A genuine poem is a tree
that breaks into blossom and shakes in the wind. George Eliot's

elaborate composition is like a vast mural design in mosaic-work, where great slabs and delicate morsels of stone are laid together with wonderful art, where there are plenty of noble lines and generous hues, but where everything is rigid, measured, and cold, — nothing dazzling, magical, and vocal. The poem contains a number of faulty lines, — lines of twelve, of eleven, and of eight syllables, — of which it is easy to suppose that a more sacredly commissioned versifier would not have been guilty. Occasionally, in the search for poetic effect, the author decidedly misses her way:

> All her being paused
> In resolution, *as some leonine wave*, etc.

A "leonine" wave is rather too much of a lion and too little of a wave. The work possesses imagination, I think, in no small measure. The description of Silva's feelings during the sojourn in the Gypsy camp is strongly pervaded by it; or if perchance the author achieved these passages without rising on the wings of fancy, her glory is all the greater. But the poem is wanting in passion. The reader is annoyed by a perpetual sense of effort and of intellectual tension. It is a characteristic of George Eliot, I imagine, to allow her impressions to linger a long time in her mind, so that by the time they are ready for use they have lost much of their original freshness and vigor. They have acquired, of course, a number of artificial charms but they have parted with their primal natural simplicity. In this poem, we see the landscape, the people, the manners of Spain as through a glass smoked by the flame of meditative vigils, just as we saw the outward aspect of Florence in *Romola*. The brightness of coloring is there, the artful *chiaroscuro*, and all the consecrated properties of the scene; but they gleam in an artificial light. The background of the action is admirable in spots, but is cold and mechanical as a whole. The immense rhetorical ingenuity and elegance of the work, which constitute its main distinction, interfere with the faithful uncompromising reflection of the primary elements of the subject.

The great merit of the characters is that they are marvelously well *understood*, — far better understood than in the ordinary picturesque romance of action, adventure and mystery. And yet they are not understood to the bottom; they retain an indefinably factitious air, which is not sufficiently justified by their position as ideal figures. The reader who has attentively read the closing scene of the poem will know what I mean. The scene shows remarkable talent; it is eloquent, it is beautiful; but it is arbitrary and fanciful, more than unreal, — untrue. The reader silently chafes and protests, and finally breaks forth and cries, "O for a blast from the outer world!" Silva and Fedalma have developed themselves so daintily and elaborately within the close-sealed precincts of the author's mind, that they strike us at last as acting not as simple human creatures, but as downright *amateurs* of the morally graceful and picturesque. To say that this is the ultimate impression of the poem is to say that it is not a great work. It is in fact not a great drama. It is, in the first place, an admirable study of character, — an essay, as they say, toward the solution of a given problem in conduct. In the second, it is a noble literary performance. It can be read neither without interest in the former respect, nor without profit for its signal merits of style, — and this in spite of the fact that the versification is, as the French say, as little *réussi* as was to be expected in a writer beginning at a bound with a kind of verse which is very much more difficult than even the best prose, — the author's own prose. I shall indicate most of its merits and defects, great and small, if I say it is a romance, — a romance written by one who is emphatically a thinker.

Edward Dowden

George Eliot

When we have passed in review the works of that great writer who calls herself George Eliot, and given for a time our use of sight to her portraitures of men and women, what form, as we move away, persists on the field of vision, and remains the chief centre of interest for the imagination? The form not of Tito, or Maggie, or Dinah, or Silas, but of one who, if not the real George Eliot, is that "second self" who writes her books, and lives and speaks through them. Such a second self of an author is perhaps more substantial than any mere human personality encumbered with the accidents of flesh and blood and daily living. It stands at some distance from the primary self, and differs considerably from its fellow. It presents its person to us with fewer reserves; it is independent of local and temporary motives of speech or of silence; it knows no man after the flesh; it is more than an individual; it utters secrets, but secrets which all men of all ages are to catch; while, behind it, lurks well pleased the veritable his-

Reprinted from the *Contemporary Review*, 20 (August 1872), 403–422.

torical self secure from impertinent observation and criticism. With this second self of George Eliot it is, not with the actual historical person, that we have to do. And when, having closed her books, we gaze outward with the mind's eye, the spectacle we see is that most impressive spectacle of a great nature, which has suffered and has now attained, which was perplexed and has now grasped the clue — standing before us not without tokens on lip and brow of the strife and the suffering, but resolute, and henceforth possessed of something which makes self-mastery possible. The strife is not ended, the pain may still be resurgent; but we perceive on which side victory must lie.

This personal accent in the writings of George Eliot does not interfere with their dramatic truthfulness; it adds to the power with which they grasp the heart and conscience of the reader. We cannot say with confidence of any one of her creations that it is a projection of herself; the lines of their movement are not deflected by hidden powers of attraction or repulsion peculiar to the mind of the author; most noteworthy is her impartiality towards the several creatures of her imagination; she condemns but does not hate; she is cold or indifferent to none; each lives his own life, good or bad; but the author is present in the midst of them, indicating, interpreting; and we discern in the moral laws, the operation of which presides over the action of each story, those abstractions from the common fund of truth which the author has found most needful to her own deepest life. We feel in reading these books that we are in the presence of a soul, and a soul which has had a history.

At the same time the novels of George Eliot are not didactic treatises. They are primarily works of art, and George Eliot herself is artist as much as she is teacher. Many good things in particular passages of her writings are detachable; admirable sayings can be cleared from their surroundings, and presented by themselves, knocked out clean as we knock out fossils from a piece of limestone. But if we separate the moral soul of any complete work of hers from its artistic medium, if we murder to dissect, we lose far more than we gain. When a work of art can be understood only by enjoying it, the art is of a high kind. The best criticism of Shakspere is not that which comes out of profound cogitation, but out of immense enjoyment; and the most valuable critic is the critic who communicates sympathy by an exquisite record of his own delights, not the critic who attempts to communicate thought. In a less degree the same is true of George Eliot. There is not a hard kernel of dogma at the centre of her art, and around it a sheath or envelope which we break and throw away; the moral significance coalesces with the narrative, and lives through the characters. . . .

In this nature, complete in all its parts, and with every part strong, the granite-like foundation of the whole is conscience, the moral perceptions and the moral will. Abstract the ethical interest from *Romola,* or from *The Spanish Gypsy,* and there is total collapse of design, characters, incidents. Other story-tellers centre our hopes and fears in the happiness or unhappiness of their chief personages; a wedding or a funeral brings to an end at once our emotional disturbance and the third volume of the novel. George Eliot is profoundly moved by the spectacle of human joy and human sorrow; death to her is always tragic, but there is something more tragic than cessation of the breath, and of the pulse; there is the slow letting go of life and the ultimate extinction of a soul; to her the marriage joys are dear, but there is something higher than the highest happiness of lovers. . . . When Tom and Maggie sink in the hurrying Floss there is left an aching sense of abrupt incompleteness, of imperious suspension, of intolerable arrest; and with this a sense of the utter helplessness of our extremest longings. The musician's hand has broken the movement in the midst, and it can never be taken up again. This is cruel to all our tender desires for joy. But there is something more dreadful. When the heavens break up over the head of Silas Marner, when the lots declare him, the innocent man, guilty in the midst of the congregation of Lantern Yard; when he goes out with despair in his soul, with shaken trust in God and man, to live for weary years a life of unsocial and godless isolation, accumulating his hoard of yellow pieces, the tragedy is deeper. When the beautiful Greek awakes from his swoon beside the Arno to find no pleasant solitary lair, but the vindictive eyes of Baldassarre looking down at him, and the eager knuckles at his throat, the real piteousness and terror is not that a young man is about to die, but that now the visible seal of finality is to be set upon that death of the soul which had already taken place.

In each tale of George Eliot's telling, if the question arise of the ruin or restoration of moral character, every other interest becomes subordinate to this. The nodes of the plot from which new developments spring are often invisible spiritual events. It is a crisis and we feel it to be such, when there falls into Maggie's hands a copy of *De Imitatione Christi;* the incident is fraught, we are at once aware, with momentous consequences. . . . The relations that human beings can form with one another which are most intimate, most full of fate, are with George Eliot not intellectual or merely social relations, but essentially moral. . . .

The conscience of George Eliot asserts itself so strongly because there are in her nature other powers strong also, and urging great claims upon the will. Her senses are framed for rich and varied pleasure. The avenues between the senses and the imagination are traversed to and fro by swift and secret intelligencers. There are blind motions in her blood, which respond to vague influences, the moral nature of which may be determined by a contingency; there are deep incalculable instincts, the heritage from past generations, which suddenly declare themselves with an energy that had not been surmised. There are zeals and ardours of the heart, eager demands and eager surrenders. There is the grasping, permitted or restrained, of a richly endowed nature after joy, — after joy from which to avert the eyes for ever is bitter as the sundering of flesh and soul. This nature, in which conscience must needs be stern, is a nature of passionate sensibility. The pure gleaming of gems, the perfect moulding of a woman's arm, the face of youth that is like a flower, and its aureole of bright hair, the strong voice of a singer that urges and controls, the exquisite movement and excitement of the dance, not one of these fails to find an answer in the large joy-embracing nature of George Eliot. We recall to mind Tito's presence in the dark library of Bardi, "like a wreath of spring dropped suddenly in Romola's young but wintry life"; and the fascination exercised over Adam by the sweet, rounded, blossom-like, dark-eyed Hetty; and Maggie borne along by the wave of arrogant baritone music too strong for her; and the wonder and worship of Rufus Lyon in presence of that miracle of grace, the Frenchwoman found by the roadside; and Fedalma circling to the booming and ringing tambourine, under the flushed clouds and in midst of the spectators of the Plaça. . . . This capacity for pure joy, this noble sensibility to beauty, are attributes, not of the lower characters of George Eliot's creating, but of the worthiest. They are felt by her to be derived from the strength of our nature, not from its weakness. Adam Bede falls in love with a woman who has nothing to recommend her but exquisite curves of cheek and neck, the liquid depth of beseeching eyes, the sweet childish pout of the lips, and he cleaves to her with almost a humility of devotion. Does George Eliot think meanly of her hero for a proceeding so unbecoming a sensible man? By no means. She perceives that "beauty has an expression beyond and far above the one woman's soul that it clothes; as the words of genius have a wider meaning than the thought that prompted them. It is more than a woman's love that moves us in a woman's eyes — it seems to be a far-off mighty love that has come near to us, and made speech for itself there; the rounded neck, the dimpled arm, move us by something more than their prettiness — by their close kinship with all we have known of tenderness and peace. The noblest nature sees the most of this *impersonal* expression in beauty." Whence sometimes, as in the case of Adam, tragic consequences.

A man or woman endowed with great susceptibility to beauty,

and prior to experience making large demands upon the world for joy, runs the risk of terrible calamity. Dissociated from the sympathetic emotions the immoderate love of beauty, as Baudelaire has well said, "leads men to monstrous and unheard of disorders." The appetite for joy consumes all that the earth can afford, and remains fierce and insatiate. It is impossible even to imagine such a calamity overtaking George Eliot, so numerous, and full of soundness and vigour are the sympathies which bind her to her fellows. There are certain artists who concentrate the light of an intense intelligence and passionate sympathy upon their two or three chief figures, which move in an oppressive glare of consciousness, while towards the rest they show themselves almost indifferent. George Eliot's sympathy spreads with a powerful and even flow in every direction. . . .

George Eliot's manifold sympathies create behind her principal figures an ample background in which they find play and find repose. An English landscape in the manner of Constable, rich with rough, soft colour, and infallible in local truth is first presented. Men, women, children, animals are seen, busy about their several concerns. The life of a whole neighbourhood grows up before us; and from this the principal figures never altogether detach themselves. Thus a perspective is produced; the chief personages are not thrust up against the eye; actions are seen passing into their effects; reverberations of voices are heard strangely altering and confused; and the emotions of the spectator are at once roused and tranquillized by the presence of a general life surrounding the lives of individuals. Hetty disappears, but the affairs of the Hall Farm still go on; Savonarola falls, but Florence remains. No more exquisite background group can be found in the literature of fiction than the Poyser household, from the little sunny-haired Totty, and her brothers as like their father as two small elephants are like a great elephant, up to Martin Poyser the elder, sitting in his arm-chair with hale, shrunken limbs, and "the quiet *outward* glance of healthy old age," which "spies out pins on the floor, and watches the flickering of the flame or the sungleams on the wall." The pathos of their shame and sorrow deepens in the presence of the unconsciousness of childhood, and the half-consciousness of self-contented age.

But the sympathies of George Eliot reach out from the slow movement of the village, from the inharmonious stir of the manufacturing town, from the Hall Farm, and from the bar of the Rainbow Inn to the large interests of collective humanity. The artistic enthusiasm of the Renaissance period, the scientific curiosity of the present century, the political life at Florence long since, the political movements of England forty years ago, and religious life in manifold forms — Catholic, Anglican, and Nonconforming, are none of them remote from her imaginative grasp. Here the heart allies itself with a vigorous intellect, the characteristics of which are its need of clearness, of precision; and its habitual turn for generalization. The "unlimited right of private haziness," so dear to many minds, is a right which George Eliot never claims on her own behalf. And in her mind facts, especially moral facts, are for ever grouping themselves into laws; the moral laws which her study of life discovers to her being definite and certain as the facts which they co-ordinate. The presence of a powerful intellect observing, defining, and giving precision explains in part the unfaltering insistence of the ethical purport of these books. It bears down upon the conscience of the reader with painful weight and tenacity.

The truths in presence of which we live, so long as the imagination of George Eliot controls our own, are not surmises, not the conjectures of prudence, not guesses of the soul peering into the darkness which lies around the known world of human destiny, nor are they attained by generous ventures of faith; they are tyrannous facts from which escape is impossible. Words which come pealing from "a glimmering limit far withdrawn," words "in a tongue no man can understand," do not greatly arouse the curiosity of George Eliot. Other teachers would fain lighten the burden of the mystery by showing us that good comes out of evil. George Eliot prefers to urge, with a force which we cannot resist, the plain and dreadful truth that evil comes out of evil — "whatsoever a man soweth that shall he also reap." No vista of a future life, no array of supernatural powers stationed in the heavens, and about to intervene in the affairs of men, lead her gaze away from the stern, undeniable facts of the actual world. "Our deeds are like children that are born to us; they live and act apart from our will. Nay, children may be strangled, but deeds never: they have an indestructible life both in and out of our consciousness." Other teachers transfigure and transmute human joys and sorrows, fears and hopes, loves and hatreds, with light from a spiritual world: the sufferings of the present time are made radiant with the coming of the glory which shall be revealed in us: in George Eliot's writings it is the common light of day that falls upon our actions and our sufferings; but each act, and each sorrow, is dignified and made important by the consciousness of that larger life of which they form a part — the life of our whole race, descending from the past, progressing into the future, surrounding us at this moment on every side. . . .

George Eliot's humour allies itself with her intellect on the one hand, and with her sympathies and moral perceptions on the other. The grotesque in human character is reclaimed from the province of the humorous by her affections, when that is possible, and is shown to be a pathetic form of beauty. The pale, brown-eyed weaver, gazing out from his cottage door with blurred vision, or poring with miserly devotion over his golden hoard, touches us, but does not make us smile. The comedy of incident, the farcical, lies outside her province; once or twice, for reasons that appear hardly adequate, the comedy of incident was attempted, and the result was not successful. The humour of George Eliot usually belongs to her entire conception of a character, and cannot be separated from it. Her humorous effects are secured by letting her mind drop sympathetically into a level of lower intelligence, or duller moral perception, and by the conscious presence at the same time of the higher self. The humorous impression exists only in the qualified organs of perception which remain at the higher, the normal point of view. What had been merely an undulation of matter, when it touches the prepared surface of the retina, breaks into light. . . .

Complete in all its parts, and strong in all, the nature of George Eliot is yet not one of those rare natures which without effort are harmonious. There is no impression made more decisively upon the reader of her books than this. No books bear upon their faces more unmistakably the pain of moral conflict, and the pain of moral victory, only less bitter than that of defeat. Great forces warring with one another; a sorrowful, a pathetic victory — that is what we discern. What is the significance of it all? . . .

The tragic aspect of life, as viewed by this great writer, is derived from the Titanic strife of egoistic desires with duties which the conscience confesses, and those emotions which transcend the interests of the individual. It seems to her no small or easy thing to cast away self. Rather the casting self away is an agony and a martyrdom. All the noblest characters she has conceived, certainly all those characters in presenting which a personal accent seems least doubtfully recognisable — the heroical feminine characters or those that might have been heroical, characters of great sensibility, great imaginative power, great fervour of feeling — Maggie, Romola, Fedalma, Armgart — cling with passionate attachment to the joy which must needs be renounced. The dying to self is the dying of young creatures full of the strength and the gladness of living. The world is indeed cruel; to be happy is so sweet. If the joy were ignoble it could be abandoned with less anguish and remorse, but it is pure and high. . . .

The same doctrine of the necessity of self-renunciation, of the obligation laid upon men to accept some other rule of conduct than the desire of pleasure, is enforced in the way of warning with terrible emphasis. Tito Melema, Arthur Donnithorne, Godfrey Cass, Maggie Tulliver, are in turn assailed by one and the same temptation — to deny or put out of sight certain duties to others, to gratify some demand for egoistic pleasure or happiness, or to avoid some wholesome necessary pain. Arthur, vain affectionate, susceptible, owed no one a grudge, and would have like to see everyone about him happy, and ready to acknowledge that a great part of their happiness was due to the handsome young landlord. Tito was clever and beautiful, kind and gentle in his manners, without a thought of anything cruel or base. And Godfrey was full of easy good nature; and Maggie of a wealth of eager love. But in the linked necessity of evil, each of these, beginning with a soft yielding to egoistic desires, becomes capable of deeds or of wishes that are base and cruel. . . .

The scientific observation of man, and in particular the study of the mutual relations of the individual and society, come to reinforce the self-renouncing dictates of the heart. To understand any individual apart from the whole life of the race is impossible. We are the heirs intellectual and moral of the past; there is no such thing as naked manhood; the heart of each of us wears livery which it cannot throw off. Our very bodies differ from those of primeval savages — differ, it may be, from those of extinct apes only by the gradual gains of successive generations of ancestors. Our instincts, physical and mental, our habits of thought and feeling, the main tendency of our activity, these are assigned to us by the common life which has preceded and which surrounds our own. "There is no private life," writes George Eliot in *Felix Holt*, "which has not been determined by a wider public life, from the time when the primeval milkmaid had to wander with the wanderings of her clan, because the cow she milked was one of a herd which had made the pastures bare." . . .

It will be readily seen how this way of thinking abolishes rights, and substitutes duties in their place. Of rights of man, or rights of woman, we never hear speech from George Eliot. But we hear much of the duties of each. The claim asserted by the individual on behalf of this or that disappears, because the individual surrenders his independence to collective humanity, of which he is a part. And it is another consequence of this way of thinking that the leadings of duty are most often looked for, not within, in the promptings of the heart, but without, in the relations of external life, which connect us with our fellow-men. Our great English novelist does not preach as her favourite doctrine the indefeasible right of love to gratify itself at the expense of law; with the correlative right, equally indefeasible, to cast away the marriage bond as soon as it has become a painful incumbrance. She regards the formal contract, even when its spirit has long since died, as sacred and of binding force. Why? Because it is a formal contract. "The light abandonment of ties, whether inherited or voluntary, because they had ceased to be pleasant, would be the uprooting of social and personal virtue." Law is sacred. Rebellion, it is true, may be sacred also. There are moments of life "when the soul must dare to act upon its warrant, not only without external law to appeal to, but in the face of a law which is not unarmed with Divine lightnings — lightnings that may yet fall if the warrant has been false." These moments, however, are of rare occurrence, and arise only in extreme necessity. . . . Maggie returns to St. Oggs: Fedalma and Don Silva part: Romola goes back to her husband's house. We can imagine how unintelligible such moral situations, and such moral solutions, would appear to a great female novelist of France. . . .

"If the past is not to bind us, where can duty lie?" As the life of the race lying behind our individual life points out the direction in which alone it can move with dignity and strength, so our own past months and years lying behind the present hour and minute deliver over to these a heritage and a tradition which it is their wisdom joyfully to accept when that is possible. . . . If no natural piety binds our days together, let us die quickly rather than die piecemeal by the slow paralyzing touch of time.

All that helps to hold our past and present together is therefore precious and sacred. It is well that our affections should twine tenderly about all material tokens and memorials of bygone days. Why should Tito keep his father's ring? Why indulge a foolish sentiment, a piece of superstition, about an inanimate object? And so Tito sells the ring, and with it closes the bargain by which he sells his soul. There is, indeed, a noble pressing forward to things that are before, and forgetting of things that are behind. George Eliot is not attracted to represent a character in which such an ardour is predominant, and the base forgetting of things behind alarms and shocks her. We find it hard to abstain from reading as autobiographical the little group of eleven poems entitled "Brother and Sister," while at the same time it is impossible to dissociate them from some of the earlier scenes of *The Mill on the Floss.* These poems are heavy with the tenderness of memory, filled with all the sweetness and sadness of lost but unforgotten days, and overbowed with the firmament of adult thought, and grief, and love.

> The wide-arched bridge, the scented elder-flowers,
> The wondrous watery rings that died too soon,
> The echoes of the quarry, the still hours
> With white robe sweeping-on the shadeless noon,
> Were but my growing self, are part of me,
> My present Past, my root of piety.

It is noted as characteristic of Hetty's shallow nature, that in her dream of the future, the brilliant future of the Captain's wife, there mingles no thought of her second parents, no thought of the children she had helped to tend, of any youthful companion, any pet animal, any relic of her own childhood. "Hetty could have cast all her past life behind her, and never cared to be reminded of it again. I think she had no feeling at all towards the old house, and did not like the Jacob's ladder and the long row of hollyhocks in the garden better than any other flowers — perhaps not so well." Jubal, after his ardent pursuit of song through the world, would return to Lamech's home, "hoping to find the former things." Silas Marner would see once more the town where he was born, and Lantern Yard, where the lots had declared him guilty. But Hetty is like a plant with hardly any roots; "lay it over your ornamental flower-pot and it blossoms none the worse." . . .

[Edith Simcox]

Middlemarch

Contemporary criticism of great works is apt to prove unsatisfactory, for even when their greatness is recognised at once, the critic labours under a double disadvantage: an unwonted sense of responsibility restrains the free expression of unmotived admiration, and the easy volubility of praise, which is enough for slighter merits, makes way for a guarded tone of respect that looks like coldness on the surface. Nor is this all; for the vocabulary of positive eulogium is soon exhausted; criticism to be significant must be comparative, and there is an obvious difficulty in estimating by old-established standards of excellence a new work that may contain within itself a fresh standard for the guidance and imitation of futurity. For the theory of art is after all only a patchwork of inference from the practice of artists, and, to quit generalities, in one clearly defined and admirable branch of imaginative art — the English novel — our ideal is simply one or other of the masterpieces of one or other of the great novelists between Fielding and George Eliot. *Tom Jones, Clarissa Harlowe, Waverley, Pride and Prejudice, Vanity Fair, Adam Bede* — to which

Reprinted from the *Academy*, 4 (1 January 1873), 1–4. It is signed with the pseudonym "H. Lawrenny."

some might wish to add *Eugene Aram, Pickwick*, and *Jane Eyre* —
are the sources from whence all theories of the novel, as a prose
narrative representation of manners, character and passion, ultimately
derive. In truth, variety, and intensity, the best of these works left
something to be supplied by excellence of a different type: there are
stronger as well as more complex passions than Fielding has drawn;
Richardson's subtlety works in a narrow field; Miss Austen's knowledge of the world was scanty, and Thackeray's theory of human
nature one-sided, while on the other hand it might be argued that an
over-systematic plot or too thrilling situations give a *primâ facie*
look of unreality to scenes of modern life. No one of course makes
it a ground of complaint against these authors that they failed to
combine incompatible perfections, but a reference to the natural
limitations of the styles in which they severally succeeded may help
to show what space was left for a fresh combination of the old
ingredients.

Middlemarch marks an epoch in the history of fiction in so far as
its incidents are taken from the inner life, as the action is developed
by the direct influence of mind on mind and character on character,
as the material circumstances of the outer world are made subordinate
and accessory to the artistic presentation of a definite passage of
mental experience, but chiefly as giving a background of perfect
realistic truth to a profoundly imaginative psychological study. The
effect is as new as if we could suppose a *Wilhelm Meister* written
by Balzac. In *Silas Marner, Romola*, and the author's other works
there is the same power, but it does not so completely and exclusively
determine the form in which the conception is placed before us. In
Silas Marner there is a natural and obvious unity in the life of the
weaver, but in *Romola* — where alone the interest is at once as varied
and as profound as in *Middlemarch* — though the historic glories of
Florence, the passions belonging to what, as compared with the nineteenth century, is an heroic age, are in perfect harmony with the
grand manner of treating spiritual problems, yet the realism, the
positive background of fact, which we can scarcely better bear to
miss, has necessarily some of the character of an hypothesis, and does
not inspire us with the same confidence as truths we can verify for
ourselves. For that reason alone, on the mere point of artistic harmony
of construction, we should rate the last work as the greatest; and to
say that *Middlemarch* is George Eliot's greatest work is to say that
it has scarcely a superior and very few equals in the whole wide range
of English fiction.

As "a study of provincial life," if it were nothing more, *Middlemarch* would have a lasting charm for students of human nature in
its less ephemeral costumes; besides the crowds of men and women

whom we have all known in real life, where, however, to our dimmer vision, they seemed less real and life-like than in the book, the relations between the different clusters, the proportions in which the different elements mix, the points of contact and the degree of isolation in the different ranks; the contented coexistence of town and country, the channels of communication between the two always open and yet so rarely used, the effect of class distinctions in varying the mental horizon and obliging the most matter-of-fact observer to see a few things in perspective, — all the subtle factors which make up the character of a definite state of society are given with inimitable accuracy and fulness of insight. The picture in its main outlines is as true of the England of today or the England of a hundred years ago as of the England of the Reform agitation. The world as we know it has its wise and good, its fools and hypocrites scattered up and down a neutral-tinted mass in much the same proportion as at Middlemarch. The only difference is that they are not so plainly recognisable, and this is perhaps the reason that a first perusal of the book seems to have an almost oppressive effect on ordinary readers, somewhat as little children are frightened at a live automaton toy. It is not natural to most men to know so much of their fellow-creatures as George Eliot shows them, to penetrate behind the scenes in so many homes, to understand the motives of ambiguous conduct, to watch "like gods knowing good and evil" the tangled course of inter-mingled lives, the remote mainsprings of impulse and the wide-eddying effects of action. Even with the author's assistance it is not easy to maintain the same height of observant wisdom for long, and since the intricacy of the subject is real, a feeling of even painful bewilderment in its contemplation is not entirely unbecoming.

But the complicated conditions of so seemingly simple a thing as provincial life are not the main subject of the work. The busy idleness of Middlemarch, its trade, its politics, its vestry meetings, and its neighbouring magnates, only form the background of relief to two or three spiritual conflicts, the scenery amongst which two or three souls spend some eventful years in working out their own salvation and their neighbours', or in effecting, with equal labour, something less than salvation for both. The story of these conflicts and struggles is the thread which unites the whole, and sympathy with its incidents is the force that reconciles the reader to the unwonted strain upon his intellectual faculties already noticed; and to the yet further effort necessary to recognise the fact that the real and the ideal sides of our common nature do coexist in just such relations, and with just such proportionate force as the author reveals. For, without this admission, it is impossible to appreciate the full literary and artistic perfection of the work as a whole; some readers

may delight spontaneously in the author's moral earnestness, and only
admire her satirical insight, while others delight in her satire and
coldly admit the excellence of the moral purpose; but the two are
only opposite aspects of the same large theory of the universe, which
is at once so charitable and so melancholy that it would be fairly
intolerable (although true) without the sauce of an unsparing humour.

Middlemarch is the story of two rather sad fatalities, of two lives
which, starting with more than ordinary promise, had to rest content
with very ordinary achievement, and could not derive unmixed
consolation from the knowledge, which was the chief prize of their
struggles, that failure is never altogether undeserved. One of the
original mottoes to the first book gives the clue to what follows:

> *1st Gent.* Our deeds are fetters that we forge ourselves.
> *2nd Gent.* Ay, truly; but I think it is the world
>   That brings the iron.

But as the action proceeds a further consciousness gathers shape:
"It always remains true that if we had been greater, circumstances
would have been less strong against us"; which is still more simply
expressed in Dorothea's "feelings that there was always something
better which she might have done, if she had only been better and
known better." The two failures, however, have little in common
but their irrevocable necessity. From one point of view, Dorothea's
is the most tragical, for the fault in her case seems to be altogether
in the nature and constitution of the universe; her devotion and
purity of intention are altogether beautiful, even when, for lack of
knowledge, they are expended in what seems to be the wrong place,
but it is a sad reflection that their beauty must always rest on a basis
of illusion because there is no right place for their bestowal. Except
in the chapter of her marriages Dorothea is a perfect woman, but for
a perfect woman any marriage is a *mésalliance*, and as such, "certainly
those determining acts of her life were not ideally beautiful." . . . To
keep society alive is perhaps a worthier mission than to cheer the
declining years of Mr. Casaubon; but to do more than keep it alive,
to make it a fit home for future Dorotheas, the present supply of such
missionaries would have to be increased; and they are born, not made.
Perhaps the strongest example of the author's instinctive truthfulness
is that she never loses sight of the limits to the exercise of the power
which she represents so vividly and values so highly. A life's growth
of empty egotism like Mr. Casaubon's cannot be melted in a year
of marriage, even to Dorothea; with a generous example close before
her, Rosamond can be almost honest for once at little expense, but
she can no more change her character than her complexion or the

colour of her eyes, or than she can unmake the whole series of circumstances which have made her life less negatively innocent than
Celia's. A little more selfishness, a little more obstinacy, a little less
good fortune, and especially life in a just lower moral atmosphere,
make all the difference between a pretty, prosaic, kittenish wife and
a kind of well-conducted domestic vampire. It is by such contrasts
as these that George Eliot contrives to preach tolerance even while
showing with grim distinctness the ineffaceableness of moral distinctions and the unrelenting force of moral obligations. If virtue is a
matter of capacity, defect calls only for pity; but defects which we
do not venture to blame may be none the less fatal to the higher
life, while the smallest shoot of virtue, if the heavens and earth chance
to be propitious to its growth, may spread into a stately tree.

Such at least is the inference suggested by another contrast, that
between Lydgate and Fred, for though marriage appears the "determining act" in their lives also, it is itself determined by certain
essential points of character and disposition. Fred's honest boyish
affection for a girl who is a great deal too good for him brings its
own reward, as that kind of virtue often will; there was enough
self-abandonment in it to deserve a generous answer, and in the
long-run people generally get their deserts. The failure of Lydgate's
intellectual aspirations, as the consequence of a marriage contracted
altogether at the bidding of his lower nature, is of course much more
elaborately treated than Fred's simple "love-problem." Unlike most
of the other characters, Lydgate does not become thoroughly intelligible till the last number of the work has been read in connection
with the first: then he appears as a masculine counterpart to Dorothea
with the relative proportions of head and heart reversed. But while
it was abstractedly impossible for Dorothea to be altogether wise,
without detriment to the peculiar and charming character of her
goodness, there was nothing but concrete human infirmity to prevent
Lydgate from combining the mind of Bichat and the morals of Fred
Vincy. Instead of such a compound the actual and very human
Lydgate is one of those men whose lives are cut in two, whose intellectual interests have no direct connection with their material
selves, and who only discover the impossibility of living according
to habit or tradition when brought by accident or their own heedless-
ness face to face with difficulties that require thought as well as resolution. There was not room in the life he contemplated for a soul
much larger than Rosamond's, and it may be doubted whether the
Rosamond he wished for would not, by a merely passive influence,
have been as obstructive to his wide speculations, for he was just,
though not expansive, and the duties entailed by one act of weakness
may multiply and branch as much as if they were of a valuable stock.

On the other hand, if the scientific ardour had been more absorbing, he might have gone on his own way, crushing all poor Rosamond's little schemes of opposition, and then she would have been the victim instead of the oppressor, but his character would have been as far from ideal excellence as before. The interest culminates when Lydgate, entangled with the consequences of his own and other people's wrongdoing, finds in Dorothea the beneficent influence that spends itself in setting straight whatever is not constitutionally crooked, but he has also of course found out by then that the events which led him to cross her path were the same that had proved fatal to his aspirations; the enlarged sympathies were gathered during the process that paralysed his original activity. The story of a man "who has not done what he once meant to do" has always a strong element of pathos, but when what he meant to do was not in itself impossible, like the realization of Dorothea's visions, there remains a twofold consolation; if possible in itself, and yet not done as proposed, it must have been impossible to the proposer, and therefore his failure is free from blame, while disappointment of his hopes, though painful, cannot be regarded as an unmitigated evil, since such fallen aspirations as Lydgate's are still something it is better to have had than to be altogether without. Natural fatality and the logic of facts are made to persuade us that all regrets are unpractical except the most unpractical of all — "if we had only known better and been better" — but the first step towards solving a problem is to state it; and one of the many merits of *Middlemarch* is that it shows the inadequacy of all other less arduous short cuts to the reformation of society. Ordinary mortals who are not fatalists have no excuse for calling a book sad which makes the redress of every one's wrongs rest in the last resort with themselves; while people whose idea of the world is already as gloomy as it well can be, cannot fail to derive some consolation from the thought that George Eliot's wider knowledge and juster perceptions find here and there a little to admire as well as much everywhere to laugh at.

There is no occasion to dwell in detail on the story, which every one has read. The studies of Casaubon and Bulstrode would each furnish matter for an ordinary review, though here we have treated them as altogether secondary to the development of the two principal characters. Besides their more direct influence on the action, both serve, with old Featherstone, to illustrate the blindness of selfish calculation. Bulstrode is none the better either for his manslaughter or for his attempt at restitution. If Mr. Casaubon's will had not drawn Dorothea and Ladislaw together, something else would; for the moral forces at work in any direction can only be arrested by other forces of the same kind, while no moral jugglery will ward off the material effects of causes set to work long before. By way of relief from such troublesome spectacles, the Garth household is invaluable, with its common-sense happiness not corrupted by an undue contempt for "notions." The choruses of slightly belated popular wisdom, the Featherstone family, Mrs. Dollop's clients, the Middlemarch teaparties, the dowager Lady Chettam's society, appear from time to time to comment with their usual insight and *à propos* on the doings of their betters. But it is perhaps a mistake to suppose the intention of this class of character to be altogether satirical. The author spends too much invention upon them for them to be quite so stupid as they look. The minds of Mrs. Waule and sister Martha, as of Mrs. Holt and the Tulliver connection, move erratically, but their reasoning is often so imaginative that it would be scarcely a compliment to suggest that they only represent, as choruses should, the opinions of the inspired *vox populi* in the process of making: they are an idealization rather than a caricature of the popular sense.

In a work that has scarcely a quality which is not a merit, it is hard to determine what points to leave unnoticed. The gift, shared only, amongst contemporaries by Mr. Browning, of choosing similes and illustrations that do really illustrate the nature of the things compared, is exercised, if anything, more freely than in the author's other works; but her style, always polished and direct, seems to have become still more sharply condensed; the dialogues, always natural, still more simple in their force. This is especially true of the scenes in the last book, where Dorothea probably uses fewer and plainer words than have ever served to express deep feeling before. Mastery like this is the best title to immortality, and posterity will only do the present generation justice if it believes that real emotion speaks so now, if it speaks at all, though in real life it more commonly observes an awkward silence. Many of the less serious conversations have the same classical perfection of finish; one, for instance, between Mary Garth and Rosamond, near the end of Part I, will show to those curious in such matters better than all Mr. Trollope's voluminous works, how girls in the nineteenth century discuss the matters in which they are privately interested. The family circle of the Vincys in the chapter before is scarcely inferior, and though we only see in it now a singularly faithful sketch from nature, there can be little doubt of its outliving the nature it represents. It is a little curious that Mr. Brooke, who represents a type, should seem, according to the general experience, to be a commoner acquaintance than Sir James Chettam, who represents a class, which we should be loth to think threatened with extinction. Both are friends of whom one does not soon weary of telling, but if we had indefinite space at command it would be better spent in quoting their sayings

or the author's own epigrams. Failing this resource, we can only
return to the point from whence we started, the natural incapacity
of criticism (or critics — "the people who have failed in literature
and art") to throw much light upon a work like *Middlemarch*.
All critics are not like Mr. Borthrop Trumbull, who "was an admirer
by nature, and would have liked to have the universe under his
hammer, feeling that it would go at a higher figure for his recom-
mendation." On the contrary, we hold that an auctioneer's catalogue
of the divers and sundry beauties, rarities, and profundities of these
admirable volumes, can add nothing to the impression which a
leisurely perusal (let no one read them in haste) will leave on the
mind of every man and woman whose mental and artistic perceptions are sound and unblunted. And if praise is unnecessary, it is
impertinent. Spontaneous admiration is one of the few pleasures of
life, but the spurious literary enthusiasm which has to be conjured
up with a bede roll of respected adjectives is a caricature of the true
feeling. In fact, for the moment, we are of Sir James Chettam's
mind. He has just said: "I don't *like* Casaubon." (Can anything be
more conclusive? if he had said: "I *like* Middlemarch!") "He did
not usually find it easy to give his reasons; it seemed to him strange
that people should not know them without being told, since he only
felt what was reasonable." Except by the amiable baronet, reasons
for *disliking* a person — or a book — are easily found; but the best
reason for an admiration of *Middlemarch* is — the book itself.

[Henry James]

George Eliot's *Middlemarch*

Middlemarch is at once one of the strongest and one of the
weakest of English novels. Its predecessors as they appeared might
have been described in the same terms; *Romola* is especially a rare
masterpiece, but the least *entraînant* of masterpieces. *Romola* sins
by excess of analysis; there is too much description and too little
drama; too much reflection (all certainly of a highly imaginative sort)
and too little creation. Movement lingers in the story, and with it

Reprinted from the *Galaxy*, 15 (March 1873), 424–428.

attention stands still in the reader. The error in *Middlemarch* is not
precisely of a similar kind, but it is equally detrimental to the total
aspect of the work. We can well remember how keenly we wondered, while its earlier chapters unfolded themselves, what turn in
the way of form the story would take — that of an organized,
moulded, balanced composition, gratifying the reader with a sense
of design and construction, or a mere chain of episodes, broken
into accidental lengths and unconscious of the influence of a plan.
We expected the actual result, but for the sake of English imaginative
literature which, in this line, is rarely in need of examples, we hoped
for the other. If it had come we should have had the pleasure of
reading, what certainly would have seemed to us in the immediate
glow of attention, the first of English novels. But that pleasure has
still to hover between prospect and retrospect. *Middlemarch* is a
treasure-house of details, but it is an indifferent whole.

Our objection may seem shallow and pedantic, and may even be
represented as a complaint that we have had the less given us rather
than the more. Certainly the greatest minds have the defects of
their qualities, and as George Eliot's mind is preëminently contemplative and analytic, nothing is more natural than that her manner
should be discursive and expansive. "Concentration" would doubtless
have deprived us of many of the best things in the book — of Peter
Featherstone's grotesquely expectant legatees, of Lydgate's medical
rivals, and of Mary Garth's delightful family. The author's purpose
was to be a generous rural historian, and this very redundancy of
touch, born of abundant reminiscence, is one of the greatest charms
of her work. It is as if her memory was crowded with antique
figures, to whom for very tenderness she must grant an appearance.
Her novel is a picture — vast, swarming, deep-colored, crowded
with episodes, with vivid images, with lurking master-strokes, with
brilliant passages of expression; and as such we may freely accept
it and enjoy it. It is not compact, doubtless; but when was a
panorama compact? And yet, nominally, *Middlemarch* has a definite
subject — the subject indicated in the eloquent preface. An ardent
young girl was to have been the central figure, a young girl framed
for a larger moral life than circumstance often affords, yearning for
a motive for sustained spiritual effort and only wasting her ardor
and soiling her wings against the meanness of opportunity. The
author, in other words, proposed to depict the career of an obscure
St. Theresa. Her success has been great, in spite of serious draw-
backs. Dorothea Brooke is a genuine creation, and a most remarkable
one when we consider the delicate material in which she is wrought.
George Eliot's men are generally so much better than the usual
trowsered offspring of the female fancy, that their merits have

perhaps overshadowed those of her women. Yet her heroines have always been of an exquisite quality, and Dorothea is only that perfect flower of conception of which her predecessors were the less unfolded blossoms. An indefinable moral elevation is the sign of these admirable creatures; and of the representation of this quality in its superior degrees the author seems to have in English fiction a monopoly. To render the expression of a soul requires a cunning hand; but we seem to look straight into the unfathomable eyes of the beautiful spirit of Dorothea Brooke. She exhales a sort of aroma of spiritual sweetness, and we believe in her as in a woman we might providentially meet some fine day when we should find our-selves doubting of the immortality of the soul. By what unerring mechanism this effect is produced — whether by fine strokes or broad ones, by description or by narration, we can hardly say; it is certainly the great achievement of the book. Dorothea's career is, however, but an episode, and though doubtless in intention, not distinctly enough in fact, the central one. The history of Lydgate's *ménage*, which shares honors with it, seems rather to the reader to carry off the lion's share. This is certainly a very interesting story, but on the whole it yields in dignity to the record of Dorothea's unresonant woes. The "love-problem," as the author calls it, of Mary Garth, is placed on a rather higher level than the reader willingly grants it. To the end we care less about Fred Vincy than appears to be expected of us. In so far as the writer's design has been to reproduce the total sum of life in an English village forty years ago, this commonplace young gentleman, with his somewhat meagre tribulations and his rather neutral egotism, has his proper place in the picture; but the author narrates his fortunes with a fulness of detail which the reader often finds irritating. The reader indeed is sometimes tempted to complain of a tendency which we are at loss exactly to express — a tendency to make light of the serious elements of the story and to sacrifice them to the more trivial ones. Is it an unconscious instinct or is it a deliberate plan? With its abundant and massive ingredients *Middlemarch* ought somehow to have depicted a weightier drama. Dorothea was altogether too superb a heroine to be wasted; yet she plays a nar-rower part than the imagination of the reader demands. She is of more consequence than the action of which she is the nominal centre. She marries enthusiastically a man whom she fancies a great thinker, and who turns out to be but an arid pedant. Here, indeed, is a disappointment with much of the dignity of tragedy; but the situation seems to us never to expand to its full capacity. It is analyzed with extraordinary penetration, but one may say of it, as of most of the situations in the book, that it is treated with too

much refinement and too little breadth. It revolves too constantly
on the same pivot; it abounds in fine shades, but it lacks, we think,
the great dramatic *chiaroscuro*. Mr. Casaubon, Dorothea's husband
(of whom more anon) embittered, on his side, by matrimonial
disappointment, takes refuge in vain jealousy of his wife's relations
with an interesting young cousin of his own and registers this
sentiment in a codicil to his will, making the forfeiture of his
property the penalty of his widow's marriage with this gentleman.
Mr. Casaubon's death befalls about the middle of the story, and from
this point to the close our interest in Dorothea is restricted to the
question, will she or will [she] not marry Will Ladislaw? The
question is relatively trivial and the implied struggle slightly factitious.
The author has depicted the struggle with a sort of elaborate
solemnity which in the interviews related in the last two books
tends to become almost ludicrously excessive.

   The dramatic current stagnates; it runs between hero and heroine
almost a game of hair-splitting. Our dissatisfaction here is provoked
in a great measure by the insubstantial character of the hero. The
figure of Will Ladislaw is a beautiful attempt, with many finely-
completed points; but on the whole it seems to us a failure. It is
the only eminent failure in the book, and its defects are therefore
the more striking. It lacks sharpness of outline and depth of color;
we have not found ourselves believing in Ladislaw as we believe
in Dorothea, in Mary Garth, in Rosamond, in Lydgate, in Mr. Brooke
and Mr. Casaubon. He is meant, indeed, to be a light creature (with
a large capacity for gravity, for he finally gets into Parliament),
and a light creature certainly should not be heavily drawn. The
author, who is evidently very fond of him, has found for him here
and there some charming and eloquent touches; but in spite of these
he remains vague and impalpable to the end. He is, we may say,
the one figure which a masculine intellect of the same power as
George Eliot's would not have conceived with the same complacency;
he is, in short, roughly speaking, a woman's man. It strikes us as an
oddity in the author's scheme that she should have chosen just this
figure of Ladislaw as the creature in whom Dorothea was to find
her spiritual compensations. He is really, after all, not the ideal
foil to Mr. Casaubon which her soul must have imperiously demanded, and if the author of the "Key to all Mythologies" sinned
by lack of [ardor], Ladislaw too has not the concentrated fervor
essential in the man chosen by so nobly strenuous a heroine. The
impression once given that he is a *dilettante* is never properly
removed, and there is slender poetic justice in Dorothea's marrying
a *dilettante*. We are doubtless less content with Ladislaw, on
account of the noble, almost sculptural, relief of the neighboring

figure of Lydgate, the real hero of the story. It is an illustration
of the generous scale of the author's picture and of the conscious
power of imagination that she has given us a hero and heroine of
broadly distinct interests — erected, as it were, two suns in her
firmament, each with its independent solar system.

Lydgate is so richly successful a figure that we have regretted
strongly at moments, for immediate interest's sake, that the current
of his fortunes should not mingle more freely with the occasionally
thin-flowing stream of Dorothea's. Toward the close, these two
fine characters are brought into momentary contact so effectively
as to suggest a wealth of dramatic possibility between them; but if
this train had been followed we should have lost Rosamond Vincy —
a rare psychological study. Lydgate is a really complete portrait
of a *man*, which seems to us high praise. It is striking evidence
of the altogether superior quality of George Eliot's imagination
that, though elaborately represented, Lydgate should be treated
so little from what we may roughly (and we trust without offence)
call the sexual point of view. Perception charged with feeling has
constantly guided the author's hand, and yet her strokes remain as
firm, her curves as free, her whole manner as serenely impersonal,
as if, on a small scale, she were emulating the creative wisdom
itself. Several English romancers — notably Fielding, Thackeray, and
Charles Reade — have won great praise for their figures of women:
but they owe it, in reversed conditions, to a meaner sort of art, it
seems to us, than George Eliot has used in the case of Lydgate; to
an indefinable appeal to masculine prejudice — to a sort of titillation
of the masculine sense of difference. George Eliot's manner is
more philosophic — more broadly intelligent, and yet her result is
as concrete, or, if you please, as picturesque. We have no space
to dwell on Lydgate's character; we can but repeat that he is a
vividly consistent, manly figure — powerful, ambitious, sagacious,
with the maximum rather than the minimum of egotism, strenuous,
generous, fallible, and altogether human. A work of the liberal scope
of *Middlemarch* contains a multitude of artistic intentions, some of
the finest of which become clear only in the meditative after-taste
of perusal. This is the case with the balanced contrast between the
two histories of Lydgate and Dorothea. Each is a tale of matrimonial
infelicity, but the conditions in each are so different and the
circumstances so broadly opposed that the mind passes from one to
the other with that supreme sense of the vastness and variety of
human life, under aspects apparently similar, which it belongs only
to the greatest novels to produce. The most perfectly successful
passages in the book are perhaps those painful fireside scenes between
Lydgate and his miserable little wife. The author's rare psychological

penetration is lavished upon this veritably mulish domestic flower. There is nothing more powerfully real than these scenes in all English fiction, and nothing certainly more *intelligent*. Their impressiveness and (as regards Lydgate) their pathos, is deepened by the constantly low key in which they are pitched. It is a tragedy based on unpaid butcher's bills, and the urgent need for small economies. The author has desired to be strictly real and to adhere to the facts of the common lot, and she has given us a powerful version of that typical human drama, the struggles of an ambitious soul with sordid disappointments and vulgar embarrassments. As to her catastrophe we hesitate to pronounce (for Lydgate's ultimate assent to his wife's worldly programme is nothing less than a catastrophe). We almost believe that some terrific explosion would have been more probable than his twenty years of smothered aspiration. Rosamond deserves almost to rank with Tito in *Romola* as a study of a gracefully vicious, or at least of a practically baleful nature. There is one point, however, of which we question the consistency. The author insists on her instincts of coquetry, which seems to us a discordant note. They would have made her better or worse — more generous or more reckless; in either case more manageable. As it is, Rosamond represents, in a measure, the fatality of British decorum.

In reading, we have marked innumerable passages for quotation and comment; but we lack space and the work is so ample that half a dozen extracts would be an ineffective illustration. There would be a great deal to say on the broad array of secondary figures, Mr. Casaubon, Mr. Brooke, Mr. Bulstrode, Mr. Farebrother, Caleb Garth, Mrs. Cadwallader, Celia Brooke. Mr. Casaubon is an excellent invention; as a dusky *repoussoir* to the luminous figure of his wife he could not have been better imagined. There is indeed something very noble in the way in which the author has apprehended his character. To depict hollow pretentiousness and mouldy egotism with so little of narrow sarcasm and so much of philosophic sympathy, is to be a rare moralist as well as a rare story-teller. The whole portrait of Mr. Casaubon has an admirably sustained greyness of tone in which the shadows are never carried to the vulgar black of coarser artists. Every stroke contributes to the unwholesome, help-lessly sinister expression. Here and there perhaps (as in his habitual diction), there is a hint of exaggeration; but we confess we like fancy to be fanciful. Mr. Brooke and Mr. Garth are in their different lines supremely genial creations; they are drawn with the touch of a Dickens chastened and intellectualized. Mrs. Cadwallader is, in another walk of life, a match for Mrs. Poyser, and Celia Brooke is as pretty a fool as any of Miss Austen's. Mr. Farebrother and his delightful "womankind" belong to a large group of figures begotten

of the superabundance of the author's creative instinct. At times
they seem to encumber the stage and to produce a rather ponderous
mass of dialogue; but they add to the reader's impression of having
walked in the Middlemarch lanes and listened to the Middlemarch
accent. To but one of these accessory episodes — that of Mr.
Bulstrode, with its multiplex ramifications — do we take exception.
It has a slightly artificial cast, a melodramatic tinge, unfriendly to
the richly natural coloring of the whole. Bulstrode himself — with
the history of whose troubled conscience the author has taken great
pains — is, to our sense, too diffusely treated; he never grasps the
reader's attention. But the touch of genius is never idle or vain.
The obscure figure of Bulstrode's comely wife emerges at the
needful moment, under a few light strokes, into the happiest reality.

All these people, solid and vivid in their varying degrees, are
members of a deeply human little world, the full reflection of whose
antique image is the great merit of these volumes. How bravely
rounded a little world the author has made it — with how dense an
atmosphere of interests and passions and loves and enmities and
strivings and failings, and how motley a group of great folk and
small, all after their kind, she has filled it, the reader must learn
for himself. No writer seems to us to have drawn from a richer
stock of those long-cherished memories which one's later philosophy
makes doubly tender. There are few figures in the book which do
not seem to have grown mellow in the author's mind. English readers
may fancy they enjoy the "atmosphere" of *Middlemarch;* but we
maintain that to relish its inner essence we must — for reasons too
numerous to detail — be an American. The author has commissioned
herself to be real, her native tendency being that of an idealist, and
the intellectual result is a very fertilizing mixture. The constant
presence of thought, of generalizing instinct, of *brain,* in a word,
behind her observation, gives the latter its great value and her whole
manner its high superiority. It denotes a mind in which imagination
is illumined by faculties rarely found in fellowship with it. In this
respect — in that broad reach of vision which would make the worthy
historian of solemn fact as well as wanton fiction — George Eliot
seems to us among English romancers to stand alone. Fielding
approaches her, but to our mind, she surpasses Fielding. Fielding
was didactic — the author of *Middlemarch* is really philosophic.
These great qualities imply corresponding perils. The first is the
loss of simplicity. George Eliot lost hers some time since; it lies
buried (in a splendid mausoleum) in *Romola.* Many of the discursive
portions of *Middlemarch* are, as we may say, too clever by half.
The author wishes to say too many things, and to say them too well;

to recommend herself to a scientific audience. Her style, rich and flexible as it is, is apt to betray her on these transcendental flights; we find, in our copy, a dozen passages marked "obscure." *Silas Marner* has a delightful tinge of Goldsmith — we may almost call it; *Middlemarch* is too often an echo of Messrs. Darwin and Huxley. In spite of these faults — which it seems graceless to indicate with this crude rapidity — it remains a very splendid performance. It sets a limit, we think, to the development of the old-fashioned English novel. Its diffuseness, on which we have touched, makes it too copious a dose of pure fiction. If we write novels so, how shall we write History? But it is nevertheless a contribution of the first importance to the rich imaginative department of our literature.

Henry James

George Eliot's *The Legend of Jubal*

When the author of *Middlemarch* published, some years since, her first volume of verse, the reader, in trying to judge it fairly, asked himself what he should think of it if she had never published a line of prose. The question, perhaps, was not altogether a help to strict fairness of judgment, but the author was protected from illiberal conclusions by the fact that, practically, it was impossible to answer it. George Eliot belongs to that class of pre-eminent writers in relation to whom the imagination comes to self-consciousness only to find itself in subjection. It was impossible to disengage one's judgment from the permanent influence of *Adam Bede* and its companions, and it was necessary, from the moment that the author undertook to play the poet's part, to feel that her genius was all of one piece. People have often asked themselves how they would estimate Shakespeare if they knew him only by his comedies, Homer if his name stood only for the *Odyssey*, and Milton if he had written nothing but "Lycidas" and the shorter pieces. The question, of necessity, inevitable though it is, leads to nothing. George Eliot is neither Homer nor Shakespeare nor Milton; but her work, like theirs, is a massive

Reprinted from the *North American Review*, 119 (October 1874), 484–489.

achievement, divided into a supremely good and a less good, and it provokes us, like theirs, to the fruitless attempt to estimate the latter portion on its own merits alone. The little volume before us gives us another opportunity; but here, as before, we find ourselves uncomfortably divided between the fear, on the one hand, of being bribed into favor, and, on the other, of giving short measure of it. The author's verses are a narrow manifestation of her genius, but they are an unmistakable manifestation. *Middlemarch* has made us demand even finer things of her than we did before, and whether, as patented readers of *Middlemarch*, we like "Jubal" and its companions the less or the more, we must admit that they are characteristic products of the same intellect. We imagine George Eliot is quite philosopher enough, having produced her poems mainly as a kind of experimental entertainment for her own mind, to let them commend themselves to the public on any grounds whatever which will help to illustrate the workings of versatile intelligence, — as interesting failures, if nothing better. She must feel they are interesting; an exaggerated modesty cannot deny that.

We have found them extremely so. They consist of a rhymed narrative, of some length, of the career of Jubal, the legendary inventor of the lyre; of a short rustic idyl in blank verse on a theme gathered in the Black Forest of Baden; of a tale, versified in rhyme, from Boccaccio; and of a series of dramatic scenes called "Armgart," — the best thing, to our sense, of the four. To these are added a few shorter pieces, chiefly in blank verse, each of which seems to us proportionately more successful than the more ambitious ones. Our author's verse is a mixture of spontaneity of thought and excessive reflectiveness of expression, and its value is generally more in the idea than in the form. In whatever George Eliot writes, you have the comfortable certainty, infrequent in other quarters, of finding an idea, and you get the substance of her thought in the short poems, without the somewhat rigid envelope of her poetic diction. If we may say, broadly, that the supreme merit of a poem is in having warmth, and that it is less and less valuable in proportion as it cools by too long waiting upon either fastidious skill or inefficient skill, the little group of verses entitled "Brother and Sister" deserve our preference. They have extreme loveliness, and the feeling they so abundantly express is of a much less intellectualized sort than that which prevails in the other poems. It is seldom that one of our author's compositions concludes upon so simply sentimental a note as the last lines of "Brother and Sister": —

But were another childhood-world my share,
I would be born a little sister there!

This will be interesting to many readers as proceeding more directly from the writer's personal experience than anything else they remember. George Eliot's is a personality so enveloped in the mists of reflection that it is an uncommon sensation to find one's self in immediate contact with it. This charming poem, too, throws a grateful light on some of the best pages the author has written, — those in which she describes her heroine's childish years in *The Mill on the Floss*. The finest thing in that admirable novel has always been, to our taste, not its portrayal of the young girl's love-struggles as regards her lover, but those as regards her brother. The former are fiction, — skilful fiction; but the latter are warm reality, and the merit of the verses we speak of is that they are colored from the same source.

In "Stradivarius," the famous old violin-maker affirms in very pregnant phrase the supreme duty of being perfect in one's labor, and lays down the dictum, which should be the first article in every artist's faith: —

> 'T is God gives skill,
> But not without men's hands: He could not make
> Antonio Stradivari's violins
> Without Antonio.

This is the only really inspiring working-creed, and our author's utterance of it justifies her claim to having the distinctly artistic mind, more forcibly than her not infrequent shortcomings in the direction of an artistic *ensemble*. Many persons will probably pronounce "A Minor Prophet" the gem of this little collection, and it is certainly interesting, for a great many reasons. It may seem to characterize the author on a number of sides. It illustrates vividly, in the extraordinary ingenuity and flexibility of its diction, her extreme provocation to indulge in the verbal license of verse. It reads almost like a close imitation of Browning, the great master of the poetical grotesque, except that it observes a discretion which the poet of Red-Cotton Nightcaps long ago threw overboard. When one can say neat things with such rhythmic felicity, why not attempt it, even if one has at one's command the magnificent vehicle of the style of *Middlemarch*? The poem is a kindly satire upon the views and the person of an American vegetarian, a certain Elias Baptist Butterworth, — a gentleman, presumably, who under another name, as an evening caller, has not a little retarded the flight of time for the author. Mr. Browning has written nothing better than the account of the Butterworthian "Thought Atmosphere." . . . All this is unfolded in verse which, if without the absolute pulse of spontaneity, has at least something that closely resembles it. It has very fine passages.

Very fine, too, both in passages and as a whole, is "The Legend of Jubal." It is noteworthy, by the way, that three of these poems are on themes connected with music; and yet we remember no representation of a musician among the multitudinous figures which people the author's novels. But George Eliot, we take it, has the musical sense in no small degree, and the origin of melody and harmony is here described in some very picturesque and sustained poetry. Jubal invents the lyre and teaches his companions and his tribe how to use it, and then goes forth to wander in quest of new musical inspiration. In this pursuit he grows patriarchally old, and at last makes his way back to his own people. He finds them, greatly advanced in civilization, celebrating what we should call nowadays his centennial, and making his name the refrain of their songs. He goes in among them and declares himself, but they receive him as a lunatic, and buffet him, and thrust him out into the wilderness again, where he succumbs to their unconscious ingratitude.

> The immortal name of Jubal filled the sky,
> While Jubal, lonely, laid him down to die.

In his last hour he has a kind of metaphysical vision which consoles him, and enables him to die contented. A mystic voice assures him that he has no cause for complaint; that his use to mankind was everything, and his credit and glory nothing; that being rich in his genius, it was his part to give, gratuitously, to unendowed humanity; and that the knowledge of his having become a part of man's joy, and an image in man's soul, should reconcile him to the prospect of lying senseless in the tomb. Jubal assents, and expires,

> A quenched sun-wave,
> The all-creating Presence for his grave.

This is very noble and heroic doctrine, and is enforced in verse not unworthy of it for having a certain air of strain and effort; for surely it is not doctrine that the egoistic heart rises to without some experimental flutter of the wings. It is the expression of a pessimistic philosophy which pivots upon itself only in the face of a really formidable ultimatum. We cordially accept it, however, and are tolerably confident that the artist in general, in his death-throes, will find less repose in the idea of a heavenly compensation for earthly neglect than in the certainty that humanity is really assimilating his productions.

"Agatha" is slighter in sentiment than its companions, and has the vague aroma of an idea rather than the positive weight of thought.

It is very graceful. "How Lisa loved the King" seems to us to have, more than its companions, the easy flow and abundance of prime poetry; it wears a reflection of the incomparable naturalness of its model in the *Decameron*. "Armgart" we have found extremely interesting, although perhaps it offers plainest proof of what the author sacrifices in renouncing prose. The drama, in prose, would have been vividly dramatic, while, as it stands, we have merely a situation contemplated, rather than unfolded, in a dramatic light. A great singer loses her voice, and a patronizing nobleman, who, before the calamity, had wished her to become his wife, retire from the stage, and employ her genius for the beguilement of private life, finds that he has urgent business in another neighborhood, and that he has not the mission to espouse her misfortune. Armgart rails tremendously at fate, often in very striking phrase. The Count, of course, in bidding her farewell, has hoped that time will soften her disappointment: —

> That empty cup so neatly ciphered, "Time,"
> Handed me as a cordial for despair.
> Time — what a word to fling as charity!
> Bland, neutral word for slow dull-beating pain, —
> Days, months, and years!

We must refer the reader to the poem itself for knowledge how resignation comes to so bitter a pain as the mutilation of conscious genius. It comes to Armgart because she is a very superior girl; and though her outline, here, is at once rather sketchy and rather rigid, she may be added to that group of magnificently generous women, — the Dinahs, the Maggies, the Romolas, the Dorotheas, — the representation of whom is our author's chief title to our gratitude. But in spite of Armgart's resignation, the moral atmosphere of the poem, like that of most of the others and like that of most of George Eliot's writings, is an almost gratuitously sad one. It would take more space than we can command to say how it is that at this and at other points our author strikes us as a spirit mysteriously perverted from her natural temper. We have a feeling that, both intellectually and morally, her genius is essentially of a simpler order than most of her recent manifestations of it. Intellectually, it has run to epigram and polished cleverness, and morally to a sort of conscious and ambitious scepticism, with which it only half commingles. The interesting thing would be to trace the moral divergence from the characteristic type. At bottom, according to this notion, the author of *Romola* and *Middlemarch* has an ardent desire and faculty for positive, active, constructive belief of the old-fashioned kind, but she has fallen upon a critical age and felt its contagion and dominion. If, with her mag-

nificent gifts, she had been borne by the mighty general current in
the direction of passionate faith, we often think that she would have
achieved something incalculably great.

[Henry James]

Daniel Deronda

In view of the deluge of criticism which is certain to be poured
out upon George Eliot's new novel when the publication is completed,
it might seem the part of discretion not to open fire upon the first
instalment. But this writer's admirers can reconcile themselves to no
argument which forbids them to offer the work a welcome, and —
putting criticism aside — we must express our pleasure in the prospect
of the intellectual luxury of taking up, month after month, the little
clear-paged volumes of *Daniel Deronda*. We know of none other
at the present time that is at all comparable to it. The quality of
George Eliot's work makes acceptable, in this particular case, a manner of publication to which in general we strongly object. It is but
just that so fine and rare a pleasure should have a retarding element
in it. George Eliot's writing is so full, so charged with reflection and
intellectual experience, that there is surely no arrogance in her giving
us a month to think over and digest any given portion of it. For
almost a year to come the lives of appreciative readers will have a
sort of lateral extension into another multitudinous world — a world
ideal only in the soft, clear light under which it lies, and most real
in its close appeal to our curiosity. It is too early to take the measure
of the elements which the author has in hand, but the imagination
has a confident sense of large and complex unfolding. The opening
chapters are of course but the narrow end of the wedge. The wedge
— as embodied in the person of Gwendolen Harleth — seems perhaps
unexpectedly narrow, but we can make no doubt that before many
weeks have gone by we shall be hanging upon this young lady's entangled destiny with the utmost tension of our highest faculties. Already we are conscious of much acuteness of conjecture as to the
balance of her potentialities — as to whether she is to exemplify the

Reprinted from the *Nation*, 22 (24 February 1876), p. 131.

harsh or the tender side of tragic interest, whether, as we may say in speaking of a companion work to *Middlemarch*, the Dorothea element or the Rosamond element is to prevail. A striking figure in these opening chapters is that of Herr Klesmer, a German music-master, who has occasion to denounce an aria of Bellini as expressing "a puerile state of culture – no sense of the universal." There could not be a better phrase than this latter one to express the secret of that deep interest with which the reader settles down to George Eliot's widening narrative. The "sense of the universal" is constant, omnipresent. It strikes us sometimes perhaps as rather conscious and over-cultivated; but it gives us the feeling that the threads of the narrative, as we gather them into our hands, are not of the usual commercial measurement, but long electric wires capable of transmitting messages from mysterious regions.

[Richard Holt Hutton]

Daniel Deronda

There are both blemishes and beauties in *Daniel Deronda* which belong exclusively to this work of its great author. No book of hers before this has ever appeared so laboured, and sometimes even so forced and feeble, in its incidental remarks. No book of hers before this has ever had so many original mottoes prefixed to the chapters which, instead of increasing our admiration for the book, rather overweight and perplex it. No book of hers before this ever contained so little humour. And no doubt the reader feels the difference in all these respects between *Daniel Deronda* and *Middlemarch*. On the other hand, no book of hers before this, unless, perhaps, we except *Adam Bede*, ever contained so fine a plot, so admirably worked out. No book of hers before this was ever conceived on ideal lines so noble, the whole effect of which, when we look back to the beginning from the end, seems to have been so powerfully given. No book of hers before this has contained so many fine characters, and betrayed so subtle an insight into the modes of growth of a better moral life within the shrivelling buds and blossoms of the selfish life

Reprinted from the *Spectator*, 49 (9 September 1876), 1131–1133.

which has been put off and condemned. And last of all, no book of
hers before this has breathed so distinctly religious a tone, so much
faith in the power which overrules men's destinies for purposes infinitely raised above the motives which actually animate them, and
which uses the rebellion, and the self-will, and the petty craft of
human unworthiness, only to perfect the execution of His higher
ends, and to hasten His day of deliverance. It is true that so far as
this book conveys the author's religious creed, it is a purified Judaism,
— in other words, a devout Theism, purged of Jewish narrowness,
while retaining the intense patriotism which pervades Judaism; and
that the hero, — who is intended for an ideal of goodness as perfect
as any to which man can reach at present, — evidently sees nothing
in the teaching of Christ which raises Christianity above the purified
Judaism of Mordecai's vision. But however much we may differ from
her here, it is not on such a difference that our estimate of the power
or art of this fine tale can turn. So far as art is concerned, there
neither is nor can be any issue of a dogmatic nature embodied in it.
But it would be as idle to say that there is no conception of Providence
or of supernatural guidance involved in the story, as to say the same
of the Oedipean trilogy of Sophocles. The art of this story is essentially religious.

The struggle between evil and good for Gwendolen, her fear of
the loneliness and vastness of the universe over which she can exert
no influence, and the selfish plunge which she makes, against all her
instincts of right and purity, into a marriage in which she fancies she
can get her own way, only to find that she has riveted on herself the
grasp of an evil nature which she cannot influence at all, though every
day makes her fear and hate that nature more; the counteracting influence for good which Deronda gains with her by venturing, — as a
mere stranger, — to warn her and help her against her gambling caprice, and thus identifying himself in her mind with those agencies
of the universe beyond the control of her will which "make for
righteousness," to use Mr. Arnold's phrase; and lastly, that disposal
of events which always brings her within reach of Deronda's influence
when she most needs it, till good has gained the victory in her, and
that influence, too, is withdrawn, to make room for a more spiritual
guidance, — all this is told with a power and a confidence in the overshadowing of human lives by a higher control which is of the essence
of the art of the story, and essentially religious. . . . Whatever the
blemishes of the story, no one who can appreciate Art of the higher
kind will deny that the history of Gwendolen's moral collapse and
regeneration, and of Deronda's mother, and her eventual submission
to that higher spirit of her father which, by its want of breadth and
sympathy with her own individual genius, had utterly alienated her,

in the brilliancy of her youth, till she strove with all her might to ignore what was noble and even grand in it, is traced with a sort of power of which George Eliot has never before given us any specimen.

At the same time, it cannot be denied that while there is more which reaches true grandeur in this story than in perhaps any other of the same writer's, there is much less equality of execution and richness of conception. The hero himself is laboured. And though in some of the closing scenes, especially those with his mother and with Gwendolen, we are compelled to admit that his picture is a noble one, so much pain has been expended on *studying* rather than on *painting* him, that throughout (say) three-quarters of the story, we are rather being prepared to make acquaintance with Deronda than actually making acquaintance with him. Again, we are not satisfied with the Jewish heroine, Mirah. After the first scene in which she appears, where in her misery she is contemplating suicide, and, with a minute forethought characteristic of time of excitement, takes care to dip her long woollen cloak in the river, in order that she may sink the more easily when she puts it on, — after this scene, we say, Mirah does not gain upon us, but rather irritates us against her by her intolerable habit of crossing her hands on her breast, in sign, we suppose, of the meekness and patience of her disposition. . . . The vagueness of the picture of the hero till within a few fine scenes of the end, and this ostentatious humility of the heroine's, seem to us real blots on the higher art of the book. . . .

Add to this that the small pedantries, like talking of "emotive memory" and a "dynamic" glance, are more numerous than ever, and that perhaps the only sketch of really great humour in the story, is the picture of the composer and pianist Klesmer, and we have shown some reason, we think, for the opinion which is so widely expressed, that at least in some respects *Daniel Deronda* falls far below the level of *Middlemarch*. On the other hand, the cynicism of the incidental irony is certainly much less, and the whole spirit of the book is wider and higher.

But what makes it, after all, uncertain whether, in spite of the much greater inequality of execution and style, *Daniel Deronda* may not rank in the estimate of the critics of the future as a greater work altogether than any which George Eliot has previously written, is the powerful construction of the plot, — almost a new feature in her stories, — and the occasional grandeur of the conceptions which she successfully works out. The whole of the seventh part and the explanation between Gwendolen and Deronda in the last, seem to us to contain perhaps the highest work George Eliot has ever given us. The scene in which Deronda's mother describes the invisible force which is upon her in her pain and weakness to make her, — involuntarily almost, — revoke her own deliberately executed and apparently successfully executed purpose, — the magnificence of the picture of the woman, half-queen, half-actress, and yet wholly real, as she discloses her unmaternal character to the son whom she admires, but neither loves nor cares to have loving her, — the shrinking and yet imploring tenderness which she awakens in her son, — the constraint and yet the passion of their mutual upbraidings, and their efforts to suppress them, — all produce an almost magical effect on the imagination, such as cannot be paralleled, we think, in any former work of this writer's. There is in this interview some of the high scenic imagination of Sir Walter Scott, blended with the greater knowledge of the individual heart possessed by George Eliot. Not so magical in its force, — we might almost say splendour, — but quite as delicate and much more subtly tender, are the later scenes between Gwendolen and Deronda, after the former has lost her husband and in the manner which makes her almost accuse herself of his death. It would be hardly possible to exceed the pathos of the parting interview, where Gwendolen suddenly becomes aware that Deronda is not only engaged to another woman, but preparing to leave for the East, to absorb himself in a life in which she has no interest or concern. There is a subtlety in the relations of the two, — relations which have never in any way been those of passion, — and a delicacy in the painting both of her forlorn sinking of the heart and of his natural tenderness for her, which seem to us among the most original conceptions of modern literature. . . .

We have avoided criticising the no doubt very prominent and important character of Mordecai, the Jewish prophet, simply because we find it very difficult to make up our mind about him. The picture in some respects is a singularly fine one. But the *ideas* and creed of the man, on which, in a case like this, so very much turns, are too indefinitely and vaguely sketched to support the character. Before such a being as Mordecai could seriously have proposed to restore nationality to the Jews, in order that they might resume their proper mission of mediating, as religious teachers at least, between East and West, he must have had a much more defined belief than any which the author chooses to communicate to us. And the result is to make us feel that he is rather a fine torso than a perfectly conceived and sculptured figure. We admire him, we revere him, we are touched by him, but we are puzzled by him. He would remind us now and then of Mr. Disraeli and the "great Asiatic mystery," if his moral nature were not so much more noble and definite than anything of which Mr. Disraeli ever caught a glimpse. On the whole, Mordecai's influence on Deronda is only half-justified. We cannot dismiss De-

ronda on his journey to the East without feeling uncomfortably that
he is gone on a wild-goose chase, — to preach ideas which have only
been hinted, and which must rest on a creed that has hardly been
hinted at all. *Daniel Deronda* thus seems to us much more unequal
than *Middlemarch*. But it rises at certain points definitely above that
great book. Its summits are higher, but its average level of power is
very much lower.

Henry James

Daniel Deronda: A Conversation

Theodora, one day early in the autumn, sat on her piazza with a
piece of embroidery, the design of which she invented as she proceeded, being careful, however, to have a Japanese screen before her,
to keep her inspiration at the proper altitude. Pulcheria, who was
paying her a visit, sat near her with a closed book, in a paper cover,
in her lap. Pulcheria was playing with the little dog, rather idly, but
Theodora was stitching, steadily and meditatively. "Well," said
Theodora, at last, "I wonder what he accomplished in the East."
Pulcheria took the little dog into her lap and made him sit on the
book. "Oh," she replied, "they had tea-parties at Jerusalem, — exclusively of ladies, — and he sat in the midst and stirred his tea and made
high-toned remarks. And then Mirah sang a little, just a little, on
account of her voice being so weak. Sit still, Fido," she continued,
addressing the little dog, "and keep your nose out of my face. But
it's a nice little nose, all the same," she pursued, "a nice little short
snub nose, and not a horrid big Jewish nose. Oh, my dear, when I
think what a collection of noses there must have been at that wedding!" At this moment Constantius steps out upon the piazza from
the long parlor window, hat and stick in hand and his shoes a trifle
dusty. He has some steps to take before he reaches the end of the
piazza where the ladies are sitting, and this gives Pulcheria time to
murmur, "Talk of snub noses!" Constantius is presented by Theodora
to Pulcheria, and he sits down and exclaims upon the admirable blue-
ness of the sea, which lies in a straight band across the green of the

Reprinted from the *Atlantic Monthly,* 38 (December 1876), 684–694.

little lawn; comments too upon the pleasure of having one side of
one's piazza in the shade. Soon Fido, the little dog, still restless, jumps
off Pulcheria's lap and reveals the book, which lies title upward. "Oh,"
says Constantius, "you have been finishing *Daniel Deronda?*" Then
follows a conversation which it will be more convenient to present
in another form.

Theodora. Yes, Pulcheria has been reading aloud the last chapters
to me. They are wonderfully beautiful.

Constantius (after a moment's hesitation). Yes, they are very
beautiful. I am sure you read well, Pulcheria, to give the fine passages
their full value.

Theodora. She reads well when she chooses, but I am sorry to
say that in some of the fine passages of this last book she took quite
a false tone. I could n't have read them aloud, myself; I should have
broken down. But Pulcheria, — would you really believe it? — when
she could n't go on, it was not for tears, but for — the contrary.

Constantius. For smiles? Did you really find it comical? One of
my objections to *Daniel Deronda* is the absence of those delightfully
humorous passages which enlivened the author's former works.

Pulcheria. Oh, I think there are some places as amusing as anything
in *Adam Bede* or *The Mill on the Floss:* for instance, where, at the
last, Deronda wipes Gwendolen's tears and Gwendolen wipes his.

Constantius. Yes, I know what you mean. I can understand that
situation presenting a slightly ridiculous image; that is, if the current
of the story does not swiftly carry you past that idea.

Pulcheria. What do you mean by the current of the story: I never
read a story with less current. It is not a river; it is a series of lakes.
I once read of a group of little uneven ponds resembling, from a
bird's-eye view, a looking-glass which had fallen upon the floor and
broken, and was lying in fragments. That is what *Daniel Deronda*
would look like, on a bird's-eye view.

Theodora. Pulcheria found that comparison in a French novel. She
is always reading French novels.

Constantius. Ah, there are some very good ones.

Pulcheria (perversely). I don't know; I think there are some very
poor ones.

Constantius. The comparison is not bad, at any rate. I know what
you mean by *Daniel Deronda* lacking current. It has almost as little
as *Romola.*

Pulcheria. Oh, *Romola* is unpardonably slow; it absolutely stagnates.

Constantius. Yes, I know what you mean by that. But I am afraid
you are not friendly to our great novelist.

Theodora. She likes Balzac and George Sand and other impure
writers.

Constantius. Well, I must say I understand that.

Pulcheria. My favorite novelist is Thackeray, and I am extremely fond of Miss Austen.

Constantius. I understand that, too. You read over *The Newcomes* and *Pride and Prejudice.*

Pulcheria. No, I don't read them over, now; I think them over. I have been making visits for a long time past to a series of friends, and I have spent the last six months in reading *Daniel Deronda* aloud. Fortune would have it that I should always arrive by the same train as the new number. I am considered a frivolous, idle creature; I am not a disciple in the new school of embroidery, like Theodora; so I was immediately pushed into a chair and the book thrust into my hand, that I might lift up my voice and make peace between all the impatiences that were snatching at it. So I may claim at least that I have read every word of the work. I never skipped.

Theodora. I should hope not, indeed!

Constantius. And do you mean that you really did n't enjoy it?

Pulcheria. I found it protracted, pretentious, pedantic.

Constantius. I see; I can understand that.

Theodora. Oh, you understand too much! Here is the twentieth time you have used that formula.

Constantius. What will you have? You know I must try to understand, it's my trade.

Theodora. He means he writes reviews. Trying *not* to understand is what I call that trade!

Constantius. Say, then, I take it the wrong way; that is why it has never made my fortune. But I do try to understand; it is my — my — (He pauses.)

Theodora. I know what you want to say. Your strong side.

Pulcheria. And what is his weak side?

Theodora. He writes novels.

Constantius. I have written *one.* You can't call that a side.

Pulcheria. I should like to read it, — not aloud!

Constantius. You can't read it softly enough. But you, Theodora, you did n't find our book too "protracted"?

Theodora. I should have liked it to continue indefinitely, to keep coming out always, to be one of the regular things of life.

Pulcheria. Oh, come here, little dog! To think that *Daniel Deronda* might be perpetual when you, little short-nosed darling, can't last at the most more than eight or nine years!

Theodora. A book like *Daniel Deronda* becomes part of one's life; one lives in it or alongside of it. I don't hesitate to say that I have been living in this one for the last eight months. It is such a complete world George Eliot builds up; it is so vast, so much-embracing! It

has such a firm earth and such an ethereal sky. You can turn into it
and lose yourself in it.

Pulcheria. Oh, easily, and die of cold and starvation!

Theodora. I have been very near to poor Gwendolen and very near
to dear little Mirah. And the dear little Meyricks, also; I know them
intimately well.

Pulcheria. The Meyricks, I grant you, are the best thing in the book.

Theodora. They are a delicious family; I wish they lived in Boston.
I consider Herr Klesmer almost Shakespearian, and his wife is almost
as good. I have been near to poor, grand Mordecai —

Pulcheria. Oh, reflect, my dear; not too near.

Theodora. And as for Deronda himself, I freely confess that I am
consumed with a hopeless passion for him. He is the most irresistible
man in the literature of fiction.

Pulcheria. He is not a man at all!

Theodora. I remember nothing more beautiful than the description
of his childhood, and that picture of his lying on the grass in the abbey
cloister, a beautiful seraph-faced boy, with a lovely voice, reading
history and asking his Scotch tutor why the Popes had so many
nephews. He must have been delightfully handsome.

Pulcheria. Never, my dear, with that nose! I am sure he had a nose,
and I hold that the author has shown great pusillanimity in her treatment of it. She has quite shirked it. The picture you speak of is very
pretty, but a picture is not a person. And why is he always grasping
his coat-collar, as if he wished to hang himself up? The author had
an uncomfortable feeling that she must make him do something real,
something visible and sensible, and she hit upon that awkward device.
I don't see what you mean by saying you have been *near* those people;
that is just what one is not. They produce no illusion. They are
described and analyzed to death, but we don't see them or hear them
or touch them. Deronda clutches his coat-collar, Mirah crosses her
feet, and Mordecai talks like the Bible; but that does n't make real
figures of them. They have no existence outside of the author's
study.

Theodora. If you mean that they are nobly imaginative, I quite
agree with you; and if they say nothing to your own imagination, the
fault is yours, not theirs.

Pulcheria. Pray don't say they are Shakespearian again. Shakespeare
went to work another way.

Constantius. I think you are both in a measure right; there is a
distinction to be drawn. There are in *Daniel Deronda* the figures
based upon observation and the figures based upon invention. This
distinction, I know, is rather a rough one. There are no figures in
any novel that are pure observation and none that are pure invention.

But either element may preponderate, and in those cases in which invention has preponderated George Eliot seems to me to have achieved at the best but so many brilliant failures.

Theodora. And are *you* turning severe? I thought you admired her so much.

Constantius. I defy any one to admire her more, but one must discriminate. Speaking brutally, I consider *Daniel Deronda* the weakest of her books. It strikes me as very sensibly inferior to *Middlemarch.* I have an immense opinion of *Middlemarch.*

Pulcheria. Not having been obliged by circumstances to read *Middlemarch* to other people, I did n't read it at all. I could n't read it to myself. I tried, but I broke down. I appreciated Rosamond, but I could n't believe in Dorothea.

Theodora (very gravely). So much the worse for you, Pulcheria. I have enjoyed *Daniel Deronda because* I had enjoyed *Middlemarch.* Why should you throw *Middlemarch* up against her? It seems to me that if a book is fine it is fine. I have enjoyed *Deronda* deeply, from beginning to end.

Constantius. I assure you, so have I. I can read nothing of George Eliot's without enjoyment. I even enjoy her poetry, though I don't approve of it. In whatever she writes I enjoy her mind – her large, luminous, airy mind. The intellectual brilliancy of *Daniel Deronda* strikes me as very great, in excess of anything the author had done. In the first couple of numbers of the book this ravished me. I delighted in its tone, its deep, rich English tone, in which so many notes seemed melted together.

Pulcheria. The tone is not English, it is German.

Constantius. I understand that – if Theodora will allow me to say so. Little by little I began to feel that I cared less for certain notes than for others. I say it under my breath – I began to feel an occasional temptation to skip. Roughly speaking, all the Jewish burden of the story tended to weary me; it is this part that produces the small illusion which I agree with Pulcheria in finding. Gwendolen and Grandcourt are admirable. Gwendolen is a masterpiece. She is known, felt, and presented, psychologically, altogether in the grand manner. Beside her and beside her husband – a consummate picture of English brutality refined and distilled (for Grandcourt is before all things brutal) – Deronda, Mordecai, and Mirah are hardly more than shadows. They and their fortunes are all improvisation. I don't say anything against improvisation. When it succeeds it has a surpassing charm. But it must succeed. With George Eliot it seems to me to succeed only partially, less than one would expect of her talent. The story of Deronda's life, his mother's story, Mirah's story are quite the sort of thing one finds in George Sand. But they are really not so good as they would be in George Sand. George Sand would have carried it off with a lighter hand.

Theodora. Oh, Constantius, how can you compare George Eliot's novels to that woman's? It is sunlight and moonshine.

Pulcheria. I really think the two writers are very much alike. They are both very voluble, both addicted to moralizing and philosophizing *à tout bout de champ*, both inartistic!

Constantius. I see what you mean. But George Eliot is solid and George Sand is liquid. When occasionally George Eliot liquefies, — as in the history of Deronda's birth, and in that of Mirah, — it is not to as crystalline a clearness as the author of *Consuelo* and *André*. Take Mirah's long narrative of her adventures, when she unfolds them to Mrs. Meyrick. It is arranged, it is artificial, old-fashioned, quite in the George Sand manner. But George Sand would have done it better. The false tone would have remained, but it would have been more persuasive. It would have been a fib, but the fib would have been neater.

Theodora. I don't think fibbing neatly a merit; and I don't see what is to be gained by such comparisons. George Eliot is pure and George Sand is impure; how can you compare them? As for the Jewish element in *Deronda*, I think it a very fine idea; it's a noble subject. Wilkie Collins and Miss Braddon would not have thought of it, but that does not condemn it. It shows a large conception of what one may do in a novel. I heard you say, the other day, that most novels are so trivial — that they had no general ideas. Here is a general idea, the idea interpreted by Deronda. I have never disliked the Jews, as some people do; I am not like Pulcheria, who sees a Jew in every bush. I wish there were one; I would cultivate shrubbery! I have known too many clever and charming Jews; I have known none that were not clever.

Pulcheria. Clever, but not charming!

Constantius. I quite agree with you as to Deronda's going in for the Jews and turning out a Jew himself being a fine subject, and this quite apart from the fact of whether such a thing as a Jewish revival is at all a possibility. If it is a possibility, so much the better — so much the better for the subject, I mean.

Pulcheria. A la bonne heure!

Constantius. I rather suspect it is not a possibility; that the Jews in general take themselves much less seriously than that. They have other fish to fry! George Eliot takes them as a person outside of Judaism — picturesquely. I don't believe that is the way they take themselves.

Pulcheria. They have the less excuse, then, for keeping themselves so dirty.

Theodora. George Eliot must have known some delightful Jews!

Constantius. Very likely; but I should n't wonder if the most delightful of them had smiled a trifle, here and there, over her book. But that makes nothing, as Herr Klesmer would say. The subject is a noble one. The idea of depicting a nature able to feel and worthy to feel the sort of inspiration that takes possession of Deronda, of depicting it sympathetically, minutely, and intimately — such an idea has great elevation. There is something very fascinating in the mission that Deronda takes upon himself. I don't quite know what it means, I don't understand more than half of Mordecai's rhapsodies, and I don't perceive exactly what practical steps could be taken. Deronda could go about and talk with clever Jews — not an unpleasant life.

Pulcheria. All that seems to me so unreal that when at the end the author finds herself confronted with the necessity of making him start for the East by the train, and announces that Sir Hugo and Lady Mallinger have given his wife "a complete Eastern outfit," I descend to the ground with a ludicrous jump.

Constantius. Unreal if you please; that is no objection to it; it greatly tickles my imagination. I like extremely the idea of Mordecai believing, without ground of belief, that if he only waits, a young man on whom nature and society have centred all their gifts will come to him and receive from his hands the precious vessel of his hopes. It is romantic, but it is not vulgar romance; it is finely romantic. And there is something very fine in the author's own feeling about Deronda. He is a very generous creation. He is, I think, a failure — a brilliant failure; if he had been a success I would call him a splendid creation. The author meant to do things very handsomely for him; she meant, apparently, to make a faultless human being.

Pulcheria. She made a dreadful prig.

Constantius. He *is* rather priggish, and one wonders that so clever a woman as George Eliot should n't see it.

Pulcheria. He has no blood in his body. His attitude at moments absolutely trenches on the farcical.

Theodora. Pulcheria likes the little gentlemen in the French novels who take good care of their attitudes, which are always the same attitude, the attitude of "conquest," and of a conquest that tickles their vanity. Deronda has a contour that cuts straight through the middle of all that. He is made of a stuff that isn't dreamt of in their philosophy.

Pulcheria. Pulcheria likes very much a novel which she read three or four years ago, but which she has not forgotten. It was Ivan Tourguéneff, and it was called *On the Eve.* Theodora has read it, I know, because she admires Tourguéneff, and Constantius has read it, I suppose, because he has read everything.

Constantius. If I had no reason but that for my reading, it would be small. But Tourguéneff is my man.

Pulcheria. You were just now praising George Eliot's general ideas. The tale of which I speak contains in the portrait of the hero very much such a general idea as you find in the portrait of Deronda. Don't you remember the young Bulgarian student, Inssaroff, who gives himself the mission of rescuing his country from its subjection to the Turks? Poor man, if he had foreseen the horrible summer of 1876! His character is the picture of a race-passion, of patriotic hopes and dreams. But what a difference in the vividness of the two figures. Inssaroff is a man; he stands up on his feet; we see him, hear him, and touch him. And it has taken the author but a couple of hundred pages — not eight volumes — to do it!

Theodora. I don't remember Inssaroff at all, but I perfectly remember the heroine, Elena. She is certainly most remarkable, but, remarkable as she is, I should never dream of calling her so wonderful as Gwendolen.

Constantius. Tourguéneff is a magician, which I don't think I should call George Eliot. One is a poet, the other is a philosopher. One cares for the reason of things and the other cares for the aspect of things. George Eliot, in embarking with Deronda, took aboard, as it were, a far heavier cargo than Tourguéneff with his Inssaroff. She proposed, consciously, to strike more notes.

Pulcheria. Oh, consciously, yes!

Constantius. George Eliot wished to show the possible picturesqueness — the romance, as it were — of a high moral tone. Deronda is a moralist, a moralist with a rich complexion.

Theodora. It is a most beautiful nature. I don't know anywhere a more complete, a more deeply analyzed portrait of a great nature. We praise novelists for wandering and creeping so into the small corners of the mind. That is what we praise Balzac for when he gets down upon all fours to crawl through the *Père Goriot* or the *Parents Pauvres.* But I must say I think it a finer thing to unlock with as firm a hand as George Eliot some of the greater chambers of human character. Deronda is in a manner an ideal character, if you will, but he seems to me triumphantly married to reality. There are some admirable things said about him; nothing can be finer than those pages of description of his moral temperament in the fourth book — his elevated way of looking at things, his impartiality, his universal sympathy, and at the same time his fear of their turning into mere irresponsible indifference. I remember some of it verbally: "He was ceasing to care for knowledge — he had no ambition for practice — unless they could be gathered up into one current with his emotions."

Pulcheria. Oh, there is plenty about his emotions. Everything about him is "emotive." That bad word occurs on every fifth page.

Theodora. I don't see that it is a bad word.

Pulcheria. It may be good German, but it is poor English.

Theodora. It is not German at all; it is Latin. So, my dear!

Pulcheria. As I say, then, it is not English.

Theodora. This is the first time I ever heard that George Eliot's style was bad!

Constantius. It is admirable; it has the most delightful and the most intellectually comfortable suggestions. But it is occasionally a little too long-sleeved, as I may say. It is sometimes too loose a fit for the thought, a little baggy.

Theodora. And the advice he gives Gwendolen, the things he says to her, they are the very essence of wisdom, of warm human wisdom, knowing life and feeling it. "Keep your fear as a safeguard, it may make consequences passionately present to you." What can be better than that?

Pulcheria. Nothing, perhaps. But what can be drearier than a novel in which the function of the hero — young, handsome, and brilliant — is to give didactic advice, in a proverbial form, to the young, beautiful and brilliant heroine?

Constantius. That is not putting it quite fairly. The function of Deronda is to have Gwendolen fall in love with him, to say nothing of falling in love himself with Mirah.

Pulcheria. Yes, the less said about that the better. All we know about Mirah is that she has delicate rings of hair, sits with her feet crossed, and talks like a book.

Constantius. Deronda's function of adviser to Gwendolen does not strike me as so ridiculous. He is not nearly so ridiculous as if he were lovesick. It is a very interesting situation — that of a man with whom a beautiful woman in trouble falls in love, and yet whose affections are so preoccupied that the most he can do for her in return is to enter kindly and sympathetically into her position, pity her, and talk to her. George Eliot always gives us something that is strikingly and ironically characteristic of human life; and what savors more of the essential crookedness of human fortune than the sad cross-purposes of these two young people? Poor Gwendolen's falling in love with Deronda is part of her own luckless history, not of his.

Theodora. I do think he takes it to himself rather too little. No man had ever so little vanity.

Pulcheria. It is very inconsistent, therefore, as well as being extremely impertinent and ill-mannered, his buying back and sending to her her necklace at Leubronn.

Constantius. Oh, you must concede that; without it there would have been no story. A man writing of him, however, would certainly have made him more peccable. As George Eliot lets herself go about him she becomes delightfully, almost touchingly feminine. It is like her making Romola go to housekeeping with Tessa, after Tito Melema's death; like her making Dorothea marry Will Ladislaw. If Dorothea had married any one after her misadventure with Casaubon, she would have married a hussar!

Theodora. Perhaps some day Gwendolen will marry Rex.

Pulcheria. Pray, who is Rex?

Theodora. Why, Pulcheria, how can you forget?

Pulcheria. Nay, how can I remember? But I recall such a name in the dim antiquity of the first or second book. Yes, and then he is pushed to the front again at the last, just in time not to miss the falling of the curtain. Gwendolen will certainly not have the audacity to marry any one we know so little about.

Constantius. I have been wanting to say that there seems to me to be two very distinct elements in George Eliot — a spontaneous one and an artificial one. There is what she is by inspiration, and what she is because it is expected of her. These two heads have been very perceptible in her recent writings; they are much less noticeable in her early ones.

Theodora. You mean that she is too scientific? So long as she remains the great literary genius that she is, how can she be too scientific? She is simply permeated with the highest culture of the age.

Pulcheria. She talks too much about the "dynamic quality" of people's eyes. When she uses such a phrase as that in the first sentence in her book she is not a great literary genius, because she shows a want of tact. There can't be a worse limitation.

Constantius (laughing). The "dynamic quality" of Gwendolen's glance has made the tour of the world.

Theodora. It shows a very low level of culture on the world's part to be agitated by a term perfectly familiar to all decently-educated people.

Pulcheria. I don't pretend to be decently educated; pray tell me what it means.

Constantius (promptly). I think Pulcheria has hit it in speaking of a want of tact. In the manner of *Daniel Deronda*, throughout, there is something that one may call a want of tact. The epigraphs in verse are a want of tact; they are sometimes, I think, a trifle more pretentious than really pregnant; the importunity of the moral reflections is a want of tact; the very diffuseness of the book is a want of tact. But it comes back to what I said just now about one's sense of the author writing under a sort of external pressure. I began to notice it in *Felix Holt;* I don't think I had before. She strikes me as a person who certainly has naturally a taste for general considerations, but who has fallen upon an age and a circle which have compelled her to give them an exaggerated attention. She does not strike me as naturally a critic, less still as naturally a skeptic; her spontaneous part is to observe life and to feel it, to feel it with admirable depth. Contemplation, sympathy, and faith, — something like that, I should say, would have been her natural scale. If she had fallen upon an age of enthusiastic assent to old articles of faith, it seems to me possible that she would have had a more perfect, a more consistent and graceful development, than she has actually had. If she had cast herself into such a current, — her genius being equal, — it might have carried her to splendid distances. But she has chosen to go into criticism, and to the critics she addresses her work; I mean the critics of the universe. Instead of feeling life itself, it is "views" upon life that she tries to feel.

Pulcheria. Pray, how can you feel a "view"?

Constantius. I don't think you can; you had better give up trying.

Pulcheria. She is the victim of a first-class education. I am so glad!

Constantius. Thanks to her admirable intellect she philosophizes very sufficiently; but meanwhile she has given a chill to her genius. She has come near spoiling an artist.

Pulcheria. She has quite spoiled one. Or rather I should n't say that, because there was no artist to spoil. I maintain that she is not an artist. An artist could never have put a story together so monstrously ill. She has no sense of form.

Theodora. Pray, what could be more artistic than the way that Deronda's paternity is concealed till almost the end, and the way we are made to suppose Sir Hugo is his father?

Pulcheria. And Mirah his sister. How does that fit together? I was as little made to suppose he was not a Jew as I cared when I found out he was. And his mother popping up through a trapdoor and popping down again, at the last, in that scrambling fashion! His mother is very bad.

Constantius. I think Deronda's mother is one of the unvivified characters; she belongs to the cold half of the book. All the Jewish part is at bottom cold; that is my only objection. I have enjoyed it because my fancy often warms cold things; but beside Gwendolen's history it is like the full half of the lunar disk beside the empty one. It is admirably studied, it is imagined, it is understood; but it is not realized. One feels this strongly in just those scenes between Deronda and his mother: one feels that one has been appealed to on rather an artificial ground of interest. To make Deronda's reversion to his native faith more dramatic and profound, the author has given him a mother who on very arbitrary grounds, apparently, has separated herself from this same faith, and who has been kept waiting in the wing, as it were, for many acts, to come on and make her speech and say so. This moral situation of hers we are invited retrospectively to appreciate. But we hardly care to do so.

Pulcheria. I don't *see* the princess, in spite of her flame-colored robe. Why should an actress and prima-donna care so much about religious matters?

Theodora. It was not only that; it was the Jewish race she hated, Jewish manners and looks. You, my dear, ought to understand that.

Pulcheria. I do, but I am not a Jewish actress of genius; I am not what Rachel was. If I were, I should have other things to think about.

Constantius. Think now a little about poor Gwendolen.

Pulcheria. I don't care to think about her. She was a second-rate English girl who spoke of her mother as "my mamma," and got into a flutter about a lord.

Theodora. I don't see that she is worse than if she were a first-rate American girl, who should speak of her female parent as "mother," and get into exactly the same flutter.

Pulcheria. It would n't be the same flutter, at all; it would n't be any flutter. She would n't be afraid of the lord.

Theodora. I am sure I don't perceive whom Gwendolen was afraid of. She was afraid of her misdeed, — her broken promise, — after she had committed it, and through that fear she was afraid of her husband. Well she might be! I can imagine nothing more vivid than the sense we get of his absolutely *clammy* selfishness.

Pulcheria. She was not afraid of Deronda when, immediately after her marriage, and without any but the most casual acquaintance with him, she begins to hover about him at the Mallingers', to drop little confidences about her conjugal woes. That seems to me very indelicate; ask any woman.

Constantius. The very purpose of the author is to give us an idea of the sort of confidence that Deronda inspired — its irresistible potency!

Pulcheria. A lay father-confessor. Dreadful!

Constantius. And to give us an idea also of the acuteness of Gwendolen's depression, of her haunting sense of impending trouble.

Theodora. It must be remembered that Gwendolen was in love with Deronda from the first, long before she knew it. She did n't know it, poor girl, but that was it.

Pulcheria. That makes the matter worse. It is very disagreeable to have her rustling about a man who is indifferent to her, in that fashion.

Theodora. He was not indifferent to her, since he sent her back her necklace.

Pulcheria. Of all the delicate attention to a charming girl that I ever heard of, that little pecuniary transaction is the most felicitous.

Constantius. You must remember that he had been *en rapport* with her at the gaming table. She had been playing in defiance of his observation, and he, continuing to observe her, had been in a measure responsible for her loss. There was a tacit consciousness of this between them. You may contest the possibility of tacit consciousness going so far, but that is not a serious objection. You may point out two or three weak spots in detail; the fact remains that Gwendolen's whole history is superbly told. And see how the girl is known, inside out, how thoroughly she is felt and understood! It is the most *intelligent* thing in all George Eliot's writing, and that is saying much. It is so deep, so true, so complete, it holds such a wealth of psychological detail, it is more than masterly.

Theodora. I don't know where the perception of character has sailed closer to the wind.

Pulcheria. The portrait may be admirable, but it has one little fault. You don't care a straw for the original. Gwendolen is not an interesting girl, and when the author tries to invest her with a deep tragic interest she does so at the expense of consistency. She has made her at the outset too light, too flimsy; tragedy has no hold on such a girl.

Theodora. You are hard to satisfy. You said this morning that Dorothea was too heavy, and now you find Gwendolen too light. George Eliot wished to give us the perfect counterpart of Dorothea. Having made one portrait she was worthy to make the other.

Pulcheria. She has committed the fatal error of making Gwendolen vulgarly, pettily, dryly selfish. She was *personally* selfish.

Theodora. I know nothing more personal than selfishness.

Pulcheria. I am selfish, but I don't go about with my chin out like that; at least I hope I don't. She was an odious young woman, and one can't care what becomes of her. When her marriage turned out ill she would have become still more hard and positive; to make her soft and appealing is very bad logic. The second Gwendolen does n't belong to the first.

Constantius. She is perhaps at the first a little childish for the weight of interest she has to carry, a little too much after the pattern of the unconscientious young ladies of Miss Yonge and Miss Sewell.

Theodora. Since when is it forbidden to make one's heroine young? Gwendolen is a perfect picture of youthfulness — its eagerness, its presumption, its preoccupation with itself, its vanity and silliness, its sense of its own absoluteness. But she is extremely intelligent and clever, and therefore tragedy *can* have a hold upon her. Her conscience does n't make the tragedy; that is an old story, and, I think, a secondary form of suffering. It is the tragedy that makes her conscience, which then reacts upon it; and I can think of nothing more powerful than the way in which the growth of her conscience is traced, nothing more touching than the picture of its helpless maturity.

Constantius. That is perfectly true. Gwendolen's history is admirably typical — as most things are with George Eliot; it is the very stuff that human life is made of. What is it made of but the discovery by each of us that we are at the best but a rather ridiculous fifth wheel to the coach, after we have sat cracking our whip and believing that we are at least the coachman in person? We think we are the main hoop to the barrel, and we turn out to be but a very incidental splinter in one of the staves. The universe, forcing itself with a slow, inexorable pressure into a narrow, complacent, and yet after all extremely sensitive mind, and making it ache with the pain of the process — that is Gwendolen's story. And it becomes completely characteristic in that her supreme perception of the fact that the world is whirling past her is in the disappointment not of a base, but of an exalted passion. The very chance to embrace what the author is so fond of calling a "larger life" seems refused to her. She is punished for being narrow and she is not allowed a chance to expand. Her finding Deronda preëngaged to go to the East and stir up the race-feeling of the Jews strikes one as a wonderfully happy invention. The irony of the situation, for poor Gwendolen, is almost grotesque, and it makes one wonder whether the whole heavy structure of the Jewish question in the story was not built up by the author for the express purpose of giving its proper force to this particular stroke.

Theodora. George Eliot's intentions are extremely complex. The mass is for each detail and each detail is for the mass.

Pulcheria. She is very fond of deaths by drowning. Maggie Tulliver and her brother are drowned, Tito Melema is drowned, Mr. Grandcourt is drowned. It is extremely unlikely that Grandcourt should not have known how to swim.

Constantius. He did, of course, but he had a cramp. It served him right. I can't imagine a more consummate representation of the most detestable kind of Englishman — the Englishman who thinks it low to articulate. And in Grandcourt the type and the individual are so happily met: the type with its sense of the proprieties, and the individual with his absence of all sense. He is the apotheosis of dryness, a human expression of the simple idea of the perpendicular.

Theodora. Mr. Casaubon in *Middlemarch* was very dry, too; and yet what a genius it is that can give us two disagreeable husbands who are so utterly different.

Pulcheria. You must count the two disagreeable wives, too — Rosamond Vincy and Gwendolen. They are very much alike. I know the author did n't mean it; it proves how common a type the worldly, *pincée*, illiberal young Englishwoman is. They are both disagreeable; you can't get over that.

Constantius. There is something in that, perhaps. I think, at any rate, that the secondary people here are less delightful than in *Middlemarch;* there is nothing so good as Mary Garth and her father, or the little old lady who steals sugar, or the parson who is in love with Mary, or the country relatives of old Mr. Featherstone. Rex Gascoigne is not so good as Fred Vincy.

Theodora. Mr. Gascoigne is admirable, and Mrs. Davilow is charming.

Pulcheria. And you must not forget that you think Herr Klesmer "Shakespearian." Would n't "Wagnerian" be high enough praise?

Constantius. Yes, one must make an exception with regard to the Klesmers and the Meyricks. They are delightful, and as for Klesmer himself, and Hans Meyrick, Theodora may maintain her epithet. Shakespearian characters are characters that are born out of the *overflow* of observation, characters that make the drama seem multitudinous, like life. Klesmer comes in with a sort of Shakespearian "value," as a painter would say, and so, in a different tone, does Hans Meyrick. They spring from a much-peopled mind.

Theodora. I think Gwendolen's confrontation with Klesmer one of the finest things in the book.

Constantius. It is like everything in George Eliot, it will bear thinking of.

Pulcheria. All that is very fine, but you cannot persuade me that *Deronda* is not a very awkward and ill-made story. It has nothing that one can call a subject. A silly young girl and a heavy, overwise young man who *don't* fall in love with her! That is the *donnée* of eight monthly volumes. I call it very flat. Is that what the exquisite art of Thackeray and Miss Austen and Hawthorne has come to? I would as soon read a German novel outright.

Theodora. There is something higher than form — there is spirit.

Constantius. I am afraid Pulcheria is sadly aesthetic. She had better confine herself to Mérimée.

Pulcheria. I shall certainly to-day read over the *Double Méprise*.

Theodora. Oh, my dear, don't!

Constantius. Yes, I think there is little art in *Deronda*, but I think there is a vast amount of life. In life without art you can find your account; but art without life is a poor affair. The book is full of the world.

Theodora. It is full of beauty and sagacity, and there is quite art enough for me.

Pulcheria (to the little dog). We are silenced, darling, but we are not convinced, are we? (The dog begins to bark.) No, we are not even silenced. It's a young woman with two band-boxes.

Theodora. Oh, it must be our muslins.

Constantius (rising to go). I see what you mean!

Edward Dowden

Middlemarch and *Daniel Deronda*

Great artists belong ordinarily to one of two chief classes — the class of those whose virtue resides in breadth of common human sympathy, or of those who, excelling rather by height than breadth, attain to rare altitudes of human thought or human passion. For the one, the large table-land, with its wealth of various life, its substantial possessions, its corn, its shadow-casting trees, and lowing kine; for the other, the mountain-summit, its thrill, its prospect, its keen air, and its inspiration. To the one we look for record, and interpretation of the average experience of men; to the other, for discoveries and deliverances of the soul, for the quickening into higher life of our finest spiritual susceptibilities, and sometimes for the rescue of our best self from the incredulity, inertia, and encumbrances which gather about it in the ways of use and wont. And Art is justified of all her children. From the first half of our century we could ill lose Scott, who represents in so distinguished a manner the class of artists who excel by breadth; we could ill lose Wordsworth or Shelley, who in different ways belongs each as distinctively to the other class. . . .

Among artists who with Shakspere unite breadth of sympathy with power of interpreting the rarer and more intense experiences of the souls of men, George Eliot must be placed. . . . In *Daniel Deronda*, for the first time, the poetical side of George Eliot's genius

Reprinted from the *Contemporary Review*, 29 (February 1877), 348–369.

obtains adequate expression, through the medium which is proper
to her — that of prose — and in complete association with the non-
poetical elements of her nature. It is the ideal creation, happier in
conception and tone, which *The Spanish Gypsy* failed to be.

The demands which such a work make upon the reader are so
large and so peculiar, that it is not a matter of surprise that at first
it should select an audience, and speak fully to only a comparatively
few. George Eliot has prefixed to one of the chapters of her novel
the beautiful lines of Whitman: —

> Surely whoever speaks to me in the right voice, him or her
> shall I follow,
> As the water follows the moon, silently, with fluid steps
> anywhere around the globe.

There are those who hear the right voice and respond to it; but the
majority of persons addressed by a new and original work of art
prefer their own impatience to its summons or challenge. . . .

To discover the central motive of *Daniel Deronda* it should be
studied in connection with its immediate predecessor, *Middlemarch*.
In externals the contrast is striking. In *Middlemarch* the prosaic or
realistic element occupies a much larger place; a great proportion
of the book is only not a satire because with the word satire we are
accustomed to associate the idea of exaggeration and malicious
purpose. The chief figures — Lydgate, Dorothea — are enveloped by
a swarm of subordinate characters, each admirably real, and to whom
we are compelled to give away a share of our interest, a share of our
admiration or our detestation. In *Daniel Deronda* the poetical or
ideal element as decidedly preponderates. We should feel the needle-
pricks of Mrs. Cadwallader's epigrams an irritating impertinence.
Our emotions are strung too tensely to permit us to yield an amused
tolerance to the fine dispersion of the idea in Mr. Brooke's discourse.
In place of a background of ugliness, — the Middlemarch streets, the
hospital, the billiard-room, the death-chamber of Peter Featherstone,
his funeral procession attended by Christian carnivora, — we have
backgrounds of beauty, the grassy court of the abbey enclosed by
a Gothic cloister, its July sunshine, and blown roses; Cardell Chase,
the changing scenery of the forest from roofed grove to open glade;
evening on the Thames at Richmond with the lengthening shadows
and the mellowing light, its darkening masses of tree and building
between the double glow of the sky and the river; the Turneresque
splendour of sunset in a great city, while the lit, expectant face is
gazing from Blackfriars Bridge, westward, where the grey day is
dying gloriously; the Mediterranean, its shores "gemlike with purple

shadows, a sea where one may float between blue and blue in an open-eyed dream that the world has done with sorrow."

These differences in externals correspond with the essential inward difference between the two works, — the one, *Middlemarch*, is critical, while its successor aims at being in a certain sense constructive. Readers of *Middlemarch* will remember that the story is preceded by a prelude which sets forth its principal theme. Dorothea Brooke is a Saint Theresa, with a passionate ideal nature which demands an epic life; but she is born out of due season into this period of faiths which are disintegrating and of social forces which are still unorganized. . . . Dorothea finds no epic life, but a life of mistakes. From the social world which hemmed her round, seeming a walled-in maze of small paths that led nowhither, she dreams for a little while that she is about to make escape into a world of large ideas impelling to far-resonant action. She is to sit at the feet of a master and prophet, who by a binding doctrine shall compel her own small life and faith into strict connection with the vast and amazing past, and occupy that life with action at once rational and ardent. Her prophet, with his Xisuthrus and Fee-fo-fum, is a pedant bringing to the great spectacle of life nothing but a small, hungry, shivering self, whose consciousness is never rapturously transformed into the vividness of a thought, the ardour of a passion, the energy of an action, who is always scholarly and uninspired, ambitious and timid, scrupulous and dim-sighted. " 'She says he has a great soul. A great bladder for dried peas to rattle in,' said Mrs. Cadwallader." No consequent doctrine of human life is discoverable by Dorothea, no satisfying action is possible for her. . . . From her failure which is pain Dorothea only passes to her failure which is happiness. From her vague ideal she lapses into the common yearning of womanhood, the need to bless one being with all good, and to receive the love of one heart. . . . Saint Theresa becomes the wife of Will Ladislaw.

But the central theme receives a second illustration in *Middlemarch*, much as the pervading sentiment of *King Lear* is developed through the stories alike of Lear and of Gloucester. Lydgate, who has received a true vocation, whose intellectual passion predestines him to far-resonant action in the world of scientific research, Lydgate, against whom the temptations of the flesh and the devil would have been idle, is subdued by that third enemy of man, the world, incarnated in the form of a creature with feminine voice, swan-like neck, perfectly turned shoulders, exquisite curves of lip and eyelid, and, hidden behind these, the hardness of a little sordid soul. George Eliot, with a hand tender and yet unfaltering, has traced the dull decay of ardour in a spirit framed for the pursuit of great ends, the lapse of slackening resolution, the creeping paralysis which seized upon an enthusiasm out of adjustment to one constant portion of the victim's life. . . . The London physician who has gained an excellent practice, and written a Treatise on Gout, is a murdered man, and Rosamond is indeed "his basil plant," which flourishes wonderfully on the murdered man's brains.

Thus *Middlemarch* closes with neither heroic joy nor noble tragic pain. The heart-beats and sobs after an unattained goodness of a Saint Theresa, foundress of nothing, "tremble off and are dispersed among hindrances instead of centering in some long-recognizable deed." The intellectual passion which might have produced a Bichat has for nett resultant a heavy insurance, and a treatise upon that disease which owns a good deal of wealth on its side. Heart and brain prove alike failures. If anything promises success in the history unfolded by the chronicler of *Middlemarch*, it is the hand of the good workman, Caleb Garth. Here is something which, even in an epoch of incoherent ideas and chaotic social forces, can yet accomplish something. Faust, despairing of all philosophies, may yet drain a marsh or rescue some acres from the sea. The religion of conscientious work is somewhat higher at least than the religion of Bulstrode, which serves but to spin a spider-web of falsehood over the foul recesses of conscience. Caleb "had never regarded himself as other than an orthodox Christian, and would argue on prevenient grace if the subject were proposed to him"; but his virtual divinities were "good practical schemes, accurate work, and the faithful completion of all undertakings; his prince of darkness was a slack workman." . . .

But *Middlemarch* is not the final word of our great imaginative teacher. Whether consciously so designed or not, *Daniel Deronda* comes to us as a counterpoise or a correlative of the work which immediately preceded it. There we saw how two natures framed for large disinterested services to humanity can be narrowed — the one into the round of the duteous sweet observances of domestic life — the other into the servitude,

> Eyeless in Gaza at the mill with slaves,

which the world imposes upon those who accept its base terms and degrading compensations. Here we are shown how two natures can be ennobled and enlarged; the one rescued through anguish and remorse, and by the grace, human if also divine, which the soul of man has power to bestow upon the soul of man, from self-centered insolence of youth, the crude egoism of a spoiled child; . . . the other, a nature of finer mould and temper than that of Lydgate, with none of the spots of commonness in it which produced a disintegrating effect on Lydgate's action, but exposed through its very plenteousness and flexibility of sympathy to peculiar dangers — the danger of neutrality in the struggle between common things and high which fills the world, the danger of wandering energy and wasted ardours; and from these dangers Deronda is delivered, he is incorporated into a great ideal life, made one with his nation and race, and there is confided to him the heritage of duty bound with love which was his forefathers', and of which it had been sought to deprive him.

Such are the spiritual histories of Gwendolen Harleth and of Daniel Deronda, told in the briefest summary. When we speak of *Middlemarch* as more realistic, and the later novel as more ideal, it is not meant that the one is true to the facts of life and the other untrue; it is rather meant that in the one the facts are taken more in the gross, and in the other there is a passionate selection of those facts that are representative of the highest (and also of the lowest) things. . . . That some clever critics should find the hero of George Eliot's last novel detestable is easily understood; that some should find him incredible proves no more than that clever critics in walking from their lodgings to their club, and from their club to their lodgings, have not exhausted the geography of the habitable globe. If "knowledge of the world" consists chiefly in a power of estimating the average force of men's vulgar or selfish appetites, instincts, and interests, it must be admitted that in such knowledge the author of *Middlemarch* and of *Felix Holt* is not deficient; but there is another knowledge of the world which she possesses, a knowledge which does not exclude from recognition the martyr, the hero, and the saint.

Daniel Deronda, however, as we meet him in the novel, has not attained to be any of these: with all the endowments needed for an eminent benefactor of men, we yet perceive how he might have failed of his true direction and function. To some readers he has seemed no thin shadow, no pallid projection from the author's imagination, but a veritable creature of flesh and blood, and his trials and dangers have seemed most real and worthy of the closest scrutiny. . . . The speciality of Deronda among the *dramatis personae* of George Eliot's art is that a pure sympathetic nature is with him innate; his freedom from egoism is a possession which has come to him without a struggle. Maggie Tulliver is tempted with a fierce temptation to sacrifice the happiness of another to her own. It is through an agony that Fedalma becomes able to slay the life within her of personal joy. Even Dorothea has a great discovery of the heart to make; she had early emerged from the moral stupidity of taking the world "as an udder to feed her supreme self. . . ."

Deronda even in childhood is sensible of the existence of independent centres of self outside himself, and can transfer his own consciousness into theirs. He is thus predestined to be a saviour and redeemer. And however incredulous persons of culture, with extensive knowledge of the world, may be as to the existence of this type among men, the heart of humanity in all ages, alike in the mystic East and the scientific West, has clung to belief in its existence as to the most precious of man's spiritual possessions. From the very fact that such persons are free from an absorbing egoism it becomes difficult to determine the precise outline of their personality. . . . A Grandcourt whose nature is one main trunk of barren egoism from which all the branches of fresh desire have withered off, is recognized forthwith to be human. But Deronda, sensitive at every point with life which flows into him and throughout him, and streams forth from him in beneficent energy, — Deronda is a pallid shadow rather than a man! For, in truth, unless the absence of egoistic greed render him an illusion, we must allow to Deronda the possession of a rich and powerful vitality. . . .

And at this point it may be worth while to notice two counter-objections which are alleged against George Eliot's work. To some readers the whole story of Mordecai and of his relation to Deronda appears fantastic and unreal — a piece of workmanship all made out of the carver's brain, or something less solid and substantial than this — a mere luminous vapour, or a phantom of the mind, which science cannot justify or even recognize. On the other hand, able critics lament over the growth, in George Eliot's writings, of scientific habits of thought and expression, and in a style of warning "eäsy and freeä," which seems to combine the authorities of "godamoighty" and "parson," bid this great thinker and artist expect the extinction of her genius. She has actually employed in a work of fiction such words as "dynamic" and "natural selection," at which the critic picks up his delicate ears and shies. If the thorough-bred critic could only be led close up to "dynamic," he would find that "dynamic" will not bite. A protest of common sense is really called for against the affectation which professes to find obscurity in words because they are trisyllabic or because they carry with them scientific associations. Language, the instrument of literary art, is an instrument of ever-extending range, and the truest pedantry, in an age when the air is saturated with scientific thought, would be to reject those accessions to language which are the special gain of the time. Insensibility to the contemporary movement in science is itself essentially unliterary, for literature with its far-reaching sensibilities should be touched, thrilled, and quickened by every vital influence of the period; and indeed it is not alone the intellect which recognizes the accuracy

and effectiveness of such scientific illustration as George Eliot
occasionally employs; the cultured imagination is affected by it, as
the imagination of Spenser's time was affected by his use of the
neoclassical mythology of the Renaissance.

But there is graver reason which justifies an artist of the present
day in drawing near to science, and receiving all it has to bestow of
ascertained truth and enlightened impulse. The normal action of the
reason upon the imagination has been happily described by Comte, —
"Elle la stimule en la réglant." This expresses with accuracy the
relation of these faculties in the nature of our English novelist, —
reason is to her imagination both law and impulse. And therefore
her art is not a mere luxury for the senses, nor a mere aesthetic
delicacy or dainty. It has chosen for its part to be founded in truth,
to nourish the affections, to reinforce and purify the will. In her
art the artist lives,

> Breathing as beauteous order that controls
> With growing sway the growing life of man.

Art dissociated from the reason and the conscience becomes before
long a finely distilled poison; while considered merely as art it has
thus declined — in however exquisite little phials it may be presented
— from its chief functions. It no longer sways or controls our being;
it painfully seeks to titillate a special sense. An indifference arises as
to what is called the substance or "content" of works of art, and
the form is spoken of as if it had a separate and independent existence.
There follows, as Comte has again observed, "the inevitable triumph
of mediocrities"; executive or technical skill, of the kind which com-
mands admiration in a period devoid of noble motive and large ideas,
being attainable by persons of mere talent. The artificial refinements
of a coterie are held to constitute the beautiful in art, and these can
be endlessly repeated. . . .

The largeness and veracity of George Eliot's own art proceed
from the same qualities which make truth-seeking a passion of her
nature; and a truth-seeker at the present day will do ill to turn a
deaf ear to the teachings of science. As little as Dante need George
Eliot fear to enter into possession of the fullest body of fact which
the age can deliver to her; nay, it is essential to the highest characteristics of her art that she should not isolate herself from the chief
intellectual movement of her time. If in the objection which has
been brought against her recent style there be any portion of truth,
it will be found in the circumstance that an occasional sentence
becomes laboured, and perhaps overloaded in her effort to charge
it fully and accurately with its freight of meaning. The manner of

few great artists — if any — becomes simpler as they advance in their career, that is, as their ideas multiply, as their emotions receive more numerous affluents from the other parts of their being, and as the vital play of their faculties with one another becomes swifter and more intricate. The later sonatas of Beethoven still perplex facile and superficial musicians. The later landscapes of Turner bewilder and amaze the profane. The difference between the languid and limpid fluency of the style of *Two Gentlemen of Verona* and the style of Shakspere's later plays, so compressed, so complex, so live with breeding imagery, is great. Something is lost but more has been gained. When the sustained *largo* of the sentences of *Daniel Deronda* is felt after the crude epigrammatic smartness of much of the writing in *Scenes of Clerical Life* we perceive as great a difference and as decided a preponderance of gain over loss.

But what renders singular the warning addressed to George Eliot that her work is undergoing a "scientific deprivation" is that the whole of her last book is a homage to the emotions rather than to the intellect of man. Her feeling finds expression not only in occasional gnomic utterances in which sentiments are declared to be the best part of the world's wealth, and love is spoken of as deeper than reason, and the intellect is pronounced incapable of ascertaining the validity of claims which rest upon loving instincts of the heart, or else are baseless. The entire work possesses an impassioned aspect, an air of spiritual prescience, far more than the exactitude of science. The main forces which operate in it are sympathies, aspirations, ardours; and ideas chiefly as associated with these. From his meditative numbness Deronda is roused, his diffused mass of feeling is rendered definite, and is impelled in a given direction, his days become an ordered sequence bound together by love and duty, his life is made one with the life of humanity. . . .

Is the objection warranted that the part assigned to Mordecai and his influence upon Deronda are a fantastic unreality which offends against our saner judgement? Is such a person as Mordecai incredible? And again, is the idea which the consumptive Jew breathes into Deronda only the hectic fever-dream of a visionary, or has it substance and validity for the imagination of the reader? And why all this concern about Jews — the stiff-necked race? . . .

But to criticize *Daniel Deronda* from the literal, prosaic point of view, would be as much a critical stupidity as to undertake the defence of Shakspere's *King Lear* from the charge of historical improbability. It is enough if the idealization is worked out upon lines which have a starting point and a direction that can be justified to the intellect, and if the imagination consents to yield credence to ideal truth. . . . We owe to the author of *Daniel Deronda* the gratitude due to one who enriches human life for her discovery in Ram's bookshop, and among the kindly-hearted mercenary Cohens, of a prophet of the Exile. . . .

But the central conception of *Daniel Deronda* is religious, and not political: religious, not in the sense which implies faith in a personal providence superintending the lives of men, or faith in the intervention of the miraculous and the supernatural, or faith in a life for each man and woman beyond the grave in other worlds than ours. . . . The religious conception of *Daniel Deronda*, as of the other writings of George Eliot, is that of a life of mankind over, above, and around the life of the individual man or woman, and to which the individual owes his loyalty and devotion, the passion of his heart, and the utmost labour of his hand. . . . Of this religion — a religion by which a man's life may become a noble self-surrender whether it contain but a portion of truth or contain the whole — Mordecai is a prophet, and Deronda is a chosen and anointed priest. The Judaic element comes second in the book — the human element first.

To any one who had attended the leading motives, the centres around which the emotions organize themselves, in the preceding writings of George Eliot, the ideas of Mordecai, and their constraining power with Deronda, cannot have appeared strange and novel. The higher, the religious life is that which transcends self, and which is lived in submission to the duties imposed upon us by the past, and the chains of those who surround us in the present, and of those who shall succeed us in time to come. To be the centre of a living multitude, the heart of their hearts, the brain from which thoughts, as waves, pass through them — this is the best and purest joy which a human creature can know. Of this kind is the glory and rapture of the artist. . . . But in its very rapture there is a danger of egoism in this joy; and of such egoism of the artist we have a conspicuous example in the rejection of the bonds of love, the claims of a father and of a child, by Deronda's mother. As Don Silva, in *The Spanish Gypsy*, for the love of one maiden would fain renounce the inheritance of honour and of duty which his past had imposed upon him, so the daughter of the Jew, Charisi, would escape from the will of her father, the traditions of her race, the clinging arms of her babe, and would live a life of freedom in her art alone. That which she resisted proves — as it proved for Don Silva — too strong for her, and in her hour of physical weakness the impersonal forces she had fled from rise within her and rise around her, the dread Erinyes of her crime.

But there is another way than the artist's of becoming the vital centre of a multitude. To be the incarnation of their highest thought, and at the same time to be the incarnation of their purest will — what nobler lot is possible to man? The epic life, the national leadership, to which — not, perhaps, without some touch of gross personal ambition — Zarca aspired, and which Fedalma accepted as the leader of a forlorn hope, this is decreed to Deronda, free from all taint of personal ambition, and free from the sorrow of anticipated failure. . . . A revolutionary writer of genius in this century of revolution, who designed for his imaginary hero an epic life, would probably represent him as the banner-bearer of some new ideas — liberty, progress, the principles of 1789 — and the youthful hero would exhale his enthusiasms upon a barricade. It is characteristic of our English novelist, who, through her imagination and affections, is profoundly conservative, that with her the epic life should be found in no breaking away from the past, no revolt against tradition. Hope and faith are with her the children of memory; the future is the offspring and heir of the past. Daniel Deronda then is a Jew, because the Jewish race is one rich with memories, possessed of far-reaching traditions, a fit object for satisfying that strong historic sympathy which is so deep a part of Deronda's nature. . . . To Deronda, the ideal of manhood in its fulness of power and beauty, the ideally perfect lot is assigned. . . .

Over against Gwendolen, the petted child, with her double nature, her layers of selfishness stifling the stray seeds of possible good, her iridescent moods, her contending passion and fear of contrite pain, her high spirit and her sudden fits of inward dread, her lack of all religious emotion, and of that piety which consists in tender, clinging affection to home and childhood, and the objects consecrated by our dead past; over against Gwendolen is set Mirah, beautiful in the singleness and purity of her soul. The clever critics have found Mirah as uninteresting as they found Deronda unreal. . . . A perfect, harmonious, still, yet richly tinted life, like the life of flowers, is that of Mirah; whatever dead substance comes in her way is either rejected or forced to take some beautiful living form; . . . her whole being possesses a flawless unity, an exquisite symmetry, every atom being bright with coherent energy. . . . Then, too, sorrow had been a familiar guest with her, and in Deronda's love there lay the joy of a blessed protectiveness. It is something less than this that Mirah was an artist witnessed to by the appalling Klesmer, who had reduced to despair Gwendolen's amateurishness, and that in all practical matters she manifests an unerring good sense. There is perpetual music in the life of him who can feel the beating of a heart so fervid and so gentle, who can bow tenderly over so dear a head.

Contrasted with Deronda, who is the sympathetic nature in its purest and highest energy, stands Grandcourt, who is the absolute of egoism. His life is the dull, low life of some monstrous reptile, coloured like the slime or dust in which he lies, seemingly torpid and indifferent to all outside himself, yet at watch with blinking eyes for every slightest motion of the one thing which interests him, — his prey; and owning a deadly power of spring and cruel constriction such as the boa can display. But there is nothing of the romantic villain in his appearance; he is only an English gentleman, with faultless manners when he did not intend them to be insolent, long narrow grey eyes, an extensive baldness surrounded by a fringe of reddish blond hair, a slight perpendicular whisker, a toneless aristocratic drawl, certain ugly secrets in the past, a strong dislike to brutes who use the wrong soap or who have ill-formed nails, a wide susceptibility to boredom, and a resolve to tolerate no damned nonsense in his wife. Let the waves wash him down to keep company with things of the monstrous world, and become a third with the ground-shark and the poulpe.

Of Gwendolen and her spiritual history, although it occupies the principal space in George Eliot's novel, little has here been said, because this portion of the story seems to have been acquiesced in with something like common consent by the majority of readers. . . . The new soul born within her through remorse and that penitential sorrow from which she had not long since so deliberately guarded herself, is sustained in its clinging infantile weakness by hands of another which are tender and strong. A living man, who is to her the best, the most real, the most worshipful of all things known, becomes her external conscience, while her inner conscience is still able to do no more than open wondering eyes, half-dazzled by the light, after its long, dark, and withering imprisonment in the airless cell of egoism. Gwendolen, with her girlish inexperience, and her slight girlish love of sway, would not be sacrificed to creatures worth less than herself, but would play the game of life with exceptional cleverness, and so conquer circumstance. It is well that the gambling at life, where her gain must be another's loss, goes against her. She had thought to conquer circumstance, and good and evil join to defeat her; Deronda, "like an awful browed angel," fixes upon her his gaze of condemnation, and Grandcourt benumbs her in the icy constringency of will.

But Gwendolen has a fulness of nature which removes her far from the Rosamond Vincy type of womanhood; she is not "one of the narrow-brained women who through life regard all their selfish demands as rights, and every claim upon themselves as an injury." It is possible for her before she loves goodness for its own sake to love goodness in a human form. This is well, though still she

remains to herself the centre of the world, and Deronda exists not
for his own sake, not for others, not for the world, but only for
her. . . .

   Daniel Deronda closes in the presence of death; *Middlemarch*
with promises of happy living; yet *Middlemarch* leaves the heart
as though in the greyness of a sweet August twilight, when we
accept the subdued colours, and the dearness of the tranquil hour.
Death, as we witness it in the concluding chapter of *Daniel Deronda*,
is solemn and beautiful as a sunset, but we see the stars come forth,
and are aware that the world is revolving into a nobler dawn.

Algernon Charles Swinburne

[On George Eliot]

   . . . Yet thus far, perhaps, we may reasonably attempt some
indication of the difference which divides pure genius from mere
intellect as by a great gulf fixed; the quality of the latter, we may
say, is constructive, the property of the former is creative. Adam
Bede, for instance, or even Tito Melema, is an example of construction — and the latter is one of the finest in literature; Edward
Rochester and Paul Emanuel are creations. And the inevitable test
or touchstone of this indefinable difference is the immediate and
enduring impression set at once and engraved for ever on the simplest
or the subtlest mind of the most careless or the most careful student.
In every work of pure genius we feel while it is yet before us — and
if we cease for a little to feel when out of sight of it for awhile, we
surely feel afresh each time our sight of it is renewed — the sense
of something inevitable, some quality incorporate and innate, which
determines that it shall be thus and not otherwise. . . . Perhaps we
may reasonably divide all imaginative work into three classes; the
lowest, which leaves us in a complacent mood of acquiescence with
the graceful or natural inventions and fancies of an honest and ingenious workman, and in no mind to question or dispute the
accuracy of his transcript from life or the fidelity of his design to

Reprinted from Algernon Charles Swinburne, *A Note on Charlotte Brontë*, London, Chatto & Windus, 1877, pp. 6–53.

the modesty and the likelihood of nature; the second, of high enough
quality to engage our judgment in its service, and make direct demand
on our grave attention for deliberate assent or dissent; the third,
which in the exercise of its highest faculties at their best neither
solicits nor seduces nor provokes us to acquiescence or demur, but
compels us without question to positive acceptance and belief. Of
the first class it would be superfluous to cite instances from among
writers of our own day, not undeserving of serious respect and of
genuine gratitude for much honest work done and honest pleasure
conferred on us. Of the second order our literature has no more
apt and brilliant examples than George Eliot and George Meredith.
Of the third, if in such a matter as this I may trust my own instinct —
that last resource and ultimate reason of all critics in every case and
on every question — there is no clearer and more positive instance
in the whole world of letters than that supplied by the genius of
Charlotte Brontë.

I do not mean that such an instance is to be found in the treatment
of each figure in each of her great three books. If this could accurately be said, it could not reasonably be denied that she might
justly claim and must naturally assume that seat by the side of
Shakespeare which certain critics of the hour are prompt alike
to assign alternately to the author of *Adam Bede* and to the author
of *Queen Mary*. . . . But without putting in a claim for the author
of *Jane Eyre* as qualified to ascend the height on which a minority
of not overwise admirers would fain enthrone a demigoddess of
more dubious divinity than hers, I must take leave to reiterate my
conviction that no living English or female writer can rationally be
held her equal in what I cannot but regard as the highest and the
rarest quality which supplies the hardest and the surest proof of a
great and absolute genius for the painting and handling of human
characters in mutual relations and reaction. . . .

If I turn again for contrast or comparison with their works to
the work of George Eliot, it will be attributed by no one above the
spiritual rank and type of Pope's representative dunces to irreverence
or ingratitude for the large and liberal beneficence of her genius at
its best. But she alone among our living writers is generally admitted
or assumed as the rightful occupant, or at least as the legitimate
claimant, of that foremost place in the front rank of artists in this
kind which none can hold or claim without challenging such comparison or such contrast. And in some points it is undeniable that
she may claim precedence, not of these alone, but of all other
illustrious women. Such wealth and depth of thoughtful and fruitful
humour, of vital and various intelligence, no woman has ever shown
— no woman perhaps has ever shown a tithe of it. In knowledge,

in culture, perhaps in capacity for knowledge and for culture, Charlotte Brontë was no more comparable to George Eliot than George Eliot is comparable to Charlotte Brontë in purity of passion, in depth and ardour of feeling, in spiritual force and fervour of forthright inspiration. It would be rather a rough and sweeping than a loose or inaccurate division which should define the one as a type of genius distinguished from intellect, the other of intellect as opposed to genius. But it would, as I venture to think, be little or nothing more or less than accurate to recognise in George Eliot a type of intelligence vivified and coloured by a vein of genius, in Charlotte Brontë a type of genius directed and moulded by the touch of intelligence. No better test of this distinction could be desired than a comparison of their respective shortcomings or failures. These will serve, by their difference in kind and import, in quality and in weight, to show the depth and width of the great gulf between pure genius and pure intellect, even better than a comparison of their highest merits and achievements. . . .

That Charlotte Brontë, a woman of the first order of genius, could go very wrong indeed, there are whole scenes and entire characters in her work which afford more than ample proof. But George Eliot, a woman of the first order of intellect, has once and again shown how much further and more steadily and more hopelessly and more irretrievably and more intolerably wrong it is possible for mere intellect to go than it ever can be possible for mere genius. Having no taste for the dissection of dolls, I shall leave Daniel Deronda in his natural place above the ragshop door; and having no ear for the melodies of a Jew's harp, I shall leave the Spanish Gipsy to perform on that instrument to such audience as she may collect. It would be unjust and impertinent to dwell much on Charlotte Brontë's brief and modest attempts in verse; but it would be unmanly and unkindly to touch at all on George Eliot's; except indeed to remark in passing that they are about equally commendable for the one and for the other of those negative good qualities which I have commended in Miss Brontë's. And from this point of difference, if from no other point here discernible, those who will or who can learn anything may learn a lesson in criticism which may perhaps be worth laying to heart: that genius, though it can put forth no better claim than intellect may assert for itself to share the papal gift of infallibility, is naturally the swifter of the two to perceive and to retrieve its errors. . . .

And now we must regretfully and respectfully consider of what quality and what kind may be the faults which deform the best and ripest work of Charlotte Brontë's chosen rival. Few or none, I should suppose, of her most passionate and intelligent admirers would

refuse to accept *The Mill on the Floss* as on the whole at once the
highest and the purest and the fullest example of her magnificent and
matchless powers — for matchless altogether, as I have already insisted,
they undoubtedly are in their own wide and fruitful field of work.
The first two-thirds of the book suffice to compose perhaps the
very noblest of tragic as well as of humorous prose idyls in the
language; comprising, as they likewise do, one of the sweetest as
well as saddest examples of dramatic analysis — a study in that kind
as soft and true as Rousseau's as keen and true as Browning's, as full
as either's of the fine and bitter sweetness of a pungent and fiery
fidelity. But who can forget the horror of inward collapse, the
sickness of spiritual reaction, the reluctant incredulous rage of disenchantment and disgust, with which he first came upon the thrice
unhappy third part? The two first volumes have all the intensity
and all the perfection of George Sand's best work tempered by all
the simple purity and interfused with all the stainless pathos of Mrs.
Gaskell's; they carry such affluent weight of thought and shine
with such warm radiance of humour as invigorates and illuminates
the work of no other famous woman; they have the fiery clarity of
crystal or of lightning; they go near to prove a higher claim and
attest a clearer right on the part of their author than that of George
Sand herself to the crowning crown of praise conferred on her by
the hand of a woman even greater and more glorious than either
in her sovereign gift of lyric genius, to the salutation given as by an
angel indeed from heaven, of "large-brained woman and large-hearted
man." And the fuller and deeper tone of colour combined with greater
sharpness and precision of outline may be allowed to excuse the
apparent amount of obligation — though we may hardly see how
this can be admitted to explain the remarkable reticence which
reserves all acknowledgment and dissembles all consciousness of
that sufficiently palpable and weighty and direct obligation — to
Mrs. Gaskell's beautiful story of *The Moorland Cottage;* in which
not the identity of name alone, nor only their common singleness of
heart and simplicity of spirit, must naturally recall the gentler
memory of the less high-thoughted and high-reaching heroine to the
warmest and the worthiest admirers of the later-born loftier-minded
Maggie; though the hardness and brutality of the baser brother
through whom she suffers be the outcome in manhood as in childhood
of mere greedy instinct and vulgar egotism, while the full eventful efflorescence of the same gracious qualities in Tom Tulliver is
tracked with incomparable skill and unquestionable certitude of
touch to the far other root of sharp narrow self-devotion and honest
harsh self-reliance.

"So far, all honour"; as Phraxanor says of Joseph in the noble poem of Mr. [Charles Jeremiah] Wells. But what shall any one say of the upshot? If we are really to take it on trust, to confront it as a contingent or conceivable possibility, resting our reluctant faith on the authority of so great a female writer, that a woman of Maggie Tulliver's kind can be moved to any sense but that of bitter disgust and sickening disdain by a thing — I will not write, a man — of Stephen Guest's; if we are to accept as truth and fact, however astonishing and revolting, so shameful an avowal, so vile a revelation as this; in that ugly and lamentable case, our only remark, as our only comfort, must be that now at least the last word of realism has surely been spoken, the last abyss of cynicism has surely been sounded and laid bare. The three master cynics of French romance are eclipsed and distanced and extinguished, passed over and run down and snuffed out on their boards. To the rosy innocence of Laclos, to the cordial optimism of Stendhal, to the trustful tenderness of Mérimée, no such degradation of female character seems ever to have suggested itself as imaginable. Iago never flung such an imputation on all womanhood; Madame de Merteuil would never have believed it. For a higher view and a more cheering aspect of the sex, we must turn back to these gentler teachers, these more flattering painters of our own; we must take up La Double Méprise — or Le Rouge et le Noir — or Les Liaisons Dangereuses.

But I for one am not prepared or willing to embrace a belief so much too degrading and depressing for the conception of those pure and childlike souls. My faith will not digest at once the first two volumes and the third volume of The Mill on the Floss; my conscience or credulity has not gorge enough for such a gulp. . . . The hideous transformation by which Maggie is debased — were it but for an hour — into the willing or yielding companion of Stephen's flight would probably and deservedly have been resented as a brutal and vulgar outrage on the part of a male novelist. But the man never lived, I do believe, who could have done such a thing as this: as the man, I should suppose, does not exist who could make for the first time the acquaintance of Mr. Stephen Guest with no incipient sense of a twitching in his fingers and a tingling in his toes at the notion of any contact between Maggie Tulliver and a cur so far beneath the chance of promotion to the notice of his horsewhip, or elevation to the level of his boot.

Here then is the patent flaw, here too plainly is the flagrant blemish, which defaces and degrades the very crown and flower of George Eliot's wonderful and most noble work; no rent or splash on the raiment, no speck or scar on the skin of it, but a cancer in the very bosom, a gangrene in the very flesh. It is a radical and mortal plague-spot, corrosive and incurable; in the apt and accurate phrase of Rabelais, "an enormous solution of continuity." The book is not the same before it and after. No washing or trimming, no pruning or purging, could eradicate or efface it; it could only be removable by amputation and remediable by cautery. It is even a worse offence against ethics, a more grievous insult to the moral sentiment or sense, because more deliberate and elaborate, than the two actual and unpardonable sins of Shakespeare: the menace of unnatural marriage between Oliver and Celia, and again between Isabella and her "old fantastical duke of dark corners." . . .

Far otherwise it is with the poor noble heroine so strangely disgraced and discrowned of natural honour by the strong and cruel hand which created her; and which could not redeem or raise her again, even by the fittest and noblest of all deaths conceivable, from the mire of ignominy into which it had been pleased to cast her down or bid her slip at the beck and call of a counter-jumping Antinous, a Lauzun of the counting-house, as vulgar as Vivien and as mean as the fellow who could gloat on the prospective degradation and anticipated unhappiness of a woman he forsooth had loved, under the wholly impossible condition of an utterly unimaginable hypothesis that the unfortunate young lady, who had at least the good fortune to escape the miserable ignominy of union with such a kinsman, might have declined on a range of lower feelings and a narrower heart than his; a supposition, as most men would think, beyond the power of omnipotence itself to realise. Surely our world would seem in danger of forgetting, under the guidance and example of its most brilliant literary chiefs, that there are characters and emotions which may not lie beyond the limits of degraded nature, but do assuredly grovel beneath the notice of undegenerate art; and that of such, most unquestionably — if any such there be — are the characters and emotions of such reptile amorists as debase by the indecent exposure of their dastardly and rancorous egotism the moral value of such otherwise admirable masterpieces as *Locksley Hall* and *The Mill on the Floss*. . . .

Another not insignificant point of difference, though less notable than this, we find in the broad sharp contrast offered by the singular perfection of George Eliot's earliest imaginative work, with its gracious union of ease and strength, its fullness and purity of outline, its clearness and accuracy of touch, its wise and tender equity, its radiant and temperate humour, its harmony and sincerity of tone, to the doubtful, heavy-gaited, floundering tread of Charlotte Brontë's immature and tentative genius, at its first start on the road to so triumphal a goal as lay ahead of it. No reader of average capacity could so far have failed to appreciate the delicate and subtle strength of hand put forth in the *Scenes of Clerical Life* as to feel any wonder mingling

with his sense of admiration when the same fine and potent hand had
gathered its latter laurels in a wider field of work; but even the wise
and cordial judgment which had discerned the note of power and
sincerity perceptible in the crude coarse outlines of *The Professor*
may well have been startled and shaken out of all judicial balance and
critical reserve at sight of the sudden sunrise which followed so fast
on that diffident uncertain dawn. . . .

   There is yet a third point of contrast which could not be passed
over without such gross and grievous injustice to the very loveliest
quality of George Eliot's work as might deservedly expose me to the
disgraceful danger of a niche in the temple of ill-fame by the side
of those reserved for the representative successors of Messrs. Gifford
and Croker. No man or woman, as far as I can recollect, outside the
order of poets, has ever written of children with such adorable fidelity
of affection as the spiritual mother of Totty, of Eppie, and of Lillo.
The fiery-hearted Vestal of Haworth had no room reserved in the
palace of her passionate and high-minded imagination as a nursery
for inmates of such divine and delicious quality. There is a certain
charm of attraction as well as compassion wrought upon us by the
tragic childhood of Jane Eyre; and no study can exceed for exquisite
veracity and pathos the subtle and faultless portrait of the child Paulina
in the opening chapters of *Villette;* but the attraction of these is not
wholly or mainly the charm of infancy, as felt either in actual fleshly
life or in simple reflection from the flawless mirror of loving and
adoring genius; it comes rather from the latent suggestion of refrac-
tion of the woman yet to be, struck sharply back or dimly shaded out
from the deep glass held up to us of a passionate and visionary childhood. We begin at once to consider how the children in Charlotte
Brontë's books will grow up; it is too evident that they are not there
for their own childish sake — a fatal infallible note of inferiority from
the baby-worshipper's point of view. What thickest-headed quarterly
section or subdivision of a human dullard ever vexed his pitifully scant
quarter of an average allowance of brains with the question how
Totty would grow up, and whether or not into a modified likeness
of her mother? She is Totty for ever and ever, a doubly immortal
little child, set in a lap of our love for the kisses and the laughter of
all time, to the last generation of possible human readers. But of
Paulina we cannot choose but take thought with Lucy Snowe how
such "a very unique child" will grow up, and what brighter or darker
chances may then bring out in full her terrible incalculable capacity
of suffering and of love. . . . Motherhood to Charlotte Brontë must
have been a more vague and dim abstraction than his camel to the
mythical sage of Germany or his seaport to the nautical king of
Bohemia. In George Eliot it is the most vivid and vital impulse which

lends to her large intelligence the utmost it ever has of the spiritual
breath and living blood of genius; and never had any such a gift more
plainly and immediately as from the very heart of heaven. Most of
her men may have been overpraised by her blatant and loose-tongued
outriders or pursuivants in the world of letters; and some also of her
women may have been praised at least up to the mark of their deserts;
not one of her little children ever can be. They are good enough to
play with the little people of the greatest among poets, from Astyanax
down to Mamillius, and onwards again even to that poor "Petit Paul"
but now baptized as in tears — "tears such as angels weep" — of
our mighty and most loving Master. None among the many and truly
great qualities of their illustrious mother seems to me so precious as
this one; so wholly of the more tender tribute paid by men's loving
thanks to something other if not lovelier, and sweeter if less rare,
than genius. . . .

[Henry James]

"The Lifted Veil" and "Brother Jacob"

In the absence of anything new from George Eliot's hand, the two
short tales included in the cheap edition of her works in course of
publication by Messrs. Blackwood and now for the first time reprinted,
may be accepted as a novelty. They appear at the end of the volume
which contains *Silas Marner*, and will doubtless procure for this
volume an extended circulation. One of them, "The Lifted Veil," was
published in *Blackwood's Magazine* in 1859; the other, "Brother
Jacob," appeared in the *Cornhill* one year later. They are extremely
different, but each is interesting, and the reader who turns to them
now will doubtless wonder why the author has not oftener attempted
to express herself within the limits of that form of fiction which the
French call the *nouvelle*. George Eliot will probably always remain
the great novelist who has written fewest short stories. As her genius
has unfolded she has departed more and more from the "short story"
standard, and become, if not absolutely the longest-winded, at least
what may be called the most spacious, of romancers. Of the two tales

Reprinted from the *Nation*, 26 (25 April 1878), 277.

in question, "Brother Jacob," which is wholly of a humorous cast, is much the better. We say it is of a humorous cast, but it is probable that like everything of George Eliot's it may be credited with something of a philosophic import — offered as it is as an example of the many forms, in the author's own words, "in which the great Nemesis hides herself." The great Nemesis here is the idiot brother of a small criminal, who brings the latter to shame and confusion by an obstinate remembrance of the sweet things he has swallowed. The guilty brother, of whose guilt he has been an accidental witness, has bribed him to secrecy by a present of sugar-plums, and when Mr. David Faux is after the lapse of years flourishing, under an assumed name, upon the indirect fruits of his misdemeanors (a petty robbery) the too appreciative Jacob reappears clamoring for more lozenges, and throwing a fatal light upon Mr. Faux's past. The story is extremely clever, but it is a little injured, perhaps, by an air of effort, by too visible an attempt to say good things, to bestrew the reader's path with epigrams. As the incident is related wholly in the ironic, satiric manner, the temptation to be pregnantly witty was, of course, particularly strong. But the figure of the diminutively mean and sneaking young man upon whom the great Nemesis descends is a real portrait; it is an admirable picture of unromantic malfeasance. Capital, too, is the fatal Jacob, who, after the manner of idiots, leaves us with a sense of his combined vagueness and obstructiveness. The minor touches are very brilliant, and the story is, generally, excellent reading.

"The Lifted Veil," which is more metaphysical, is, we think, less successful. It relates the history of a young man who, growing up in morbid physical conditions, acquires a mysterious intellectual foresight of the things that are to happen to him; together with that of a wicked lady, his wife, whose guilt is brought to light by the experiment of infusing blood into the heart of a person just dead, who revives for an instant and denounces her. The tale is wofully sombre, and there is a want of connection between the clairvoyance of the hero and the incidents we have just related. Each of these things is very wonderful, but in conjunction they are rather violent. "The Lifted Veil," however, is a fine piece of writing; and if they were interesting for nothing else, these two tales would be interesting as the *jeux d'esprit* of a mind that is not often — perhaps not often enough — found at play.

William E. A. Axon

George Eliot's Use of Dialect

A literary form may be given to the dialectal words and expressions that constitute the folk-speech of a district either from a scientific or from an artistic motive. When Prince Lucien Bonaparte caused the Song of Solomon to be translated into various dialects, his purpose was purely scientific. When Shakspere, Scott, or George Eliot use dialect to give local colour or rustic flavour, the intention is purely artistic. The scientific method aims at the illustration of the dialect itself, with its historical associations and philological affinities. The artistic uses it for the elucidation of character, and by the aid of its minute touches increases the individuality of the portrait. Most dialect writers aim as a first object at the display of the dialect itself, and this not infrequently leads them into exaggeration. Thus Tim Bobbin noted all the uncommon and quaint-sounding phrases that he heard anywhere, and pressed them into his "Lancashire Dialogue." The effect is that his work cannot be taken as a faithful representation of the common speech of the county at any particular time or place. George Eliot's use of dialect was distinctly artistic. She used just so much of it as was necessary to give point and finish to the personages of rural life who live and breathe in her pages. Thus, in *Adam Bede*, the very opening chapter shows her skill and discretion; for the men, all engaged in the free and unconstrained talk of the workshop, not only vary in the degree in which they use dialectal expressions, but there is a certain individuality in their way of employing it which marks them off from each other. That George Eliot fully appreciated the value of dialect is shown in the complacent speech of Mr. Casson, the host of the "Donnithorne Arms":

> "I'm not this countryman you may tell by my tongue, sir; they're cur'ous talkers i' this country, sir; the gentry's hard work to hunderstand 'em. I was brought hup among the gentry, sir, an' got the turn o' their tongue when I was a bye. Why, what do you think the folks here says for 'hevn't you'? — the gentry, you know, says 'hevn't you' — well, the people about here says 'hanna yey.' It's what they call the dileck as is spoke hereabout, sir. That's what

Reprinted from the English Dialect Society, *Miscellanies*, No. IV, Trübner & Co., London, 1880, pp. 37–43.

I've heard Squire Donnithorne say many a time; 'it's the dileck,' says he."

This delightful passage is suggestive in many ways. The ignorance of Casson is perhaps less due to self-conplacency than to want of intellectual grasp, especially in so unaccustomed a field of mental inquiry. The difference between his speech and that of his neighbours has struck him as an interesting phenomenon, but his effort to ascertain the causes of the variance only results in his accepting as a solution what is only a restatement of the problem in a to him scholastic and authoritative form. When Squire Donnithorne says that the country people speak a dialect, he merely tells Casson in a unaccustomed phrase a fact which the former butler's perceptive powers have already ascertained. Casson, however, contentedly accepts the mere word as the key of the mystery. In this he probably resembles many other arrested inquirers who deceive themselves by juggling with mere words, and who fancy they have found effectual answers, when in point of fact they have merely restated momentous problems in unfamiliar words. Casson's perceptive faculty, although equal to noting the broader discrepancies between his own fashion of speaking and that of the rustics around him, is incapable of discriminating between his own style and that of the gentry amongst whom he "was brought up." The departure from conventional English is in this case a note of *caste*. The English gentry as a body have a flavour of public school education and university culture, and yet their household dependants speak in another tongue. The drawing-room and the servants' hall have each their own vocabulary and grammar, and a philological gulf is fixed between the two, though one might at least suppose that the yawning chasm would easily be bridged over by a little educational effort on either side.

With the reticence of genius George Eliot obtains her effects with the slightest possible expenditure of material. She contrives to give the impression of provincial speech without importing any great number of unfamiliar words into the text. Thus old Joshua Rann stands before us as a pronounced Mercian, although not a dozen of his words are unknown to the dictionary. . . . Yet George Eliot does use words that have not found the sanctuary of the dictionary, although the horns of its altar have been grasped by greater lingual offenders. Amongst these we name, at random, the following: — Curchey, chapellin, overrun (run away), dawnin' (morning), nattering, plash, coxy, queechy, franzy, megrim, fettle. It is needless to attempt a complete list, as George Eliot's dialect words appear to be all included in the *Leicestershire Glossary* of Dr. [A. B.] Evans [1881], who states that "None of the Leicestershire writers are so rich in illustrations of the Leicestershire dialect as Shakspere and Drayton; while in our own time by far its best literay exponent is the War-wickshire author of *Adam Bede* and *Middlemarch*." A writer in the *Quarterly Review* (October, 1860), amongst some unjust criticism, bears testimony to the excellence of her presentation of folk-speech.

Thus the most serious characters make the most solemn and most pathetic speeches in provincial dialect and ungrammatical construc-tions, although it must be allowed that the authoress has not ven-tured so far in this way as to play with the use and abuse of the aspirate. And her dialect appears to be very carefully studied, although we may doubt whether the Staffordshire provincialisms of *Clerical Life* and *Adam Bede* are sufficiently varied when the scene is shifted in the latest book to the Lincolnshire side of the Humber. But where a greater variation than that between one mid-land dialect and another is required, George Eliot's conscientious-ness is very curiously shown. There is in "Mr. Gilfil's Love-Story" a gardener of the name of Bates, who is described as a Yorkshire-man; and in *Adam Bede* there is another gardener, Mr. Craig, whose name would naturally indicate a Scotchman. Each of these horti-culturists is introduced into the dialogue, and of course the reader would naturally think one to talk Yorkshire and the other some Scotch. But the authoress apparently did not feel herself mistress of either Scotch or Yorkshire to such a degree as would have warranted her in attempting them; and, therefore, before her char-acters are allowed to open their mouths, she, in each case, is careful to tell us that we must moderate our expectations: "Mr. Bates's lips were of a peculiar cut, and I fancy this had something to do with the peculiarity of his dialect, which, as we shall see, was in-dividual rather than provincial." "I think it was Mr. Craig's pedi-gree only that had the advantage of being Scotch, and not his 'bringing up,' for except that he had a stronger burr in his accent, his speech differed little from that of the Loamshire people around him."

The reviewer's *dicta* are open to some objection alike as to fact and deduction. Mr. Casson, for instance, both uses and abuses the aspirate in his utterances, and the amount of literary material both in "Scotch" and "Yorkshire" would easily have enabled her to become familiar with the general character and structure of those forms of speech. Surely this would have been a small matter compared to her resur-rection of a dead age of Italian history.

Whatever uncertainty may have existed as to the varieties of our English folk-speech uttered by the characters of George Eliot must be set at rest by a letter to Professor Skeat, in which George Eliot has expounded her own theories as to the artistic use of the dialect.

She says: "It must be borne in mind that my inclination to be as close as I could to the rendering of dialect, both in words and spelling, was constantly checked by the artistic duty of being generally intelligible." This, it will be seen, is the chief distinction between the scientific method which addresses either philological experts or a public — however small — thoroughly familiar with the dialect itself. "But for that check," continues George Eliot,

> I should have given a stronger colour to the dialogue in *Adam Bede*, which is modelled on the talk of North Staffordshire and the neighbouring part of Derbyshire. The spelling, being determined by my own ear alone, was necessarily a matter of anxiety, for it would be as possible to quarrel about it as about the spelling of Oriental names. The district imagined as the scene of *Silas Marner* is in North Warwickshire; but here, and in all my other presentations of life except *Adam Bede*, it has been my intention to give the general physiognomy rather than a close portraiture of the provincial speech as I have heard it in the Midland or Mercian region. It is a just demand that art should keep clear of such specialities as would make it a puzzle for the larger part of its public; still one is not bound to respect the lazy obtuseness or snobbish ignorance of people who do not care to know more of their native tongue than the vocabulary of the drawing-room and the newspaper.

This last sentence may be commended alike to those who write in any dialect and to those superfine critics who have not skill to discern the difference between provincial words and mere vulgarisms.

It may be asked why Dinah Morris, the saintly Methodist woman preacher, although on the same social and educational plane as the dialect-speaking characters of *Adam Bede*, is rarely represented as employing any provincial words or phrases. The reason is that such intensely religious natures nurturing mind and soul upon the pure English of the Bible have their entire diction permeated by the influence of its words, which have always a certain dignity and sometimes the truest grandeur and poetic force. Elizabeth Evans, the original of Dinah Bede, has left an autobiography extending over several pages, and this narrative, though highly charged with religious fervour, contains only one word that can be regarded as unfamiliar to conventional English. There is another reason why George Eliot would have been justified in not putting dialect words into the mouth of her fair saint. When we see any one possessed of and possessed by a spirit of intense religious earnestness and seeking for the good of others, we do not notice the strange or uncouth fashion in which their message may be delivered. The accidents of speech and manner are burned up like dross in the fire of their zeal, and only the real gold is left behind. Their mannerisms, whether of action or of speech, do not affect us and are unnoticed. We are not conscious of this or that imperfect form of words, but hear only that higher language in which soul calls to soul.

Leslie Stephen

George Eliot

Had we been asked, a few weeks ago, to name the greatest living writer of English fiction, the answer would have been unanimous. No one — whatever might be his special personal predilections — would have refused that title to George Eliot. To ask the same question now would be to suggest some measure of our loss. In losing George Eliot we have probably lost the greatest woman who ever won literary fame, and one of the very few writers of our day to whom the name "great" could be conceded with any plausibility. We are not at a sufficient distance from the object of our admiration to measure its true elevation. We are liable to a double illusion on the morrow of such events. In political life we fancy that all heroism is extinct with the dead leader, whilst there are within the realm five hundred good as he. Yet the most daring optimist can hardly suppose that consolatory creed to be generally true in literature. If contemporaries sometimes exaggerate, they not unfrequently underestimate their loss. When Shakespeare died, nobody imagined — we may suspect — that the English drama had touched its highest point. When men are crossing the lines which divide one of the fruitful from one of the barren epochs in literature, they are often but faintly conscious of the change. It would require no paradoxical ingenuity to maintain that we are even now going through such a transition. The works of George Eliot may hereafter appear as marking the termination of the great period of English fiction which began with Scott. She may hereafter be regarded as the last great sovereign of a literary dynasty, who had to bequeath her sceptre to a comparatively petty line of successors: though — for anything that we can say to the contrary —

Reprinted from the *Cornhill Magazine,* 43 (February 1881), 152–168.

it may also be true that the successor may appear to-morrow, or may even be now amongst us in the shape of some writer who is struggling against a general want of recognition. . . .

Putting aside Scott, hardly any great English writer has left a greater quantity of work representing the highest level of the author's capacity than is equivalent to the *Scenes of Clerical Life, Adam Bede, The Mill on the Floss, Silas Marner, Romola,* and *Middlemarch.* Certainly, she might have done more. She did not begin to write novels till a period at which many popular authors are already showing symptoms of exhaustion, and indulging in the perilous practice of self-imitation. Why, it may be said, did not George Eliot write immortal works in her youth, instead of translating German authors of a heterodox tendency? If we could arrange all such things to our taste, and could foresee a writer's powers from the beginning, we might have ordered matters differently. Yet one may observe that there is another side to the question. Imaginative minds often ripen quickly; and much of the finest poetry in the language derives its charm from the freshness of youth. But writers of the contemplative order — those whose best works represent the general experience of a rich and thoughtful nature — may be expected to come later to their maturity. The phenomenon of early exhaustion is too common in these days to allow us to regret an occasional exception. If during her youth George Eliot was storing the thoughts and emotions which afterwards shaped themselves into the *Scenes of Clerical Life,* we need not suppose that the time was wasted. . . . I think that there is nothing preposterous in the supposition that George Eliot's work was all the more powerful because it came from a novelist who had lain fallow through a longer period than ordinary.

If it is rather idle to pursue such speculations, it is still more idle to indulge in that kind criticism which virtually comes to saying that George Eliot ought to have been Walter Scott or Charlotte Brontë. You may think her inferior to those writers; you may dislike her philosophy or her character; and you are fully justified in expressing your dislike. But it is only fair to ask whether the qualities which you disapprove were mere external and adventitious familiarities or the inseparable adjunct of those which you admire. It is important to remember this in considering some of the common criticisms. The poor woman was not content simply to write amusing stories. She is convicted upon conclusive evidence of having indulged in ideas; she ventured to speculate upon human life and its meaning, and still worse, she endeavoured to embody her convictions in imaginative shapes, and probably wished to infect her readers with them. This was, according to some people, highly unbecoming in a woman and very inartistic in a novelist. I confess that, for my part, I am rather glad to find ideas anywhere. They are not very common; and there are a vast number of excellent fictions which these sensitive critics may study without the least danger of a shock to their artistic sensibilities by anything of the kind. But if you will permit a poor novelist to indulge in such awkward possessions, I cannot see why he or she should not be allowed occasionally to interweave them in her narrative, taking care of course to keep them in their proper place. Some of that mannerism which offends many critics represents in fact simply George Eliot's way of using this privilege. We are indeed told dogmatically that a novelist should never indulge in little asides to the reader. Why not? One main advantage of a novel, as it seems to me, is precisely that it leaves room for a freedom in such matters which is incompatible with the requirements, for example, of dramatic writing. I can enjoy Scott's downright story-telling, which never reminds you obtrusively of the presence of the author; but with all respect for Scott, I do not see why his manner should be the sole type and model for all his successors. I like to read about Tom Jones or Colonel Newcome; but I am also very glad when Fielding or Thackeray puts his puppets aside for the moment and talks to me in his own person. A child, it is true, dislikes to have the illusion broken, and is angry if you try to persuade him that Giant Despair was not a real personage like his favourite Blunderbore. But the attempt to produce such illusions is really unworthy of work intended for full-grown readers. The humorist in particular knows that you will not mistake his puppet-show for reality, nor does he wish you to do so. He is rather of opinion that the world itself is a greater puppet-show, not to be taken in too desperate earnest. . . .

What is it, in fact, which makes us conscious that George Eliot had a position apart; that, in a field where she had so many competitors of no mean capacity, she stands out as superior to all her rivals; or that, whilst we can easily imagine that many other reputations will fade with a change of fashion, there is something in George Eliot which we are confident will give delight to our grandchildren as it has to ourselves? To such questions there is one obvious answer at hand. There is one part of her writings upon which every competent reader has dwelt with delight, and which seems fresher and more charming whenever we come back to it. There is no danger of arousing any controversy in saying that the works of her first period, the *Scenes of Clerical Life, Adam Bede, Silas Marner,* and *The Mill on the Floss,* have the unmistakable mark of high genius. They are something for which it is simply out of the question to find any substitute. Strike them out of English literature, and we feel that there would be a gap not to be filled up; a distinct vein of thought and feeling unrepresented; a characteristic and delightful type of social development left without any adequate interpreter. A second-rate writer can be more or less replaced. When you have read Shakespeare, you can do very well without Beaumont and Fletcher, and a study of the satires of Pope makes it unnecessary to plod through the many volumes filled by his imitators. But we feel that, however much we may admire the other great English novelists, there is none who would make the study of George Eliot superfluous. The sphere which she has made specially her own is that quiet English country life which she knew in early youth. It has been described with more or less vivacity and sympathy by many observers. Nobody has approached George Eliot in the power of seizing its essential characteristics and exhibiting its real charm. She has done for it what Scott did for the Scotch peasantry, or Fielding for the eighteenth century Englishman, or Thackeray for the higher social stratum of his time. Its last traces are vanishing so rapidly amidst the changes of modern revolution, that its picture could hardly be drawn again, even if there were an artist of equal skill and penetration. And thus, when the name of George Eliot is mentioned, it calls up, to me at least, and, I suspect, to most readers, not so much her later and more ambitious works, as the exquisite series of scenes so lovingly and vividly presented in the earlier stage. . . .

So far, indeed, it can hardly be said that George Eliot is unique. She has been approached, if she has not been surpassed, by other writers in her idyllic effects. But there is something less easily paralleled in the peculiar vein of humour which is the essential complement of the more tender passages. Mrs. Poyser is necessary to balance the solemnity of Dinah Morris. Silas Marner would lose half his impressiveness if he were not in contrast with the inimitable party in the "Rainbow" parlour. Omit the few pages in which their admirable conversation is reported, and the whole harmony of the book would be altered. The change would be as fatal as to strike out a figure in some perfect composition, where the most trifling accessory may really be an essential part of the whole design. It might throw some light upon George Eliot's peculiar power if we could fairly analyse the charm of that little masterpiece. Psychologists are very fond of attempting to define the nature of wit and humour. Hitherto they have not been very successful, though, of course, their failure cannot be due to any want of personal appreciation of those qualities. But I should certainly despair of giving any account of the pleasure which one receives from that famous conflict of rustic wits. . . . One can understand at a proper distance how a clever man comes to say a brilliant thing, and it is still more easy to understand how he can say a thoroughly silly thing, and, therefore, how he can simulate stupidity. But there is something mysterious in the power possessed by a few great humorists of converting themselves for the nonce into that peculiar condition of muddle-headedness dashed with grotesque flashes of common-sense which is natural to a half-educated mind. It is less difficult to draw either a perfect circle or a purely arbitrary line than to see what will be the proportion of the regular figure on some queer, lop-sided, and imperfectly-reflecting surface. And these quaint freaks of rustic intelligence seem to be rags and tatters of what would make wit and reason in a cultivated mind, but when put together in this grotesque kaleidoscopic confusion suggests, not simple nonsense, but a ludicrous parody of sense. To reproduce the effect, you have not simply to lower the activity of the reasoning machine, but to put it together on some essential plan, so as to bring out a new set of combinations distantly recalling the correct order. We require not a new defect of logic, but a new logical structure.

There is no answer to this as to any other such problems. It is enough to take note of the fact that George Eliot possessed a vein of humour, of which it is little to say that it is incomparably superior, in depth if not in delicacy, to that of any feminine writer. It is the humour of a calm contemplative mind, familiar with wide fields of knowledge, and capable of observing the little dramas of rustic life from a higher standingpoint. . . .

There is the breadth of touch, the large-minded equable spirit of loving contemplative thought, which is fully conscious of the narrow limitations of the actor's thoughts and habits, but does not cease on that account to sympathise with his joys and sorrows. We are on a petty stage, but not in a stifling atmosphere, and we are not called upon to accept the prejudices of the actors or to be angry with them, but simply to understand and be tolerant. We have neither the country idyl of the sentimentalist which charms us in some of George Sand's stories of French life, but in which our enjoyment is checked by the inevitable sense of unreality, nor the caricature of the satirist who is anxious to proclaim the truth that base passions and grovelling instincts are as common in country towns as in court and city. Everything is quietly set before us with a fine sense of its wider relations, and yet with a loving touch, significant of a pathetic yearning for the past, which makes the whole picture artistically charming. . . .

Everybody has noticed how admirably George Eliot has portrayed certain phases of religious feeling with which, in one sense, she had long ceased to sympathize. Amongst the subsidiary actors in her stories, none are more tenderly and lovingly touched than the old-fashioned parsons and dissenting preachers — Barton and Gilfil and Tryan, and Irwine and Dinah Morris in *Adam Bede*, and Mr. Lyon in *Felix Holt*. I do not know that they or their successors would have much call to be grateful. For, in truth, it is plain enough that the interest is in the kindly old-fashioned parson, considered as a valuable factor in the social system, and that his creed is not taken to be the source of his strength; whilst the few Methodists and the brethren in Lantern Yard are regarded as attaining a very imperfect and stammering version of truths capable of being very completely dissevered from their dogmatic teaching. In any case, her breach with the creed of her youth involved no breach of the ties formed by early reverence for its representatives. The change involved none of the bitterness which is sometimes generated by a spiritual revolt. Dickens — who is sometimes supposed to represent the version of modern Christianity — could apparently see nothing in a dissenting preacher but an unctuous and sensual hypocrite — a vulgarised Tartuffe such as Stiggins and Chadband. If George Eliot had been the mere didactic preacher of mere critics, she might have set before us mere portraits of spiritual pride or clerical charlatanism. But, whatever her creed, she was too deep a humorist, too thoughtful and too tender, to fall into such an error. . . .

The so-called masculine quality in George Eliot — her wide and calm intelligence — was certainly combined with a thoroughly feminine nature; and the more one reads her books and notes her real triumphs, the more strongly this comes out. The poetry and pathos which she seeks to reveal under commonplace surroundings is found chiefly in feminine hearts. Each of the early books is the record of an ordeal endured by some suffering woman. In the *Scenes of Clerical Life* the interest really centres in the women whose fate is bound up with the acts of the clerical heroes; it is Janet and Milly Barton in whom we are really interested; and if poor little Tina is too weak to be a heroine, her vigorous struggle against the destinies is the pivot of the story. That George Eliot succeeded remarkably in some male portraits, and notably in Tom Tulliver, is undeniable. Yet the men were often simply women in disguise. The piquancy, for example, of the famous character of Tito is greatly due to the fact that he is the voluptuous, selfish, but sensitive character, not unfamiliar in the fiction which deals with social intrigues, but generally presented to us in feminine costume. We are told of Daniel Deronda, upon whose character an extraordinary amount of anaylsis is expended, that he combined a feminine affectionateness with masculine inflexibility. To our perceptions, the feminine vein becomes decidedly the most prominent; and this is equally true of such characters as Philip Wakem and Mr. Lyon. Adam Bede, indeed, to mention no one else, is a thorough man. He represents, it would seem, that ideal of masculine strength which Miss Brontë used with curious want of success to depict in Louis Moore — the firm arm, the offer of which (as we are told *à propos* of Maggie Tulliver and the offensive Stephen Guest) has in

it "something strangely winning to most women." Yet if Adam Bede
had shown less Christian forbearance to young Squire Donnithorne,
we should have been more convinced that he was of masculine fibre
throughout. . . .

Balzac — or somebody else — said, or is said to have said — that there
were only seven possible plots in fiction. Without pledging oneself
to the particular number, one may admit that the number of rad-
ically different motives is remarkably small. It may be added that
even great writers rarely show their highest capacity in more than
one of these typical situations. It is not hard to say which is George
Eliot's favourite theme. We may call it — speaking with proper reserve — the woman in need of a confessor. We may have the comparatively shallow nature, the poor wilful little Tina, or Hetty or
Tessa — the mere plaything of fate, whom we pity because in her
childish ignorance she is apt, like little Red Ridinghood, to mistake
the wolf for a friend, though not exactly to take him for a grandmother. Or we have the woman with noble aspirations — Janet, or
Dinah, or Maggie, or Romola, or Dorothea, or, may we add, Daniel
Deronda — who recognises more clearly her own need of guidance,
and even in failure has the lofty air of martyrdom. It is in the setting
such characters before us that George Eliot has achieved her highest
triumphs, and made some of her most unmistakable failures. It is
here that we meet the complaint that she is too analytic; that she takes
the point of view of the confessor rather than the artist; and is more
anxious to probe the condition of her heroines' souls, to give us an
accurate diagnosis of their spiritual complaints, and an account of
their moral evolution, than to show us the character in action. If I
must give my own view, I must venture a distinction. To say that
George Eliot's stories are interesting as studies of human nature, is
really to say little more than that they deserve serious attention.
There are stories — and very excellent and amusing stories — which
have comparatively little to do with character. . . . Still, every serious
writer must derive his power from his insight into men and women.
A Cervantes or Shakespeare, a Scott, a Fielding, a Richardson or
Thackeray, command our attention by forcible presentation of certain
types of character; and, so far, George Eliot's does not differ from
her predecessors'. Nor, again, would any truly imaginative writer
give us mere abstract analyses of character, instead of showing us the
concrete person in action. If George Eliot has a tendency to this error
it does not appear in her early period. We can see any of her best
characters as distinctly, we know them by direct vision as intimately,
as we know any personage in real or fictitious history. We are not
put off with the formulae of their conduct, but persons are themselves
revealed to us. Yet it is, I think, true that her stories are pre-eminently

studies of character in this sense, that her main and conscious purpose is to set before us the living beings in what may be called, with due apology, their statical relations — to show them, that is, in their quiet and normal state, not under the stress of exceptional events. When we once know Adam Bede or Dinah Morris, we care comparatively little for the development of the plot. Compare, for example, *Adam Bede* with the *Heart of Midlothian*, the first half of which seems to me to be one of the very noblest of all fictions, though the latter part suffers from the conventional madwoman and the bit of commonplace intrigue which Scott fancied himself bound to introduce. Jeanie Deans is, to my mind, a more powerfully drawn and altogether a more substantial and satisfactory young woman than Dinah Morris, who, with all her merits, seems to me, I will confess, to be a bit of a prig. The contrast, however, to which I refer is in the method rather than in the characters or the situation. Scott wishes to interest us in the magnificent trial scene, for which all the preceding narrative is a preparation; he is content to set the Deans family before us with a few amazingly vigorous touches, so that we may thoroughly enter into the spirit of the tremendous ordeal through which poor Jeanie Deans is to pass in the conflict between affection and duty. We first learn to know her thoroughly by her behaviour under that overpowering strain. But in *Adam Bede* we learn first to know the main actors by their conduct in a number of little scenes, most admirably devised and drawn, and serving to bring out, if not a more powerful, a more elaborate and minute manifestation of their inmost feelings. When we come to the critical parts in the story, and the final catastrophe, they are less interesting and vivid than the preliminary detail of apparently insignificant events. The trial and the arrival of the reprieve are probably the weakest and most commonplace passages; and what we really remember and enjoy are the little scenes on the village green, in Mrs. Poyser's dairy, and Adam Bede's workshop. We have there learnt to know the people themselves, and we scarcely care for what happens to them. The method is natural to a feminine observer who has learnt to interpret character by watching its manifestations in little every-day incidents, and feels comparatively at a loss when having to deal with the more exciting struggles and calamities which make a noise in the world. And therefore, as I think, George Eliot is always more admirable in careful exposition — in setting her personages before us — than in dealing with her catastrophes, where, to say the truth, she sometimes seems to become weak just when we expect her full powers to be exerted.

This is true, for example, of *Silas Marner*, where the inimitable opening is very superior to the sequel. It is still more conspicuously true of *The Mill on the Floss*. The first part of that novel appears to me to mark the culmination of her genius. So far, it is one of the rare books which it is difficult to praise in adequate language. We may naturally suspect that part of the singular vividness is due to some admixture of an autobiographical element. The sonnets called *Brother and Sister* — perhaps her most successful poetical effort — suggest that the adventures of Tom and Maggie had some counterpart in personal experience. In any case, the whole account of Maggie's childhood, the admirable pathos of the childish yearnings, and the quaint chorus of uncles and aunts, the adventure with the gipsies, the wanderings by the Floss, the visit to Tom in his school, have a freshness and brilliance of colouring showing that the workmanship is as perfect as the sentiment is tender. But when Maggie ceases to be the most fascinating child in fiction, and becomes the heroine of a novel, the falling off is grievous. The unlucky affair with Stephen Guest is simply indefensible. It may, indeed, be urged — and urged with plausibility — that it is true to nature; it is true, that is, that women of genius — and, indeed, other women — do not always show that taste in the selection of lovers which commends itself to the masculine mind. There is nothing contrary to experience in the supposition that the imagination of an impulsive girl may transfigure a very second-rate young tradesman into a lover worthy of her; but this does not excuse the author for sharing the illusion. It is painfully true that some women, otherwise excellent, may be tempted, like Janet Dempster, to take to stimulants. But we should not have been satisfied if her weakness had been represented as a creditable or venial peculiarity, or without a sense of the degradation. So it would, in any case, be hardly pleasant to make our charming Maggie the means of illustrating the doctrine that a woman of high qualities may throw herself away upon a low creature; but when she is made to act in this way, and the weakness is not duly emphasized, we are forced to suppose that George Eliot did not see what a poor creature she has really drawn. Perhaps this is characteristic of a certain feminine incapacity for drawing really masculine heroes, which is exemplified, not quite so disagreeably, in the case of Dorothea and Ladislaw. But it is a misfortune, and all the more so because the error seems to be gratuitous. If it was necessary to introduce a new lover, he should have been endowed with some qualities likely to attract Maggie's higher nature, instead of betraying his second-rate dandyism in every feature. But the engagement to Philip Wakem, who is at least a lovable character, might surely have supplied enough tragical motive for a catastrophe which would not degrade poor Maggie to common clay. As it is, what promises to be the most perfect story of its kind ends most pathetically indeed, but yet with a strain which jars most painfully upon the general harmony.

The line so sharply drawn in *The Mill on the Floss* is also the boundary between two provinces of the whole region. With Maggie's visit to St. Ogg's, we take leave of that part of George Eliot's work which can be praised without important qualification — of work so admirable in its kind that we have a sense of complete achievement. In the later stories we come upon debatable ground: we have to recognise distinct failure in hitting the mark, and to strike a balance between the good and bad qualities, instead of simply recognising the thorough harmony of a finished whole. What is the nature of the change? The shortcomings are, as I have said, obvious enough. We have, for example, the growing tendency to substitute elaborate analysis for direct presentation; there are such passages, as one to which I have referred, where we are told that it is necessary to understand Deronda's character at five-and-twenty in order to appreciate the effect of after-events; and where we have an elaborate discussion which would be perfectly admissible in the discussion of some historical character, but which, in a writer who has the privilege of creating history, strikes us as an evasion of a difficulty. When we are limited to certain facts, we are forced to theorise as to the qualities which they indicate. Real people do not always get into situations which speak for themselves. But when we can make such facts as will reveal character, we have no right to give the abstract theory for the concrete embodiment. We perceive when this is done that the reflective faculties have been growing at the expense of the imagination, and that, instead of simply enriching and extending the field of interest, they are coming into the foreground and usurping functions for which they are unfitted. The fault is palpable in *Romola*. The remarkable power not only of many passages but of the general conception of the book is unable to blind us to the fact that, after all, it is a magnificent piece of cram. The masses of information have not been fused by a glowing imagination. The fuel has put out the fire. If we fail to perceive this in the more serious passages, it is painfully evident in those which are meant to be humorous or playful. People often impose upon themselves when they are listening to solemn rhetoric, perhaps because, when we have got into a reverential frame of mind, our critical instincts are in abeyance. But it is not so easy to simulate amusement. And if anybody, with the mimicry of Mrs. Poyser or Bob Jakin in his mind, can get through the chapter called "A Florentine Joke" without coming to the conclusion that the jokes of that period were oppressive and wearisome ghosts of the facetious, he must be one of those people who take in jokes by the same faculty as scientific theorems. If we are indulgent, it must be on the ground that the historical novel proper is after all an elaborate blunder. . . .

Yet the situation was not so much the cause as the symptom of a change. When George Eliot returned to her proper ground, she did not regain the old magic. *Middlemarch* is undoubtedly a powerful book, but to many readers it is a rather painful book, and it can hardly be called a charming book to any one. The light of common day has most unmistakably superseded the indescribable glow which illuminated the earlier writings.

The change, so far as we need consider it, is sufficiently indicated by one circumstance. The "prelude" invites us to remember Saint Theresa. Her passionate nature, we are told, demanded a consecration of life to some object of unselfish devotion. She found it in the reform of a religious order. But there are many modern Theresas who, with equally noble aspirations, can find no worthy object for their energies. They have found "no coherent social faith and order," no sufficient guidance for their ardent souls. And thus we have now and then a Saint Theresa, "foundress of nothing, whose loving heart-beats and sobs after an unattained goodness tremble off and are dispersed among hindrances instead of centering in some long recognisable deed." This, then, is the keynote of *Middlemarch*. We are to have one more variation on the theme already treated in various forms; and Dorothea Brooke is to be the Saint Theresa with lofty aspirations to pass through a searching ordeal, and, if she fails in outward results, yet to win additional nobility from failure. And yet, if this be the design, it almost seems as if the book were intended for elaborate irony. Dorothea starts with some admirable, though not very novel, aspirations of the social kind, with a desire to improve drainage and provide better cottages for the poor. She meets a consummate pedant, who is pitilessly ridiculed for his petty and hidebound intellect, and immediately takes him to be her hero and guide to lofty endeavour. She fancies, as we are told, that her spiritual difficulties will be solved by the help of a little Latin and Greek. "Perhaps even Hebrew might be necessary — at least the alphabet and a few roots — in order to arrive at the core of things and judge soundly on the social duties of the Christian." She marries Mr. Casaubon, and of course is speedily undeceived. But, curiously enough, the process of enlightenment seems to be very partial. Her faith in her husband receives its death-blow as soon as she finds out — not that he is a wretched pedant, but that he is a pedant of the wrong kind. Will Ladislaw points out to her that Mr. Casaubon is throwing away his labour because he does not know German, and is therefore only abreast of poor old Jacob Bryant in the last century, instead of being a worthy contemporary of Prof. Max Müller. Surely Dorothea's error is almost as deep as ever. Casaubon is a wretched being because he has neither heart nor brains — not because his reading has been confined to the wrong set of books. Surely a man may be a prig and a pedant, though he is familiar with the very last researches of German professors. The latest theories about comparative mythology may be familiar to a man with a soul comparable only to a dry pea in a bladder. If Casaubon had been all that Dorothea fancied, if his knowledge had been thoroughly up to the mark, we should still have pitied her for her not knowing the difference between a man and a stick. Unluckily, she never seems to find out that in this stupendous blunder, and not in the pardonable ignorance as to the true value of his literary labours, is the real source of her misfortune. In fact, she hardly seems to grow wiser even at the end; for when poor Casaubon is as dead as his writings, she takes up with a young gentleman, who appears to have some good feeling, but is conspicuously unworthy of the affections of a Saint Theresa. Had *Middlemarch* been intended for a cutting satire upon the aspirations of young ladies, who wish to learn Latin and Greek when they ought to be nursing babies and supporting hospitals, these developments of affairs would have been in perfect congruity with the design. As it is, we are left with the feeling that aspirations of this kind scarcely deserve a better fate than they meet, and that Dorothea was all the better for getting the romantic aspirations out of her head. Have not the commonplace people the best of the argument?

It would be very untrue to say that the later books show any defect of general power. I do not think, for example, that there are many passages in modern fiction so vigorous as the description of poor Lydgate, whose higher aspirations are dashed with a comparatively vulgar desire for worldly success, gradually engulfed by the selfish persistence of his wife, like a swimmer sucked down by an octopus. On the contrary, the picture is so forcible and so lifelike that one reads it with a sense of actual bitterness. And as in *Daniel Deronda*, though I am ready to confess that Mordecai and Daniel are to my mind intolerable bores, I hold the story of Grandcourt and Gwendolen to be, though not a pleasant, a singularly powerful study of the somewhat repulsive kind. And it may certainly be said both of *Romola* and *Middlemarch* that they have some merits of so high an order that the defects upon which I have dwelt are felt as blemishes, not as fatal errors. If there is some misunderstanding of the limits of her own powers, or some misconception of true artistic conditions, nobody can read them without the sense of having been in contact with a comprehensive and vigorous intellect, with high feeling and keen powers of observation. Only one cannot help regretting the loss of that early charm. In reading *Adam Bede*, we feel first the magic, and afterwards we recognise the power which it implies. But in *Middlemarch* we feel the power, but we ask in vain for the charm. Some such change passes over any great mind which goes through a genuine process of development. It is not surprising that the reflective powers should become more predominant in later years; that reasoning should to some extent take the place of intuitive perception; and that experience of life should give a sterner and sadder tone to the implied criticism of human nature. We are prepared to find less spontaneity, less freshness of interest in the little incidents of life, and we are not surprised that a mind so reflective and richly stored should try to get beyond the charmed circle of its early successes, and to give us a picture of wider and less picturesque aspects of human life. But this does not seem to account sufficiently for the presence of something jarring and depressing in the later work.

Without going into the question fully, one thing may be said: the modern Theresa, whether she is called Dorothea, or Maggie, or Dinah, or Janet, is the central figure in the world of George Eliot's imagination. We are to be brought to sympathise with the noble aspirations of a loving and unselfish spirit, conscious that it cannot receive any full satisfaction within the commonplace conditions of this prosaic world. How women are to find a worthier sphere of action than the mere suckling of babes and chronicling of small beer is a question for the Social Science Associations. Some people answer it by promising to give women votes or degrees, and others would tell us that such problems can only be answered by reverting to Saint Theresa's method. The solution in terms of actual conduct lies beyond the proper province of the novelist. She has done all that she can do if she has revealed the intrinsic beauty of such a character, and its proper function in life. She should make us fall in love with Romola and Maggie, and convert us to the belief that they are the true salt of the earth. . . .

But as soon as Maggie has left her quiet fields and reached even such a centre of civilisation as St. Ogg's, there is a jar and a discord. *Romola* is in presence of a great spiritual disturbance where the highest aspirations are doomed to the saddest failure; and when we get to *Middlemarch* we feel that the charm has somehow vanished. Even in the early period, Mrs. Poyser's bright common-sense has some advantages over Dinah Morris's high-wrought sentiment. And in *Middlemarch* we feel more decidedly that high aspirations are doubtful qualifications; that the ambitious young devotee of science has to compound with the quarreling world, and the brilliant young Dorothea to submit to a decided clipping of her wings. Is it worth while to have a lofty nature in such surroundings? The very bitterness with which the triumph of the lower characters is set forth seems to betray a kind of misgiving. And it is the presence of this feeling, as well as the absence of the old picturesque scenery, that gives a tone of melancholy to the later books. . . .

Undoubtedly we must admit that, wherever the fault lies, our Theresas have some difficulty in fully manifesting their excellence. But with all their faults, we feel that they embody the imperfect influence of a nature so lofty in its sentiment, so wide in its sympathies, and so keen in its perceptions, that we may wait long before it will be adequately replaced. . . . Lower minds escape the difficulty because they are lower; and even to be fully sensitive to the deepest searchings of heart of the time is to possess a high claim on our respect. At lowest, however, we may differ from George Eliot's teaching on many points, we feel her to be one who, in the midst of great perplexities, has brought great intellectual powers to setting before us a lofty moral ideal, and, in spite of manifest shortcomings, has shown certain aspects of a vanishing social phase with a power and delicacy unsurpassed in her own sphere.

Algernon Charles Swinburne

The Deaths of Thomas Carlyle
and George Eliot

Two souls diverse out of our human sight
  Pass, followed one with love and each with wonder:
  The stormy sophist with his mouth of thunder,
Clothed with loud words and mantled with the might
Of darkness and magnificence of night;
  And one whose eye could smite the night in sunder,
  Searching if light or no light were thereunder,
And found in love of loving-kindness light.
Duty divine and Thought with eyes of fire
Still following Righteousness with deep desire
  Shone sole and stern before her and above,
Sure stars and sole to steer by; but more sweet
Shone lower the loveliest lamp for earthly feet,
  The light of little children, and their love.

Reprinted from the *Athenaeum*, 30 April 1881, p. 591.

Anthony Trollope

[On George Eliot]

At the present moment George Eliot is the first of English novelists, and I am disposed to place her second of those of my time. She is best known to the literary world as a writer of prose fiction, and not improbably whatever of permanent fame she may acquire will come from her novels. But the nature of her intellect is very far removed indeed from that which is common to the tellers of stories. Her imagination is, no doubt, strong, but it acts in analysing rather than in creating. Everything that comes before her is pulled to pieces so that the inside of it shall be seen, and be seen, if possible, by her readers as clearly as by herself. This searching analysis is carried so far that, in studying her latter writings, one feels one's self to be in company with some philosopher rather than with a novelist. I doubt whether any young person can read with pleasure either *Felix Holt*, *Middlemarch*, or *Daniel Deronda*. I know that they are very difficult to many that are not young.

Her personifications of character have been singularly terse and graphic, and from them has come her great hold on the public, — though by no means the greatest effect which she has produced. The lessons which she teaches remain, though it is not for the sake of the lessons that her pages are read. Seth Bede, Adam Bede, Maggie and Tom Tulliver, old Silas Marner, and, much above all, Tito, in *Romola*, are characters which, when once known, can never be forgotten. I cannot say quite so much for any of those in her later works, because in them the philosopher so greatly overtops the portrait-painter, that, in the dissection of the mind, the outward signs seem to have been forgotten. In her, as yet, there is no symptom whatever of that weariness of mind which, when felt by the reader, induces him to declare that the author has written himself out. It is not from decadence that we do not have another Mrs. Poyser, but because the author soars to things which seem to her to be higher than Mrs. Poyser.

It is, I think, the defect of George Eliot that she struggles too hard to do work that shall be excellent. She lacks ease. Latterly the signs of this have been conspicuous in her style, which has

Reprinted from Anthony Trollope, *An Autobiography*, 1883, Chapter 13.

always been and is singularly correct, but which has become
occasionally obscure from her too great desire to be pungent. It
is impossible not to feel the struggle, and that feeling begets a
flavour of affectation. In *Daniel Deronda*, of which at this moment
only a portion has been published,[1] there are sentences which I
have found myself compelled to read three times before I have been
able to take home to myself all that the writer has intended.
Perhaps I may be permitted here to say, that this gifted woman was
among my dearest and most intimate friends. As I am speaking
here of novelists, I will not attempt to speak of George Eliot's merit
as a poet.

[1] *Daniel Deronda* was published in eight parts, February–September 1876.
The following sentence was perhaps added after George Eliot's death in
1880.

Lord Acton

George Eliot's Life

If it is true that the most interesting of George Eliot's characters
is her own, it may be said also that the most interesting of her books
is her Life. Mr. Cross has made known what is in fact the last
work of the great Englishwoman. . . . The usual attractions of
biography are wanting here. We see the heroine, not reflected
from other minds, but nearly as she saw herself and cared to be
known. Her own skilled hand has drawn her likeness. In books
variously attributable to a High Church curate and to a disciple of
Comte the underlying unity of purpose was not apparent. For
valid reasons they invite interpretation as much as *Faust* or the
Paradiso. The drift and sequence of ideas, no longer obscured by
irony, no longer veiled under literary precautions or overlaid with
the dense drapery of style, is revealed beyond the risk of error now
that the author has become her own interpreter.

The Life, while it illustrates the novels, explains what they do
not indicate, the influences which produced the novelist. George
Eliot was no spontaneous genius, singing unbidden with unpre-

Reprinted from the *Nineteenth Century*, 17 (March 1885), 464–485.

meditated art. Her talents ripened successively and slowly. No
literary reputation of this century has risen so high after having
begun so late. The even maturity of her powers, original and acquired,
lasted only thirteen years, and the native imagination was fading
when observation and reflection were in the fulness of their prime.
Mr. Cross's first volume describes the severe discipline of life and
thought, the trials and efforts by which her greatness was laboriously
achieved.

Marian Evans spent the first thirty years of her life in a rural
shire, and received her earliest and most enduring impressions in
a region of social stability, among inert forces, away from the
changing scenes that attend the making of history. Isolation, the
recurring note of her existence, set in early, for her urgent craving
for love and praise was repelled by the relations around her, and
her childhood was unhappy. We are assured that she was affectionate,
proud, and sensitive in the highest degree; and the words are
significant, because they bear the concurrent testimony of her brother
and her husband. . . .

Evangelical and Baptist teachers had imbued her with practical
religion, and she enjoyed the writings proper to the school. . . .
Respect for the logic of Calvinism survived most of her theology,
and it was attended originally by a corresponding aversion for what
pertains to Rome. She reads the Oxford tracts, and unconsciously
applying a noted saying of St. Thomas, detects the Satanic canker
amidst so much learning and devotion.

This seriousness is the most constant element which early education
supplied to her after career. She knew, not from hearsay or habit,
but from the impress of inward experience, what is meant by conversion, grace, and prayer. Her change was not from external
conformity to avowed indifference, but from earnest piety to explicit
negation, and the knowledge of many secrets of a devout life
accompanied her through all vicissitudes. Writers of equal celebrity
and partly analogous career, such as Strauss and Renan, have made
the same claim, somewhat confounding theological training with
religious insight, and deliberate conviction or devotional feeling
with faith. But George Eliot continued to draw the best of her
knowledge from her own spiritual memories, not from a library of
local divinity, and she treated religion neither with learned analysis
nor with a gracious and flexible curiosity, but with a certain grave
sympathy and gratitude. Her acquaintance with books had been
restricted by the taste or scruples of teachers who could not
estimate the true proportions or needs of her mind, and the defect
was not remedied by contact with any intelligent divine. Such
instruction as she obtained has supported thousands faithfully in

the trials of life, but for an inquisitive and ambitious spirit, gifted with exceptional capacity for acquiring knowledge, it was no adequate protection under the wear and tear of study.

In the summer of 1841 the thought quickens, the style improves, and a new interest is awakened in disputed questions. She already aspired after that reconciliation of Locke with Kant which was to be the special boast of one of her most distinguished friends, and she was impressed by Isaac Taylor's *Ancient Christianity*, allowing some drawback for his treatment of the Fathers. At this point, while still a trusted member of the Church, Miss Evans was introduced at Coventry to a family of busy and strenuous freethinkers [the Brays]. . . . The revolution was sudden, but it was complete. For a time she continued to speak of eternal hope and a beneficent Creator; in deference to her father she even consented, uneasily, to go to church. But from that momentous November until her death it would appear that no misgiving favorable to Christianity ever penetrated her mind, or shook for an instant its settled unbelief. There was no wavering and no regret. And when George Eliot had become a consummate expert in the pathology of conscience, she abstained from displaying the tortures of doubt and the struggles of expiring faith. . . .

Strauss himself never made so important a proselyte. . . . She was more thorough in her rejection of the Gospels, and she at once rejected far more than the Gospels. For some years her mind travelled in search of rest, and, like most students of German thought before the middle of the century, she paid a passing tribute to pantheism. But from Jonathan Edwards to Spinoza she went over at one step. The abrupt transition may be accounted for by the probable action of Kant, who had not then become a buttress of Christianity.

Miss Evans translated the *Leben Jesu* from the fourth edition, in which Strauss betrayed the feeling roused by the violence of the conflict, and withdrew the concessions which his ablest opponents had wrung from him. It was not a labour of love to the translator. In her judgment the problem was exhausted. She had her own more radical solution, which the author did not reach for twenty years, and she shared neither his contentious fervour, his asperity, nor his irresolution. The task was accomplished under a sense of growing repulsion. One of her friends even says that she gathered strength to write on the Crucifixion by gazing on the crucifix, and we may infer from this remark that some confusion of thought prevailed at Coventry. . . . In the life of George Eliot Strauss is an episode, not an epoch. She did not take him up to satisfy doubts or to complete an appointed course. These studies were carried no further, and she was not curious regarding the future of the famous school whose influence extended from Newman and Ritschl to Renan and Keim. But there is no writer on whom she bestowed so large a share of the incessant labour of her life. Two years spent in uncongenial contact with such a mind were an effectual lesson to a woman of twenty-six, unused to strict prosaic method and averse from the material drudgery of research. She could learn from Strauss to distrust the royal road of cleverness and wit, to neglect no tedious detail, to write so that what is written shall withstand hostile scrutiny. . . .

Beyond the pleasures of literature arose the sterner demand for a certain rule of life in place of the rejected creeds. The sleepless sense that a new code of duty and motive needed to be restored in the midst of the void left by lost sanctions and banished hopes never ceased to stimulate her faculties and to oppress her spirits. After the interrupted development and the breach with the entire past, only her own energy could avail in the pursuit that imparted unity to her remaining life. It was the problem of her age to reconcile the practical ethics of unbelief and of belief, to save virtue and happiness when dogmas and authorities decay. To solve it she swept the realm of knowledge and stored up that large and serious erudition which sustains all her work, and in reality far exceeded what appears on the surface of the novels or in the record of daily reading. For an attentive observer there are many surprises like that of the mathematician who came to give her lessons and found that she was already in the differential calculus. It is her supreme characteristic in literature that her original genius rested on so broad a foundation of other people's thoughts; and it would be hard to find in her maturer life any parallel to Mr. Spencer's historic inacquaintance with Comte, or to the stranger ignorance of Mr. Spencer's own existence avowed in 1881 by Michelet, the legendary mantle-bearer of Hegel.

George Eliot always read with a purpose before her, and there was no waste and little raw material in her learning. But her acquirements were mainly those of a person who had taught herself, and might not have satisfied University tests. The Latin is dubious in *Romola* and the Italian in "Mr. Gilfil's Love Story." The Princess of Eboli, who is supposed in the *Life* to have been a beauty, wore a patch over her eye. A questionable date is assigned to the Platonic anniversary in *Romola*, and the affair of the Appeal is misunderstood. There is a persistent error regarding the age of Pico; and Savonarola, instead of proclaiming that he went straight to heaven, gave his evidence the other way. These and all other mistakes which the patience of readers has detected are immeasurably trivial compared to those which occur in the most famous historical novels, such as *Ivanhoe* and *John Inglesant*.

Caution and vigilance in guarding even the vestige of inaccuracy are apparent in other ways than the trip to Gainsborough and the consultation with Mr. Harrison on the legal obscurities of *Felix Holt*. Ladislaw's fatal allusion to German scholarship, which shattered Dorothea's belief in her husband, was an audacious hyperbole. Comparative mythology was as backward in Germany as elsewhere, besides which the *Aglaophamus* was written in Latin and the *Symbolik* was already appearing in French. But George Eliot takes care to warn us that Ladislaw did not know what he was talking about, and that Casaubon scorned to learn from a German even writing in Latin. Macchiavelli, in *Romola*, blows hot and cold on the Frate, but the inconsistency is faithfully taken from his writings. While the enthusiasts prevailed he went easily with the tide; but after he had been ruined and tortured for the Republic, and had become the officious expounder of Borgian theory to Medicean experts, he spoke as became him of the man who had the blood feud with Borgias and Medicis. The discovery of a single epithet, of a single letter (*versuto* for *versato*), has determined his real opinion since George Eliot wrote. The supreme test of the solidity of her work is the character of Savonarola. She possibly under-estimates the infusion of artifice in the prophecies, but no historian has held more firmly the not very evident answer to the question how a man who denounced the Pope as fiercely as Luther, who was excommunicated and consigned to death by Rome, should nevertheless have left such a reputation behind him, that, within eleven years of his execution, Julius the Second declared him a true martyr and was willing to canonise him, that Paul the Third suspected any man who should venture to accuse him, that he was honoured among the saints in the liturgy of his Order. The answer is that Savonarola assailed the intruder, not the institution. He was no reformer of the prerogative, and would have committed full powers to a pontiff of his choice. He upheld the Papal authority against the usurper of the Papacy. Three false popes were once upon a time removed to make way for Clement the Third, for the same reason for which Savonarola deemed Alexander an illegitimate pretender, who ought to be made to yield his place to a better man.

The essential articles of George Eliot's creed were the fruit of so much preceding study that she impresses us less than some other writers by originality in the common sense of invention. She was anxious to make it known that her abiding opinions were formed before she settled in London. Mr. Spencer confirms the claim, and it is proved by her first paper in the *Westminster Review*. The doctrine that neither contrition nor sacrifice can appease Nemesis, or avert the consequences of our wrongdoing from ourselves and others, filled a very large space indeed in her scheme of life and literature. From the bare diagram of *Brother Jacob* to the profound and finished picture of *Middlemarch*, retribution is the constant theme and motive for her art. It helped to determine her religious attitude, for it is only partly true that want of evidence was her only objection to Christianity. She was firmly persuaded that the postponement of the reckoning blunts the edge of remorse, and that repentance, which ought to be submission to just punishment, proved by the test of confession, means more commonly the endeavour to elude it. She thought that the world would be infinitely better and happier if men could be made to feel that there is no escape from the inexorable law that we reap what we have sown. When she began to write, this doctrine was of importance as a neutral space, as an altar of the Unknown God, from which she was able to preach her own beliefs without controversy or exposure. For whilst it is the basis of morals under the scientific reign, it is a stimulant and a consolation to many Christians. . . .

This fundamental principle, that the wages of sin are paid in ready money, was borne in upon her by all her early environment. Bray had written a book in its defence, and the strength of Dawson's moral teaching was largely ascribed to the firmness with which he held it. Combe had said that obedience to each natural law has its peculiar reward, and disobedience its appropriate punishment; and Emerson stated his theory of Compensation in these terms: "The specific stripes may follow late upon the offence, but they follow, because they accompany it. Crime and punishment grow out of one stem. We cannot do wrong without suffering wrong." The same law, that evil ensues of necessity from evil deeds, is the pivot of Spinoza's ethics, and it was the belief of Strauss. George Eliot accepted it, and made it bright with the splendour of genius. Other portions of her system, such as altruism and the reign of the dead, exhibit her power of anticipating and of keeping abreast with the quicker movements of the age. In this she plainly followed, and she followed the lead of those who happened to be near. . . .

George Eliot retired from the management of the [*Westminster*] *Review* without having found her vocation or struck a vein of ore. She employed herself in translating Spinoza and Feuerbach. The *Essence of Christianity* had been published more than twelve years, and expressed neither a prevailing phase of philosophy nor the last views of the author. More than any other work it had contributed to the downfall of metaphysics, and it contained an ingenious theory of the rise and growth of religion and of the relation of the soul to God, while denying the existence of either. Feuerbach repudiated Christianity so decisively that Strauss was distanced and stranded for thirty years; and it would have been difficult to introduce to the British public any work of the same kind written with as much ability. It met no demand and was received with cold reserve. . . . The book appeared in July 1854, and immediately after she accepted Lewes, who was completing the Life of Goethe, and they started for Weimar and Berlin.

Mr. Cross has judged it unnecessary to explain a step which is sufficiently intelligible from the whole tenour of George Eliot's life. The sanctions of religion were indifferent to her after rejecting its doctrines; and she meant to disregard not the moral obligation of marriage, but the social law of England. Neither the law which assigns the conditions of valid marriage, nor that which denied the remedy of divorce, was of absolute and universal authority. Both were unknown in some countries and inapplicable to certain cases; and she deemed that they were no more inwardly binding upon everybody than the royal edicts upon a Huguenot or the penal laws upon a Catholic.

George Eliot can neither be defended on the plea that every man must be tried by canons he assents to, nor censured on the plea that virtue consists in constant submission to variable opinion. The first would absolve fanatics and the other would supersede conscience. It is equally certain that she acted in conformity with that which, in 1854, she esteemed right, and in contradiction to that which was the dominant and enduring spirit of her own work. She did not feel that she was detracting from her authority by an act which gave countenance to the thesis that associates rigid ethics with rigid dogma, for she claimed no authority and did not dream of setting an example. The idea of her genius had not dawned. That she possessed boundless possibilities of doing good to men, and of touching hearts that no divine and no philosopher could reach, was still, at thirty-five, a secret to herself. At first she was astonished that anybody who was not superstitious could find fault with her. To deny herself to old friends, to earn with her pen an income for her whose place she took, to pass among strangers by a name which was not her due, all this did not seem too high a price for the happiness of a home. She urged with pathetic gravity that she knew what she was losing. She did not know it. Ostensibly she was resigning a small group of friends and an obscure position in literature. What she really sacrificed was liberty of speech, the foremost rank among the women of her time, and a tomb in Westminster Abbey. . . . Long retirement prepared her to suspect a snare in conventional gentility, as if company manners concealed a defect of genuine humanity and served to keep classes apart. She would not have assented to the definition of a gentleman that he is one who will bear pain rather than inflict it. This is the angle at which a faint echo of Carlyle strikes the ear. She pursues with implacable vengeance the easy and agreeable Tito. Her chosen hero goes bare-necked and treads on corns. She will not see that Harold Transome is a brute, and salves over his inconsiderate rudeness by asserting, in parabasis, his generosity and goodness of heart. Garth, who might have sent in his resignation by post, prefers an interview which compels a cruel explanation. No rumours preserved in a family of land agents could justify the picture of Grandcourt; but his odiousness is requisite in order to contrast the wife's momentary flash of guilty delectation when he goes overboard with the ensuing expiation. The same discordant note appears in Gwendolen's impatience under the burden of gratitude. . . .

The visit to Germany opened out wider horizons. . . . She saw *Nathan der Weise*, not in vain. "Our hearts swelled and the tears came into our eyes as we listened to the noble words of dear Lessing, whose great spirit lives immortally in this crowning work of his." Twenty years later she explained the design of *Deronda* by the reasons given in the preface to the *Juden*. The altered attitude towards the Jews, which gradually prepared her last novel, began at this time; and she must have heard Humboldt's saying that Judaism is more easily reconcilable with science than other religions. . . . If Lessing was the favourite, Goethe was the master. Life at Weimar, with the sublime tradition, closed for George Eliot the season of storm and strain. Although she never practised art for its own sake, or submitted to the canon that poetry is aimless song, Goethe's gospel of inviolate serenity was soothing to a spirit disabled by excess of sensibility, and taught her to be less passionately affected either by sympathy or sorrow. The contrast is great between the agonising tones of the earlier life and the self-restraint and composure that succeeded. . . .

The Italian journey reveals that weakness of the historic faculty which is a pervading element in her life. Her psychology was extracted from fortuitous experience, from observations made on common people in private life, under the sway of thoughtless habit and inherited stupidity, not from the heroic subjects, the large questions and proportions of history. Italy was little more to her than a vast museum, and Rome, with all the monuments and insti-tutions which link the old world with the new, interested her less than the galleries of Florence. She surveys the grand array of tombs in St. Peter's, and remarks nothing but some peasants feeling the teeth of Canova's lion.

Travel supplied the later books with the materials which came at first from home. *The Spanish Gypsy* was derived from a Venetian

picture. The celestial frescoes in Savonarola's home at San Marco
suggested the argument of *Romola*. A Dresden Titian haunted her
for years. It became the portrait of her latest hero, whose supposed
resemblance to our Lord gives intensity to the contrast between a
Jew who sacrificed his people for religion, and a Christian who goes
back to Judaism, renouncing his religion in obedience to the hereditary
claim of race. When she was writing *Adam Bede* at Munich, a
Moldavian Jew came with introductions to her friends, intent on
the same vague errand of national redemption upon which Deronda
disappears from sight. Liszt, whom they had known at Weimar,
became Klesmer; and a young lady over whom George Eliot wept
in the gambling rooms at Homburg, and who remembers the
meeting, served as the model of Gwendolen.

After many years characterised by mental independence and resistance to control, George Eliot inclined to that system which is
popular among men who "yield homage only to eternal laws."
The influence of Comte began early and grew with the successive
study of his works, until the revolutionary fervour of 1848 was
transformed into the self-suppression of *The Spanish Gypsy*, and
the scorn for Liberality and Utilitarianism which appears in *Felix
Holt*. It was the second Comte, the dogmatising and emotional
author of the *Politique Positive*, that she revered; and she has not a
word for the arch-rebel Littré. Positivists deem that she never
thoroughly conformed. But she renounced much of her unattached
impartial freedom for an attitude of doctrinal observance, and submitted her mind to discipline, if not to authority. She continued to
analyse and to illustrate with an increasing fertility and accuracy;
but she was in the clasp of the dead hand, and the leading ideas
recur with constant sameness. That the yoke was ever shaken does
not appear. We learn from the *Life* that she never became a party
politician, and refused to admit that political differences are, what
religious differences are not, founded on an ultimate diversity of
moral principles.

Comte, who was averse to popular Protestantism, who excluded
the Reformers from his Calendar, and acknowledged the provisional
services rendered to the mediaeval phase of the progress of society
by the Church, encouraged the growing favour which she showed
to Catholicism. The *Imitation*, which is the most perfectly normal
expression of Catholic thought, as it bears the least qualifying impress
of time and place, and which Comte never wearied of reading and
recommending, prepared the sympathy. It had been in her hands
when she translated Spinoza, and afterwards when she wrote *The
Mill on the Floss*. No thought occurs more often in her writings
than that of the persecuted Jews; but she spares the persecutors.

Romola suggests that Catholic life and history is guided by visions; but the stroke is aimed at other religions as well. The man who, for the pure love of holiness, became a brother of the order of Torquemada, led up to the central problem of Catholicism, how private virtue and public crime could issue from the same root. Comte has extolled De Maistre, the advocate of the Inquisition; and when, in her next work, George Eliot approaches the subject, it was done with reserve, and without advancement of learning. Although she preferred the Protestant Establishment to Sectarianism, Catholicism to Protestantism, and Judaism to Christianity, the margin of liking was narrow, and she was content to say that the highest lot is to have definite beliefs. . . .

She has said of herself that her function is that of the aesthetic, not the doctrinal teacher — the rousing of the nobler emotions which make mankind desire the social right, not the prescribing of special measures. The supreme purpose of all her work is ethical. Literary talent did not manifest itself until she was thirty-seven. In her later books the wit and the descriptive power diminish visibly, and the bare didactic granite shows through the cultivated surface. She began as an essayist, and ended as she had begun, having employed meanwhile the channel of fiction to enforce that which, propounded as philosophy, failed to convince. If the doctrine, separate from the art, had no vitality, the art without the doctrine had no significance. There will be more perfect novels and truer systems. But she has little rivalry to apprehend until philosophy inspires finer novels, or novelists teach nobler lessons of duty to the masses of men. If ever science or religion reigns alone over an undivided empire, the books of George Eliot might lose their central and unique importance, but as the emblem of a generation distracted between the intense need of believing and the difficulty of belief, they will live to the last syllable of recorded time. Proceeding from a system which had neglected Morals, she became the pioneer in that movement which has produced the *Data of Ethics* and the *Phänomenologie*. Her teaching was the highest within the resources to which Atheism is restricted, as the teaching of the *Fioretti* is the highest within the Christian limits. In spite of all that is omitted, and of specific differences regarding the solemn questions of Conscience, Humility, and Death, there are few works in literature whose influence is so ennobling; and there were people divided from her in politics and religion by the widest chasm that exists on earth, who felt at her death what was said of the Greek whom she had most deeply studied — σκότον εἶναι τεθνηκότος.

William Ernest Henley

[On George Eliot]

It was thought that with George Eliot the Novel-with-a-Purpose had really come to be an adequate instrument for the regeneration of humanity. It was understood that Passion only survived to point a moral or provide the materials of an awful tale, while Duty, Kinship, Faith were so far paramount as to govern Destiny and mould the world. A vague, decided flavour of Liberty, Equality, and Fraternity was felt to pervade the moral universe, a chill but seemly halo of Golden Age was seen to play soberly about things in general. And it was with confidence anticipated that those perfect days were on the march when men and women would propose — (from the austerest motives) — by the aid of scientific terminology.

To the Sceptic — (an apostate, and an undoubted male) — another view was preferable. He held that George Eliot had carried what he called the "Death's-Head Style" of art a trifle too far. He read her books in much the same spirit and to much the same purpose that he went to the gymnasium and diverted himself with parallel bars. He detested her technology; her sententiousness revolted while it amused him; and when she put away her puppets and talked of them learnedly and with understanding — instead of letting them explain themselves, as several great novelists have been content to do — he recalled how Wisdom crieth out in the street and no man regardeth her, and perceived that in this case the fault was Wisdom's own. He accepted with the humility of ignorance, and something of the learner's gratitude, her women generally, from Romola down to Mrs. Pullet. But his sense of sex was strong enough to make him deny the possibility in any stage of being of nearly all the governesses in revolt it pleased her to put forward as men; for with very few exceptions he knew they were heroes of the divided skirt. To him Deronda was an incarnation of woman's rights; Tito an "improper female in breeches"; Silas Marner a good, perplexed old maid, of the kind of whom it is said that they have "had a disappointment." And Lydgate alone had aught of the true male principle about him.

Epigrams are at best half-truths that look like whole ones. Here

Reprinted from William Ernest Henley, *Views and Reviews: Essays in Appreciation*, London, 1890, 130–132.

is a handful about George Eliot. It has been said of her books — ("on several occasions") — that "it is doubtful whether they are novels disguised as treatises, or treatises disguised as novels"; that, "while less romantic than Euclid's Elements, they are on the whole a great deal less improving reading"; and that "they seem to have been dictated to a plain woman of genius by the ghost of David Hume." Herself, too, has been variously described: as "An Apotheosis of Pupil-Teachery"; as "George Sand *plus* Science and *minus* Sex"; as "Pallas with prejudices and a corset"; as "the fruit of a caprice of Apollo for the Differential Calculus." The comparison of her admirable talent to "not the imperial violin but the grand ducal violoncello" seems suggestive and is not unkind.

Oscar Browning

[On George Eliot]

From the first there was a tone of sadness in her stories. She set herself to describe ordinary life and to sympathize with common joys and sorrows. She had no respect for that art which deals only with polite society, and overlooks the struggles of the humdrum people with whom we are perpetually in contact. Nor did she seek approval by making her heroes happy. We have been told by experienced playwrights that the catastrophe of a play has much to do with its success. There are some stories which the public will not allow to end unhappily, however much such an end may be demanded by the truth of art. Deep in human nature lies the instinct of compensation, the confidence that everything must be for the best; that misery in this world is certain to be made right in the next; and that very probably in our present condition there will be something to set off on the other side. George Eliot's nature rejected with scorn this easy method of making things pleasant. She knew too well that everything is not always for the best; she regarded this unfounded confidence as one of the most fruitful sources of immoral action. She was never tired of repeating that the good and

Reprinted from Oscar Browning, *Life of George Eliot*, London, 1890, pp. 147–167.

evil which exist in the world are the outcome of good and bad actions done by generations of human beings. Our lives are certain to add something to the sum on one side or the other; let us be on our guard, not only that our actions are positively good, but that they are so directed as to interfere as little as possible with the good which others are trying to effect. The worst evil is often wrought by those who are free from the most repugnant qualities. Stupidity, and, above all, an easy, self-indulgent disposition, may bring ruin on its possessor, and on all who come into contact with him. Such men are favourites in the world, and are not considered to be bad. They are described as well-meaning, and as "no man's enemy but their own." Yet Goethe and George Eliot warn us with persistent iteration that by characters such as this the best lives are wasted. One thoughtless moment of Arthur Donnithorne brings ruin and death to Hetty. Tito sinks by slow gradations of easy selfishness into a villain and a murderer. Edward, in the *Wahlverwandtschaften* of Goethe, ruins characters far nobler than his own. Werther is of the same type, but the glamour of the artist has endowed him with such attractiveness that he rather invited imitators than gave a warning. George Eliot did not intend her novels to wear a robe of sombre melancholy. Nothing was more foreign to her than the belief that most lives must be failures; no feeling would she less have desired to generate than despair of good and distrust of effort. Her personal influence was stimulating; to many souls she was a prophetess, inspiring them with hope for the struggle of life, ordering their careers, marshalling their forces, making them see the honour of a humble task and an obscure function. Her voice was like that of a great captain which cheers not only those who are in the forefront of the conflict, but those who, set to guard the women and the stuff, hear the roar of warfare from afar. There lay undoubtedly a deep gloom in the recesses of her own nature, and this dark background may have appeared in her writings in spite of herself. She once said to her friend with deep solemnity that she regarded it a wrong and a misery that she ever had been born. But her self-command would have crushed this pessimism had she supposed that it could have injuriously affected others. . . .

This, then, I take to be the key-note of George Eliot's art: — to paint the lives of those she saw about her, to describe their joys and sorrows, their successes and failures, and, by insisting on the deep importance of this world to teach us to hinder as little as possible the good which is burgeoning around us. This, I say, is the germ; but how did this art develop? She died in the fulness of her powers. There is no failure in grasp of intellect or cunning of style. Gwendolen is as complicated and difficult a character as she ever painted.

Is it not reasonable to believe that, in the maturity of her mind and the height of her influence, she would in writing *Deronda* have braced herself to a supreme effort, have nerved herself to satisfy the claims of the highest art, and to soar with no common or slender pinion beyond the Aonian mount? . . .

Which of George Eliot's novels do we rank the highest? If I have at all carried my readers with me in my reasoning, they will agree with me that there is a gradual progression from first to last, that during her twenty-five years of literary production she was ever conceiving deeper views of the problem of life, and was filled with a stronger sense of the responsibilities of her mission. She strove more and more to grasp the difficulties of complex characters such as she met in the course of her London life, and such as she learnt to have more sympathy for; to express not only their appearance and their manners, but the very inmost secrets and battles of their hearts. In one of her essays there is a criticism of Dickens, which has been but little noticed. She says: —

> We have one great novelist who is gifted with the utmost power of rendering the external traits of our town population; and if he could give us their psychological character, their conceptions of life, and their emotions with the same truth as their dress and manners, his books would be the greatest contribution art has ever made to the awakening of social sympathies. But . . . he scarcely ever passes from the humourous and external to the emotional and the tragic without becoming as transcendent in his unreality as he was a moment before in his artistic truthfulness.

George Eliot never failed to deal with the inner nature of her characters. But what a chasm there is between her first story and her last! In "The Sad Fortunes of the Reverend Amos Barton" there are but few characters, and those of the humblest kind. An underbred clergyman of very ordinary appearance and capacity, a loving wife and mother, a countess who had been a governess, her brother a retired tradesman, a sympathetic neighbour, an outspoken country servant — these make up the whole of the *dramatis personae*. Others are indicated with marvelous truth, but they hardly enter into the action. They are all simple characters, such as may be met with any day in any country town. Compared with this, *Deronda* assumes the proportions of an epic poem. It is of great length, and the plot is of rare complexity. There are episodes which might be detached from the main action. The simplest characters, the Gascoignes and the Meyricks, have a touch of rareness and elevation; whereas the main actors are played upon by the stormiest passion which can influence humanity in these modern days. How complicated is the character of Gwendolen, how difficult to grasp, her feet on the well-known ground of vanity and ambitious selfishness, yet endowed with a nature which led her at once to acknowledge the supremacy of Deronda, and yield herself to his guidance. Mirah, a tender plant reared among the worst surroundings, charming Deronda as the pearl of womanhood, yet in her despair tempted to suicide as Gwendolen was to murder; Mordecai, the embodiment of a strange religion, his frail life at once consumed and sustained by an absorbing yearning; Deronda, far different, indeed, to the ordinary product of a public school or a university, yet so like nature that his prototype has often been recognized; Klesmer, the embodiment of German culture, so little sympathetic to Englishmen; Deronda's mother, so powerfully drawn, a fiery nature well fitted for the weird fortunes of her youth; Sir Hugo, now the trusted man of common sense, with the romance of his young life buried deep beneath its ashes: — all these characters, created, not only in their external appearance, but in their inmost souls, and woven together in an intricacy of plot which is the true representation of real life, such as few authors have the courage to describe, just as few painters dare to paint with realistic accuracy the true colours of a glowing sunset.

This, as it is the sum and glory of George Eliot's art, is also one of the great masterpieces of our literature. But it is not a book which he who runs may read, and it may be better understood fifty years hence than it is at the present day. It deals with persons and problems which are only possible in a highly civilized society, and become more common as civilization advances. Literature began with Homer, with strife and battles, the virtues and the vices of semi-savage tribes. Human nature is there, but human nature in germ. The Greeks of the Homeric age are with us still; they are to be found in South Africa and the Soudan; we have spent several millions in killing them with Remington rifles and Gatling guns. But you will not find among them a Faust, a Wilhelm Meister, a Deronda, or a Gwendolen. Living art must deal with the circumstances which environ it, with the deepest problems of advanced humanity, not only with the joys and sorrows common to all human beings. To do this well and worthily is the privilege of the highest genius, and it was to this stupendous task that two of the greatest writers of this century set themselves in the maturity of their powers. The attempt to compass this, perhaps the partial failure, will link together indissolubly for future ages the names of Goethe and George Eliot.

166

George Saintsbury

[On George Eliot]

Twenty years ago it required, if not a genuine strength of mind, at any rate a certain amount of "cussedness," not to be a George-Eliotite. All, or almost all, persons who had "got culture" admired George Eliot, and not to do so was to be at best a Kenite among the chosen people, at worst an outcast, a son of Edom and Moab and Philistia. Two very different currents met and mingled among the worshippers who flocked in the flesh to St. John's Wood, or read the books in ecstasy elsewhere. There was the rising tide of the aesthetic, revering the creator of Tito. There was the agnostic herd, faithful to the translator of Strauss and the irregular partner of Mr. G. H. Lewes. I have always found myself most unfortunately indisposed to follow any fashion, and I never remember having read a single book of George Eliot's with genuine and whole-hearted admiration. Yet an experience which I once went through enables me, I think, to speak about her at least without ignorance. When *Daniel Deronda* appeared, my friend, the late Dr. Appleton, asked me to review it for the *Academy*. My hands were the reverse of full at the time, and as there were some books of the author's which I had not read, and others which I had not read for some time, I thought it might be worth while to get an entire set and read it through in chronological order, and so "get the atmosphere" before attacking that Ebrew Jew. I have spent many days with less pleasure and less profit than those which I spent on this task. And when I had finished it, I came to an opinion which I have since seen little reason to change.

Something of what has been already said about Charlotte Brontë will apply also to this very different contemporary and craftsfellow of hers. Neither of them seems to have had in any great degree the male faculties of creation and judgment. Both, and Miss Evans especially, had in no ordinary degree the female faculty of receiving, assimilating, and reproducing. During a long and studious youth she received and assimilated impressions of persons, of scenes, of books. At a rather belated crisis of feeling she experienced what I suppose must be called Love, and at the same time was exposed to a fresh

Reprinted from George Saintsbury, *Corrected Impressions: Essays on Victorian Writers*, New York, 1895, pp. 162–172.

current of thought, such as it was. She travelled and enriched her store; she frequented persons of distinction and was influenced by them. And then it came out in novels, at first pretty simple, and really powerful; then less simple, but ingeniously reproductive of certain phases of thought and sentiment which were current; last of all reflective of hardly anything (save in scattered and separate scenes where she always excelled) except strange crotchets of will-worship, which she had taken up to replace the faith that she had cast out, but that was evidently more or less necessary to her.

She began with those *Scenes of Clerical Life*, which some very fervent worshippers of hers, I believe, put at the head of all her work in merit as in time, but which I should rank decidedly below the best parts of *Adam Bede* and the wonderful opening of *Silas Marner*. Then came the great triumph, *Adam Bede*, itself. Of course it is extremely clever; but no one who calls himself a critic can afford to forget the circumstances in which it appeared. Dickens's best work was done, and his mannerism was already disgusting some readers. Thackeray, though at his very best, had not reached full popularity, and was entirely different in style and subject. Charlotte Brontë was dead or dying, — I forget which; there was nobody else who could even pretend to the first class. How could *Adam Bede* fail?

The Mill on the Floss was not likely, the circumstances being still the same, to diminish the author's vogue, and I suppose it is her best book, though it may not contain her best scenes. The objection which is often made and still oftener felt to the repulsiveness of Maggie's worship of a counter-jumping cad like Stephen, is somewhat uncritical. I suspect that most women resent it, because they feel the imputation to be true: and most men out of a not wholly dissimilar feeling which acts a little differently. *Silas Marner* again has qualities of greatness, though the narrative and characters are slight for a book. But between these earlier novels and the later batch a great gulf is fixed. Hardly after *Silas* do we find anything, except in patches and episodes, that is really "genial" in George Eliot's work. *Felix Holt* and *Middlemarch* are elaborate studies of what seemed to the author to be modern characters and society, — studies of immense effort and erudition not unenlightened by humour, but on the whole dead. *Romola* is an attempt — still more Herculean, and still more against the grain — to resuscitate the past. As for *Daniel Deronda*, it is a kind of nightmare, — a parochial and grotesque idea having thoroughly mastered the writer and only allowed her now and then to get free in the character of Grandcourt and (less often) in that of Gwendolen. I think *Theophrastus Such* has met with rather undeserved contempt, due to the fact that *Deronda* had already begun to sap the foundations of its author's popularity. The poems are laboured and thoroughly unpoetical expositions of crotchet and theory. The essays are neither better nor worse than a vast number of essays by quite second-rate authors. . . .

But there was another influence of the first importance which has not yet been noticed. I never knew anything personally of Mr. G. H. Lewes. But he was certainly a very clever man: and as a literary trainer, with a view to the present success of the still more clever companion whom accident threw in his way, he was really consummate. I think George Eliot might possibly have occupied a higher place in literary history if she had never met him at all; but it is rather more probable that she might have occupied none whatever. As it was, he managed to put her literary faculties in a kind of forcing-house. . . .

In a certain other way the result was disastrous. She never lived in the open. . . . And so there was, even from the first, a taint of the morbid and the unnatural upon her. The flowers forced from her in this non-natural atmosphere and by this non-natural treatment had, as is customary in such cases, no small *éclat* and attraction at first, but their colour and their form grew less and less lifelike as time went on, and their inherent weakness caused them to fade sooner and sooner. That this would have been the case anyhow I do not doubt, but the Nemesis of the *liaison* with Lewes exhibited itself in an even more unmistakable fashion than this. The scientific phraseology to which he himself was more or less sincerely devoted invaded his companion's writing with a positive contagion, and what many independent critics had been saying for years became the public voice on the appearance of *Daniel Deronda*. Coterie admiration lasted a little longer; and that popular reflex which a well-engineered fame always brings with it, a little longer still. And then it all broke down, and for some years past George Eliot, though she may still be read, has more or less passed out of contemporary critical appreciation. There are, of course, a few obstinate and "know-nothing" worshippers; perhaps there are some who kept their heads even in the heyday, and who can now say *sunt lachrymae rerum*, as they contemplate a fame once so great, in part so solidly founded, and yet now to a greater extent than strict justice can approve almost utterly vanished away.

Arnold Bennett

[On George Eliot]

Wednesday, May 13th [1896]. I dipped into *Adam Bede*, and my impression that George Eliot will never be among the classical writers was made a certainty. Her style, though not without shrewdness, is too rank to have any enduring vitality. People call it "masculine." Quite wrong! It is downright, aggressive, sometimes rude, but genuinely masculine, never. On the contrary it is transparently feminine — feminine in its lack of restraint, its wordiness, and the utter absence of feeling for form which characterizes it. The average woman italicizes freely. George Eliot, of course, had trained herself too well to do that, at least formally; yet her constant, undue insistence springs from the same essential weakness, and amounts practically to the same expedient. Emily and Charlotte Brontë are not guiltless on this count, but they both had a genuine, natural appreciation of the value of words, which George Eliot never had.

Wednesday, July 8th [1896]. Miss Symonds lamented the decadence of the novel since Thackeray and George Eliot, and I retorted that in future years the present would be regarded as a golden age of fiction. She regretted the lapse of that custom which made it lawful for authors to intersperse their narratives by personal reflections, opinions, moralizings. In the case of a great author, she said, these constituted for her frequently the chief charm of a novel.

Which shows that sensible people are capable of holding the most bizarre views.

Reprinted from *The Journals of Arnold Bennett*, compiled by Newman Flower, The Viking Press, New York, 1932, pp. 5–6, 11. Copyright 1932, 1933 by The Viking Press, Inc. Reprinted by permission of Mrs. Dorothy Cheston Bennett and Doubleday & Company, Inc.

W. C. Brownell

George Eliot

How long is it since George Eliot's name has been the subject of even a literary allusion? What has become of a vogue that only yesterday, it seems, was so great? Of course, every day has its own fiction — even ours, such as it is. But this does not exclude popular interest in august survival — Thackeray, Dickens, Jane Austen, Reade, Trollope, Charlotte Brontë, every one but Bulwer and George Eliot, I should say. As to Bulwer, perhaps, speculation would be surplusage. The neglect, however, into which so little negligible a writer as George Eliot has indubitably fallen is one of the most curious of current literary phenomena, and an interesting one to consider, since considering it involves also a consideration at the same time of the remarkable genius that is the subject of it. It is probably largely due to the fact that from a purely intellectual point of view people, in books or out of them, are both less interesting and less idiosyncratic than we were wont to suppose when George Eliot's fame was at its height.

The novelty of psychological fiction was a powerful source of attraction, in the first place. For any such fiction as hers, which keeps one actively thinking not only some but all of the time, the stimulus of novelty is requisite, because only under such stimulus does the mind experience the zest that alone sustains the needed alertness of appreciation. In the second place, its *ex vi termini* superiority — surely no stuff of fiction could have the dignity and the significance of the human mind! — gave it an irrefutable claim on our esteem. The novelty has disappeared. We have had a surfeit of psychological fiction since George Eliot's day. Psychology, too, has entered as an element into almost every other variety of fiction. And the glamour of novelty gone, we have been able to discern the defects, once obscured by the qualities, of the purely intellectual element of fiction when it wholly overshadows all others. We now recognize that science had invaded the domain of literature — *dona ferens* and undistrusted. The current reaction, started perhaps, exemplified certainly, by Stevenson — the significance of whose work is purely

Reprinted from W. C. Brownell, *Victorian Prose Masters*, New York, Scribner's Sons, 1901, pp. 99–145, 249–250.

"literary" — is so great as to have sacrificed seriousness along with science. But it is not necessary to exalt the puerile in order to establish the insufficiency of the pedantic. And to pedantry, however obscurely felt or unconsciously manifested, disproportionate preoccupation with the intellectual element in fiction is apt, popularly, to be ascribed.

George Eliot certainly stands at the head of psychological novelists, and though within far narrower limits she has here and there been equalled — by Mr. Hardy, for example; and in highly differentiated types, in the subtleties and *nuances* of the *genre* by Mr. Henry James — it is probable that the *genre* itself will decay before any of its practitioners will, either in depth or range, surpass its master spirit. . . . She is, thus, and is likely to remain, a unique figure. More than any other writer's her characters have — and for the serious readers of the future will continue to have — the specifically intellectual interest. This interest, indeed, is so marked in them that one is tempted to call it the only one they possess. What goes on in their minds is almost the sole concern of their creator. Our attention is so concentrated on what they think that we hardly know how they feel, or whether — in many cases, at least, where we nevertheless have a complete inventory of their mental furniture — they feel at all. They are themselves also prodigiously interested in their mental processes. They do a tremendous lot of thinking. . . . But the drama itself of George Eliot's world is largely an intellectual affair. The soul, the temperament, the heart — in the scriptural sense — the whole nature, plays a subordinate part. The plot turns on what the characters think. The characters are individualized by their mental complexions; their evolution is a mental one; they change, develop, deteriorate, in consequence of seeing things differently. Their troubles are largely mental perplexities. . . .

One consequence of this intellectual preoccupation and point of view is incontestable: whatever one's predilections, one cannot gainsay that it is fatal to action. In George Eliot's world nothing ever happens, one is tempted to say; certainly less, very much less, than in the world of any other writer of fiction of the first rank. . . .

It is undoubtedly partly true that George Eliot shrank instinctively from the melodramatic. "At this stage of the world if a man wants to be taken seriously he must keep clear of melodrama," she makes Deronda observe. She certainly wanted to be taken seriously, and she certainly has been; even solemnly. But her instinctive feeling in this respect was greatly reinforced by her practice of limiting the field of her fiction as she did. The drama with which she was concerned was the interior drama, the successive mental changes whereby a person gradually attains his or her development; and to this any-

thing like elaborateness or complication of plot, any narrative of
events or record of incidents which play so important a part in fiction,
even when they are merely the background that sets off the characters concerned in them, seems inapposite. Her themes are in general
so high and her treatment so serious, the moral so inevitable, so like
the moral of life itself — the life and reality of which any book of
hers is the equivalent in literature — that even tragedy, where she employs it, seems a little artificial, a little contrived and arranged. . . .

An analogous but more important trait is the lack of creative
imagination that is implied, as the lack of action is involved, in the
scientific turn of her genius. Whatever dramatic demands upon a
novelist's characters one may forgo, the vivid and enduring interest
of the characters themselves requires an imaginative differentiation.
Otherwise they lose in concrete effect very much in proportion to
their abstract interest, which in George Eliot's characters is very
great. And it is the concrete effect that, in any work of art, is of
fundamental value. George Eliot's world is certainly less concrete
than its moral inspiration, which is often as definite as a proposition.
Her characters are thus, it is true, perfectly typical — in spite of the
extent to which they are psychologically individualized. And this
constitutes for them a family distinction of importance. The characters of no other novelist are discriminated so nicely at the same time
that they have also a clear representative value. They occupy a middle
ground in this respect, one may say, between the personages of
Thackeray, who is accused latterly of having no psychology, and
those of Hawthorne, which, as Mr. James points out, are never types.
This is, perhaps, why they are so rarely our companions, our inti-
mates, as the characters of even inferior novelists are, though I imagine the reason is mainly that they are mentally instead of tempera-
mentally individualized, and that it is the sense, the volitions and the
emotions rather than the intellect of people which, in fiction as in
life, attach them to us and give them other than a quasi-scientific
interest for us. . . . We do not, I think, sufficiently *feel* with George
Eliot's personages. They have too much a speculative, and too little
an imaginative, origin and suggestion. . . .

It was doubtless in thinking mainly of George Eliot, whose aptest
pupil he was, that more than a score of years ago Mr. Hardy spoke
of fiction as having "taken a turn, for better or worse, for analyzing
rather than depicting character and emotion." It was certainly George
Eliot who more than any other practitioner gave fiction this turn —
a turn still followed, with whatever modifications, and illustrated in
all serious examples of the art, so much so that a novel without the
psychological element is almost as much of a solecism, as a picture
with a conventional *chiaroscuro*. Analyzing, synthetizing — the terms

do not matter much; in any mental exercise of importance, both processes are involved. Nothing could be more systematically synthetic than the patient way in which, having arrived, deductively, no doubt, from the suggestions of observation, at the idea of a character, and then analytically induced the traits which belong to it, George Eliot puts these together in orderly demonstration of the validity of her original theorem. This, to be sure, relates to the mental process of the artist rather than to the technic, which is certainly analytic enough in the case of George Eliot. But it is worth while, perhaps, in accepting Mr. Hardy's expression as practically adequate enough to indicate to us the turn in fiction that he had in mind, nevertheless to remember that with George Eliot, at least, analysis has no tyrannical preponderance over other faculties of the mind, and that, so far from being allowed in unchecked monopoly to unravel its material into uninteresting and unrelated shreds, it merely co-operates with these to a truly creative end. A character of George Eliot is never picked to pieces, in a word. It is perfectly coherent and original — as original and coherent as a character of Dickens, for example, which is not analyzed at all.

It is, however, not the product of the imagination. Its conception — let us say, rather, its invention — is less irresponsible and spontaneous than if it were; itself, therefore, has, on the whole, less vitality — less reality, which is the vitality of a character of fiction. It is the result of the travail of the mind, the incarnation of an idea, not the image of a vision. . . . Gwendolen is imperfectly exteriorized. Always in exteriorization George Eliot's touch shows less zest than in examination. At times it is fatigued, often infelicitous, and now and then grotesque; Deronda's mother, with her orange dress and black lace and bare arms, is a caricature, a mere postulate of her profession of public singer. And not only is Gwendolen ineffectively presented: she is incompletely realized as an individual, in virtue of her creator's absorption in her typical significance. You are impressed by her interest in her own personality as a significant moral trait, but you are more interested in the trait than in the personality; the personality is more elusive, not quite varied enough; what else does she do, think, feel, say, besides explicitly exhibit egoism? one asks. Like every other character of her extraordinary creator, she is thoroughly *in* character. She is conceived and exhibited with an absolutely informing consistency, and with a strictness unusual even in psychological fiction. Mr. Hardy, for instance (such stress does he lay on the *ewig Weibliche*), makes two women, whom he takes pains to show as of the most disparate organizations, do the same thing — act in a way which if natural to one of them, would, for that very reason, be out of character in the other.

But consistency is not only not completeness, not fulness, not variety, not productive of special interest and pleasure: it is a decidedly inferior element in the production of illusion, the illusion that is a condition of vitality in a character of fiction. Beside unexpectedness it is, in this regard, of no merit whatever. The consistency of Bulstrode, Tito, Felix Holt, ends by boring us. You want a personage in a book as out of it to act in a way that you cannot everlastingly prefigure. To surprise but not shock expectant intelligence involves, however, the aid of the creative imagination. And we have only to turn from Gwendolen to Daniel Deronda himself to realize how much George Eliot's other faculties exceed her imagination. She is for once unhampered by any scientific subscription to the laws of reality. . . . She has made Deronda out of whole cloth. She has done everything for him, and spared no pains to make him attractive and personal. He has a "grand face," though a young man; his smile is occasional and, therefore, "the reverse of the continual smile that discredits all expression." He is just what she wants to make him — her imaginative ideal. He is no more real than Charlotte Brontë's Rochester. We owe him entirely to his author's creative imagination. The result is aptly enough implied in a letter written — obviously in Scotch — by Stevenson to a reviewer friend [A. P. Martin], when the book came out. "Did you — I forget," he says, "did you have a kick at the stern works of that melancholy puppy and humbug, Daniel Deronda himself? the Prince of Prigs; the literary abomination of desolation in the way of manhood; a type which is enough to make a man forswear the love of women, if that is how it is to be gained." The whole structure and color of the book indeed (Gwendolen and her affairs apart) may be said to be George Eliot's one explicit imaginative flight and — shall we say therefore? — her one colossal failure.

The irresponsible imagination has certainly much to answer for as an element of fiction and a factor in its composition. But at the present day it is plainly superfluous to dwell on the fact. The weight of current criticism is altogether against it, whatever the practice of the hour. And not only in fiction but in plastic art the errors for which it is no doubt justly held responsible have come to wear the aspect of solecisms. The application of a realistic standard is become almost instinctive. What is imaginative seems imaginary, and beauty that is not also obviously truth has lost its intimate appeal. There are signs of reaction, and no doubt the "image-making" faculty will again receive the recognition that for the moment more or less exclusively rewards the observation which normally — and notably in most very notable works of art — has the humbler role of verification and correction. . . . In all art worth talking about, therefore, the imagination is inevitably present. . . . And its absence means an ar-

tistic vacuum. With George Eliot it certainly counts for propor-
tionally less than it does in any great writer of fiction. Of course
there are compensations, as I have endeavored to indicate. One need
not prefer *Monte Cristo* to *Middlemarch.*

Apparently in this respect of the imagination, as in others, she did
not herself sufficiently recognize the genuineness of her vocation as
a novelist. At all events she did not depend on it. Yet there are
characters and situations, there are in fact whole novels, among her
works which show that it would have triumphantly withstood any
strain she might have put on it. *The Mill on the Floss*, the *Scenes of
Clerical Life*, show what her genius left to itself could, unaided, accomplish. But she was not content to leave it to itself. She had other
ambitions — ambitions which she could attain, which a woman with
less intellect (there have been none with more) could not, which
would attract less a man of equal genius, which the very circumstance
of her sex — given her environment on the one hand and her powers
on the other — teased her toward with a fatal explicitness. . . . The
result is a certain dryness, a certain mechanical effect for which unimaginative is just the epithet. She brought her mind to bear on
everything, and almost ceremoniously, so to say. This was clearly
enough instinctive with her. There is nothing artificial in it. And
this saves it from pedantry. She was intellectually very high-bred.
There is not a hint, a shadow of vulgarity in any of her books. She
is at home with the very best and has no inclination for anything
else; she has no moments when her sense for the excellent relaxes and
sags into irresponsibility. Without austerity — without much humor,
too, surely, except in so far as the appreciation implies the possession of
it — she is never tempted into caricature. She has no excess of high
spirits thus to mislead her, but in any case her taste is a sure reliance.
Her taste, indeed, is the part of her intellectual equipment that is
perhaps most clearly instinctive. . . . And this spontaneity she may
be said to have so instinctively alloyed with reflection, so transmuted
by thought, that often she seems to lack it altogether.

Its absence is particularly apparent in her style. One may speak
of George Eliot's style as of the snakes in Ireland. She has no style.
Her substance will be preserved for "the next ages" by its own
pungency or not at all. No one will ever read her for the sensuous
pleasure of the process. . . . It is inspired by the wish to be pointed,
to be complete, to give an impeccable equivalent in expression for
the content of thought, to be adequately articulate. In her aim at
exactness she neglects even energy. Her statements are scientific, but
never even rudimentarily rhetorical, if we except the use of irony,
in which she was sometimes very happy. Of modulation she never
seems to have thought. Any element of periodic quality, of rhythm,

of recurrence, of alternation, succession, inversion, for the sake of effect, decorating instead of merely expressing significance, she would no doubt have eschewed had any ever occurred to her, as plainly it never did. Rhetoric of any degree, in short, probably seemed to her meretricious if — which one doubts — she ever considered it at all. She was the slave of the meaning, hypnotized apparently by the sense, and deaf to the sound, of what she wrote. Her taste was noticeably good in avoiding the pretentious, but her tact was insufficient to save her from the complicated and the awkward. Her puritan predilections should have suggested simplicity to her, but simplicity is the supreme quality which she not only wholly lacks, but never even strives for; the one salient characteristic of her style — of her manner of writing, that is to say — is its complexity. . . . Every sentence stands by itself; by its sententious self, therefore. The "wit and wisdom" of the author are crystallized in phrases, not distilled in fluid diction. Their truth strikes us sharply, penetrates us swiftly; the mind tingles agreeably under the slight shock, instead of flowing in expansive accord and dilating with gradual conviction. Often these sentences have the force, the ring, of proverbs — of those of Solomon, too, rather than those of Sancho Panza. Some of them, on the other hand, have the air less of the Sibyl than of "saws," and suggest the wiseacre more than the philosophic moralist. At times they have the trenchant crispness of La Rochefoucauld; at others, even in the novels, the unravelled looseness premonitory of the appalling Theophrastus Such. . . .

At times, certainly, the sense of humor failed her equally with the aesthetic sense, of which in a large — or strict — sense it is, of course, a subdivision; and the artist who could objectively reproduce such humor as that of *Adam Bede* and *The Mill on the Floss* could also, when it came to self-expression, illustrate the very acme of dulness. Her facetiousness is, at its worst, as bad as Dickens's; and, at her worst, she writes as badly, without the mitigation of his extraordinary high spirits and infectious hilarity. Without, too, his bad taste, though with, as I said, the tactlessness which is the next thing to it. The moral element in taste involves self-respect. And in anything moral George Eliot is never deficient. Her intelligence saves her; it is too serious, it has too much poise, and it sees temptation as a kind of sophistry — temptation, I mean, to put up with the second rate on account of its tinsel, for example. But the tact that shows one when he is hitting and when he is missing the mark, she does not infallibly possess, and often when, apparently, she seems to herself to be exhibiting the light touch, she is bravely ponderous. With a little more tact, a little more humor, a little more aesthetic sense, some of her significance might have been even more striking, and certainly some of it would not have seemed so absolutely flat.

But why discuss her style at all, one asks one's self. No one can have any doubt that, though, in general, it serves her well enough, and sometimes expresses adequately the most searching subtleties of observation and reflection, nevertheless its idiosyncrasies are defects. And of style in any large sense surely no great writer ever had so little. Her constant references in her letters to her "art" have an odd sound. Yet even here one's last word must be a recognition of the extraordinary way in which her intellect atones for sensuous deficiencies. Could two better words be found, for a slight example, to characterize the first impression Rome makes on the stranger than "stupendous fragmentariness"? One of her characters, "like most tyrannous people, had that dastardly kind of self-restraint which enabled him to control his temper where it suited his convenience to do so." The adjective is felicity itself. And in her letters one can see how safely her intelligence guides her through the museum maze of plastic art for which she had so little native feeling, but in which, less than many an aesthetic temperament, is she either imposed upon or unappreciative. In art, as in life, she has an acute sense, if not a sensitive feeling, for what is distinctly worth while. . . .

Had George Eliot not fallen in love with science; had not her feeling for the world of her girlhood atrophied with the loss of faith in its standards, so that she got more and more domesticated in a foreign environment, and even predisposed to exotic themes, suggested by intellectual and acquired rather than native and sentimental interests; . . . had she not given the rein to her curiosity and become absorbed in a world of books, of literature rather than its raw material, which she could nevertheless handle to such admirable ends; had she not, as it were, made herself over into an intelligent force from being a person with idiosyncrasies, and expressly subordinated the susceptibility in which, not only as a woman, but as an individual, she was so strong, to the more purely intellectual development which she could only share with so many masters, we should have had works of undoubtedly more charm, and, such was the native force of her genius, of equal power. We should have had, in fine, more books like *The Mill on the Floss; Middlemarch* would have been more condensed; *Felix Holt* would have been dramatic; we should have lost *Romola*, perhaps, but we should have escaped *Daniel Deronda*. . . . *Middlemarch* any one can praise. It is probably the "favorite novel" of most "intellectual" readers among us — at least those who are old enough to remember its serial appearance. It is, indeed, a half-dozen novels in one. Its scale is cyclopaedic, as I said, and it is the microcosm of a community rather than a story concerned with a unified plot and set of characters. And it is perhaps the writer's fullest expression of her philosophy of life. . . .

This world was not to her the pure spectacle it is to the pure artist, nor even the profoundly moving and significant spectacle it is to the reflective and philosophic artist. Its phenomena were not *disjecta membra* to be impressionistically reproduced or combined in agreeable and interesting syntheses. They were data of an inexorable moral concatenation of which it interested her to divine the secret. What chiefly she sought in them was the law of cause and effect, the law of moral fatality informing and connecting them. Since the time of the Greek drama this law has never been brought out more eloquently, more cogently, more inexorably or — may one not say, thinking of Shakespeare? — more baldly. But at the same time she makes human responsibility perfectly plain. No attentive reader can hope for an acquittal at her hands in virtue of being the plaything of destiny. She is more than mindful, also, of the futilities as well as the tragedies of existence, and, indeed, gives them a tragic aspect. *Middlemarch*, for example, read in the light — the sombre light — of its preface, is a striking showing of her penetration into the recesses of the commonplace, and of the else undiscovered deeps which there reward her subtlety; with the result, too, of causing the reader to reflect on infinity, as he does after a look through the telescope or microscope — an effect only to be produced by a master. But in neither the tragic nor the trifling does she engage the freedom of the individual, and if she shows the victim in the toils of fate, she shows also with relentless clearness how optionally he got there. Her central thought is the tremendous obligation of duty. Duty is in a very special way to her "the law of human life." The impossibility of avoiding it, the idleness of juggling with it, the levity of expecting with impunity to neglect it, are so many facets of her persistent preoccupation. The fatality here involved she states and enforces on every occasion. . . . The "note" appears again and again. It is a diapason whose slow and truly solemn vibrations, communicated to their own meditations, all of her thoughtful readers must recall.

Her books are apt to close in gloom, but they leave you with courage. They contain the tonic of stoicism; and no one can be ungrateful to stoicism who has experienced the *soundness* of its solace in dark hours. At the same time, whatever one's personal predilections in such a matter, one must admit that stoicism itself has experienced the vicissitude of evolution, and the modern stoic has, ancestrally at least, passed through the phase of Christianity. . . At all events, it is certain that her mature philosophy does not take account of the miracle of grace. As a moralist this is her great defect,

or rather deficiency. . . . The miracle of grace, in a word, is a common enough and prominent enough factor in the universal moral
problem to reward if not exact the attention of the artist who is also
a moralist, and in excluding it the modern stoic exhibits a real
limitation.

Its exclusion from the consideration of so eminent a moralist as
George Eliot is undoubtedly due to the lack of imagination and
the predominance of intellect already noted in her genius and her
practice. . . .

But with whatever limitations, her position as a classic is doubtless
assured. There are types of human character of which she has fixed
the image in striking individual incarnation for all time; and her
philosophy is of an ethical cogency and stimulant veracity that make
her fiction one of the notablest contributions ever made to the criticism of life. It is none the less true, to be sure, that her survival will
mean the surmounting of such obstacles to enduring fame as a limited
imaginative faculty, a defective sense of art, and an inordinate ag-
grandizement of the purely intellectual element in human character,
which implies an imperfect sense of the completeness of human nature
and the comprehensiveness of human life. But no other novelist gives
one such a poignant, sometimes such an insupportable, sense that life
is immensely serious, and no other, in consequence, is surer of being
read, and read indefinitely, by serious readers.

[From Brownell's essay on Meredith, pp. 249–250.]

George Eliot's genius for generalization is, considering its scope and
its seriousness, certainly not inferior to Mr. Meredith's, but she is
mistress of it, and though it limits the elasticity of her characters, it
is never allowed to dilute their individuality. On the contrary, it intensifies it. Tito illustrates an idea as completely, as exclusively, as
Mr. Meredith's Egoist does, for example; but he incarnates it also.
You get so much of the idea that you would perhaps be glad of a
diversion, but it is because Tito himself is so interpenetrated with it
that it is an idea active, moving and alive. Patterne is in comparison
a symbol. Setting aside the fact that the whole question is begged by
describing him as vastly more winning than he is shown to be, half
his psychology is commentary, and before long the reader is admiring
the penetration of the author into human character in general, his
detection of egoism under its multifarious disguises, the justice he
renders the quality even in exposing it, and so on. Tito, on the other
hand, has the actual, almost palpable force of the traditional "awful
example." As for Maggie Tulliver or any of George Eliot's notablest
successes, none of Meredith's are at all in the same class with them

any more than they are with Thackeray's. His discursiveness and his
kind of discursiveness are fatal obstacles. Whatever may be said of
the art of Thackeray's moralizing or of George Eliot's philosophizing,
neither is discursive in the sense of diminishing the vitality of the
characterizations it accompanies.

Henry H. Bonnell

[George Eliot's Language]

No student of [George Eliot's] work ever joins in the usual dis-
praise of *Theophrastus*, as that book carries us into her workshop,
as it were, and we see the artificer surrounded by her tools. Each
essay has a clearly defined end, which is pursued with vigor and
humor; and each essay contains also the germ of a story which, you
feel, could be well worked out if the author had the time. Without
Theophrastus we should not have the whole of George Eliot. It is
folly to resent a book of essays from the pen of a novelist; concerning such things as are treated in *Theophrastus*, the best novelist ought
to make the best essayist. . . . "A book," says Mr. Birrell, in one of
his delightful touch-and-go papers, "which we were once assured
well-nigh destroyed the reputation of its author, but which would
certainly have established that of most living writers upon a surer
foundation than they at present occupy."

She has the three essential characteristics of the fine essayist: penetration of vision, clearness of expression, sympathy of judgment. . . .
This clearness condenses into a single happy word at times, which
does duty for a sentence. There is a perfect picture in her metaphorical adjective describing Casaubon's *"sandy"* absorption of his
wife's care. Fred Vincy is in the *"pink-skinned"* stage of typhoid
fever; in almost everybody else's hands he would have been "trembling
on the verge" of it. A *"violoncello"* voice is a novel inspiration for
"barytone," and a *"chiaroscuro"* parentage is a stroke of genius. The
sense of Baldassarre's weakness pressed on him like a *"frosty"* ache.

Reprinted from Henry H. Bonnell, *Charlotte Brontë, George Eliot, Jane
Austen: Studies in Their Works*, Longmans, Green, and Co., New York,
London, and Bombay, 1902, pp. 227–237.

Mr. Vincy's florid style is contrasted with the *"Franciscan"* tints of Bulstrode. *"Ethereal* chimes" is worthy of Charlotte Brontë. Her dramatic sense prompted the sure adjective at critical moments. As the French army approached Florence, the dark grandeur of the moving mass overwhelmed the onlookers with its "long-winding *terrible* pomp." And there is a fine recklessness, suitable to a wild acceptance of the future as a result of a delirious pleasure in the present, in her *"hell-braving* joy."

She is not afraid to use a word usually stamped as vulgar if circumstances justify. "There was something very fine in Lydgate's look just then, and any one might have been encouraged to *bet* on his achievement." That is just the right word; none other would do at all. She employs "kick" and "roast" in the same manner. She is fortunate in her choice of words with the prefix *un*, — as "unapplausive audience," "uncherishing years"; although "unfecundated egg" is perhaps unnecessary, as the more recognizable "unfruitful" (she does not mean "unhatched") would have answered. "Otherworldliness" is not her invention, Lewes having used it in his *History of Philosophy*, and, it may be, others before him.

One has the frequent feeling in reading George Eliot that in this happy selective ability the one correct word is found to describe what must otherwise be described only by circumlocution, and that no synonym could have been used without weakening the picture. Mrs. Poyser's dairy is described as "a scene to sicken for with a sort of *calenture*" in hot and dusty streets. "Fever" would have been altogether too tame and too generalizing. . . . If you know your George Eliot, your sickening for the country at such a season will be heightened by recollections of her "gleams and *greenth* of summer." What other word would so vividly represent the *living* green for which you long? "Verdure," after that, sounds almost as unreal as Mrs. Henry Wood's "pellucid tear of humanity." . . .

She is not a constant neologist, like De Quincey, and her invention of new, or employment of forgotten, words has not always the immediately appreciated value of that master, who uses "parvanimity" and "dyspathy" with a reason difficult to apply to George Eliot's "innutrient," with a choice already at hand between "innutritive" and "innutritious." She shares the rewards, however, as well as the penalties, of the fearless, as may be noted by the quotation of this sentence from her works in all the dictionaries, in illustration of the underscored word: "Has any one ever pinched into its *pilulous* smallness the cobweb of prematrimonial acquaintanceship?"

In her descriptions of the varying moods of nature, the functional power of the adjective is especially noticeable. A sky has the *"woolly"* look which comes before snow. She speaks of the *"dewy"* starlight as

a "*baptismal*" epoch. The still lanes on a bright spring day are filled
with a "*sacred silent* beauty like that of fretted aisles." The snow
falls from the laurels and fir trees with a "*shuddering*" sound. (You
see it falling, and then close your eyes to listen for the dear familiar
sound.) Gwendolen was married on a "*rimy*" morning in November.
The sunlight stealing through the boughs plays about Tito and Tessa
"like a *winged* thing." . . .

George Eliot was the reverse of a pedant. She had no regard for
futile learning, as her treatment of Casaubon shows; and her seemingly
pedantic use of scientific words, now and then, is but the accidental
overflow of her vast reading. Luke, the miller, is "subdued by a
general mealiness, like an *auricula*" — the fruit of her zoölogical
studies by the seaside with Lewes. She makes "*laches*" stand for
"negligence" (having Macaulay's authority there), and "*opodeldoc*"
for "liniment"; "*praeterite*" for "past," and "*loobies*" for the better
known "gawks" or "lubbers." A type is spoken of as presenting
a "brutish *unmodifiableness*." Jermyn wishes to "*smoothen*" the
current of talk, which is unnecessarily Old English; and "*contra-
dictiously*" is grafted upon an obsolete adjective. But what is really
the matter with the "*dynamic*" glance of Gwendolen, which has
raised such a hubbub? The word was seized with peculiar power at
a time when electricity was revealing new possibilities of energy;
and the idea of force production, of a disturbed equilibrium, of
energy not static but in active motion, could not be emphasized by
any other term. Nor have we any quarrel with her "systole and
diastole," either in *Middlemarch*, when applied to rational conversation, or in *Deronda*, when applied to blissful companionship. And
who but a purist would object to the humorous dash she gives to
the word "*chancy*," — her invention, I believe, in this significance
of "untrustworthy" and which she used more than once, as, *e.g.*,
"By a roundabout course even a gentleman may make of himself
a chancy personage." She forgets, once in a while, that her readers
may not be as learned as herself; but this is a compliment which it is
ungracious in us to fling back at her, — as much of a compliment as
when she supposes us sufficiently acquainted with literature to accept
without question her metaphors of "Laputan," "Mawworm," and
"Harpagons." . . .

Nobody denies her occasional obscurity. . . . "Moment-hand,"
in "His mind glanced over the girl-tragedies that are going on in the
world hidden, unheeded, as if they were but tragedies of the copse
or hedgerow, where the helpless drag wounded wings forsakenly,
and streak the shadowed moss with the red moment-hand of their
own death," has given commentators some trouble. But I am weak
enough to think the sentence fine in its illustrative suggestion of

unutterable pathos in the fate of tender human beings, so unheeded that it can only be likened to a shot bird in the forest, — its death a thing hidden from the great outside-world, and forgotten at the *moment* of its consummation.

But there are no purposely invented Meredithian darknesses; and meeting her obscurity, one has the sensation of inevitableness, not of teasing deceit. You guess that Browning is playing with you; you know that George Eliot is not. . . .

[Virginia Woolf]

George Eliot

To read George Eliot attentively is to become aware of how little one knows about her. It is also to become aware of the credulity, not very creditable to one's insight, with which, half consciously and partly maliciously, one had accepted the late Victorian version of a deluded woman who held phantom sway over subjects even more deluded than herself. At what moment, and by what means her spell was broken it is difficult to ascertain. Some people attribute it to the publication of her *Life*. Perhaps George Meredith, with his phrase about "the mercurial little showman" and the "errant woman" on the dais, gave point and poison to the arrows of thousands incapable of aiming them so accurately, but delighted to let fly. She became one of the butts for youth to laugh at, the convenient symbol of a group of serious people who were all guilty of the same idolatry and could be dismissed with the same scorn. Lord Acton had said that she was greater than Dante; Herbert Spencer exempted her novels, as if they were not novels, when he banned all fiction from the London Library. She was the pride and paragon of her sex. Moreover, her private record was not more alluring than her public. Asked to describe an afternoon at the Priory, the story-teller always intimated that the memory of those

This essay first appeared upon the occasion of George Eliot's centenary in the *Times Literary Supplement*, 18 (20 November 1919), 657–658, from which this text is taken, and was included in *The Common Reader*, copyright, 1925, by Harcourt, Brace & World, Inc.; renewed, 1953, by Leonard Woolf. Reprinted by permission of the publishers.

serious Sunday afternoons had come to tickle his sense of humour.
He had been so much alarmed by the grave lady in her low chair;
he had been so anxious to say the intelligent thing. Certainly, the
talk had been very serious, as a note in the fine clear hand of the
great novelist bore witness. It was dated on the Monday morning,
and she accused herself of having spoken without due forethought
of Marivaux when she meant another; but no doubt, she said, her
listener had already supplied the correction.[1] Still, the memory of
talking about Marivaux to George Eliot on a Sunday afternoon was
not a romantic memory. It had faded with the passage of the years.
It had not become picturesque. . . .

In all these records one feels that the recorder, even when he
was in the actual presence, kept his distance and kept his head, and
never read the novels in later years with the light of a vivid, or
puzzling, or beautiful personality dazzling in his eyes. In fiction,
where so much of personality is revealed, the absence of charm is a
great lack; and her critics, who have been, of course, mostly of the
opposite sex, have resented, half consciously perhaps, her deficiency
in a quality which is held to be supremely desirable in women.
George Eliot was not charming; she was not strongly feminine; she
had none of those eccentricities and inequalities of temper which
give to so many artists the endearing simplicity of children. One
feels that to most people, as to Lady Ritchie, she was "not exactly a
personal friend, but a good and benevolent impulse." But if we
consider these portraits more closely we shall find that they are all
the portraits of an elderly celebrated woman, dressed in black satin,
driving in her victoria, a woman who had been through her struggle
and issued from it with a profound desire to be of use to others, but
with no wish for intimacy, save for the little circle who had known
her in the days of her youth. We know very little about the
days of her youth; but we do know that the culture, the philosophy,
the fame, and the influence were all built upon a very humble
foundation — she was the granddaughter of a carpenter. . . .

Her development was very slow and very awkward, but it had
the irresistible impetus behind it of a deep-seated and noble ambition.
Every obstacle at length was thrust from her path. She knew every
one. She read everything. Her astonishing intellectual vitality had
triumphed. Youth was over, but youth had been full of suffering.
Then, at the age of thirty-five, at the height of her powers, and
in the fullness of her freedom, she made the decision which was of
such profound moment to her and still matters even to us, and
went to Weimar, alone with George Henry Lewes.

  [1] This note, to Virginia Woolf's father Leslie Stephen, dated 7 January
1878, is found in *The George Eliot Letters*, VII, 3. — Ed.

The books which followed so soon after her union testify in the fullest manner to the great liberation which had come to her with personal happiness. In themselves they provide us with a plentiful feast. Yet at the threshold of her literary career one may find in some of the circumstances of her life influences that turned her mind to the past, to the country village, to the quiet and beauty and simplicity of childish memories and away from herself and the present. We understand how it was that her first book was *Scenes of Clerical Life,* and not *Middlemarch.* Her union with Lewes had surrounded her with affection, but in view of the circumstances and of the conventions it had also isolated her. "I wish it to be understood," she wrote in 1857, "that I should never invite any one to come and see me who did not ask for the invitation." She had been "cut off from what is called the world," she said later, but she did not regret it. By becoming thus marked, first by circumstances and later, inevitably, by her fame, she lost the power to move on equal terms unnoted among her kind; and the loss for a novelist was serious. Still, basking in the light and sunshine of *Scenes of Clerical Life,* feeling the large mature mind spreading itself with a luxurious sense of freedom in the world of her "remotest past," to speak of loss seems inappropriate. Everything to such a mind was gain. All experience filtered down through layer after layer of perception and reflection, enriching and nourishing. The utmost we can say, in qualifying her attitude towards fiction by what little we know of her life, is that she had taken to heart certain lessons not usually learnt early, if learnt at all, among which, perhaps, the most branded upon her was the melancholy virtue of tolerance; her sympathies are with the everyday lot, and play most happily in dwelling upon the homespun ordinary joys and sorrows. She has none of that romantic intensity which is connected with a sense of one's own individuality, unsated and unsubdued, cutting its shape sharply upon the background of the world. What were the loves and sorrows of a snuffy old clergyman, dreaming over his whisky, to the fiery egotism of Jane Eyre? The beauty of those first books, *Scenes of Clerical Life, Adam Bede, The Mill on the Floss,* is very great. It is impossible to estimate the merit of the Poysers, the Dodsons, the Gilfils, the Bartons, and the rest with all their surroundings and dependencies, because they have put on flesh and blood and we move among them, now bored, now sympathetic, but always with that unquestioning acceptance of all that they say and do, which we accord to the great originals only. The flood of memory and humour which she pours so spontaneously into one figure, one scene after another, until the whole fabric of ancient rural England is revived, has so much in common with a

natural process that it leaves us with little consciousness that there
is anything to criticise. We accept; we feel the delicious warmth
and release of spirit which the great creative writers alone procure
for us. As one comes back to the books after years of absence
they pour out, even against our expectation, the same store of energy
and heat, so that we want more than anything to idle in the warmth
as in the sun beating down from the red orchard wall. If there is
an element of unthinking abandonment in thus submitting to the
humours of Midland farmers and their wives, that, too, is right
in the circumstances. We scarcely wish to analyse what we feel
to be so large and deeply human. And when we consider how
distant in time the world of Shepperton and Hayslope is, and how
remote the minds of farmer and agricultural labourers from those of
most of George Eliot's readers, we can only attribute the ease and
pleasure with which we ramble from house to smithy, from cottage
parlour to rectory garden, to the fact that George Eliot makes us
share their lives, not in a spirit of condescension or of curiosity, but
in a spirit of sympathy. She is no satirist. The movement of her
mind was too slow and cumbersome to lend itself to comedy. But
she gathers in her large grasp a great bunch of the main elements of
human nature and groups them loosely together with a tolerant
and wholesome understanding which, as one finds upon re-reading,
has not only kept her figures fresh and free, but has given them an
unexpected hold upon our laughter and tears. There is the famous
Mrs. Poyser. It would have been easy to work her idiosyncrasies to
death, and, as it is, perhaps, George Eliot gets her laugh in the
same place a little too often. But memory, after the book is shut,
brings out, as sometimes in real life, the details and subtleties which
some more salient characteristic has prevented us from noticing at
the time. We recollect that her health was not good. There were
occasions upon which she said nothing at all. She was patience itself
with a sick child. She doted upon Totty. Thus one can muse and
speculate about the greater number of George Eliot's characters
and find, even in the least important, a roominess and margin where
those qualities lurk which she has no call to bring from their
obscurity.

But in the midst of all this tolerance and sympathy there are,
even in the early books, moments of greater stress. Her humour
has shown itself broad enough to cover a wide range of fools and
failures, mothers and children, dogs and flourishing midland fields,
farmers, sagacious or fuddled over their ale, horse-dealers, innkeepers,
curates, and carpenters. Over them all broods a certain romance,
the only romance that George Eliot allowed herself — the romance
of the past. The books are astonishingly readable and have no trace

of pomposity or pretence. But to the reader who holds a large stretch of her early work in view it will become obvious that the mist of recollection gradually withdraws. It is not that her power diminishes, for, to our thinking, it is at its highest in the mature *Middlemarch*, the magnificent book which with all its imperfections is one of the few English novels written for grown-up people. But the world of fields and farms no longer contents her. In real life she had sought her fortunes elsewhere; and though to look back into the past was calming and consoling, there are, even in the early works, traces of that troubled spirit, that exacting and questioning and baffled presence who was George Eliot herself. In *Adam Bede* there is a hint of her in Dinah. She shows herself far more openly and completely in Maggie in *The Mill on the Floss*. She is Janet in *Janet's Repentance*, and Romola, and Dorothea seeking wisdom and finding one scarcely knows what in marriage with Ladislaw. Those who fall foul of George Eliot do so, we incline to think, on account of her heroines; and with good reason; for there is no doubt that they bring out the worst of her, lead her into difficult places, make her self-conscious, didactic, and occasionally vulgar. Yet if you could delete the whole sisterhood you would leave a much smaller and a much inferior world, albeit a world of greater artistic perfection and far superior jollity and comfort. In accounting for her failure, in so far as it was a failure, one recollects that she never wrote a story until she was thirty-seven, and by the time she was thirty-seven she had come to think of herself with a mixture of pain and something like resentment. For long she preferred not to think of herself at all. Then, when the first flush of creative energy was exhausted and self-confidence had come to her, she wrote more and more from the personal standpoint, but she did so without the unhesitating abandonment of the young. Her self-consciousness is always marked when her heroines say what she herself would have said. She disguised them in every possible way. She granted them beauty and wealth into the bargain; she invented, more improbably, a taste for brandy. But the disconcerting and stimulating fact remained that she was compelled by the very power of her genius to step forth in person upon the quiet bucolic scene.

The noble and beautiful girl who insisted upon being born into *The Mill on the Floss* is the most obvious example of the ruin which a heroine can strew about her. Humour controls her and keeps her lovable so long as she is small and can be satisfied by eloping with the gipsies or hammering nails into her doll; but she develops; and before George Eliot knows what has happened she has a full-grown woman on her hands demanding what neither gipsies nor dolls, nor St. Ogg's itself is capable of giving her. First Philip Wakem is produced, and later Stephen Guest. The weakness of the one and the coarseness of the other have often been pointed out; but both, in their weakness and coarseness, illustrate not so much George Eliot's inability to draw the portrait of a man, as the uncertainty, the infirmity, and the fumbling which shook her hand when she had to conceive a fit mate for a heroine. She is in the first place driven beyond the home world she knew and loved, and forced to set foot in middle-class drawing-rooms where young men sing all the summer morning and young women sit embroidering smoking-caps for bazaars. She feels herself out of her element, as her clumsy satire of what she calls "good society" proves.

> Good society has its claret and its velvet carpets, its dinner engagements six weeks deep, its opera, and its faëry ball rooms, . . . gets its science done by Faraday and its religion by the superior clergy who are to be met in the best houses; how should it have need of belief and emphasis?

There is no trace of humour or insight there, but only the vindictiveness of a grudge which we feel to be personal in its origin. But terrible as the complexity of our social system is in its demands upon the sympathy and discernment of a novelist straying across the boundaries, Maggie Tulliver did worse than drag George Eliot from her natural surroundings. She insisted upon the introduction of the great emotional scene. She must love; she must despair; she must be drowned clasping her brother in her arms. The more one examines the great emotional scenes the more nervously one anticipates the brewing and gathering and thickening of the cloud which will burst upon our heads at the moment of crisis in a shower of disillusionment and verbosity. It is partly that her hold upon dialogue, when it is not dialect, is slack; and partly that she seems to shrink with an elderly dread of fatigue from the effort of emotional concentration. She allows her heroines to talk too much. She has little verbal felicity. She lacks the unerring taste which chooses one sentence and compresses the heart of the scene within that. "Whom are you going to dance with?" asked Mr. Knightley, at the Westons' ball. "With you, if you will ask me," said Emma; and she has said enough. Mrs. Casaubon would have talked for an hour and we should have looked out of the window.

Yet, dismiss the heroines without sympathy, confine George Eliot to the agricultural world of her "remotest past," and you not only diminish her greatness but lose her true flavour. That greatness is here we can have no doubt. The width of the prospect, the large strong outlines of the principal features, the ruddy light of the early books, the searching power and reflective richness of the later tempt us to linger and expatiate beyond our limits. But it is upon the heroines that we would cast a final glance. "I have always been finding out my religion since I was a little girl," says Dorothea Casaubon. "I used to pray so much — now I hardly ever pray. I try not to have desires merely for myself. . . ." She is speaking for them all. That is their problem. They cannot live without religion, and they start out on the search for one when they are little girls. Each has the deep feminine passion for goodness, which makes the place where she stands in aspiration and agony the heart of the book — still and cloistered like a place of worship, but that she no longer knows to whom to pray. In learning they seek their goal; in the ordinary tasks of womanhood; in the wider service of their kind. They do not find what they seek, and we cannot wonder. The ancient consciousness of woman, charged with suffering and sensibility, and for so many ages dumb, seems in them to have brimmed and overflowed and uttered a demand for something — they scarcely know what — for something that is perhaps incompatible with the facts of human existence. George Eliot had far too strong an intelligence to tamper with those facts, and too broad a humour to mitigate the truth because it was a stern one. Save for the supreme courage of their endeavour, the struggle ends, for her heroines, in tragedy, or in a compromise that is even more melancholy. But their story is the incomplete version of the story of George Eliot herself. For her, too, the burden and the complexity of womanhood were not enough; she must reach beyond the sanctuary and pluck for herself the strange bright fruits of art and knowledge. Clasping them as few women have ever clasped them, she would not renounce her own inheritance — the difference of view, the difference of standard — nor accept an inappropriate reward. Thus we behold her, a memorable figure, inordinately praised and shrinking from her fame, despondent, reserved, shuddering back into the arms of love as if there alone were satisfaction and, it might be, justification, at the same time reaching out with "a fastidious yet hungry ambition" for all that life could offer the free and inquiring mind and confronting her feminine aspirations with the real world of men. Triumphant was the issue for her, whatever it may have been for her creations, and as we recollect all that she dared and achieved, how with every obstacle against her — sex and health and convention — she sought more knowledge and more freedom till the body, weighted with its double burden, sank worn out, we must lay upon her grave whatever we have it in our power to bestow of laurel and rose.

Oliver Elton

[On George Eliot]

The ebb of George Eliot's fame after her death in 1880 was sadly noted by the true believers. Nor was this wholly the fault of her last essays, *Impressions of Theophrastus Such*, a personage most unlike that light sharp observer Theophrastus of Lesbos. *Daniel Deronda* had already cooled the public, and the writer had to pay for the zeal of her devotees. A typical eulogy was administered by Richard Holt Hutton, of the *Spectator*:

> If she cannot paint the glow of human enterprise like Scott, or sketch with the easy rapidity of Fielding, she can do what neither of them can do — see and explain the relation of the broadest and commonest life to the deepest springs of philosophy and religion.

The letters of Henry Sidgwick show how seriously George Eliot was taken, as a teacher, by some of the best minds. Edmond Scherer exalted her, but then dry severe critics are apt to go far when they once give a loose to their rare enthusiasms. Lord Acton, while making his reserves, said that she "justly seemed the most illustrious figure that had arisen in literature since Goethe." This judgement sounds strange enough to-day. Lord Acton was amazed, he explains, that an "atheist," brought up in a school distinguished by its "ethical impotence," should have evolved a "new and puissant morality" which "was even preferable in some ways to that of the current religion. It had no weak places, no evil champions, no bad purpose, to screen or excuse, unlike almost all forms of Christianity." So George Eliot "has little rivalry to apprehend until philosophy inspires finer novels or moralists teach nobler lessons to the mass of mankind." Strange, ambiguous credentials for an artist! More than this is needed, if the work is to stand.

But of this admiration she was not all unworthy. Let those who are now young think of their own chief private enthusiasm, what-

Reprinted from Oliver Elton, *A Survey of English Literature, 1830–1880*, 2 vols., Edward Arnold Ltd., London, 1920, II, 258–275, by permission of the publishers.

ever it be, and let them salute in sympathy that old far-away one
of the Eighties, which is only to be comprehended by those who
grew up in it. I recall without apology the fervid, overcharged
view of George Eliot. She was a sibyl; she read the surface and
the depths alike infallibly. *Middlemarch*, above all, was an image
of life; and if it was a gloomy one, so much the worse for life. . . .
And the writer had her own consolations, though not of the ordinary
kind. She had cast off the current doctrines; she had managed
to "do without opium." The "religion of humanity," the voices of
the "choir invisible," sounded in the ear, though their comfort was
of a far-off and grimmish order. And then George Eliot had, or
so it appeared, unique claims as a writer. Dickens often "sat on
the piano"; Thackeray (I still cite the headlong immature notion)
was apt to maunder, and had no philosophy or sense of beauty;
the experience of the Haworth sisters was intense but limited. But
George Eliot's canvas was broad, her ideas were broader still; her
people were alive and real, and innumerable; and the play of motive
in her tales, the course itself of the action, revealed the spiritual
issues that shape even the humblest fates.

So ardent an estimate could scarcely last, though no mean writer
and no charlatan could have inspired it. Critical protests had been
already heard, and some unhallowed noises. Swinburne had made
a sonnet to her who (in contrast to Carlyle) had "found, in love
of lovingkindness, light"; but in prose he was less enthusiastic. In
much rougher strain, the poet and journalist, William Ernest Henley,
talked of the "Apotheosis of Pupil-Teachery"; and his "sense of sex,"
so he confided to the reader, led him to deny the attributes of
manhood to the "governesses in revolt whom it had pleased her to
put forward as men." George Eliot was "the fruit of a caprice of
Apollo for the differential calculus." Sir Leslie Stephen's book
(1902) did something to restore the critical balance, if not the old
popularity or worship. Stephen's doubts and abatements were all
the more forcible, that he had much sympathy with George Eliot's
point of view, and himself professed a lay religion. But in truth
the reaction against her fame was only one symptom of a long-
brewing change that came over English thought as the century
wore on. It may be briefly described as the emergence, on one side,
of the cult of pure force, and, on another, as the cult of pure
art. . . ; enough that an idealist like George Eliot, who declared
for charity and fraternity, and was an avowed teacher, came to be
at a discount. Any one who tried to bring a heavy park of ethical
ordnance into the sacred territory must expect to be severely ex-
amined at the frontier, and probably to be turned back. And there
was a further check to George Eliot's reputation: two other masters

of fiction came into fuller view. George Meredith was her contemporary, but his wider fame was established far later than hers;
and Mr. Thomas Hardy only began to publish in the Seventies.
Each of these novelists saw the world of men and women more
freely than George Eliot had done; and they brought into relief
one of her greatest deficiencies, namely, that while exhaustively
describing life, she is apt to miss the spirit of life itself. Its unashamed
passion, its careless gaiety, the intoxication of sunshine — so far as she
understands these things, she leaves us with the feeling that she
rather distrusts them. We can but ask once more how she weathers
all such criticism. . . .

[*Middlemarch*] is almost one of the great novels of the language.
A little more ease and play and simplicity, a little less of the anxious
idealism which ends in going beyond nature, and it might have
been one of the greatest. Some of the figures, like Ladislaw, are
mere pasteboard; but there is still a dense throng of persons whom
we all might have known, perhaps too well. Some of the men
whose inner crises are described with most labour and travail are
the least real; such are the pedant Mr. Casaubon and the banker
Bulstrode. But the whole is like some piece of experience that we
might wish to but cannot forget. There is no plan, but there is no
confusion. The "three love-problems" are held firmly in hand.
Dorothea, Lydgate, the Garth and Vincy families, meet and part,
they pair and quarrel, they suffer and resign themselves, in what
the authoress well calls an embroiled medium — say a kind of
birdlime — yet solidly and distinctly; and the illusion holds out. The
insignificant, like Fred Vincy, are made happy; the superior natures
suffer. If they prospered, there would be no story: who could write
a novel about the Brownings? George Eliot insists on making such
persons suffer, above all in marriage. "Retribution," said Lord Acton,
"is the constant theme and motive of her art." Lord Acton did
not exactly mean this in commendation; he held, himself, that
"virtue on earth is not much happier than crime." However that
may be, the retribution, in George Eliot's last two stories, is a
visitation upon matrimonial blindness or folly, and not on crime.
The folly of Dorothea in choosing Mr. Casaubon is not made quite
credible, and the immense pains taken in explaining it may betray
a certain sense of the difficulty. But once the fact is granted, we
foresee from the first the slow march of tragic disappointment. "No
one would ever know what she thought of a wedding journey to
Rome." The case is worse with Dr. Lydgate, who wishes to become
a second Bichat; it is worse, because his crampfish of a wife outlives
him; whereas Mr. Casaubon does die and makes room for Ladislaw.

The strain of these sombre histories is relieved by the picture of the minor households, and by the invaluable Mr. Brooke, one of George Eliot's most cheerful creations. . . . *Middlemarch* is a precious document for the provincial life of that time, vaguely astir with ideas, but promptly sinking back into its beehive routine.

Daniel Deronda (1876), which unsealed the lips of the scorner, shows misguidance rather than failure of power; but the book can easily be undervalued. It is duly blamed for its excess of dissertation and dissection; and, what is worse, there seems to be a wrong twist in the moral sympathies of the great moralist. Gwendolen Harleth is another victim of folly in marriage. Her pride and humbling, her agony of helpless hatred for her husband, are drawn with bitter strength; of all George Eliot's ladies she is the most alive. The authoress drops on her a load of brickbats, and seems to wish to leave the impression that Gwendolen deserves them. But then she does not deserve them. Her worst fault is to be handsome. She is young and rather hard, sprightly and rather domineering. We feel that she would have made better terms with the aristocratic boa-constrictor, Grandcourt. Some critics have hinted, with justice, that George Eliot's upbringing hardly qualified her to draw the Wicked *Blasé* Swell. But at all costs the young lady's moral nature must be awakened. She is almost as much tormented by her lay confessor, Deronda (who assures us that he is "not a priest"), as by her husband. She explains how a sudden, paralysing impulse (all too human) had kept her from throwing a rope to the drowning Grand-court. Deronda remarks that he would probably anyhow have sunk with the cramp; but he practically adds that Gwendolen must all the same treat herself as a murderess in heart and intention, and must flagellate her soul; which she duly does, and her life is broken for a time. As for the intent to murder, we know what the verdict of a French jury would have been; and it would be a more truly moral one than Deronda's. However, Grandcourt never really existed; how then, we may frivolously add, could he be murdered? One may yawn, laugh, or cry over the whole Judaic business in this novel; it has found few to praise it, in spite, as Sir Leslie Stephen pleasantly says, of "the approval of learned Jews." People have mocked at the enormous satisfaction shown by an English gentleman who finds out that he is a Jew: "Feelings had lately been at work within him which had very much modified the reluctance he would formerly have had to think of himself as probably a Jew." I would rather say that Deronda is not a Jew. He has no resemblance within or without, to a Jew good or bad. All Jews are salient; he is featureless. They love arguing, they are dialecticians even in the family circle; he preaches, no doubt with a certain taste for casuistry. His very ethics are occidental. The little boy Jacob and the thieving old sponger Lapidoth (*Schnorrer* is, I believe, the correct word) are much more satisfactory. George Eliot protested well against vulgar anti-Semitism; she studied, she appreciated, the loftier dreams of modern Israel; but she could not embody them. Yet it is not safe to leave the book unread. The old skill is there in the light sketches of the country gentry. The gambling scene at the outset makes us hope for an honest, full-blown romance; and some sound melodrama, some healthy violence, we do get in the scenes with Grandcourt's cast mistress and the fatal diamonds. It is singular to think of the inventress of these things enjoying walks and philosophic talks with the author of *Social Statics*. . . .

She well knew that the old Adam in us, whatever his failings, is quite a good judge of story and incident, and that these things he must have. Observation and analysis leave him unsatisfied, while admiring; he must have "moments," and crises, and violence: and he is right. George Eliot takes much care to meet his wishes, and her power to do so has often been overlooked. Critics have pointed out how the use and appreciation of crime in fiction, as a mainspring of the plot, marked the age of Dickens, Wilkie Collins, and Reade; how Dickens himself came to elaborate this interest more and more; and how even Trollope was deflected by the same impulse, from his task of portraying archdeacons. The fight in *Adam Bede*, suggested by Lewes, is sound, but brief and unprofessional. *Felix Holt* leads up to the well-arranged moment when the prosperous gentleman finds he is the unlawful son of a brutal attorney whom he has just whipped; and, catching sight of himself in a mirror, sees "the hated fatherhood asserted." There is a high melodramatic scene in *Silas Marner*, in the passage where Eppie chances on the discovery of the long-murdered body. The meetings of Tito and Baldassarre in *Romola* have a similar quality. Most of these climaxes are prepared in a workmanlike way. In *Middlemarch* the interest of crime passes into that of casuistry; the moral psychologist warms to her work, and certainly rivets the attention. Bulstrode, a banker known for charities and good works, formal, repellent, and a semiconscious Tartuffe, is blackmailed by a bad fellow, Raffles, who knows of Bulstrode's shady past, long since repented of. Raffles has delirium tremens, and Bulstrode watches him. Lydgate, the doctor, contrary to the old-fashioned medical views of the place, forbids Raffles to have alcohol. Bulstrode, after a struggle of conscience, does not "strive officially to keep alive" the patient; but on the contrary, lets the housekeeper give a dram to the patient, who duly dies. Lydgate, though surprised at the death, signs the certificate with little ado. It seems a weak point that he should never question the housekeeper. But the bailiffs were in Lydgate's house, and Bulstrode, on the eve of the crime, had unexpectedly lent him a thousand pounds, having before refused monetary aid. But all is in vain; the shady past comes out, there is a public scandal, and Bulstrode is wrecked. People, knowing of the loan, gossip about Lydgate's motives; and he, naturally, tortures himself with the question whether, but for the thousand pounds, he would not have been more inquisitive. I dwell on this episode, for it tells us much of George Eliot. She shows a real power of pinning down a moral problem; she has a lawyer's grasp of the facts and a psychologist's vision of the motives. She loves a self-deceiver, and also relishes Bulstrode's religious lingo. She loves still more to get into the mind of Lydgate, the half-innocent accessory. She cares more for these things than for the mystery or its detection; but her carpentry of the plot is excellent. Bulstrode, it is true, is not quite alive, but he is a carefully complicated puppet. The best scene of unregenerate passion is found in *The Mill on the Floss*. Old Mr. Tulliver, like a man in a saga, cares only for his vengeance, satisfies some of it on his deathbed, and instructs his son to be unforgiving. The pledge is recorded in the family Bible — the last touch of paganism in the transaction. The ferocity, like the pathos, of dull and puzzled minds is recorded with much force.

Indeed, stupidity plays a great part in the novels, and its presence on this earth is much insisted on. George Eliot's treatment of it varies, and may serve as one test of her powers as a humourist. She possibly becomes more acidulous as time goes on. . . . Her tolerant understanding sympathy with common people is a source of her power and of her humour. It is seen at its purest in the talk of Adam Bede's mother, or of the drinkers in the Rainbow at Raveloe. It has often been wondered where she picked this up, unless she was hidden, like the lady among the Free-masons, in the clock. A Westminster Reviewer is rarely a master, and still more rarely a mistress, of tavern talk. Yet we who have the freedom of the taproom could not report it so well. But this is one of the sleights of the craft. Given the genius and observing power, the stage setting can be managed at second-hand. George Eliot's boors drinking, her "Dutch interiors," may be a little short of spontaneous, but they are actual. She must have had a kindly relish for tinkers and potmen to begin with. She does not patronise them; she is like a queen who is easy-going with the people, but sharp and exacting with the court ladies. George Eliot is apt to be hard on the upper bourgeois, and Trollope's light unassuming way with his parsons and lawyers is really sounder than hers. But her satire is often excellent, and also her delineation of satiric persons, like the high-nosed, high-coloured Mrs. Cadwallader in *Midddlemarch*. Her true business, no doubt, is to transcribe the mother-wit of her Mrs. Poysers, or the prejudice of her Aunt Gleggs and Pullets. They are none the worse for the touch of caricature. Such personages come from the deeper stratum of her memories, out of the reach of her reading and theorising, and emerge in the generous light of pure comedy; which is blended, in such figures as Dolly Winthrop in *Silas Marner*, with pathos and humanity.

Of course George Eliot is melancholy. She is melancholy, not because she lacks the consolations of the accepted religion, for such persons are often the cheeriest of all; nor simply because she has a wide and tragic vision of the human lot. She is melancholy because of her painful, uneasy turn for analysis, because she hears what she calls, in a noted phrase, "the roar that lies on the other side of silence"; that is, the minute, unspoken play of motive that lies behind an ordinary conversation; and also the sorrows or bewilderments of simple inarticulate persons, like Hetty Sorrel. And for this kind of analysis she has a genius: a heavy, German, relentless sort of genius, but still a genius. It is seen also in her irony and humour. In *Daniel Deronda* there are two whole pages in which the talk is thus punctuated: Grandcourt says to Gwendolen Harleth:

"You would perhaps like tiger-hunting or pig-sticking. I saw some of that for a season or two in the East. Everything here is poor stuff after that."

"*You* are fond of danger, then?"

(Pause, wherein Gwendolen speculated on the probability that the men of coldest manners were the most adventurous, and felt the strength of her own insight, supposing the question had to be decided.)

"One must have something or other. But one gets used to it."

"I begin to think I am very fortunate, because everything is new to me: it is only that I can't get enough of it. I am not used to anything except being dull, which I should like to leave off as you have left off shooting."

(Pause, during which it occurred to Gwendolen that a man of cold and distinguished manners might possibly be a dull companion; but on the other hand she thought that most persons were dull, that she had not observed husbands to be companions — and after all she was not going to accept Grandcourt.)

And so on; it is all most workmanlike, granted the characters. The man may be an unreal stick, but the girl is natural enough. The weight of the irony cannot be denied; but O, shade of Voltaire!

O, light-handed Jane Austen! George Eliot uses this method for serious, for pathetic, even for dreadful matter, and uses it with signal power. But we feel instinctively that there is something wrong with the method, and not merely with the style. If you apply to life a microscope of too high a power, you will see life wrong. When the lens is directed upon a woman, the male mind (I will speak for no other) recoils, much as Gulliver did from the maids of honour in Brobdingnag: "their skins appeared so coarse and uneven, so variously coloured when I saw them near, with a mole here and there as broad as a trencher, etc." We by no means object (to change the figure) to hearing the bitter truth; but let it be at the right distance for hearing distinctly. Here George Eliot is sometimes oppressive.

But her art cannot be separated from her ethical habit of mind. I have mentioned her passion for making studies in retribution. This may have been rooted in her Calvinistic training; the crude doctrine of necessity was also preached, untheologically, by her friends at Coventry. But there was also, newly in the air, the scientific conception of law and order, as extended to the world of character. This conception, secular and rationalistic, transforms the visitations of God into the self-acting law of moral consequence, or *Karma*, in the human soul. It is a law that may be signally unjust, indeed not moral at all. The innocent suffer with the guilty, and the guilt itself may be mere blindness. The sin of Tito is that of Judas, namely, the betrayal of benefactors; the fault of Mrs. Transome is youthful impulse; the error of Gwendolen is little more than inexperience. Some at least of these personages are scourged out of all proportion. It may seem that in such a lowering picture the chance of lucky escapes hardly receives its due weight. The atmosphere, however, is relieved by flashes of ordinary or of unusual goodness. This suggests another way in which George Eliot's philosophy affects her representations.

Her notions of charity and well-doing, and the quality of her sympathy, are different from those of Dickens. They are less easy and buoyant altogether, and they are part of her creed and her self-discipline. She had herself a more than common hunger for sympathy and kindness; she made a religion of kindness — of the need of getting outside the *ego*. The Positivist cult attracted her closely, and though she never became a professed member of the body, its tenets coloured her vision of the world. For the world being a grim place full of traps, and ready to avenge the least false moral step, some sort of loop-hole, some ground for hope, is imperiously wanted. George Eliot finds it in "morality touched by emotion"; in the practice of sympathetic perception, painfully

sharpened till it can detect the most silent and humble suffering, or
the oddest and proudest distress. Sometimes this temper is exhibited
with peculiar intensity. . . . If we think that the tension of such a
mood is excessive, it is best to remember that George Eliot is
a woman, and that her sensibility is true to the better habit of her
sex, even if it will not do for our rougher one. Some of her
chapters may strike us as less like food than like medicine. But then
most people are never likely to take an overdose of it. Most people
are the better for a little of it; and let them try it, and profit; and
then let them go and play, let them return to Scott and Dumas and
gaiety and the highways of the world. Looking back, they will
admit that they have visited, not merely an anxious physician, but
a rare spirit, and also an artist — not a flawless or quite disinterested
artist, but an artist still.

The two sides of George Eliot's talent, the more and the less
spontaneous, are reflected in her style. Often we exclaim that every
one in her books talks well except the author. She is surest of her
diction when she is some one else. The chorus is not so good as the
characters — a frequent phenomenon in fiction. Every one deplored
the increase of ponderous abstract English in her later stories; but
this criticism applies, if we look closer, chiefly to the commentary
and not to the dialogue. Where the latter is at fault, it is not on
the score of diction, except when the speaker is himself markedly
unreal. . . . Her descriptive style, at any rate up to the date of
Romola, is signally pure. The things seen and heard are drawn from
the memories of her youth in the country, and from her untrammelled
sense of beauty. *The Mill on the Floss* is full of such writing, as
every one knows; and the cadence, correspondingly, is simple and
happy, and scans well. . . .

This limpid English does not disappear in the later stories, though
it tends to be thrust out. The picture of the country house where
Deronda is brought up, and the rare glimpses of Middlemarch
scenery "under the quiet light of a sky marbled with high clouds,"
have the same kind of excellence. And if the chorus tends to
become heavier, the dialogue is always liable to remain good. Mr.
Raffles and the Garth family talk as naturally as Trollope's people.
And whatever may be said against George Eliot, there is a strong
mind at the back of all that she may write. Frequently her strength
gets in her way, and therefore in ours. It may not make for lightness.
But it is equal even to denying itself, and it is wonderful, when her
humour comes uppermost, how sterling it can be, and how easy
its language. . . .

But George Eliot's language also claims to be judged when she is taxing it to the utmost, for solemn or passionate situations. Here, no doubt, it is more uncertain, and its possibilities of weakness have been sufficiently hinted. But she can excel in one specially difficult and risky kind of writing. She has a singular fondness for scenes that may be called confessional; where some slight or limited personage, or as she would say "nature," is swept away and spiritualised, if only for a moment, by a stronger and fuller one. This subject recurs again and again. The interview in prison between Dinah Morris and Hetty was suggested by a real event, and here the dialect is evangelical. But it becomes purely human and secular in the appeals made by Felix Holt to Esther Lyon, or by Dorothea to Rosamond Lydgate. It is none the less impressive. We may not much like the speaker; but the dramatic truth and energy, and the mastery of the right words where a word wrong would be disaster, are undeniable. This is but one of the reasons why George Eliot's work, when all is said, stands so firmly. She is considered, and sometimes is, more laborious than inspired; but she herself knew when the mysterious powers were at play. . . .

Lord David Cecil

George Eliot

. . . George Eliot, though she was a thinker, was not a particularly original thinker. And her conception of life was that held by the dominant school of thought in "advanced" circles of her day. She was a thoroughgoing Victorian rationalist. She was not religious: the progress of thought and discovery to her made it impossible to believe in the supernatural; she had given up the Puritan theology of her childhood. But the moral code founded on that Puritan theology had soaked itself too deeply into the fiber of her thought and feeling for her to give it up as well. . . .

Nor did she think man was excused for his failure to follow the right code by the removal of its supernatural sanction. The second

Reprinted from David Cecil, *Early Victorian Novelists: Essays in Revaluation*, Bobbs-Merrill Co., Indianapolis and New York, [1935], pp. 309–336, by permission of Bobbs-Merrill Co. and Constable and Co., Ltd. Copyright 1935 by Bobbs-Merrill Co., Inc.; 1962 by Lord David Cecil.

fundamental in her philosophy is a belief in free will. She thought every man's character was in his own hands to mold into the right shape or the wrong; and she thought that all his strength should be put forward to mold it right. Matthew Arnold thought that conduct was three-fourths of life; George Eliot went further, she thought it was four-fourths. Activities were right in so far as they assisted you to be good, they were wrong in so far as they prevented you. And such activities as were neither right nor wrong, were frivolous, unworthy of the attention of a serious person.

Finally she believed that her code was justified by results. The third fundamental of her philosophy is a conviction that life is just. She was sure that those who live a virtuous life are essentially contented, that those who live a vicious are essentially discontented. However well-meaning you might be or however lucky, she was sure that you cannot escape the consequences of your own actions; that your sins find you out, that the slightest slip will be visited on you, if not immediately then later.

It is in the light of these views that George Eliot constructs her novels. The "ideas" which are their germ are all moral ideas; the conflicts which are the mainspring of their action are always moral conflicts. They divide themselves into two classes. In some, "Janet's Repentance," *Adam Bede, Silas Marner,* the moral course is clear. The characters are in a position to do what they think right, only they are tempted to do something wrong instead; and the conflict turns on the struggle between their principles and their weaknesses. . . . In *The Mill on the Floss* George Eliot confronts another problem. How should one act if one wants to do right but cannot find a satisfactory method of doing it? Maggie Tulliver thirsts after righteousness, but she finds no way to satisfy her thirst in the materialist provincial world in which she lives; and such efforts as she makes only result in annoying everyone around her. Part of *Middlemarch* is concerned with a similar theme. Dorothea Brooke wants to live a life of self-sacrifice for the good of others, but she cannot find scope for it in humdrum Middlemarch. However *Middlemarch,* George Eliot's masterpiece, has a bigger subject, the biggest subject of any English classical novel. Like Tolstoy in *War and Peace,* she shows us the cosmic process, not just in a single drama but in several; not only in an individual but in a whole society. The principles of moral strength and weakness which in her view are the determining forces of life, exhibit themselves at their work in the lives of four diverse and typical representatives of the human race. . . .

George Eliot's serious characters, then, are envisaged exclusively in their moral aspect. They are portraits of the inner man, but portraits not designed like Charlotte Brontë's to exhibit the color of his temperament, but the principles of his conduct — his besetting sin, his presiding virtue. Such a portrait inevitably omits many of those aspects of a man — his manner, his mood, his face — which make living most of the great figures of fiction. All the same, George Eliot's concentration on the moral side of human nature is the chief source of her peculiar glory, the kernel of her precious unique contribution to our literature. Her imagination is not a distorting glass like Dickens', vitalizing her figures by accentuating their personal idiosyncrasies, nor is it, like Charlotte Brontë's, a painted window suffusing them with the color of her own live temperament; it is an X-ray, bringing them to life by the clearness with which she penetrates to the secret mainspring of their actions.

Once more it is her intellect which is the source of her success. Her power of drawing conclusions gave her a naturally sharp eye for symptoms of moral strength and weakness, taught her to discern them in all their varying modes of expression in well-brought-up girls, in men of the world, a poor weaver, a lusty young man, to note that Doctor Lydgate did not take trouble with an ugly woman, that Hetty Sorrel always avoided being left to look after the children. She could also distinguish between different varieties of the same characteristic; see how Dorothea's sense of duty differed from Mary Garth's, Godfrey Cass's self-indulgence from that of Arthur Donnithorne. And she took advantage of her observation. She traced these expressions of virtue and weakness to their original source in the character, discovered the spark of nobility, the streak of weakness which are their origin. Finally her disciplined generalizing intelligence taught her to see the significance of her discoveries. Having analyzed a character into its elements, she was able to distinguish their relative force and position. She could deduce its central principle so that, however complex and inconsistent it might appear, she saw it as a unity. It is this grasp of psychological essentials which gives her characters their reality. We may not *see* Godfrey Cass as we *see* Pickwick, but we understand him. We get behind the clock face and see the works, locate the mainspring, discover how it makes the wheels turn. We know just how he will behave and why; we know exactly what special mixture of common human ingredients makes him act differently from other people.

This clear-sighted vision of the essentials of character gives George Eliot certain advantages over the other Victorians. For one thing it means that her characters, unlike theirs, are always consistent. . . . George Eliot's characters act inevitably, under the irresistible force of their directing principle: so that they are always true to themselves. Through every change of fortune, every variety of circumstance, they remain the same clear recognizable individual moral entities.

But it is not only in this consistency that George Eliot's intellectual understanding of her characters gives her an advantage over the other Victorians. It also enables her to describe aspects of human nature which they cannot. It gives her the power which won her the admiration of Proust, the power to describe successfully how a character develops. This is very rare among novelists. When they want to describe a good man going to the bad, for instance, they generally cut him into two; we are shown a good man in the first part of the book, and a bad man in the second. But they do not seem the same man. We have seen nothing in the first to lead us to understand how he becomes the second. In their efforts to show the change that overtook him, they forget to maintain those constant characteristics which keep him one person. Not so George Eliot. For her perception of these characteristics is the root of her whole conception. Lydgate, on his first appearance in *Middlemarch*, is an enthusiastic and disinterested young doctor, only intent on extending the boundaries of knowledge and with a scorn for the worldly prizes that his profession might enable him to gain. At the end he is a fashionable physician with no interest in discovery, content only to maintain a prosperous practice. George Eliot portrays the evidences of this change with extraordinary acuteness of observation. We see how it has lowered his spirits, slackened his scruples, embittered his tongue. But for all that he is so altered, we recognize him as the same Lydgate as we saw at first; nor do we find the change inexplicable. For, from his entry on the scene, we have been made aware of the weak spot in Lydgate's character, his dislike of doing something disagreeable to himself, and we can see that in difficult circumstances this weakness will render impotent his strongest ambitions. Moreover, George Eliot knows just how to show how this is most likely to have happened. The situations in which she has involved Lydgate are precisely those most likely to find out his weakness; and she can exhibit exactly the mode by which, step by step, he gives way to it, readjusts his principles to suit his practice, till imperceptibly he is transformed to the man of his final phase. . . .

Again, George Eliot's grip on psychological essentials enables her to draw complex characters better than her predecessors. Novelists who draw from the outside like Trollope have no difficulty in making a simple character convincing; for the reader has only to see its outside clearly to be able to deduce its elements for himself. But when they come to a complex character they fail; for the outer manifestations of such a character are so inconsistent that unless the reader is given some key to them he simply does not feel that they are expressions of the same person. He cannot understand what sort of woman Lady Ongar is, when her actions seem to contradict one another so sharply. George Eliot's peculiar power makes her able to surmount this difficulty. Drawing from the inside out, starting with the central principle of the character, she is able to show how it reveals itself in the most apparently inconsistent manifestations, can give to the most vari-colored surface of character that prevalent tone which marks it as the expression of one personality. Her characters always hang together, are of a piece, their defects are the defects of their virtues. . . . George Eliot can follow the windings of motive through the most tortuous labyrinths, for firmly grasped in her hand is always the central clue.

Her power to describe mixed characters extends to mixed states of mind. Indeed, the field of her most characteristic triumphs is the moral battle-field. Her eagle eye can penetrate through all the shock and the smoke of struggle, to elucidate the position of the forces concerned, reveal the trend of their action. We are shown exactly how the forces of temptation deploy themselves for the attack, how those of conscience rally to resistance, the ins and outs of their conflict, how inevitably in the given circumstances one or the other triumphs. She is particularly good at showing how temptation triumphs. No other English novelist has given us so vivid a picture of the process of moral defeat, the gradual steps by which Mr. Bulstrode is brought to further Raffles' death, Arthur Donnithorne's gradual yielding to his passion for Hetty, Maggie Tulliver's to hers for Stephen Guest. With an inexorable clearness she reveals how temptation insinuates itself into the mind, how it retreats at the first suspicious movement of conscience, how it comes back disguised, and how, if once more vanquished, it will sham death only to arise suddenly and sweep its victim away on a single irresistible gust of desire when he is off his guard. With an extraordinary subtlety she describes Arthur Donnithorne's yielding to his desire to meet Hetty once more: how he conceals his true object even from himself by pretending that he does it only to say farewell, persuades himself that he will be committing an act of gratuitous cruelty if he refuses to see Hetty; or how Maggie's passion for Stephen steals into her inexperienced mind, imperceptibly, so that she only realizes it when it has become such an obsession that she is unable to see it in its true proportions. Alone in her room she can make the strongest resolutions, but when Stephen appears the violence of her desire so overwhelms her that she cannot see her conduct in perspective at all. She lives only in the present, and in the present she is only conscious that she is happy and must at all costs prolong her happiness. With equal insight George Eliot can portray the moral chaos that takes possession of the mind after wrong has been done. She exposes all the complex writhings of a spirit striving to make itself at ease on the bed of a disturbed conscience, the desperate casuistry by which it attempts to justify itself, its inexhaustible ingenuity in blinding itself to unpleasant facts, the baseless hopes it conjures up for its comfort; she can distinguish precisely how different an act looks before it is done, shrouded in the softening darkness of the secret heart, and after, exposed in all its naked ugliness to the harsh daylight of other people's judgment. Arthur Donnithorne is left to contemplate his conduct toward Hetty after he has realized that Adam Bede has got to know something of it. [A long passage from Ch. 29 follows.]

With what certain penetration does George Eliot in this picture isolate and detect the various warring elements in Arthur's mind, his genuine compunction, his horror of being disapproved of, his instinctive resentment at disapproval, however justifiable, his inextinguishable hope that things will come right in the end, his irrational conviction that with him at least, things always must come right. One grows quite uncomfortable as one watches so merciless, so delicate an exposure of human weakness. The truth it embodies is universal. In exposing Arthur Donnithorne, she also exposes her reader.

This insight into the moral consciousness makes George Eliot's picture of human nature far more homogeneous than that of a writer like Dickens. She divides the world into saints and sinners quite as definitely as he does. But her sinners are not made of a different clay from her saints. They are for the most part amiable, well-intentioned people who mean to be good, just as much as the saints do; only they have not the same strength of mind, there is a flaw in the metal of their virtue. And in difficult circumstances this flaw leads them into error, even into crime.

Arthur Donnithorne is a young man, and George Eliot is a woman. It is worth noting that she is one of the few women novelists whose great characters include young men. Once again this is due to her intellectual approach. Instinctive writers create from their impressions of life; and a woman's impression of a man's life is, as a rule, necessarily a scrappy one. However clearly she may see him, she sees him only as he appears from time to time in female society. But George Eliot draws not from instinct but mind, not from impression but knowledge. So that the fact she has herself seen little of a man's life does not incapacitate her from drawing it. Over her official heroes, indeed, her hand did falter. All her learning and her conscientious impartiality could not make her wholly immune from the frailties of her sex; like every woman novelist she tends to draw heroes less from life, than in the image of her desire. Adam Bede is a little too manly and protecting to be human; Ladislaw, flinging himself down on the hearth-rug with an enchanting impetuosity, wilfully tossing back his charming curls, is a schoolgirl's dream, and a vulgar dream at that. But when George Eliot's emotions are not involved, when Lydgate or Donnithorne or Godfrey Cass are her subjects, her portrait is as convincing and foursquare and well found as any in her gallery.

It is in the treatment of character that George Eliot's more active intellect gives her her most conspicuous advantage over the typical Victorians. But in two other respects her work is a pleasant contrast to theirs. Her level of merit is far more consistently maintained. . . . With her greater consistency goes a greater command of form. Dickens' form or Charlotte Brontë's is imperfect because it is no part of their inspiration, it is a mere make-shift frame-work to hold their inspiration together; and as often as not it holds it together very badly. Inessential characters and scenes bulge over its edges, deforming its symmetry, concealing its intention. But George Eliot's structure is the very substance of her primary conception. She begins with her situation; her characters and scenes are developed from it. Each has its part to play in her general purpose and none is permitted to play more than this part. No minor character swells to gigantic proportions in George Eliot's novels, dwarfing the principals, her most memorable scenes are always turning points in the action. All is co-ordinated, all is proportion, all is tidy. For her books are as better organized than Charlotte Brontë's, as the material of which they are composed is larger.

Yet she is not admired so much as Charlotte Brontë; she is not even admired so much as Trollope. In spite of the variety of her talents and the width of her scope, in spite of the fact that she is the only novelist of her time who writes on the scale of the great continental novelists, the only novelist who holds the same conception of her art which is held today, her reputation has sustained a more catastrophic slump than that of any of her contemporaries. It is not just that she is not read, that her books stand on the shelves unopened. If people do read her they do not enjoy her. It certainly is odd. All the same it is explicable. The temper of our time has somthing to do with it. For though she is nearer to us in form and subject than the other Victorians, in point of view she is quite as distant. Indeed, we find her point of view even more alien. This is natural enough. An exclusively moral point of view is, at any time, a bleak and unsatisfying affair. Life is altogether too complex and masterful and mysterious to be ordered into tidy little compartments of right and wrong; and any attempt so to order it inevitably leaves a good deal outside that is both interesting and delightful. Moreover, George Eliot's compartments are conspicuously inadequate ones. The virtues of her admiration, industry, self-restraint, conscientiousness, are drab, negative sort of virtues; they are school-teachers' virtues. George Eliot does confront human nature a little like a school-teacher; kindly but just, calm but censorious, with birchrod in hand to use as she thinks right, and lists of good and bad conduct marks pinned neatly to her desk. And when we see all the vivid disorderly vitality of human nature ranged before her for carefully measured approval or condemnation, we tend to feel rebellious and resentful. . . .

George Eliot's imagination had to scrape what nourishment it could from the bare bones of Puritan ethics; her narrow way led beneath a dull sky into darkness; she had to persuade herself that a life of self-denial was sufficiently rewarded by the consciousness of virtue. In theory she managed to do this satisfactorily enough; but she was too clear-sighted and too honest not to find it difficult to feel a lively conviction of it, in practice. Even in the stories of her ardent youth, she does not paint the satisfactions of a good conscience in very glowing colors. And when in *Middlemarch* she turned to survey the spectacle of human life in the harsh disillusioning light of mature experience, she clearly found it all she could do to believe that a good conscience was much satisfaction at all. She would not admit this. Desperately she reiterates the articles of her creed, anxiously tries to convince us that Dorothea's unselfish devotion to husband and children made up for her failure to realize her youthful dreams. But she does not even convince herself. Do what she will, she cannot disguise the fact that the thought of Dorothea's life leaves her disappointed, disheartened and depressed. And she communicates her depression to her readers.

Still, George Eliot's point of view should not put us off her books. To let it do so indeed is to fall into her error, to judge things by too exclusively moral a standard. A book is not good in proportion as its moral standard is a right one. . . . All the same George Eliot's loss of reputation is not wholly undeserved. Even if we do strain ourselves to acquiesce in her point of view, we do not feel her the supreme novelist that her contemporaries did. Her books never give us that intense unalloyed pleasure we get from the greatest masters. Though like Tolstoy she is an interesting critic of life, though she constructs well like Jane Austen, though like Dickens she creates a world, yet when we set her achievement in any of these lines beside those of these famous competitors, we feel something lacking. Somehow we are dissatisfied.

It is easy to see why she fails to stand a comparison with Tolstoy. Her vision of life is smaller. She knows about life in provincial nineteenth-century England, life in Middlemarch, the life of merchants and doctors and squires and humble clergymen and small town politicians; she does not know about the savage or sophisticated, about artists and adventurers and the world of fashion and affairs. Even in *Middlemarch*, there are certain things she does not see. Her assiduously intellectual view made her oblivious of the irrational instinctive aspects of human nature. She can enter into its deliberate purposes and its conscientious scruples, but not into its caprices, its passions, its mysticism. . . . Moreover, like all Victorian rationalists, she is a Philistine. She pays lip-service to art, but like Dorothea Brooke confronted with the statues of the Vatican, she does not really see why people set such a value on it. Constructed within so confined an area of vision, it is inevitable that her criticism of life is inadequate. Compared to Tolstoy's it seems petty, drab, provincial. *Middlemarch* may be the nearest English equivalent to *War and Peace*, but it is a provincial sort of *War and Peace*.

It is also easy to see why her form does not satisfy us as Jane Austen's does. Life is chaotic, art is orderly. The novelist's problem is to evolve an orderly composition which is also a convincing picture of life. It is Jane Austen's triumph that she solves this problem perfectly, fully satisfies the rival claims of life and art. Now George Eliot does not. She sacrifices life to art. Her plots seem too neat and symmetrical to be true. We do not feel them to have grown naturally from their situation like a flower, but to have been put together deliberately and calculatedly like a building. For, in spite of her determination that her story should develop logically, she has not that highest formal faculty which makes development appear inevitable, she has to twist facts to make them fit her purpose. For instance, it is an essential part of her design that Godfrey Cass's marriage should not turn out perfectly happy. For it was only made possible by an act of moral weakness on his part: and her object is to show that such acts always bring their punishment. It should have been quite easy for her to make this seem inevitable. The same weakness that inspired Godfrey's act might have alienated his wife; or his mind might have been poisoned by remorse. But George Eliot vindicates the moral law by making him childless. This is not in the least an inevitable consequence of his act. There is no inherent reason in the nature of things why a morally feeble man should not beget twenty children. In consequence we feel Godfrey's discontent to be no inevitable expression of the moral law, but a gratuitous piece of poetic justice imposed on him by the arbitrary will of his creator. Again, the marriage between Dinah and Adam, which provides the happy ending for *Adam Bede*, does not strike us as inevitable; indeed what we have learned of Adam's taste in women leads us to think it very unlikely. But the moral purpose which directs the story demands that Adam and Dinah, the two virtuous characters in the book, should be adequately rewarded for their virtue. And marrying them to each other seems the handiest reward in the circumstances. In order to achieve structural symmetry George Eliot has been forced to relax her vigilant grip on truth.

However, she might have constructed badly and criticized life inadequately and yet have been as satisfying an author as Dickens. He constructed much worse, and only offered us the most rudimentary criticism of life. Yet she is not as satisfying as he is. For she is as inferior to him in his distinguishing quality as she is to Tolstoy and Jane Austen in theirs: she is inferior to him in creative imagination. She had one, as we have seen. But, like Trollope's, it was a relatively mild imagination; it does not unite with its subject to generate the highest intensity of aesthetic life. So that when its creations are set beside those of a white-hot imagination like Dickens's, they look pale and lifeless. Her settings, for instance, are as substantial as his and as individual. No other English novelist has revealed the English countryside in the light of its past. But her imagination is not powerful enough to make this light a very vivid one. Compared with Dickens' London, George Eliot's Warwickshire shows a little devitalized — not a first-hand painting but a careful colored engraving.

Her characters, again, are more variously conceived than his, more consistently constructed and observed more accurately. Lydgate is far more like a real man than Mr. Micawber: we know much more about him; he never acts, as Mr. Micawber does, out of character. But — he is not so alive. Beside Micawber he looks wooden, static, inanimate. For no aspect of his nature, not even that moral aspect where George Eliot's genius shows itself at its most concentrated, is informed by the highest creative vitality. Or, compare Dorothea Brooke with Elena in Turgenev's *On the Eve*. It is an illuminating comparison. For, national differences apart, they are almost the same character; each is a young girl, noble, romantic, passionate, austere, intolerant of triviality and frivolity, possessed by the desire to sacrifice herself to some altruistic ideal. George Eliot stands the comparison much better than might be expected. Dorothea is as substantial and convincing a character as Elena. Her every side is as clearly apprehended. But she is not so individual, she lacks Elena's unmistakable personal flavor; for, though George Eliot has assembled the elements of her character, she has not been able to fire them with that Promethean spark which fuses them together in the substance of a single personality. It is significant that the inhabitants of George Eliot's world, with the exception of her comic characters, are most real to us when they are not talking. George Eliot's analysis of Maggie Tulliver and Dorothea clearly defines the difference between them.

But separate two passages of their conversation from their context, and who shall tell which is speaking? And though in analysis they are individual, even there they are not alive in the intensest sense. They are bodies laid out in the dissecting-room, not moving flesh-and-blood human beings. They never seem, as the greatest figures in fiction do, to have got free from their creators, and to be acting and speaking of their own volition. Behind the puppets we always see the shadow of the puppet master manipulating the strings.

Indeed — and here we come to the root cause of her failure to attain that supreme rank to which she aspired — there was something second-rate in the essential quality of George Eliot's inspiration. Her genius was built on the same grand scale as that of the greatest novelists; but it was not, as theirs was, compounded of the best material. She had more talents than most writers; but they were none of them of the finest caliber. So that though she seeks success in so many fields — and never wholly fails to find it — in none, even at her best, does she reach the level of the masterpieces in that particular kind.

Still, this is not enough to account for the peculiar feeling of dis-satisfaction that her books give us. Trollope had a second-rate talent, and, within his limitations, he is perfectly satisfying. . . . Her imagi-nation was quite wide enough to cover the ground explored by a domestic novel like *Doctor Thorne*. But it was not wide enough to cover the ground needed for an adequate criticism of life. And her intellect spurred her to attempt such criticism. Again, her sense of form was quite strong enough to have achieved success on the lines of an ordinary conventional plot. It was not strong enough to carry through an action only conditioned by the logical development of the situation. And her intellect inspired her to try such an action. Finally, her intellect tended to reduce such imaginative vitality as she had. For all that Trollope's imagination was as weak as hers, he does now and again achieve a greater intensity of creative life, be-cause he lets it have its head. George Eliot could not let her imagi-nation have its head. Her intellect was always at its side, tugging at the reins, diverting it from its course, weighing it down with a great load of analytic comment.

Yet we cannot regret her intellect. For it is the source of her most original characters and her most memorable passages. In it is en-gendered that penetration into the moral nature of man, which is her peculiar contribution to our literature. No, the truth is that there was a congenital disproportion in the original composition of George Eliot's talent. It had two sides, intellectual and imaginative. And they were inextricably connected. The intellect was the engine which started the machinery of the imagination working. But the engine was too powerful for the machine: it kept it at a strain at which it could not run smoothly and easily. So that it never produced a wholly satisfactory work of art.

All the same, her achievement is a considerable one, more considerable than that of many more accomplished writers. *Middlemarch* may never give us the same feeling of unalloyed pleasure as *Wives and Daughters* does, but rouses far deeper emotions, sets the mind far more seriously astir. For though she was not a supreme artist, George Eliot was not a minor one; laboriously but surely her insight, her integrity, her sad, mature wisdom, lifted her to the region of major art. When all is said and done she is a great writer; no unworthy heir of Thackeray and Dickens, no unworthy forerunner of Hardy and Henry James. She stands at the gateway between the old novel and the new, a massive caryatid, heavy of countenance, uneasy of attitude; but noble, monumental, profoundly impressive.

V. S. Pritchett

George Eliot

Two of George Eliot's novels, it seems to me, will have a permanent place in English literature. As time goes by *Adam Bede* looks like our supreme novel of pastoral life; and I cannot see any novel of the nineteenth century that surpasses *Middlemarch* in range or construction. . . . No Victorian novel approaches *Middlemarch* in its width of reference, its intellectual power, or the imperturbable spaciousness of its narrative. It is sometimes argued by critics of contemporary literature that a return to Christianity is indispensable if we are to produce novels of the Victorian scale and authority, or indeed novels of any quality at all; but there are the novels of unbelievers like George Eliot and Hardy to discountenance them. The fact is that a wide and single purpose in the mind is the chief requirement outside of talent; a strong belief, a strong unbelief, even a strong egoism will produce works of the first order. If she had any religious leanings, George Eliot moved toward Judaism because of its stress on law; and

Reprinted from V. S. Pritchett, *The Living Novel*, Reynal & Hitchcock, New York, [1947], pp. 91–102, by permission of the author.

if we think this preference purely intellectual and regard worry, that profoundly English habit of mind, as her philosophy, the point is that it was strong, serious, comprehensive worry. A forerunner of the psychologists, she promises no heaven and threatens no hell; the best and the worst we shall get is Warwickshire. Her world is the world of will, the smithy of character, a place of knowledge and judgments. So, in the sense of worldly wisdom, is Miss Austen's. But what a difference there is. To repeat our earlier definition, if Miss Austen is the novelist of the ego and its platitudes, George Eliot is the novelist of the idolatries of the super-ego.

We find in a book like *Middlemarch*, not character modified by circumstance only, but character first impelled and then modified by the beliefs, the ambitions, the spiritual objects which it assimilates. Lydgate's schemes for medical reform and his place in medical science are as much a part of his character as his way with the ladies. And George Eliot read up her medical history in order to get his position exactly right. Dorothea's yearning for a higher life of greater usefulness to mankind will stay with her all her days and will make her a remarkable but exasperating woman; a fool for all her cleverness. George Eliot gives equal weight to these important qualifications. Many Victorian novelists have lectured us on the careers and aspirations of their people; none, before George Eliot, showed us the unity of intellect, aspiration and nature in action. Her judgment on Lydgate as a doctor is a judgment on his fate as a man:

> He carried to his studies in London, Edinburgh, and Paris the conviction that the medical profession as it might be was the finest in the world; presenting the most perfect interchange between science and art; offering the most direct alliance between intellectual conquest and the social good. Lydgate's nature demanded this combination: he was an emotional creature, with a flesh-and-blood sense of fellowship which withstood all the abstractions of special study. He cared not only for "cases," but for John and Elizabeth, especially Elizabeth.

The Elizabeth, who was not indeed to wreck Lydgate's life, but (with far more probability) to corrupt his ideals and turn him into the smart practitioner, was Rosamond, his wife. Yet, in its own way, Rosamond's super-ego had the most distinguished ideals. A provincial manufacturer's daughter, she too longed idealistically to rise; the desire was not vulgar until she supposed that freedom from crude middle-class notions of taste and bearing could only be obtained by marriage to the cousin of a baronet; and was not immoral until she made her husband's conscience pay for her ambitions. The fountain, George Eliot is always telling us, cannot rise higher than its source.

Such analyses of character have become commonplace to us. When one compares the respectable Rosamond Lydgate with, say, Becky Sharp, one sees that Rosamond is not unique. Where *Middlemarch* is unique in its time is in George Eliot's power of generalization. The last thing one accuses her of is unthinking acceptance of convention. She seeks, in her morality, the positive foundation of natural law, a kind of Fate whose measures are as fundamental as the changes of the seasons in nature. Her intellect is sculptural. The clumsiness of style does not denote muddle, but an attempt to carve decisively. We feel the clarifying force of a powerful mind. Perhaps it is not naturally powerful. The power may have been acquired. There are two George Eliots: the mature, experienced, quiet-humored Midlander who wrote the childhood pages of *The Mill on the Floss;* and the naïve, earnest and masterly intellectual with her half-dozen languages and her scholarship. But unlike the irony of our time, hers is at the expense not of belief, but of people. Behind them, awful but inescapable to the eye of conscience, loom the statues of what they ought to have been. Hers is a mind that has grown by making judgments — as Mr. Gladstone's head was said to have grown by making speeches.

Middlemarch resumes the observation and experience of a lifetime. Until this book George Eliot often strains after things beyond her capacity, as Dorothea Casaubon strained after a spiritual power beyond her nature. But now in *Middlemarch* the novelist is reconciled to her experience. In Mr. Casaubon George Eliot sees that tragedy may paralyze the very intellect which was to be Dorothea's emancipation. Much of herself (George Eliot said, when she was accused of portraying Mark Pattison) went into Casaubon, and I can think of no other English novel before or since which has so truthfully, so sympathetically and so intimately described the befogged and grandiose humiliations of the scholar, as he turns at bay before the vengeance of life. Casaubon's jealousy is unforgettable, because, poisonous though it is, it is not the screech of an elderly cuckold, but the voice of strangled nature calling for justice. And notice, here, something very characteristic; George Eliot's pity flows from her moral sense, from the very seat of justice, and not from a sentimental heart.

Middlemarch is the first of many novels about groups of people in provincial towns. They are differentiated from each other not by class or fortune only, but by their moral history, and this moral differentiation is not casual, it is planned and has its own inner hierarchy. Look at the groups. Dorothea, Casaubon and Ladislaw seek to enter the highest spiritual fields — not perhaps the highest, for us, because, as we have seen, the world of George Eliot's imagination was prosaic and not poetic — still, they desire, in their several ways, to influence the standards of mankind. There is Lydgate, who is devoted to science and expects to be rewarded by a career. He and his wife are practical people, who seek power. The pharisaical Bulstrode, the banker, expects to rise both spiritually and financially at once, until he sits on the right hand of God, the Father; a businessman with a bad conscience, he is the father of the Buchmanites and of all success-religions. The Garths, being country people and outside all this urban world, believe simply in the virtue of work as a natural law and they are brought up against Fred Vincy, Rosamond's brother. He, as a horsey young man educated beyond his means, has a cheerful belief in irresponsible Style and in himself as a thing of pure male beauty with a riding crop. We may not accept George Eliot's standards, but we can see that they are not conventional, and that they do not make her one-sided. She is most intimately sympathetic to human beings and is never sloppy about them. When Vincy quarrels with Bulstrode about Fred's debts, when Casaubon's jealousy of Ladislaw secretes its first venom, when Lydgate tries vainly to talk about money to his wife or Fred goes to his mad old uncle for a loan, vital human issues are raised. The great scenes of *Middlemarch* are exquisite, living transpositions of real moral dilemmas. Questions of principle are questions of battle; they point the weapons of the human comedy, and battle is not dull. In consequence, George Eliot's beliefs are rarely boring, because they are a dynamism. They correspond to psychological and social realities, though more especially (on the large scale) to the functions of the will; they are boring only when, in the Victorian habit, she harangues the reader and pads out the book with brainy essays.

I see I have been writing about *Middlemarch* as though it was a piece of engineering. What about the life, the humor, the pleasure? There are failures: Dorothea and Ladislaw do not escape the fate of so many Victorian heroes and heroines who are frozen by their creator's high-mindedness. Has George Eliot forgotten how much these two difficult, sensitive and proud people will annoy each other by the stupidity which so frequently afflicts the intellectual? Such scruples, such play-acting! But Lydgate and Rosamond quarreling about money; Rosamond quietly thwarting her husband's decisions, passing without conscience to love affairs with his friends and ending as a case-hardened widow who efficiently finds a second father for her family — these things are perfect. Mary Garth defying the old miser is admirable. But the most moving thing in the book — and I always think this is the real test of a novelist — is given to the least likeable people. Bulstrode's moral ruin, and his inability to confess to his dull wife, is portrayed in a picture of dumb human despondency which recalls a painting by Sickert. One hears the clock tick in the silence that attends the wearing down of two lives that can cling together but dare not speak.

The humor of George Eliot gains rather than loses by its mingling with her intellect. Here we feel the sound influence of her girlish reading of the eighteenth-century novelists who were above all men of education. This humor is seen at its best in scenes like the one where the relations of the miser come to his house, waiting to hear news of his will; and again in the sardonic description of the spreading of the scandal about Bulstrode and Lydgate. George Eliot followed causes down to their most scurrilous effects. She is good in scandal and public rumor. Her slow tempo is an advantage, and it becomes exciting to know that she will make her point in the minor scenes as surely as she will make it in the great ones. Mrs. Dollop of The Tankard has her short paragraph of immortality: she had "often to resist the shallow pragmatism of customers disposed to think their efforts from the outer world were of equal force with what had 'come up' in her mind." Mr. Trumbull, the auctioneer, is another portrait, a longer one, smelling of the bar and the saleroom. Dickens would have caricatured this gift from heaven. George Eliot observes and savors. Characteristically she catches his intellectual pretensions and his offensive superiority. We see him scent the coming sale and walk over to Mary Garth's desk to read her copy of Scott's *Anne of Geierstein*, just to show that he knows a book when he sees one: "The course of four centuries," he reads out unexpectedly, "has well-nigh elapsed since the series of events which are related in the following chapters took place on the Continent." That moment is one of the funniest in the English novel, one of those mad touches like the insertion of a dog stealing a bone, which Hogarth put into his pictures.

There is no real madness in George Eliot. Both heavy feet are on the ground. Outside of *Wuthering Heights* there is no madness in Victorian fiction. The Victorians were a histrionic people who measured themselves by the Elizabethans; and George Eliot, like Browning and Tennyson, was compared to Shakespeare by her contemporaries. The comparison failed, if only because madness is lacking. Hysteria, the effect of the exorbitant straining of their wills, the Victorians did, alas, too often achieve. George Eliot somehow escapes it. She is too level-headed. One pictures her, in life, moralizing instead of making a scene. There is no hysteria in *Middlemarch;* perhaps there are no depths because there is so much determination. But there is a humane breadth and resolution in this novel which offers neither hope nor despair to mankind but simply the necessity of fashioning a moral life. . . .

Vernon Rendall

George Eliot and the Classics

GREEK AND NEMESIS

George Eliot was a capable classical scholar and in her allusions of this sort I found some years ago a point of special interest in the presentation of her characters. This has hardly been appreciated by her earlier critics. I looked at the volume on her in the English Men of Letters, by Leslie Stephen, and the notice of it by Herbert Paul in his *Stray Leaves*. These supply brief and reasonable comments on a writer who is supposed to have fallen into the background. *Middlemarch* is a solid monument of story which cannot easily be deprived of readers by the denigrators of to-day. I begin with a passage from *The Life and Letters of Sir R. C. Jebb*, Chap. 7. At Cambridge in 1873 he wrote to the lady who later became his wife that he had met George Eliot not for the first time and had made great friends with her. He asked her how Sophocles had influenced her and her answer startled him. He had noted long before that she was the modern dramatist, in the large sense, most like Sophocles, probably in the "outlining of the first emotions." She said, "in the delineation of the great primitive emotions." Jebb did not tell her of this curious corroboration of his views. What exactly he meant I am not sure. I am not much interested in *The Spanish Gipsy*. No true poet, as Herbert Paul remarks, begins writing verse at the age of forty-four, an age for ceasing to write it, not for beginning it. I take it that the phrase about her drama refers to her stories. Perhaps the similitude is on these lines. In dealing with such primitive emotions as fear and love Sophocles does not let himself go, like the other two great dramatists. George Eliot never lets herself go. She is much more restrained than George Sand, whose work she admired. She wrote with difficulty and perhaps was cautious because she felt herself to be a teacher. As Herbert Paul says, "She never made any pretence of not having a moral." The plays of Sophocles were in a world in which the divine overlordship is not queried, as by Aeschylus, or scouted, as by Euripides. George Eliot has always a high sense of

Reprinted from *Notes and Queries*, 192 (13 and 27 December 1947), 544–546, 564–565; and 193 (3 April, 26 June 1948), 148–149, 272–274, by permission of the Oxford University Press.

morality, but by the time she wrote she had ceased to believe in the
Christian religion. She believed in the sure retribution of Nemesis
amply exhibited in the fresh drama. It includes many shades of
women, who are generally secluded from notice, as in the famous
speech of Pericles. Such quotations are unusual in English fiction, or
in English literature in general, if I may trust a wide and long survey
of this particular sign of interest in Greek ideas.

George Eliot's early fiction quotes Sophocles in Greek: "Amos
Barton," Chap. 4. The Countess had serious thoughts of being *quite*
pious when she had once secured her carriage and establishment. "Let
us do this one sly trick," says Ulysses to Neoptolemus, "and we will
be perfectly honest ever after." This is from *Philoctetes*, 81, which
Whitelaw translates:

> Yet, for the prize, success, is sweet to win
> Consent: some other day shall prove our truth.

The heading of Chap. 42 of *Felix Holt* has two passages of Sophocles
in English from the *Electra* (642) in which Electra declares that her
strange language is due to her mother's acts, and a larger one from
the *Ajax* (520) in which Tecmessa pleads that a man should remember
where he had delight, and kindness should lead to kindness. In "Janet's
Repentance," Chap. 13, her mother is said to be right about one cause
of half her misery. She had no children:

> "Mighty is the force of motherhood," says the great tragic poet
> to us across the ages, finding, as usual, the simplest words for the
> sublimest fact — δεινὸν τὸ τίκτειν ἐστιν.

This is from the *Electra* of Sophocles (770, Jebb). In *The Mill on
the Floss*, Book I, Chap. 7, when Maggie had cut off her hair and
Tom laughed at her, "She sat as helpless and despairing among her
black locks as Ajax among the slaughtered sheep." He had in his
madness taken them for human foes and killed their guardians as
well, and when he knew what he had done, his despair was terrible,
Ajax, 307. In Book II, Chap. 6, when Tom, swaggering about with
a sword, had wounded himself badly and was laid up, Philip Wakem
told him the story of Philoctetes, who had a terrible wound and cried
out so dreadfully about it. In the play of Sophocles he uses such
words as "Ah me!" and "Alas" seven times within a few words. Jebb,
the most careful of translators, finds it impossible to render all of
these lamentations. At the end of Book I, Chap. 13, a good-natured
streak in Mr. Tulliver and his impulsion to deeper borrowing due to
a remark of his wife entangled him further towards ruin. So he "had

a destiny as well as Oedipus, and in this case he might plead, like Oedipus, that his deed was inflicted on him rather than committed by him."

In *Daniel Deronda*, Chap. 32, Mirah says, "it is so much easier to me to share in love than in hatred," and recalls a heroine saying something of the sort in a play she had read in German. Deronda supplies the name, *Antigone*. The beautiful line of Sophocles, *Antigone*, 528, is a masterpiece of conciseness impossible in English. Sophocles is evidently a favourite. I have never seen so many references to him in the writings of any other author.

But it is to the earlier great dramatist that George Eliot turns for the doctrine of Nemesis, and she emphasizes it by alterations the Greek does not justify. *Felix Holt*, Chap. 48, has the heading:

> 'Tis law as steadfast as the throne of Zeus —
> Our days are heritors of days gone by.
> Aeschylus' *Agamemnon*.

Turning to that play, 1540 (Paley), I find the first line rendered well enough but the second should run:

> That the doer should suffer: it is ordinance.

George Eliot has always a vivid sense of the past in the present. She can reproduce with satisfying detail the enthusiasms of a child and the gardens and scenery of her earlier days; so it is with her characters. She is often thinking back about them. In "Mr. Gilfil's Love-Story," she begins in Chap. 1 with the reflection that we poor mortals are often little better than wood-ashes with small signs of the sap and leafy freshness which, we know, belonged to the early fulness of life: "I, at least, hardly ever look at a bent old man, or a wizened old woman, but I see with my mind's eye, that Past of which they are the shrunken remnant." She goes back to their earlier thoughts as well as their physical appearance. Chap. 70 of *Middlemarch* has the heading:

> Our deeds still travel with us from afar,
> And what we have been makes us what we are.

With wrong-doers this sense of the past is for George Eliot always vivid. She believes with Horace that "Punishment, though lame of foot, has seldom quitted the criminal who goes before." In *Adam Bede* Arthur Donnithorne had his chance to escape from the entanglement with Hetty. He even decided to confess to his old friend from

childhood, Parson Irwine, and then did not go through with it, Chap.
16. Irwine was at breakfast with the first volume of the Foulis
Aeschylus at his elbow. Arthur was told to "fall in love in the right
place," and Irwine adds: "I dare say, now, even a man fortified with
a knowledge of the classics might be lured into an imprudent marriage, in spite of the warning given him by the chorus in the Prometheus [906, Paley]." A discussion follows about temptations. Irwine
talks of "the inward suffering which is the worst form of Nemesis.
Consequences are unpitying. Our deeds carry their terrible consequences, quite apart from any fluctuations that went before — consequences that are hardly ever confined to ourselves." Then follows
a question whether Arthur is considering some private danger of his
own, and no answer, with a paragraph suggesting that he hardly
realised himself the motives responsible for this fatal reticence. Later,
on the day of the Birthday Feast, Chap. 22, Irwine spoke to Arthur
about "ἀπέρωτος ἔρως, as old Aeschylus calls it." This "inordinate love"
is from the *Choephoroe*, 590 (Paley). But Arthur went on with
Hetty, Chap. 27, till they were discovered together by Adam, who
fought him and knocked him down. The next morning he "would
so gladly have persuaded himself that he had done no harm! And if
no one had told him the contrary, he could have persuaded himself
so much better. Nemesis can seldom forge a sword for herself out
of our consciences — out of the suffering we feel in the suffering we
may have caused: there is rarely metal enough there to make an
effective weapon." In a page or two comes George Eliot's special
comment:

> There is a terrible coercion in our deeds which may first turn the
> honest man into a deceiver, and then reconcile him to the change;
> for this reason — that the second wrong presents itself to him in
> the guise of the only practical right. The action which before
> commission has been seen with that blended common-sense and
> fresh untarnished feeling which is the healthy eye of the soul, is
> looked at afterwards with the lens of apologetic ingenuity, through
> which all things that men call beautiful and ugly are seen to be
> made up of textures very much alike.

Lord David Cecil in his *Early Victorian Novelists* (1934) quotes
this passage. If earlier critics make little or nothing of such analysis
and discussion, he sees its importance. He is not concerned with the
Greek that I give, but he states firmly that "George Eliot's concentration on the moral side of human nature is the chief source of her
peculiar glory, the kernel of her precious unique contribution to our
literature." The ideas at the back of her novels and the conflicts she
develops in her characters are always moral. This consistency gives

her an advantage over other writers of the Victorian period. In fact, there is one sort of novel before George Eliot and another after her. In *Romola* Tito is an adroit, intensely selfish scoundrel, commended by nothing but his beauty and his scholarship. His case leads George Eliot to her most elaborate analysis of Nemesis, and a quotation from the final play of the great trilogy, the *Eumenides*, 491 (Paley). She exposes at length this ingenious reasoning that Baldassarre has no claim on him and continues (Chap. 11):

> His mind was destitute of that dread which has been erroneously decried as if it were nothing higher than a man's animal care for his own skin: that awe of Divine Nemesis which was felt by religious pagans, and, though it took a more positive form under Christianity, is still felt by the mass of mankind simply as a vague fear at anything which is called wrong-doing. Such terror of the unseen is so far above mere sensual cowardice that it will annihilate that cowardice; it is the initial recognition of a moral law restraining desire, and checks the hard bold scrutiny of imperfect thought into obligations which can never be proved to have any sanctity in the absence of feeling.

Then follows the translation from the Greek:

> "It is good," sing the old Eumenides, in Aeschylus, "that fear should sit as the guardian of the soul, forcing it into wisdom — good that men should carry a threatening shadow in their hearts under the full sunshine; else, how should they learn to revere the right?"

The passage is in the rather rough Greek of the chorus, 491 (Paley), which George Eliot shortens a little. That is reasonable enough, but she also adds, as I noted in the quotation from the *Agamemnon* above, a detail to suit her views. The reading is a little uncertain at one point, but the sense is clear, and "a threatening shadow" is not in the Greek at all. More could be added of this sort, of reflection and comment, but I hope that I have given enough to show George Eliot's deep interest in Nemesis and the feelings involved in a moral breakdown. Not all her characters yield to the strain. In "Janet's Repentance" the heroine is saved by a preacher, and Gwendolen in *Daniel Deronda* was taught to live a better life, in spite of the final shock which parted her from the man who had always helped and influenced her.

Florence at the date of *Romola*, 1492, thought a great deal of the classics and particularly of Greek. George Eliot was equal to the occasion. She knew of Valla's translation of Thucydides and how much the Pope paid for it. Her Tito is familiar with Pausanias, a

guide-book little read by many scholars, unless they are archaeol-
ogists, and the sight of a page in the *Messenica* brings back to him,
though the light is too poor for reading, the stoning of Aristocrates
— he had betrayed the Arcadians to the Spartans and a monument was
erected with verses on the traitor's doom. The learned Bardo in his
blindness recalled his emendations in Nonnus and knew very well
after many years a passage in his fifth Book, which he asks Romola
to read. Peacock quotes the *Dionysiaca* frequently but I do not recall
anyone else who remembers anything of that interminable poem.
Bardo also quotes Epictetus. "For men are disturbed not by things
themselves, but by their opinions or thoughts concerning those things."
This is from the *Enchiridion*, Chap. 5, and if George Eliot had read
Tristram Shandy, she might have recalled it in Greek on the title-
page.[1]

In her other books a wide range of Greek is to be found. In *The
Mill on the Floss*, Book I, chap. 10, Maggie was full of anger and
jealousy because Tom entertained Lucy and neglected her. "There
were passions at war in Maggie at that moment to have made a
tragedy, if tragedies were made by passion only; but the essential
$\tau\iota\ \mu\acute{\epsilon}\gamma\epsilon\theta os$ which was present in the passion was wanting to the action."
This is from Aristotle's famous definition of tragedy, *Poetics*, VI, 2, as
"the imitation of an action that is important, complete, and of a
certain magnitude."

There is another reference to the *Poetics* at the beginning of Book
VI of *Daniel Deronda*, and Book VII, Chapter 57 has at its head: "The
unripe grape, the ripe, and the dried. All things are changes, not into
nothing, but into that which is not at present. Marcus Aurelius
(XI, 37)." Two references from *Middlemarch* will be enough to add.
In Chap. 6, Sir James Chettam was "not one of those gentlemen who
languish after the unattainable Sappho's apple that laughs from the
topmost bough." The charming fragment, 93 (Teubner text), runs:
"Like the honey-apple that reddens on the top of the bough, topping
the topmost, and the apple-gatherers forget it. Nay, they did not
utterly forget it; they could not reach it." When in *Middlemarch*,
Chap. 11, Fred Vincy is discussing slang with his sister, the conversation goes thus:

> "Well tell me whether it is slang or poetry to call an ox a *leg-
> plaiter?*"
> "Of course you can call it poetry if you like."
> "Aha, Miss Rosy, you don't know Homer from slang."

See the "shambling kine" of *Iliad* IX. 466.

[1] George Eliot knew *Tristram Shandy* well, and read it aloud to Lewes
in 1859 and again in 1873. — Ed.

George Eliot was, indeed, a determined student. When she acquired Greek is not stated in the earliest volume of the *Life* published
by her husband. She was busy with French, German and Italian as
well as housework and various reading and letter-writing. But no
letter of hers mentions Greek until she wants to complete a set of
Xenophon in 1846. She began with the *Antigone* in the winter of
1855, and the *Ajax* at the end of 1856. The next year she wrote: "I
rush on the slightest pretext to Sophocles and am as excited about
blind old Œdipus as any young lady can be about the latest hero with
magnificent eyes." In that year "Amos Barton" in *Blackwood's* included, as I have noted, a Greek couplet from the *Philoctetes*, and she
went on to a garland of Greek which I have not seen equalled in the
writings of any author, inside or outside fiction.

LATIN

This "quiet, anxious, sedentary, serious, invalidical English lady," as
Henry James calls her, did pretty well in Latin. In her time, and in
the earlier periods of which she wrote, Latin was much more valued
than now. It was the common mark of the gentleman; it supplied tags
for Parliament and for writers of books. "A quotation or two adorns
the whole man," wrote Heine, and George Eliot, always an intellectual
in her stories, felt this. In "Amos Barton," Chap. 5, she writes naively:

> And now here is an opportunity for an accomplished writer to
> apostrophise calumny, to quote Virgil, and to show that he is
> acquainted with the most ingenious things which have been said
> on that subject in polite literature. But what is opportunity to
> the man who can't use it? . . . So, as my memory is ill-furnished,
> and my note-book still worse, I am unable to show myself either
> erudite or eloquent. . . .

She had no Priscian, who with his vast storehouse of Latin quotations,
helped writers to them at second-hand for centuries. The *Aeneid*
at IV, 173, would have supplied plenty about *Fama*. In "Mr. Gilfil's
Love Story," Chap. 1, his wife's tablet over the vicarage pew had a
Latin inscription which none of the rustics could read. In Chap. 4,
ad libitum is used, also in Chap. 9 of "Janet's Repentance." One of
these quotations might appear in the *OED*, which has only a single
musical usage in the nineteenth century. In Chap. 3, the Miss Linnets
are credited with "their seven or eight lustrums," which seems a little
pedantic for 35 or 40. The Latin word, doubtless due to its use in
Horace, is given an English plural, perhaps following Young in his
Night Thoughts, which, in earlier years, George Eliot had read with

attention. In Chap. 18, a lad of nine is "prematurely invested with the *toga virilis*, or smock-frock."

I have already noted the Greek quotations in these stories. Perhaps George Eliot with this learning wished to encourage the idea of a male author. So, many thought her, but not Dickens. Any critic of observation and experience should have noticed the elaborate descriptions of feminine costume as due to a woman. In *Adam Bede*, at the Harvest Supper, Chap. 53, the shepherd and an invaluable labourer were not on easy terms. "When Tityrus and Meliboeus happen to be on the same farm, they are not sentimentally polite to each other." The Latin pair appear in Virgil's first Eclogue and stand for his pastoral talkers. In *The Mill on the Floss*, Book I, Chap. 3, Mr. Riley, the auctioneer, had made a juvenile contact with the *De Senectute* and the Fourth Book of the *Aeneid*, and thought he understood Latin generally, so he advised the schooling of the unwilling Tom under a classical tutor. Mr. Stelling put him on to the Eton Latin Grammar. He was very slow at it, though it fascinated Maggie, which may be an autobiographical reminiscence. Tom could boast later, Book II, Chap. 3, of having got as far as the *Propria qua maribus*. Here is a scrap of Latin well known in English literature which has not reached the quotation books. It is the beginning of one of the rules in hexameters which the Eton book preserved from the grammar of Colet and Lily, the first High-master of St. Paul's School. It dominated the teaching of Latin for three and a half centuries in almost all the schools of England.

Horace is far more quoted than Virgil, or any other Latin writer. To George Eliot he was a familiar friend, as, apart from the references in her stories, her letters show. In 1840 she writes to a friend: "I have adopted as my motto — *Certum voto pete finem* — Seek a sure end." (*Ep.* I, 2, 56.) In 1845, on translating Strauss: "You must really expect me, if not to sleep and snore *aliquando*, at least to nod in the course of some thousand pages." This is Homer sometimes nodding, *Ars Poetica*, 359, with the common substitution of "aliquando" for "quandoque." In 1848, "I have tired myself with trying to write cleverly, *invitâ Minervâ*. . . ." (*Ars Poetica*, 385.)

Her journal notes in 1859, after the success of *Adam Bede:* Blackwood writes to say that I am "a popular as well as a great author." . . . I happened this morning to be reading the 30th Ode, Book III of Horace — *non omnis moriar*.

Arthur Donnithorne in *Adam Bede*, Chap. 16, has forgotten most of his classics and says: "It's well if I can remember a little inapplicable Latin to adorn my maiden speech in Parliament six or seven years hence. 'Cras ingens iterabimus aequor' (*Odes* I, 7, 32), and a few shreds of that sort will perhaps stick to me, and I shall arrange my opinions so as to introduce them." It is not worth while to note in detail other hackneyed things such as "aes triplex" and "in medias res." In *Middlemarch*, Chap. 34, the lazy and hazy Mr. Brooke can only produce three words "Omne tulit punctum" of a well-worn commonplace (*Ars Poetica*, 343) and is wise in calling in Ladislaw's help for that sort of thing. In Chap. 38 he can ask, "But what is that in Horace? — *fiat justitia, ruat*, something or other." It does not occur to him that the words are hopelessly unmetrical.

I notice some more obscure references. In Book II, Chap. 1 of *The Mill on the Floss*, Tom prayed for help in the irregular verbs of Latin but "it seemed clear that Tom's despair under the caprices of the present tense did not constitute a *nodus* worthy of interference." The Latin word standing alone looked rather pedantic, though Carlyle had used it so in his *French Revolution*, Book V, Chap. 2. It would be more reasonable to give "dignus vindice nodus," a "difficulty worth a solver," *Ars Poetica*, 191. Later, Book II, Chap. 4, it is suggested that his tutor was not one of the best, with his broad chest and ambitious intentions, probably because "these stalwart gentlemen are rather indolent, their *divinae particulum aurae* being obstructed from soaring by a too hearty appetite." It should be *particulam* (*Sat.* II, 2, 79).

In the *Essays* under "Evangelical Teaching," the glib, unscrupulous, and prophesying Dr. Cumming is firmly assured of his mediocrity. "His motto apparently is *Christianitatem, quocunque modo, Christianitatem*." He will take any means to promote his Calvinistic Protestantism. Who would suspect an adaptation of Horace here? Yet George Eliot was thinking of his

rem facias, rem,

si possis, recte, si non, quocumque modo, rem.

Here, *Ep.* I, 1, 65–6, he suggests that you must get money, honestly, if you can; if not, money by any method.

In *Daniel Deronda*, Chap. 15, Deronda's guardian suspects him of a tendency to fall in love with Gwendolen: "What! are you a little touched with the sublime lash? . . . Are you inclined to run after her?" The "sublime lash" seems nonsense. The adjective is copied from the Latin of *Odes* IV, 26, end, where it means "uplifted." Horace wishes the uplifted lash applied just once to the haughty Chloe.

In *Adam Bede*, Mrs. Poyser is always a joy, and, as Parson Irwine remarks, delightfully original. But when in Chap. 6 she criticizes Dinah's views of the claims of religion at some length, she perceives at last that her objections are a waste of time: "You'd make me the same answer at the end. I might as well talk to the running brook, and tell it to stand still." Here, her creator had, perhaps, at the back of her mind Horace's rustic waiting for the brooks to run dry, *Ep.* i, 2, 42. *Romola* is full of classical allusions, clogged with them, some think. The intelligentsia of Florence in 1492 prized the Greek scholar and welcomed the Latinist with critical appreciation. Nello, the lively, talkative barber, practises his art at the sign of "Apollo and the Razor," Chap. 3, and remembers that Juvenal supplied the "audacia perdita" which Politian ascribes to the swarm of Greeks. Tito quotes the passage in Latin, iii, 73, and thinks it wise to laugh about it. In Chap. 5, Bardo, the erudite scholar, who is blind, insists on handling his own copy of Nonnus. He prefers to printing the manuscript "over which we scholars have bent with that insight into the poet's meaning which is closely akin to the *mens divinior* of the poet himself." (Horace, *Sat.* i, 4, 43.) Chap. 6 includes four references to Horace. Nello twice talks of *tonsor inaequalis*, a barber who cuts awry, *Ep.* i, 1, 94, while Bardo, after quoting Quintilian and Plautus, calls Nello *abnormis sapiens*, an unschooled philosopher, like Ofellus in Horace, *Sat.* ii, 2, 3. Again Bardo recalls him twice in Chap. 12, praising Tito for his readiness to walk uphill, not shrinking "from labour, without which, the poet has wisely said, life has given nothing to mortals [*Sat.* i, 9, 59], it is too often the 'palma sine pulvere,' the prize of glory without the dust of the race, that attracts young ambition." (*Ep.* i, v, 51.) Oddly enough, the neat brevity of the last three words has not made the phrase a commonplace. I have never seen it quoted elsewhere.

Chap. 7, "A Learned Squabble," provides the chief array of scholarship. Herbert Paul calls it a "brilliant picture," though he notes one mistake in the Latin. Bardo had complained in the previous chapter that "I, myself, for having shown error in a single preposition, had an invective written against me wherein I was taxed with treachery, fraud, indecency, and even hideous crimes." The two combatants each had their advantages. Politian was an accomplished scholar with a high reputation, while Scala had a handsome palace and had been for twenty years secretary of the Florentine Republic and had attained all the honours a citizen could desire. But he had an itch for learned authorship, and handed about trifles he had composed in Latin, though, George Eliot notes, "the terrible Joseph Scaliger" was in the next century to proclaim him "totally ignorant of Latinity." Politian did not love him, having tried in vain to marry his daughter. So a Latin epigram of his was duly scarified and one was returned, explaining pleasantly that *culex, a gnat,* was not feminine. Scala replied in Latin about Politian's unsuccessful suit in a supposed imitation of a Greek epigram. Politian replied with a neat frankness about the *culex,* suggesting that, "like

Venus, it was born from the waters." Scala then defended his own
Latin and doubted the reference to Venus. This was Politian's
chance. George Eliot was scholar enough to know that Virgil's poem
about the gnat who saved the shepherd from a snake introduces it
as the "*alumnus* of the waters" (*Culex*, 183). Politian was impreg-
nable, and when he called the Greeks "transmarine," could have
cited in support of the word Livy, who was much admired and
copied at the time. Scala had to fall back on a general criticism of
Politian's arrogance, his perverse tastes, and questionable criticisms:
"He was fond of saying pungent things about the men who thought
they wrote like Cicero because they ended every sentence with 'esse
videtur.'" This comment on an ending Cicero overdoes comes from
Tacitus, *De Oratoribus*, 23, but the last word should be "videatur,"
making a good rhythm, which the dactyl with "videtur" does not. Pitt
used this spirited discussion by Tacitus for a memorable phrase,
but I knew several good scholars who had not bothered to read
it. Such a mistake is unusual with George Eliot and raises for
me some questions. Did she write "videatur," which the printers,
always bothered with Latin, made into "videtur"? A reader of
the Press could not be expected to query an obscure reference in
Latin. I know nothing of the legibility of her handwriting, but I
note that her books in the authentic editions are admirably printed
and free from small slips. I suppose that she herself was a careful
proof-reader. She considered her wording elaborately in her translation of Strauss.

There is another possibility. Did she write "videtur" and mean
to write it, since the passage tells us what Scala said to his friends
(and he was just the man to make such a blunder)? It is a dangerous
game, I know, to make your characters speak wrong on purpose.
Reviewers will seize a chance to expose your ignorance of the
right word.

I add one more quotation. In *Daniel Deronda*, chap. 52, Hans
Meyrick, the artist, writes a tediously lengthy letter, in which, concluding that he must give up historic and poetic subjects and take
to mere portrait-painting, he addresses himself thus: "Fate, my
friend, has made you the hinder wheel — *rota posterior curras, et
in axe secundo* — run behind, because you can't help it." This is
from Persius, V, 72.

I have not made this list of references exhaustive, but it goes well
beyond that of the *George Eliot Dictionary*. As a novelist, she is
not peculiar in showing a lively interest in Greek and Latin, but in
adding to it many references to the advance of Science. A paragraph may include the hemlock which cut short the life of a great
teacher and James Watt's steam-engine. Great writers of the nine-

teenth century, such as Meredith and Hardy, expect their readers to understand and appreciate the old classics. Even the wildly romantic Ouida blunders over similar touches. In the twentieth century, Greek has been dismissed from education, or let off with a caution. But if it is not compulsory, it still supplies the terminology for the latest medical research. It has even been quoted in Parliament. Our stage and a host of new translations and popular abstracts of philosophy show that it has not lost its hold on the English mind.

Joan Bennett

Vision and Design

When we read George Eliot's novels for the first time we are likely to be too much absorbed in the unfolding of the story to be conscious of any peculiar characteristics of her vision of life or her method of presenting it. Like most of the great Victorian novelists, she has the spell-binding power of the Ancient Mariner; we are forced to attend, the world in which her characters move becomes the real world, unquestioningly accepted. The principal characters take their place in the foreground, our sympathies are firmly engaged for them and we are carried forward by that curiosity which novel readers share with children, the desire to know what happens next. Only when the book is closed and we cease to participate in the life of Hayslope, St Ogg's or Middlemarch can we begin to inquire what makes up the characteristic impression of a George Eliot novel; by then the spell is broken. But it is well to remember that her books are great works of fiction, partly because they have this magic; no analysis can reproduce it any more than an analysis of a poem can reproduce the effect of poetry. With fiction as with poetry the first necessity (if the work is to become an effective part of our own experience) is to submit to the spell: intellectual appreciation and evaluation follow after. It is, of course,

Reprinted from Joan Bennett, *George Eliot: Her Mind and Her Art*, Cambridge, 1948, pp. 77–101, by permission of the Cambridge University Press.

the story, not the mere plot, that works the spell. The plot is preconceived by the author and can be summarized by the critic, but the stories, George Eliot herself tells us, "grow in me like plants." It is the growth of the plant, the gradual unfolding of character in its environment, that compels attention, not the mere concatenation of events. The story-teller works her will on us because we are convinced that these people and this town or village exist. The novels, like any other stories that beguile us, provide us with the pleasure of disinterested sympathy. When we read of the sufferings of fictitious, or, for that matter, of historical characters, we can indulge in the natural human tendency to sympathize without any possibility of being required to act. In so far as an unimaginative hardness of heart is normal, it is probably the result of unconscious self-protection against such a demand, and the satisfaction following upon reading a fiction or witnessing a drama suggests that, when there is no need to be on the defensive, we enjoy being made to understand our fellow-sufferers. The ultimate value of such aesthetic experience will depend upon how far the pleasurable exercise — playing at sympathy — can affect our conduct in the workaday world. The immediate effect of reading George Eliot's novels is, then, one which her works have in common with all successful fiction, it is hard to put the book down. . . .

Adam Bede is the earliest and simplest example of the typical George Eliot form. The life of Hayslope envelops the tragedy. We come to know all grades of its society, artisans, labourers, farmers, rector, schoolmaster, innkeeper and squire. It is an active community in which most men or women have work to do and their character is affected by that work. That character is also the product of religious influences; we become aware of the impact of Methodism upon the inhabitants of Hayslope and of the more subtly pervasive influence of traditional Anglicanism. In the Third Book the whole community is assembled at Donnithorne Chase to celebrate the young squire's coming of age; by that time the pattern of living out of which the central characters emerge is clearly established and their drama is already under way. After the climax, when Hetty Sorrel has been condemned to death, reprieved and deported, and another author would feel that the work was complete, there is a Sixth Book, balancing the Third. In it the rhythm of Hayslope life is re-established and, with the inevitable gaps made by the intervening event, a Harvest supper reassembles the same community as celebrated the young squire's birthday. The central tragedy is intimately connected with this background. The full effect of Arthur Donnithorne's yielding to the sensuous appeal of the pretty child-like Hetty and of all that ensues depends upon the relation of both characters to their world. The pride and well-grounded self-respect of the Poysers, established in the reader's mind by the vivid pictures of their surroundings, their working day, their home life, their Sunday observance, and the neighbours' opinion of them, all play their part in causing the tragedy and in heightening the bitterness of its effect. It is the social background the Poysers have provided for their niece and the standard of conduct imbibed from it that make it inevitable for Hetty to take flight before the birth of her baby; it is the esteem in which they are held by which the reader measures their shame and it is the clear sense he acquires of their identification with Hayslope by which he measures the anguish as well as the probability of their contemplated uprooting when the shame is known to them. Similarly, it is Arthur's upbringing, his relations with his grandfather, the squire, his high conception of the love and esteem he will earn from all his dependents when he inherits the land, that define the price he pays for his weakness. There is no part of what we have learnt of the outer circle that does not affect our sense of the inner. The cultured benignity of the rector, the moral enthusiasm of the Methodists, the simple ignorance of the country-folk, all make their own impact on the central characters and help to determine the events. Although the impression while we read is of a leisurely sequence of naturalistic scenes of comedy or of pathos and of a world richly populated with entertaining characters, when we look back we find that every individual scene or character is directly or indirectly related to the simple story at the core of the book, of the carpenter's betrothed betrayed by the squire's grandson. In its setting this commonplace story becomes widely significant. The simple, well-contrived pattern conveys the sense of a social structure enclosing four human beings as completely as the soil encloses the roots of a growing plant and, in so doing, it illustrates one aspect of the author's vision of life.

Although the formal pattern is not elsewhere so simple and symmetrical as in *Adam Bede* — where the assembly of the villagers on the green to hear the preaching in Book I, their assembly at the birthday feast in Book III and at the Harvest supper in Book VI provide rests that divide the composition into almost equal parts — the general character of the design, an individual tragedy surrounded by the life of a community, is similar in all George Eliot's novels, except *Daniel Deronda*, where the absence of such an enclosing community is an important part of her conception. In her own view the lack of symmetry in *The Mill on the Floss* was responsible for her imperfect fulfilment of her intention, and for the dissatisfaction that most readers feel about the end of that novel:

. . . the tragedy is not adequately prepared. This is a defect which I felt even while writing the third volume, and have felt ever since the MS. left me. The *Epische Breite* into which I was beguiled by love of my subject in the first two volumes, caused a want of proportionate fullness in the treatment of the third, which I shall always regret.

The regret is justified in so far as the compression of the Maggie and Stephen episode contributes to its faulty presentation. Yet the epic breadth of the first two volumes is warranted by the completeness with which we come to understand the pressure of her surroundings on Maggie's developing personality which will, in turn, condition the central drama. We are brought to a full realization of those surroundings because, in a series of scenes, each with their own intrinsic value as social comedy, or drama, we grow familiar with a number of households and their way of life, which is both in-dividual and representative. There is, for instance, the financially precarious home life of the Tullivers themselves; Mr Tulliver speculative, perplexed and, compared with his wife, adventurous, and Mrs Tulliver, foolish and faithful, torn between loyalty to her own family and to the proud conventions of her Dodson upbringing. Then there are the prosperous middle-class homes of her sisters; Mrs Glegg's home at St Ogg's with its "front and back parlour so that she had two points of view from which she could observe the weakness of her fellow-beings, and reinforce her thankfulness for her own exceptional strength of mind," and the elegant home of Mrs Pullet with its "front door mats by no means intended to wipe shoes on: the very scraper had a deputy to do its dirty work"; and we are shown the well-conducted home life of Tom's ambitious clerical tutor, or, in contrast to all of these, the home of Mr Tulliver's sister, Aunt Moss, who struggles to feed and clothe a large family on the proceeds of a farm starved of capital, since she has committed the indiscretion of marrying solely for love. All these aspects of life that the reader encounters as they impinge on Maggie's childhood, and that he relishes for their own vivid humour or pathos, convey the breadth of the world that surrounds an individual life and the narrowness of the space in which such a life can freely grow.

The difference in quality between George Eliot's novels is closely related to the degree of success with which she gives life to the social world surrounding her central characters. In her first period, from the *Scenes of Clerical Life* to *Silas Marner* she plants those characters in the environment with which she had been familiar since her childhood, and, for many readers, it is these novels that give the most delight. Certainly in them her characteristic humour, com-pounded of compassion, a sense of the incongruous, and an ear for dialogue that is both racy and individual, has the freest play. But when she returned, in *Middlemarch*, with a more assured command of her art, to the environment she most fully understood, she achieved her masterpiece. It is true that this great novel lacks some of the qualities of the first period; it has less spontaneous gaiety, partly because the provincial town gave her less scope for comedy than did the rural environment. There is also an aspect of her genius, absent here, which is more often found in the poet than the prose artist, an ability to simplify without distorting human truths, so that they can be presented symbolically as they are in the legend of *Silas Marner*. The impulse towards such simplification is intrusive at the close of *The Mill on the Floss*, where the reunion in death of Maggie and Tom is out of key with the rest of the work, and a similar discord between two modes of treatment distorts *Daniel Deronda*. But in *Silas Marner* the naturalistic treatment and the legendary story are happily combined and produce a minor masterpiece. Nevertheless, though certain excellencies must be sought elsewhere, *Middlemarch* is her widest and deepest study of the interpenetration between the life of a community and the individual lives that compose it. . . .

The humour in George Eliot's novels, more prevalent in the earlier than in the later works, is as direct a product of her vision of life as is the way she shapes her stories. It arises out of a profound and sympathetic understanding of the world she creates and it expresses itself predominantly in the dialogue which bears the stamp both of the individual speaker and of the race and class. Behind the words spoken and the characteristic idiom lie the accumulated misconstructions of inherited beliefs, or the complex of prejudices, experience and common sense which make up rural wisdom. Mrs Poyser's gift for vivid self-expression, for instance, is more than a delightful idiosyncrasy. The metaphors that enrich her language spring from the soil in which she was nurtured. They reflect her own character and also the habits, the daily work, the religious tradition and the social conventions and assumptions of her time and class. . . . The speech of George Eliot's rustic or provincial characters is racy because it represents personalities steeped in the history of the race. The variety of religious beliefs assimilated into the pieties and prejudices of the countryside is one aspect of this history and some of the humour in the novels arises out of consequent incongruities; for instance, Mrs Patten's shocked surprise, despite her regular church attendance, at being considered a "miserable sinner." . . . Felix Holt's mother, a member of the General Baptist Connection, has a similar "proper pride" in her own deserving. . . . The author's attitude towards these women is not satirical. It is true that a sense of superior understanding contributes to the reader's enjoyment; but he is seldom allowed to feel contempt; and his amusement is often compatible with the reverse of this. He can, for instance, feel nothing but respect for Dolly Winthrop when she comes to help Silas with the baby and advocates baptism and " 'noculation as equivalent prophylactics against harm. Such confusions of thought are characteristic of rural life, and we are made to feel that Dolly Winthrop's human kindness is no less so. In the same novel the lucubrations of the philosophical Mr Macey evoke as much respect for his good sense as amusement over his elaborately imperfect logic. Mr Macey is, as clerk of the parish, well versed in the Prayer Book, but he interprets it in the light of his own experience and concludes that, if Silas Marner's knowledge of curative herbs owes something to the devil, no one, except the village doctor will be any the worse off for that. . . . Social conventions provide a similar source of amusement; even the oddest of them are obviously accepted by their inheritors as a part of the order of nature. Moral and religious principles are not more binding than they are, nor are they indeed distinguishable from them. In this the Dodsons and Tullivers are typical of their kind.

> . . . The religion of the Dodsons consisted in revering whatever was customary and respectable: it was necessary to be baptised, else one could not be buried in the churchyard, and to take the sacrament before death, as a security against more dimly understood perils; but it was of equal necessity to have the proper pall-bearers and well-cured hams at one's funeral, and to leave an unimpeachable will. A Dodson would not be taxed with the omission of anything that was becoming, or that belonged to that eternal fitness of things which was plainly indicated in the practice of the most substantial parishioners, and in the family traditions — such as obedience to parents, faithfulness to kindred, industry, rigid honesty, thrift, the thorough scouring of wooden and copper utensils, the hoarding of coins likely to disappear from the currency, the production of first-rate commodities for the market, and the general preference for whatever was home-made. (*Mill on the Floss*, Bk. iv, ch. 1.)

This complex and inflexible Dodson code underlies the eccentricities of the individual sisters and permeates their behaviour at every turn of the story so that, delightfully surprising though they are, they are always recognizably in character.

The early books are necessarily richer in this humour arising out of intimacy with a tradition, since in them George Eliot is recreating the world in which she was born and bred. Yet even in *Daniel Deronda* there is an area in which her characteristic sense of comedy

comes into play. The Cohen family are amusing and sympathetic in
the same fashion as the Poysers or the Dodsons, and for the same
reason. Their behaviour bears the stamp of race and tradition; and,
as the reader gains intimacy with the Cohen family life, he respects
and sympathizes with them while, at the same time, he relishes
their incongruous mixture of generosity and greed, candor and
cunning, moral rectitude and an eye for the main chance. The Cohens,
like the Dodsons, have a streak of vulgarity — both families attach
undue importance to their possessions as tokens of wealth and therefore of worth — but the Cohen vulgarities are specifically Jewish.
Young Mrs Cohen wears "a string of large artificial pearls wound
round and round her neck," the baby sleeps under a scarlet counter-
pane and the two children, Adelaide Rebekah and Jacob Alexander,
are dressed respectively in braided amber and in "black velveteen
with scarlet stockings" when Daniel calls one afternoon at five
o'clock. All this is as racial as is little Jacob's precocious sharpness
over the transaction of "shwopping" a corkscrew for Deronda's
penknife with a white handle and a hook. No less so is the family
affection and the pride of the grandmother and the mother in their
offspring. But perhaps the quality of the Cohen family and the
nature of the amusement they afford the reader can best be illustrated
by the dialogue that takes place when Mordecai is to leave the
household. — After Deronda had broken the news to the assembled
family:

> There was silence for a moment or two before the grandmother
> said in a wailing tone —
> "Well, well! and so you're going away from us, Mordecai."
> "And where there's no children as there is here," said the mother,
> catching the wail.
> "No Jacob, and no Adelaide, and no Eugenie!" wailed the
> grandmother again.
> "Ay, ay, Jacob's learning 'ill all wear out of him. He must
> go to school. It'll be hard times for Jacob," said Cohen, in a tone
> of decision. (*Daniel Deronda*, Bk. vi, ch. 46.)

Mordecai, in return for the Cohens' hospitality, has been teaching
the boy. The accumulating sense of woe in the remarks of the
family affects the children and the father's "hard times for Jacob"
is the last straw; Jacob sets up a wail, and his sister who "always
cried when her brother cried, now began to howl with astonishing
suddenness, whereupon baby awaking contributed angry screams
and required to be taken out of the cradle." In this general turmoil
Cohen, "sensible that the master of the family must make some
apology for all this weakness, and that the occasion called for a

speech, addressed Deronda with some elevation of pitch, squaring his elbows and resting a hand on each knee. . . ." The full flavour of this speech of Cohen's and its rich revelation of character is not the product of mere knowledge or of thought about racial characteristics. It is an imaginative recreation. George Eliot has identified herself with Cohen, so that she reproduces the cadence of his speech and the inconsequent twists and turns of his mind. He is self-assertive, acute, has an eye to the main chance (which includes earning the approval of his God). But he is also warm hearted, proud of the family he rules and not without dignity in his *apologia* for it. He is half ashamed (as a business man) and half proud (as a family man) to own that what really troubles them all in Mordecai's departure is not the loss of any profit, material or spiritual, but the loss of a friend they have grown to like. . . .

George Eliot's novels have in them all the elements expected by nineteenth-century novel readers. They were written within the tradition and she proved to have all the talents that Lewes knew she would need if she was to succeed in the genre. From one point of view her novels continue in the tradition evolved from Fielding, but which had gradually become less picaresque and more strictly narrative. She tells a story with a beginning, middle and end. The main interest is focussed on a small group of characters the development of whose fortunes is laid out. They move towards a crisis or tangle which is unravelled before the end so that in the last chapter a *dénouement* is reached. All the fortunes with which the reader has been concerned are tidied up. The story ends in a marriage or a death and the future of the survivors is indicated. The reader is persuaded that the story is complete. Within this framework there is scope for the narrator to comment on the action and the characters and so to expound his "philosophy" or sense of moral values. "Wit," both in the commentary and in the dialogue, contributes to the reader's delight and communicates the author's sense of proportion; "descriptive powers" evoke the surroundings in which the action takes place, while "dramatic powers" enable the author to recreate the scenes of the story in terms of dialogue and action. But from another point of view George Eliot is an innovator. The organic or living form of her novels, within the expected framework, is different from anything that had gone before. It resembles, in some respects, Jane Austen's form in so far as the central characters are deeply rooted in their social environment which determines their story as much as does their individual character. The difference is that the social environment is wider, more complex, made up of a greater variety of minor characters drawn from many more social and economic levels, and also that the display of this outer circle or environment is more conscious. Jane Austen took her social *milieu* for granted; its manners and traditions were, for her, as little open to question as the laws of nature. George Eliot was aware of the ethical, religious and social conventions of the world she paints as a product of history, evolved in time and changing with time. She was consciously interested in the pressure all these exert on individual lives and in the existence of a problem concerned with resisting or succumbing to that pressure. She shares the modern consciousness of man in a changing and developing society. Consequently, the organic form of her novels — an inner circle (a small group of individuals involved in a moral dilemma) surrounded by an outer circle (the social world within which the dilemma has to be resolved) — is more significant than in any preceding fiction. Furthermore, her perception of individual human beings is more complex than that of her predecessors. She never suggests a simple division of characters into good and bad. The individual, like the environment, has evolved and is still evolving; his or her behaviour at any given moment is the inevitable result of all that has gone before; therefore, while the action can itself be judged, both in relation to its consequences and to its aesthetic beauty (an action that pleases or displeases) the doer is not presented judicially but compassionately. In her discourse George Eliot sometimes deviates from this attitude and her novel suffers accordingly. But whenever her reflective powers are in due subordination to her creative gift, wherever, as usually happens in the dialogue, she responds to her characters rather than thinks about them, the reader feels with them and the total effect of her novel is an increase of understanding and of compassion.

F. R. Leavis

George Eliot

I. THE EARLY PHASE

There is general agreement that an appraisal of George Eliot must be a good deal preoccupied with major discriminations — that the body of her work exhibits within itself striking differences not merely of kind, but between the more and the less satisfactory, and exhibits them in such a way that the history of her art has to be seen as something less happy in its main lines than just an unfolding of her genius, a prosperous development of her distinctive powers, with growing maturity. It is generally assumed that this aspect of her performance is significantly related to the fact of her having displayed impressive intellectual gifts outside her art, so that she was a distinguished figure in the world of Herbert Spencer and the *Westminster Review* before she became a novelist. And there is something like a unanimity to the effect that it is distinctive of her, among great novelists, to be peculiarly addicted to moral preoccupations.

The force of this last — what it amounts to or intends, and the significance it has for criticism — is elusive; and it seems well to start with a preliminary glance at what, from his hours with the critics, the reader is likely to recall as a large established blur across the field of vision. Henry James seems to me to have shown finer intelligence than any one else in writing about George Eliot, and he, in his review of the Cross *Life* of her, tells us that, for her, the novel "was not primarily a picture of life, capable of deriving a high value from its form, but a moralized fable, the last word of a philosophy endeavoring to teach by example." The blur is seen here in that misleading antithesis, which, illusory as it is, James's commentary insists on. What, we ask, is the "form" from which a "picture of life" derives its value? As we should expect, the term "aesthetic," with its trail of confusion, turns up in the neighbourhood (it is a term the literary critic would do well to abjure). James notes, as characterizing "that side of George Eliot's nature which

Reprinted from F. R. Leavis, *The Great Tradition*, New York [1948], pp. 28–47, 79–125, by permission of New York University Press and of Chatto & Windus, Ltd.

was weakest," the "absence of free aesthetic life," and he says that her "figures and situations" are "not *seen* in the irresponsible plastic way." But, we ask, in what great, in what interesting, novel *are* the figures and situations seen in an "irresponsible plastic way" (a useful determination of one of the intentions of "aesthetic")? Is there any great novelist whose preoccupation with "form" is not a matter of his responsibility towards a rich human interest, or complexity of interests, profoundly realized? — a responsibility involving, of its very nature, imaginative sympathy, moral discrimination and judgment of relative human values? . . .

That the antithesis I quote from Henry James is unsatisfactory and doesn't promote clear thinking is no doubt obvious enough. And the reader may note that James's essay dates sixty years back. Yet his handling of the matter seems to me representative: I don't know of anything written about George Eliot that, touching on this matter of her distinctive moral preoccupation, does anything essentially more helpful towards defining the distinctive quality of her art. James, then, is a critic one reads with close attention, and, coming on so challenging a formulation in so intelligent a context, one is provoked to comment that, while, among the great novelists, George Eliot must certainly have her difference, it can hardly be of the kind such an antithetical way of putting things suggests. Though such formulations may have their colourable grounds, there must, one reflects, be something more important to say about the moral seriousness of George Eliot's novels; otherwise she would hardly be the great novelist one knows her to be. There are certain conditions of art from which she cannot be exempt while remaining an artist.

A tentative comparison or two may help to define the direction in which the appraising critic should turn his inquiries. Consider her against, not Flaubert, but two novelists concerning whose greatness one has no uneasy sense of a need to hedge. In her own language she ranks with Jane Austen and Conrad, both of whom, in their different ways, present sharp contrasts to her. . . .

James speaks of a "philosophy endeavouring to teach by example": perhaps, it may be suggested, the clue we want is to be found in the "philosophy"? And the context shows that James does, in attempting to define her peculiar quality, intend to stress George Eliot's robust powers of intellectual labour and her stamina in the realm of abstract thought — he speaks elsewhere of her "exemption from cerebral lassitude." But actually it is not easy to see how, in so far as her intellectual distinction appears in the strength of her art, it constitutes an essential difference between her and Conrad. She has no more of a philosophy than he has, and he, on the other

hand, is, in his work, clearly a man of great intelligence and confirmed intellectual habit, whose "picture of life" embodies much
reflective analysis and sustained thought about fundamentals.

What can, nevertheless, be said, with obvious truth, is that Conrad
is more completely an artist. It is not that he had no intellectual
career outside his art — that he did nothing comparable to translating
Strauss, Spinoza and Feuerbach, and editing *The Westminster Review*.
It is that he transmutes more completely into the created work the
interests he brings in. . . . But it must not be concluded that the
point about her is that her novels contain unabsorbed intellectual
elements — patches, say, of tough or drily abstract thinking un-
digested by her art. The relevant characteristic, rather, is apt to
strike the reader as something quite other than toughness or dryness;
we note it as an emotional quality, something that strikes us as the
direct (and sometimes embarrassing) presence of the author's own
personal need. . . . At her best she has the impersonality of genius,
but there is characteristic work of hers that is rightly admired where
the quality of the sensibility can often be felt to have intimate
relations with her weakness.

That is, the critic appraising her is faced with a task of discrimination. I began by reporting general agreement to this effect. The
point of my comparison is to suggest that the discriminating actually
needing to be done will be on different lines from those generally
assumed.

And that is equally the conclusion prompted by a comparative
glance at Jane Austen. Though the fashionable cult tends to suggest
otherwise, she doesn't differ from George Eliot by not being
earnestly moral. The vitality of her art is a matter of a preoccupation
with moral problems that is subtle and intense because of the pressure
of personal need. As for the essential difference (leaving aside the
differences in the nature of the need and in range of interests),
is it something that can be related to the fact that Jane Austen,
while unmistakably very intelligent, can lay no claim to a massive
intellect like George Eliot's, capable of maintaining a specialized
intellectual life? Perhaps; but what again strikes us in the intellectual
writer is an emotional quality, one to which there is no equivalent
in Jane Austen. And it is not merely a matter of a difference of
theme and interest — of George Eliot's dealing with (say) the agonized
conscience and with religious need as Jane Austen doesn't. There
could be this difference without what is as a matter of fact associated
with it in George Eliot's work: a tendency towards that kind of
direct presence of the author which has to be stigmatized as
weakness. . . .

Going back in one's mind over the earlier works, what can one note as their attractions and their claims? There is *Scenes of Clerical Life*, which is to-day, perhaps, not much read. And indeed only with an effort can one appreciate why these stories should have made such an impact when they came out. One of them, "Mr. Gilfil's Love-Story," is charming in a rather slight way. Without the charm the pathos would hardly be very memorable, and the charm is characteristic of the earlier George Eliot: it is the atmospheric rich- ness of the past seen through home tradition and the associations of childhood. Of the other two, "The Sad Fortunes of the Rev. Amos Barton" and "Janet's Repentance," one feels that they might have appeared in any Victorian family magazine. This is unfair, no doubt; the imaginative and morally earnest sympathy that finds a moving theme in the ordinariness of undistinguished lives — there we have the essential George Eliot; the magazine writer would not have had that touch in pathos and humour, and there is some justice in Leslie Stephen's finding an "indication of a profoundly reflective intellect" in "the constant, though not obtrusive, suggestion of the depths below the surface of trivial life." But *Scenes of Clerical Life* would not have been remembered if nothing had followed.

George Eliot did no more prentice-work (the greater part of the *Scenes* may fairly be called that): *Adam Bede* is unmistakably qualified to be a popular classic — which, in so far as there are such to-day, it still is. There is no need here to offer an appreciation of its attractions; they are as plain as they are genuine, and they have had full critical justice done them. Criticism, it seems to me, is faced with the ungrateful office of asking whether, much as *Adam Bede* deserves its currency as a classic (and of the classical English novels it has been among the most widely read), the implicit valuation it enjoys in general acceptance doesn't represent something more than justice. The point can perhaps be made by suggesting that the book is too much the sum of its specifiable attractions to be among the great novels — that it is too resolvable into the separate interests that we can see the author to have started with. Of these, a main one, clearly, is given in Mrs. Poyser and that mellow presentation of rustic life (as George Eliot recalled it from her childhood) for which Mrs. Poyser's kitchen is the centre. This deserves all the admiration it has received. And this is the moment to say that juxtaposition with George Eliot is a test that disposes finally of the "Shakespearean" Hardy: if the adjective is to be used at all, it applies much more fitly to the rich creativeness of the art that seems truly to draw its sap from life and is free from all suspicion of Shakespeareanizing. George Eliot's rustic life is convincingly real even when most charming (and she doesn't always mellow her presentation of it with charm).

We have another of the main interests with which George Eliot started in Dinah, that idealized recollection of the Methodist aunt. Dinah, a delicate undertaking, is sufficiently successful, but one has, in appraising her in relation to the total significance of the book, to observe, with a stress on the limiting implications of the word, that the success is conditioned by the "charm" that invests her as it does the world she moves in and belongs to. She is idealized as Adam is idealized; they are in keeping. Adam, we know, is a tribute to her father; but he is also the Ideal Craftsman, embodying the Dignity of Labour. He too is *réussi*, but compare him with George Eliot's other tribute to her father, Caleb Garth of *Middlemarch*, who is in keeping with *his* context, and the suggestion that the idealizing element in the book named after Adam involves limiting judgments for the critic gets, I think, an obvious force.

Mrs. Poyser, Dinah and Adam — these three represent interests that George Eliot wanted to use in a novel. To make a novel out of them she had to provide something else. The Dinah theme entails the scene in prison, and so there had to be a love-story and a seduction. George Eliot works them into her given material with convincing skill; the entanglement of Arthur Donnithorne with Hetty Sorrel — the first casual self-indulgence, the progressive yielding to temptation, the inexorable Nemesis — involves a favourite moral-psychological theme of hers, and she handles it in a personal way. And yet — does one want ever to read that large part of the book again? does it gain by re-reading? doesn't this only confirm one's feeling that, while as Victorian fiction — a means of passing the time — the love-story must be granted its distinction, yet, judged by the expectations with which one approaches a great novelist, it offers nothing proportionate to the time it takes (even if we cut out the large amount of general reflection)? . . .

It is a related point that if "charm" prevails in *Adam Bede* (and, as Henry James indicates, in *Silas Marner*), there should be another word for what we find in *The Mill on the Floss*. The fresh directness of a child's vision that we have there, in the autobiographical part, is something very different from the "afternoon light" of reminiscence. This recaptured early vision, in its combination of clarity with rich "significance," is for us, no doubt, enchanting; but it doesn't idealize, or soften with a haze of sentiment (and it can't consort with "art"). Instead of Mrs. Poyser and her setting we have the uncles and aunts. The bearing of the change is plain if we ask whether there could have been a Dinah in this company. Could there have been an Adam? They both belong to a different world.

In fact, the Gleggs and the Pullets and the Dodson clan associate, not with the frequenters of Mrs. Poyser's kitchen, but with the tribe that forgathers at Stone Court waiting for Peter Featherstone to die. The intensity of Maggie's naïve vision is rendered with the convincing truth of genius; but the rendering brings in the intelligence that goes with the genius and is *of* it, and the force of the whole effect is the product of understanding. This is an obvious enough point. I make it because I want to observe that, although the supremely mature mind of *Middlemarch* is not yet manifested in *The Mill on the Floss,* the creative powers at work here owe their successes as much to a very fine intelligence as to powers of feeling and remembering — a fact that, even if it is an obvious one, the customary stress nevertheless leaves unattended to, though it is one that must get its full value if George Eliot's development is to be understood. I will underline it by saying that the presentment of the Dodson clan is of marked sociological interest — not accidentally, but because of the intellectual qualifications of the novelist.

But of course the most striking quality of *The Mill on the Floss* is that which goes with the strong autobiographical element. It strikes us as an emotional tone. We feel an urgency, a resonance, a personal vibration, adverting us of the poignantly immediate presence of the author. Since the vividness, the penetration and the irresistible truth of the best of the book are clearly bound up with this quality, to suggest that it also entails limitations that the critic cannot ignore, since they in turn are inseparable from disastrous weaknesses in George Eliot's handling of her themes, is perhaps a delicate business. But the case is so: the emotional quality represents something, a need or hunger in George Eliot, that shows itself to be insidious company for her intelligence — apt to supplant it and take command. The acknowledged weaknesses and faults of *The Mill on the Floss,* in fact, are of a more interesting kind than the accepted view recognizes.

That Maggie Tulliver is essentially identical with young Mary Ann Evans we all know. She has the intellectual potentiality for which the environment into which she is born doesn't provide much encouragement; she has the desperate need for affection and intimate personal relations; and above all she has the need for an emotional exaltation, a religious enthusiasm, that shall transfigure the ordinariness of daily life and sweep her up in an inspired devotion of self to some ideal purpose. There is, however, a difference between Maggie Tulliver and Mary Ann Evans: Maggie is beautiful. She is triumphantly beautiful, after having been the ugly duckling. The experience of a sensitive child in this latter rôle among insensitive adults is evoked with great poignancy: George Eliot had only to remember. The glow that comes with imagining the duckling turned swan hardly needs analysing; it can be felt in every relevant page,

and it is innocent enough. But it is intimately related to things in
the book that common consent finds deplorable, and it is necessary
to realize this in order to realize their nature and significance and
see what the weaknesses of *The Mill on the Floss* really are.

There is Stephen Guest, who is universally recognized to be a
sad lapse on George Eliot's part. He is a more significant lapse, I
think, than criticism commonly allows. Here is Leslie Stephen
(*George Eliot*, p. 104):

> George Eliot did not herself understand what a mere hairdresser's
> block she was describing in Mr. Stephen Guest. He is another
> instance of her incapacity for portraying the opposite sex. . . .
> We cannot help regretting Maggie's fate; she is touching and
> attractive to the last; but I, at least, cannot help wishing that the
> third volume could have been suppressed. . . .

That the presentment of Stephen Guest is unmistakably feminine
no one will be disposed to deny, but not only is the assumption of
a general incapacity refuted by a whole gallery of triumphs, Stephen
himself is sufficiently "there" to give the drama a convincing force.
Animus against him for his success with Maggie and exasperation
with George Eliot for allowing it shouldn't lead us to dispute that
plain fact — they don't really amount to a judgment of his unreality. To call him a "mere hairdresser's block" is to express a
valuation — a valuation extremely different from George Eliot's.
And if we ourselves differ from her in the same way (who doesn't?),
we must be careful about the implication of the adjective when we
agree that her valuation is surprising. For Leslie Stephen Maggie's
entanglement with Stephen Guest is an "irrelevant and discordant
degradation." — Irrelevant to what and discordant with what? —

> The whole theme of the book is surely the contrast between the
> "beautiful soul" and the commonplace surroundings. It is the
> awakening of the spiritual and imaginative nature and the need
> of finding some room for the play of the higher faculties, whether
> in the direction of religious mysticism or of human affection.

— It is bad enough that the girl who is distinguished not only by
beauty but by intelligence should be made to fall for a provincial
dandy; the scandal or incredibility (runs the argument) becomes
even worse when we add that she is addicted to Thomas à Kempis
and has an exalted spiritual nature. Renunciation is a main theme
in her history and in her daily meditations; but — when temptation
takes the form of Mr. Stephen Guest! It is incredible, or insufferable
in so far as we have to accept it, for temptation at this level can

have nothing to do with the theme of renunciation as we have become familiar with it in Maggie's spiritual life — it is "irrelevant and discordant." This is the position.

Actually, the soulful side of Maggie, her hunger for ideal exaltations, as it is given us in the earlier part of the book, is just what should make us say, on reflection, that her weakness for Stephen Guest is not so surprising after all. It is commonly accepted, this soulful side of Maggie, with what seems to me a remarkable absence of criticism. It is offered by George Eliot herself — and this of course is the main point — with a remarkable absence of criticism. There *is*, somewhere, a discordance . . . not between her ability to present Maggie's yearnings and her ability to present Stephen Guest as an irresistible temptation, but between her presentment of those yearnings on the one hand and her own distinction of intelligence on the other.

That part of Maggie's make-up is done convincingly enough; it is done from the inside. One's criticism is that it is done too purely from the inside. Maggie's emotional and spiritual stresses, her exaltations and renunciations, exhibit, naturally, all the marks of immaturity. . . . There is nothing against George Eliot's presenting this immaturity with tender sympathy; but we ask, and ought to ask, of a great novelist something more. "Sympathy and understanding" is the common formula of praise, but understanding, in any strict sense, is just what she doesn't show. To understand immaturity would be to "place" it, with however subtle an implication, by relating it to mature experience. But when George Eliot touches on these given intensities of Maggie's inner life the vibration comes directly and simply from the novelist, precluding the presence of a maturer intelligence than Maggie's own. It is in these places that we are most likely to make with conscious critical intent the comment that in George Eliot's presentment of Maggie there is an element of self-idealization. The criticism sharpens itself when we say that with the self-idealization there goes an element of self-pity. George Eliot's attitude to her own immaturity as represented by Maggie is the reverse of a mature one.

Maggie Tulliver, in fact, represents an immaturity that George Eliot never leaves safely behind her. . . . This "blind, unconscious yearning" never, for all the intellectual contacts it makes as Maggie grows up and from which it acquires a sense of consciousness, learns to understand itself: Maggie remains quite naïve about its nature. She is quite incapable of analysing it into the varied potentialities it associates. . . .

Obviously there is a large lack of self-knowledge in Maggie — a very natural one, but shared, more remarkably, by George Eliot.

Maggie, it is true, has the most painful throes of conscience and they ultimately prevail. But she has no sense that Stephen Guest (apart, of course, from the insufficient strength of moral fibre betrayed under the strain of temptation — and it is to Maggie he succumbs) is not worthy of her spiritual and idealistic nature. There is no hint that, if Fate had allowed them to come together innocently, she wouldn't have found him a pretty satisfactory soul-mate; there, for George Eliot, lies the tragedy — it is conscience opposes. Yet the ordinary nature of the fascination is made quite plain, . . . And it is quite plain that George Eliot shares to the full the sense of Stephen's irresistibleness — the vibration establishes it beyond a doubt:

> For hours Maggie felt as if the struggle had been in vain. For hours every other thought that she strove to summon was thrust aside by the image of Stephen waiting for the single word that would bring him to her. She did not *read* the letter: she heard him uttering it, and the voice shook her with its old strange power. . . . And yet that promise of joy in the place of sadness did not make the dire force of the temptation to Maggie. It was Stephen's tone of misery, it was the doubt in the justice of her own resolve, that made the balance tremble, and made her once start from her seat to reach the pen and paper, and write "Come!" [vii, 5]

There is no suggestion of any antipathy between this fascination and Maggie's "higher faculties," apart from the moral veto that imposes renunciation. The positive counterpart of renunciation in the "higher" realm to which this last is supposed to belong is the exaltation, transcending all conflicts and quotidian stalenesses, that goes with an irresistibly ideal self-devotion. It is significant that the passages describing such an exaltation, whether as longed for or as attained — and there are many in George Eliot's works — have a close affinity in tone and feeling with this (from the chapter significantly headed, *Borne along by the tide*):

> And they went. Maggie felt that she was being led down the garden among the roses, being helped with firm tender care into the boat, having the cushion and cloak arranged for her feet, and her parasol opened for her (which she had forgotten) — all by this stronger presence that seemed to bear her along without any act of her own will, like the added self which comes with the sudden exalting influence of a strong tonic — and she felt nothing else (vi, 13).

— The satisfaction got by George Eliot from imaginative participation in exalted enthusiasms and self-devotions would, if she could suddenly have gained the power of analysis that in these regions she lacked, have surprised her by the association of elements it represented.

The passage just quoted gives the start of the expedition with Stephen in which chance, the stream and the tide are allowed, temporarily, to decide Maggie's inner conflict. It has been remarked that George Eliot has a fondness for using boats, water and chance in this way. But there are distinctions to be made. The way in which Maggie, exhausted by the struggle, surrenders to the chance that leaves her to embark alone with Stephen, and then, with inert will, lets the boat carry her down-stream until it is too late, so that the choice seems taken from her and the decision compelled — all this is admirable. *This* is insight and understanding, and comes from the psychologist who is to analyse for us Gwendolen Harleth's acceptance of Grandcourt. But the end of *The Mill on the Floss* belongs to another kind of art. Some might place it under the "art" referred to by Henry James. And it is certainly a "dramatic" close of a kind congenial to the Victorian novel-reader. But it has for the critic more significance than this suggests: George Eliot is, emotionally, fully engaged in it. The qualifying "emotionally" is necessary because of the criticism that has to be urged: something so like a kind of daydream indulgence we are all familiar with could not have imposed itself on the novelist as the right ending if her mature intelligence had been fully engaged, giving her full self-knowledge. The flooded river has no symbolic or metaphorical value. It is only the dreamed-of perfect accident that gives us the opportunity for the dreamed-of heroic act — the act that shall vindicate us against a harshly mis-judging world, bring emotional fulfilment and (in others) changes of heart, and provide a gloriously tragic curtain. Not that the sentimental in it is embarrassingly gross, but the finality is not that of great art, and the significance is what I have suggested — a re-vealed immaturity.

The success of *Silas Marner*, that charming minor masterpiece, is conditioned by the absence of personal immediacy; it is a success of reminiscent and enchanted re-creation: *Silas Marner* has in it, in its solid way, something of the fairy-tale. That "solid" presents itself because of the way in which the moral fable is realized in terms of a substantial real world. But this, though re-seen through adult experience, is the world of childhood and youth — the world as directly known then, and what is hardly distinguishable from that, the world as known through family reminiscence, conveyed in anecdote and fireside history. The mood of enchanted adult remi-niscence blends with the re-captured traditional aura to give the world of *Silas Marner* its atmosphere. And it is this atmosphere that conditions the success of the moral intention. We take this intention quite seriously, or, rather, we are duly affected by a realized moral significance, the whole history has been conceived in a profoundly and essentially moral imagination. But the atmosphere precludes too direct a reference to our working standards of probability — that is, to our everyday sense of how things happen. . . . There is nothing that strikes us as false about the story; its charm depends upon our being convinced of its moral truth. But in our description of the satisfaction got from it, "charm" remains the significant word.

The force of the limiting implication may be brought out by a comparative reference to another masterpiece of fiction that it is natural to bring under the head of "moral fable": Dickens's *Hard Times*. The heightened reality of that great book (which combines a perfection of "art" in the Flaubertian sense with an un-Flaubertian moral strength and human richness) has in it nothing of the fairy-tale, and is such as to preclude pleasantness altogether; the satisfaction given depends on a moral significance that can have no relations with charm. But the comparison is of course unfair: *Hard Times* has a large and complex theme, involving its author's profoundest response to contemporary civilization, while *Silas Marner* is modestly conscious of its minor quality.

The unfairness may be compensated by taking up Leslie Stephen's suggestion, that "*Silas Marner* is . . . scarcely equalled in English literature, unless by Mr. Hardy's rustics in *Far from the Madding Crowd* and other works." Actually, the comparison is to George Eliot's advantage (enormously so), and to Hardy's detriment, in ways already suggested. The praises that have been given to George Eliot for the talk at the Rainbow are deserved. It is indeed remarkable that a woman should have been able to present so convincingly an exclusively masculine *milieu*. It is the more remarkable when we recall the deplorable Bob Jakin of *The Mill on the Floss*, who is so obviously and embarrassingly a feminine product.

Silas Marner closes the first phase of George Eliot's creative life. She finds that, if she is to go on being a novelist, it must be one of a very different kind. And *Romola*, her first attempt to achieve the necessary inventiveness, might well have justified the conviction that her creative life was over.

III. "DANIEL DERONDA" AND "THE PORTRAIT OF A LADY"

In no other of her works is the association of the strength with the weakness so remarkable or so unfortunate as in *Daniel Deronda*. It is so peculiarly unfortunate, not because the weakness spoils the strength — the two stand apart, on a large scale, in fairly neatly separable masses — but because the mass of fervid and wordy unreality seems to have absorbed most of the attention the book has ever had, and to be all that is remembered of it. That this should be so shows, I think, how little George Eliot's acceptance has rested upon a critical recognition of her real strength and distinction, and how unfair to her, in effect, is the conventional overvaluing of her early work. For if the nature of her real strength had been appreciated for what it is, so magnificent an achievement as the good half of *Daniel Deronda* could not have failed to compel an admiration that would have established it, not the less for the astonishing badness of the bad half, among the great things in fiction.

It will be best to get the bad half out of the way first. This can be quickly done, since the weakness doesn't require any sustained attention, being of a kind that has already been thoroughly discussed. It is represented by Deronda himself, and by what may be called in general the Zionist inspiration. . . . The Victorian intellectual certainly has a large part in her Zionist inspirations, but that doesn't make these the less fervidly emotional; the part is one of happy subordinate alliance with her immaturity. . . . A distinguished mind and a noble nature are unquestionably present in the bad part of *Daniel Deronda*, but it *is* bad; and the nobility, generosity, and moral idealism are at the same time modes of self-indulgence. . . .

The kind of satisfaction George Eliot finds in Deronda's Zionism is plain. " 'The refuge you are needing from personal trouble is the higher, the religious life, which holds an enthusiasm for something more than our own appetites and vanities.' " But since poor Gwendolen is not in a position to discover herself a Jewess, and so to find her salvation in Deronda's way, she might in time — when Deronda has gone off to Palestine with Mirah — come to reflect critically upon the depth and general validity of his wisdom. We, at any rate, are obliged to be critical of the George Eliot who can so unreservedly endorse the account of the "higher, the religious life" represented by Deronda. A paragon of virtue, generosity, intelligence and disinterestedness, he has no "troubles" he needs a refuge from; what he feels he needs, and what he yearns after, is an "enthusiasm" — an enthusiasm which shall be at the same time a "duty." Whether or not such a desire is necessarily one to have it both ways needn't be discussed; but it is quite plain that the "duty" that Deronda embraces — " 'I considered it my duty — it is the impulse of my feeling — to identify myself . . . with my hereditary people' " — combines moral enthusiasm and the feeling of emotional intensity with essential relaxation in such a way that, for any "higher life" promoted, we may fairly find an analogy in the exalting effects of alcohol. The element of self-indulgence is patent. And so are the confusions. There is no equivalent of Zionism for Gwendolen, and even if there were — :

the religion of heredity or race is not, as a generalizable solution of
the problem, one that George Eliot herself, directly challenged, could
have stood by. In these inspirations her intelligence and real moral
insight are not engaged. But she is otherwise wholly engaged – how
wholly and how significantly being brought further home to us when
we note that Deronda's racial mission finds itself identified with his
love for Mirah, so that he is eventually justified in the "sweet irresistible hopefulness that the best of human possibilities might befall him
– the blending of a complete personal love in one current with a
larger duty. . . ."

All in the book that issues from this inspiration is unreal and
impotently wordy in the way discussed earlier in connection with
Dorothea – though *Middlemarch* can show nothing to match the
wastes of biblicality and fervid idealism ("Revelations") devoted to
Mordecai, or the copious and drearily comic impossibility of the
working-men's club (Ch. 42), or the utterly routing Shakespearean
sprightliness of Hans Meyrick's letter in Ch. 52. The Meyricks who,
while not being direct products of the prophetic afflatus, are subordinate ministers to it, are among those elements in George Eliot that
seem to come from Dickens rather than from life, and so is the pawn-
broker's family: the humour and tenderness are painfully trying, with
that quality they have, that obviousness of intention, which relates
them so intimately to the presiding solemnity they subserve.

No more need be said about the weak and bad side of *Daniel
Deronda*. By way of laying due stress upon the astonishingly con-
trasting strength and fineness of the large remainder, the way in
which George Eliot transcends in it not only her weakness, but what
are commonly thought to be her limitations, I will make an assertion
of fact and a critical comparison: Henry James wouldn't have written
The Portrait of a Lady if he hadn't read *Gwendolen Harleth* (as I
shall call the good part of *Daniel Deronda*), and, of the pair of closely
comparable works, George Eliot's has not only the distinction of
having come first; it is decidedly the greater. The fact, once asserted,
can hardly be questioned. Henry James wrote his "Conversation"
on *Daniel Deronda* in 1876, and he began *The Portrait of a Lady*
"in the spring of 1879." No one who considers both the intense
appreciative interest he shows in *Gwendolen Harleth* and the extraordinary resemblance of his own theme to George Eliot's (so that *The
Portrait of a Lady* might fairly be called a variation) is likely to
suggest that this resemblance is accidental and non-significant.

Isabel Archer is Gwendolen and Osmond is Grandcourt – the
parallel, in scheme, at any rate, is very close and very obvious. As
for the individual characters, that Osmond is Grandcourt is a proposition less likely to evoke protest than the other. And there are certainly

more important differences between Isabel and Gwendolen than between Osmond and Grandcourt — a concession that, since the woman
is the protagonist and the centre of interest, may seem to be a very
favourably significant one in respect of James's originality. The differences, however, as I see them are fairly suggested by saying that
Isabel Archer is Gwendolen Harleth seen by a man. And it has to be
added that, in presenting such a type, George Eliot has a woman's
advantage.

To say that, in the comparison, James's presentment is seen to be
sentimental won't, perhaps, quite do; but it is, I think, seen to be
partial in both senses of the word — controlled, that is, by a vision
that is both incomplete and indulgent; so that we have to grant George
Eliot's presentment an advantage in reality. Here it may be protested
that James is *not* presenting Gwendolen Harleth, but another girl, and
that he is perfectly within his rights in choosing a type that is more
wholly sympathetic. That, no doubt, is what James intended to do
in so far as he had Gwendolen Harleth in mind. But that he had her
in mind at all consciously, so that he thought of himself as attempting
a variation on George Eliot's theme, seems to me very unlikely. The
inspiration, or challenge, he was conscious of was some girl encountered in actual life: "a perfect picture of youthfulness — its eagerness,
its presumption, its preoccupation with itself, its vanity and silliness,
its sense of its own absoluteness. But she is extremely intelligent and
clever, and therefore tragedy *can* have a hold on her."

This, as a matter of fact, is James's description of Gwendolen (given
through Theodora, the most sympathetic of the three *personae* of
the "Conversation," who is here — as the style itself shows — endorsed
by the judicially central Constantius): there seems no need to insist
further that there is point in saying that Isabel Archer is Gwendolen
Harleth seen by a man — or that Gwendolen is Isabel seen by a woman.
For clearly, in the girl so described there must have been (even if
we think of her as Isabel Archer — in whom James doesn't *see* vanity
or silliness) expressions of her "preoccupation with self" and her
"sense of her own absoluteness" justifying observations and responses
more critical and unsympathetic than any offered by James. It isn't
that George Eliot shows any animus towards Gwendolen; simply, as
a very intelligent woman she is able, unlimited by masculine partiality
of vision, and only the more perceptive because a woman, to achieve
a much *completer* presentment of her subject than James of his. The
strength which manifests itself in sum as completeness affects us
locally as a greater specificity, an advantage which, when considered,
turns out to be also an advantage over James in consistency. And, as
a matter of fact, a notable specificity marks the strength of her mature
art in general.

This strength appears in her rendering of country-house and "county" society compared with James's. Here we have something that is commonly supposed to lie outside her scope. Her earlier life having been what it was, and her life as a practising novelist having been spent with G. H. Lewes, "cut off from the world" ("the loss for a novelist was serious," says Mrs. Woolf), what can she have known of the "best society where no one makes an invidious display of anything in particular, and the advantages of the world are taken with that high-bred depreciation which follows from being accustomed to them" (her own words)? The answer is that, however she came by her knowledge, she can, on the showing of *Daniel Deronda* present that world with such fulness and reality as to suggest that she knows it as completely and inwardly as she knows *Middlemarch*. James himself was much impressed by this aspect of her strength. Of the early part of George Eliot's book he says (through Constantius): "I delighted in its deep, rich English tone, in which so many notes seemed melted together."

The stress should fall on the "many notes" rather than on the "melted," for what James is responding to is the specificity and completeness of the rendering, whereas "melted" suggests an assimilating mellowness, charming and conciliating the perceptions; a suffusing richness, bland and emollient. George Eliot's richness is not of that kind; she has too full and strong a sense of the reality, she sees too clearly and understandingly, sees with a judging vision that relates everything to her profoundest moral experience: her full living sense of value is engaged, and sensitively responsive. It isn't that she doesn't appreciate the qualities that so appeal to Henry James: she renders them at least as well as he — renders them better, in the sense that she "places" them (a point very intimately related to the other, that her range of "notes" is much wider than his). It is true that, as Virginia Woolf says, "She is no satirist." But the reason given, "The movement of her mind was too slow and cumbersome to lend itself to comedy," shows that Mrs. Woolf hadn't read *Daniel Deronda* — and can't have read other things at all perceptively. If George Eliot is no satirist it is not because she hasn't the quickness, the delicacy of touch and the precision. And it certainly is not that she hasn't the perceptions and responses that go to make satire. Consider, for instance, the interview between Gwendolen and her uncle, the Reverend Mr. Gascoigne ("man of the world turned clergyman"), in Ch. 13. . . .

This is Samuel Butler's matter, and taken by itself, not, in effect, altogether remote from Samuel Butler's mode. The presentment of the Rector here is directly satirical — at any rate, it might very well have come from a satirical novel. But even within the passage quoted there are signs (notably in the short narrative passage describing

Gwendolen's state of mind) adverting us that the author isn't a satirist. And we know from his appearances elsewhere that her total attitude towards Mr. Gascoigne is very far from being satirical; she shows him as an impressive and, on the whole, admirable figure: "cheerful, successful worldliness," she tells us, "has a false air of being more selfish than the acrid, unsuccessful kind, whose secret history is summed up in the terrible words, 'Sold, but not paid for.'" And Mr. Gascoigne not only has strong family feeling and a generous sense of duty, but shows himself in adversity not only admirably practical, but admirably unselfish. George Eliot sees too much and has too strong a sense of the real (as well as too much self-knowledge and too adequate and constant a sense of her own humanity) to be a satirist.

The kind of complexity and completeness, the fulness of vision and response, represented by her Mr. Gascoigne characterizes her rendering in general of the world to which he belongs. Henry James's presentment of what is essentially the same world is seen, in the comparison, to have entailed much excluding and simplifying. His is a subtle art, and he has his irony; but the irony doesn't mean inclusiveness — an adequacy to the complexities of the real in its concrete fulness; it doesn't mark a complex valuing process that has for upshot a total attitude in which all the elements of a full response are brought together. His art (in presenting this world in *The Portrait of a Lady*, I mean) seems to leave out all such perceptions as evoke the tones and facial expressions with which we register the astringent and the unpalatable. The irony is part of the subtlety of the art by which, while being so warmly concrete in effect, he can, without challenge, be so limited and selective, and, what is an essential condition of his selectiveness, so lacking in specificity compared with George Eliot. His world of "best society" and country-house is, for all its life and charm, immeasurably less real (the word has a plain enough force here, and will bear pondering) than George Eliot's. He idealizes, and his idealizing is a matter of not seeing, and not knowing (or not taking into account), a great deal of the reality. And it seems to me that we have essentially this kind of idealizing in his Isabel Archer; she stands to Gwendolen Harleth as James's "best society" does to George Eliot's.

In saying this, of course, I am insisting on the point of comparing Gwendolen with Isabel. The point is to bring out the force of James's own tribute (paid through Constantius) to the characteristic strength of George Eliot's art as exhibited in her protagonist: "And see how the girl is known, inside out, how thoroughly she is felt and understood. It is the most *intelligent* thing in all George Eliot's writing; and that is saying much. It is so deep, so true, so complete, it holds such a wealth of psychological detail, it is more than masterly." It would hardly be said of Isabel Archer that the presentment of her is complete; it is characteristic of James's art to have made her an effective enough presence for his purpose without anything approaching a "wealth of psychological detail." Her peculiar kind of impressiveness, in fact, is conditioned by her *not* being known inside out, and — we have to confess it — could *not* have been achieved by George Eliot: she knows too much about that kind of girl. For it is fair to say that if James had met Gwendolen Harleth (at any rate, an American one) he would have seen Isabel Archer; he immensely admired George Eliot's inwardness and completeness of rendering, but when he met the type in actual life and was prompted to the conception of *The Portrait of a Lady*, he saw her with the eyes of an American gentleman. One must add — an essential point — that he saw *her* as American.

It is, of course, possible to imagine a beautiful, clever and vital girl, with "that sense of superior claims which made a large part of her consciousness" (George Eliot's phrase for Gwendolen, but it applies equally to Isabel), whose egoism yet shouldn't be as much open to the criticism of an intelligent woman as Gwendolen's. But it is hard to believe that, in life, she could be as free from qualities inviting a critical response as the Isabel Archer seen by James. Asking of Gwendolen, why, though a mere girl, she should be everywhere a centre of deferential attention, George Eliot says (Ch. 4): "The answer may seem to lie quite on the surface: — in her beauty, a certain unusualness about her, a decision of will which made itself felt in her graceful movements and clear unhesitating tones, so that if she came into the room on a rainy day when everybody else was flaccid and the use of things in general was not apparent to them, there seemed to be a sudden, sufficient reason for keeping up the forms of life." James might very well have been glad to have found these phrases for his heroine. But George Eliot isn't satisfied with the answer: she not only goes on, as James would hardly have done, to talk about the girl's "inborn energy of egoistic desire," she is very specific and concrete in exhibiting the play of that energy — the ways in which it imposes her claims on the people around her. And it is not enough to reply that James doesn't need to be specific to this effect — even granting, as we may, that the two authors are dealing with different girls: it is so plain that George Eliot knows more about hers than he about his, and that this accounts for an important part of the ostensible difference. . . .

George Eliot's genius appears in the specificity with which she exhibits the accompaniments in Gwendolen of the kind of conscious advantage she resembles Isabel in enjoying. There is the conversation with Mrs. Arrowpoint that comes just before Herr Klesmer has the opportunity to produce that "softening air of silliness," a conversation that illustrates one of the disabilities of egoism: "self-confidence is apt to address itself to an imaginary dulness in others; as people who are well off speak in a cajoling tone to the poor, and those who are in the prime of life raise their voice and speak artificially to seniors, hastily conceiving them to be deaf and rather imbecile." We have hardly here a writer the movement of whose mind is "too slow and cumbersome for comedy" and whose "hold upon dialogue is slack." When she is at her best, as she is on so large a scale in *Gwendolen Harleth,* there is no writer of whom these criticisms are less true. Nowhere is her genius more apparent than in the sensitive precision of her "hold on dialogue"; a hold which, with the variety of living tension she can create with it, is illustrated in the scene between Gwendolen and her mother that follows on the arrival of Grand-court's self-committing note [Ch. 26], and in the decisive *tête-à-tête* with Grandcourt [Ch. 27.] It is essentially in her speech that Gwendolen is made a concrete presence — Gwendolen, whose "ideal it was to be daring in speech and reckless in braving danger, both moral and physical"; of whom it is hard to say whether she is more fitly described as tending to act herself or her ideal of herself; "whose lively venturesomeness of talk has the effect of wit" ("it was never her aspiration to express herself virtuously so much as cleverly — a point to be remembered in extenuation of her words, which were usually worse than she was"). . . .

It is in the scene between Gwendolen and Grandcourt that George Eliot's mastery of dialogue is most strikingly exhibited. We have it in the brush that follows, in Ch. 11, on their being introduced to each other. It is shown in the rendering of dramatic tension in Ch. 13, where Gwendolen takes evasive action in the face of Grandcourt's clear intent to propose. I will save quotation for the marvelously economical passage (reference to it will be in place later) in which she finds that she has placed herself in a position in which she can't not accept, and acceptance seems to determine itself without an act of will. There is a good example of light exchange between them in the following Chapter (28).

At the moment, what has to be noted is that, though James's Pulcheria of the "Conversation" says "they are very much alike" ("it proves how common a type the worldly, *pincée,* selfish young woman seemed to her"), Gwendolen is decidedly not another Rosamond Vincy: her talk is enough to establish that; as Theodora says, she is intelligent. It is with Mrs. Transome that she belongs, being qualified in the same kind of way as Mrs. Transome had been in youth to enact the rôle of daringly brilliant beauty: "she had never dissociated happiness from personal pre-eminence and *éclat*." She is intelligent – in Mrs. Transome's way. . . .

It is only when compared with George Eliot herself that she is (like Mrs. Transome) to be classed with Rosamond Vincy: none of these three *personae* is at all like Dorothea, or represents any possibility of the Dorothea relation to the novelist. As James's Theodora says, she is intelligent, "and therefore tragedy *can* have a hold on her." She is a young Mrs. Transome, in whom disaster forces a development of conscience; for, in George Eliot's phrase, "she has a root of conscience in her." . . .

Here, of course, we have a difference between her and Isabel Archer: remorse – it doesn't belong to James's conception of his young woman that she shall have any need for that. She is merely to make a wrong choice, the wrongness of which is a matter of an error in judgment involving no guilt on her part, though it involves tragic consequences for her. As Mr. Yvor Winters sees it in his essay on him in *Maule's Curse*, James is concerned, characteristically, to present the choice as free – to present it as pure choice. "The moral issue, then, since it is primarily an American affair, is freed in most of the Jamesian novels, and in all of the greatest, from the compulsion of a code of manners." This certainly has a bearing on the difference between Gwendolen and Isabel; between the English young lady in her proper setting of mid-Victorian English "best society," one who in her "venturesomeness" "cannot conceive herself as anything else than a lady," and the "free" American girl, who moves on the Old World stage as an indefinitely licensed and privileged interloper. But there is a more obviously important difference: "The moral issue is also freed from economic necessity. . . . Isabel Archer is benevolently provided with funds after her story opens, with the express purpose that her action shall thereafter be unhampered."

The contrast offered by George Eliot's preoccupation is extreme. All her creative power works to the evoking of a system of pressures so intolerable to Gwendolen, and so enclosing, that her final acceptance of Grandcourt seems to issue, not from her will, but from them; if she acts, it is certainly not in freedom, and she hasn't even the sense of exercising choice. Economic necessity plays a determining part. In the earlier phase of the history she has, as much as Isabel Archer in respect of Lord Warburton and Gilbert Osmond, a free choice in front of her: does she, or does she not, want to marry Grandcourt? But after the meeting with Mrs. Glasher and Grandcourt's children she recoils in disgust and horror from the idea of marriage with him; she recoils from the wrong to others, and from the insult (she feels) offered herself. Then comes the financial disaster, engulfing her family. The effect on Gwendolen, with her indocile egoism and her spoilt

child's ignorance of practical realities, and the consequences for her —
these are evoked with vivid particularity. There is, pressed on her
by the kind and efficient Rector, her uncle, as a duty that is at the
same time a gift of fortune she can't fail to accept with grateful
gladness, the situation of governess with Mrs. Mompert, the Bishop's
wife — who, as a woman of "strict principle" such as precludes her
from "having a French person in the house," will want to inspect
even the Rector's nominee before appointing her: the sheer impossibility of such a "situation" for Gwendolen is something we are made
to feel from the inside. The complementary kind of impossibility, the
impossibility of her own plan of exploiting with *éclat* her talents and
advantages and becoming a great actress or singer, is brought home
to her with crushing and humiliating finality by Herr Klesmer (Ch.
23). It is immediately after this interview, which leaves her with no
hope of an alternative to Mrs. Mompert and the "episcopal peniten-
tiary," that Grandcourt's note arrives, asking if he may call. No
better illustration of George Eliot's peculiar genius as a novelist — a
kind of genius so different from that she is commonly credited with
— can be found for quoting than the presentment of Gwendolen's
reactions. Here we have the most subtle and convincing analysis
rendered, with extraordinary vividness and economy, in the concrete;
the shifting tensions in Gwendolen are registered in her speech and
outward movements, and the whole is (in an essentially novelistic
way) so dramatic that we don't distinguish the elements of description and commentary as such: [The long passage from Ch. 26 is found
in the Harper Torchbook ed., 1961, pp. 217–219.]

Reading this, it is hard to remember that George Eliot was contemporary with Trollope. What later novelist has rendered the inner
movement of impulse, the play of motive that issues in speech and
act and underlies formed thought and conscious will, with more penetrating subtlety than she? It is partly done *through* speech and action.
But there is also, co-operating with these, a kind of psychological
notation that is well represented in the passage quoted above, and is
exemplified in "Quick, quick, like pictures in a book beaten open
with a sense of hurry . . . ," and "yet in the dark seed-growths of
consciousness a new wish was forming itself . . . ," and "The young
activity within her made a warm current through her terror . . . ,"
and "All the while there was a busy under-current in her, like the
thought of a man who keeps up a dialogue while he is considering
how he can slip away" — and so much else. This notation is one of
the distinctive characteristics of her mature style, doing its work always with an inevitable rightness — and *Daniel Deronda* (with *Middlemarch*) was written in the earlier 'seventies. But remarkable as it is,
and impressive as would be the assemblage of instances that could be

quickly brought together, it is better not to stress it without adding that, as she uses it, it is inseparable from her rendering of "psychology" in speech and action. It doesn't seem to me that her genius as exhibited in these ways has been anything like duly recognized. . . .

We note, with regard to Gwendolen's attitude towards what she sees as the strong moral ground for refusing Grandcourt, that "in the dark seed-growths of consciousness a new wish was forming itself — 'I wish I had never known it.'" There is much concrete psychological notation to this effect, deriving from the insight of a great novelist; that it has a moral significance, a relation to that ostensibly mechanical and unwilled 'Yes,' is plain. But it is possible to overstress Gwendolen's guilt in the matter of Mrs. Glasher, a guilt that is so very conscious. George Eliot's appreciation of the moral issues doesn't coincide with that of her protagonist — or of the conventional Victorian moralist. For George Eliot the essential significance of Gwendolen's case lies in the egoism expressed here. . . .

> The prospect of marrying Grandcourt really seemed more attractive to her than she had believed beforehand that any marriage could be: the dignities, the luxuries, the power of doing a great deal of what she liked to do, which had now come close to her, and within her choice to secure or to lose, took hold of her nature as if it had been the strong odour of what she had only imagined and longed for before. And Grandcourt himself? He seemed as little of a flaw in his fortunes as a lover and husband could possibly be. Gwendolen wished to mount the chariot and drive the plunging horses herself, with a spouse by her side who would fold his arms and give her his countenance without looking ridiculous. [Ch. 13]

So much pride and courage and sensitiveness and intelligence fixed in a destructive deadlock through false valuation and self-ignorance — this is what makes Gwendolen a tragic figure. And as George Eliot establishes for our contemplation the complexities of inner constitution and outer conditions that make Gwendolen look so different from Isabel Archer, she is exhibiting what we recognize from our most intimate experience to be as much the behaviour of a responsible moral agent, and so as much amenable to moral judgment, as any human behaviour can be. Not, of course, that our attitude is that of the judge towards the prisoner in the dock; but neither is it that of *tout comprendre, c'est tout pardonner*. It is, or should be (with George Eliot's help), George Eliot's own, which is that of a great novelist, concerned with human and moral valuation in a way proper to her art — it is a way that doesn't let us forget that what is being lit up for us lies within. . . .

James's marvelous art is devoted to contenting us with very little in the way of inward realization of Isabel, and to keeping us interested, instead, in a kind of psychological detective work — keeping us intently wondering from the outside, and constructing, on a strict economy of evidence, what is going on inside. And, if we consider, we find that the constructions to which we are led are of such a kind as not to challenge, or to bear with comfort, any very searching test in terms of life. The difference between James and George Eliot is largely a matter of what he leaves out. . . .

Actually, we can see that the trouble is that he derives so much more from George Eliot than he suspects: he largely mistakes the nature of his inspiration, which is not so much from life as he supposes. He has been profoundly impressed by the irony of Gwendolen's married situation, and is really moved by a desire to produce a similar irony. But he fails to produce the fable that gives inevitability and moral significance. He can remain unaware of his failure because he is so largely occupied (a point that can be illustrated in detail) in transposing George Eliot, whose power is due to the profound psychological truth of her conception, and the consistency with which she develops it. . . .

If any doubt should linger as to whether one is justified in talking about "what James does with *Gwendolen Harleth*," it should be settled finally by a consideration of Osmond in relation to Grandcourt: Osmond so plainly *is* Grandcourt, hardly disguised, that the general derivative relation of James's novel to George Eliot's becomes quite unquestionable. It is true that Grandcourt is no aesthetic connoisseur, but Osmond's interest in articles of *virtù* amounts to nothing more than a notation of a kind of cherished fastidiousness of conscious, but empty, superiority that is precisely Grandcourt's: "From the first she had noticed that he had nothing of the fool in his composition but that by some subtle means he communicated to her the impression that all the folly lay with other people, who did what he did not care to do." That might very well be an account of the effect of Osmond on Isabel, but it comes from George Eliot. Grandcourt, as an English aristocrat whose status licenses any amount of languid disdain, doesn't need a symbolic dilettantism. [Ch. 54, pp. 504–5]. This equally describes Osmond, of whom it might equally well be said that "he is a man whose grace of bearing has long been moulded on an experience of boredom," and that "he has worn out all his healthy interest in things." All either cares about is to be assured that he feels superior; and the contemptible paradox of a superiority that is nothing unless assured of itself by those whose judgment it affects to despise is neatly "placed" by George Eliot. . . .

The diamonds, it may be noted at this point, exemplify George

Eliot's characteristic subtle and inevitable use of symbolism. They are his mother's diamonds, "long ago" given Lydia to wear. His demanding them back for Gwendolen is his means of announcing to Lydia that the relations they symbolize — marital, virtually — are to cease. But he can't force her to give them up when she refuses; her strength is that they were given to her as his wife, and she has been that, in all but legal form and social recognition. "Her person suited diamonds, and made them look as if they were worth some of the money given for them" — the natural validity of the relation is suggested there. They come to Gwendolen on the night of her wedding-day with the enclosed message that turns them to poison (Ch. 31): "I am the grave in which your chance of happiness is buried. . . ." Gwendolen has a hysterical fit: the diamonds are for her the consciousness of that past of Grandcourt's with Lydia which precludes any possibility of good married relations between him and herself. . . . The first glimpse we have of Gwendolen in public after her marriage, she is wearing the diamonds. We are told that her "belief in her power of dominating had utterly gone." And again and again, with inevitable naturalness, they play their pregnantly symbolic part. They come to represent Nemesis: they are what Gwendolen married Grandcourt for, and her punishment is having to wear them.

James's use of symbols, famous as he is for it, looks weak in comparison with George Eliot's. They are thought out independently of the action and then introduced. We have an instance in the valuable coffee-cup, "precious" to Madame Merle but "attenuated," that Osmond, in the show-down scene with Madame Merle (Ch. 49), picks up and observes, "dryly," to be cracked. It symbolizes very obviously, in its *ad hoc* way, the relations between the two, the crack being the resentment Osmond feels against Madame Merle for the "service" she had done him in marrying him to Isabel. And here, it is worth noting, we have the first form of the celebrated Golden Bowl symbol, which, in the novel, called after it, is used for so many purposes, but which, for all the modish esteem it enjoys, is always applied elaborately from the outside, with an effect of strain. The introduction of George Eliot's diamonds arises naturally from the social drama, and they play a natural part in the action. The turquoise necklace that represents Gwendolen's relations with Deronda is a symbol of the same order. . . .

George Eliot's greatness is of a different kind from that she has been generally credited with. And by way of concluding on this emphasis I will adduce once again her most intelligently appreciative critic, Henry James:

> She does not strike me as naturally a critic, less still as naturally a sceptic; her spontaneous part is to observe life and to feel it, to

feel it with admirable depth. Contemplation, sympathy and faith
— something like that, I should say, would have been her natural
scale. If she had fallen upon an age of enthusiastic assent to old
articles of faith, it seems to me possible that she would have had
a more perfect, a more consistent and graceful development than
she has actually had.

There is, I think, a complete misconception here. George Eliot's
development may not have been "perfect" or "graceful," and "consistent" is not precisely the adjective one would choose for it; yet she
went on developing to the end, as few writers do, and achieved the
most remarkable expression of her distinctive genius in her last work:
her art in *Gwendolen Harleth* is at its maturest. And her profound
insight into the moral nature of man is essentially that of one whose
critical intelligence has been turned intensively on her faiths. A sceptic
by nature or culture — indeed no; but that is not because her intelligence, a very powerful one, doesn't freely illuminate all her interests
and convictions. That she should be thought depressing (as, for instance, Leslie Stephen thinks her) always surprises me. She exhibits
a traditional moral sensibility expressing itself, not within a frame of
"old articles of faith" (as James obviously intends the phrase), but
nevertheless with perfect sureness, in judgments that involve confident
positive standards, and yet affect us as simply the report of luminous
intelligence. She deals in the weakness and ordinariness of human
nature, but doesn't find it contemptible, or show either animus or
self-deceiving indulgence towards it; and, distinguished and noble as
she is, we have in reading her the feeling that she is in and of the
humanity she presents with so clear and disinterested a vision. For
us in these days, it seems to me, she is a peculiarly fortifying and
wholesome author, and a suggestive one: she might well be pondered
by those who tend to prescribe simple recourses — to suppose, say,
that what Charlotte Yonge has to offer may be helpfully relevant — in
face of the demoralizations and discouragements of an age that isn't
one of "enthusiastic assent to old articles of faith."

As for her rank among novelists, I take the challenge from a representative purveyor of currency, Oliver Elton. . . . He says in discussing the "check to George Eliot's reputation" given by the coming
"into fuller view" of "two other masters of fiction" — Meredith and
Hardy: "Each of these novelists saw the world of men and women
more freely than George Eliot had done; and they brought into relief
one of her greatest deficiencies, namely, that while exhaustively describing life, she is apt to miss the spirit of life itself." I can only say
that this, for anyone whose critical education has begun, should be
breath-taking in its absurdity, and affirm my conviction that, by the
side of George Eliot — and the comparison shouldn't be necessary —

Meredith appears as a shallow exhibitionist (his famous "intelligence" a laboured and vulgar brilliance) and Hardy, decent as he is, as a provincial manufacturer of gauche and heavy fictions that sometimes have corresponding virtues. For a positive indication of her place and quality I think of a Russian; not Turgènev, but a far greater, Tolstoy — who, we all know, is pre-eminent in getting "the spirit of life itself." George Eliot, of course, is not as transcendently great as Tolstoy, but she *is* great, and great in the same way. The extraordinary reality of *Anna Karenina* (his supreme masterpiece, I think) comes of an intense moral interest in human nature that provides the light and courage for a profound psychological analysis. This analysis is rendered in art (and *Anna Karenina, pace* Matthew Arnold, is wonderfully closely worked) by means that are like those used by George Eliot in *Gwendolen Harleth* — a proposition that will bear a great deal of considering in the presence of the text. Of George Eliot it can in turn be said that her best work has a Tolstoyan depth and reality.

Basil Willey

George Eliot

F. W. H. Myers, in an oft-quoted passage, has recorded a conversation with George Eliot at Cambridge in 1873, and I venture, on account of its high relevance, to quote it once again as a text for this chapter:

> I remember how, at Cambridge, I walked with her once in the Fellows' Garden of Trinity, on an evening of rainy May; and she, stirred somewhat beyond her wont, and taking as her text the three words which have been used so often as the inspiring trumpet-calls of men, — the words *God, Immortality, Duty,* — pronounced, with terrible earnestness, how inconceivable was the *first*, how unbelievable the *second*, and yet how peremptory and absolute the *third*. Never, perhaps, have sterner accents affirmed the sovereignty of impersonal and unrecompensing Law. I listened, and night fell; her grave, majestic countenance turned towards me like a sibyl's in the

Reprinted from Basil Willey, *Nineteenth Century Studies*, London, Chatto & Windus, 1949, pp. 204–207, 237–250, by permission of the publishers.

gloom; it was as though she withdrew from my grasp, one by one, the two scrolls of promise, and left me the third scroll only, awful with inevitable fates. And when we stood at length and parted, amid that columnar circuit of the forest-trees, beneath the last twilight of starless skies, I seemed to be gazing, like Titus at Jerusalem, on vacant seats and empty halls, — on a sanctuary with no Presence to hallow it, and heaven left lonely of a god (*Essays — Modern* [1883], pp. 268–9).

In the present book, which attempts to follow some of the main currents of thought and belief in nineteenth century England, George Eliot must needs occupy a central place. Probably no English writer of the time, and certainly no novelist, more fully epitomizes the century; her development is a paradigm, her intellectual biography a graph, of its most decided trend. Starting from evangelical Christianity, the curve passes through doubt to a reinterpreted Christ and a religion of humanity: beginning with God, it ends in Duty. George Eliot's representative quality is due largely to her unique position, amongst imaginative writers, as a focus for the best (and the worst) that was being said and thought in her time, in Europe as well as at home. No one was more thoroughly abreast of the newest thought, the latest French or German theory, the last interpretations of dogma, the most up-to-date results in anthropology, medicine, biology or sociology; it is she who first translates Strauss's *Life of Jesus* and Feuerbach's *Essence of Christianity;* if a Mackay writes *The Progress of the Intellect* (1850), it is Miss Evans who must review it for the *Westminster.* She was the first English writer to bring an intellect of that calibre to the service of fiction, and the wonder perhaps is that this preponderant cerebration did not devour her creative instinct more completely than it did. But as with Wordsworth, whom she greatly reverenced and in some ways resembled, the heart in her was kept alive by the recollection of her early life, and of the scenes and people associated with the feelings of childhood. In a sense her early novels are her *Prelude,* that is, the means by which she pierced below the hard crust formed by the years of translating, reviewing and mental overforcing, to the quickening beds of heartfelt memory which lay beneath. Having achieved this recovery of time past, she was then able to see in truer perspective the relations between advancing intellect and backward-yearning affections. From the very outset, however, she showed the instinct — which was deeply imbedded in the consciousness of the century as a whole — to see both sides of any question: to tolerate the ordinary while admiring the ideal, to cling to the old while accepting the new, to retain the core of traditions while mentally criticizing their forms. She succeeded, better than

J. S. Mill, in uniting what he described as the two main streams of
the nineteenth century mind — its two kinds of onesidedness — the
Benthamite, which stands outside and tests all received opinions, and
the Coleridgean, which tries from within to discover what is true in
them. We see this action and reaction going on both in her own
life and in the novels. . . .

In what follows I hope to suggest that this "conservative-reforming"
impulse was the leading *motif* of her life: that her lifelong quest, as
it was Comte's and the century's, was for a reconcilement between
these opposites, a synthesis (as Comte would say) between the Static
and Dynamic principles, between Order and Progress, Tradition and
Enlightenment, the heart and the head. In the foregoing chapter I
have considered Comte as at once a symbol and a producer of the
intellectual climate of the mid-century — of that climate in which,
after emerging from her provincial-evangelical chrysalis, George Eliot
lived and moved. Though Comte made his impact upon her in due
time (mainly, at first, through G. H. Lewes), this was not until the
shape of her mind had already been formed in other moulds. I want
now to consider three of these early formative influences, in the order
in which they affected her: Charles Hennell, D. F. Strauss and Ludwig
Feuerbach. . . .

Whoever has been reading George Eliot will recognize that with
most of the underlying principles of Strauss, Comte and Feuerbach
she was in agreement. The supersession of God by Humanity, of
Faith by Love and Sympathy, the elimination of the supernatural, the
elevation of the natural, the subordination of intellect to heart, thought
to feeling — these may all be found in her novels as well as in her
letters. Heaven will not help us, so we must help one another; this
realization tinges our whole life with anguish, but it is the cross which
the new elect must bear: "The 'highest calling and election' is to *do
without opium*, and live through all our pain with conscious, clear-
eyed endurance."[1] But her studies, as well as her own inmost
propensities, inclined her to rely upon truth of feeling, and this
engendered a wide tolerance and reverence for all religious forms
which have expressed, and still express, the primary needs of the
human heart. To her "conservative-reforming intellect," the merely
negative kinds of "free-thinking" were hateful: "I have a growing
conviction," she writes to Sara Hennell, while at work on *Scenes of
Clerical Life*, "that we may measure true moral and intellectual culture by the comprehension and veneration given to all forms of

[1] J. W. Cross, *George Eliot's Life*, [3 vols., 1885], II, 283 (letter to Mme
Bodichon, Dec. 26, 1860).

thought and feeling which have influenced large masses of mankind
— and of all intolerance the intolerance calling itself philosophical is
the most odious to me."[2] And again, to Charles Bray (July 5, 1859):
"people are, for the most part, so incapable of comprehending the
state of mind which cares for that which is essentially human in all
forms of belief, and desires to exhibit it under all forms with loving
truthfulness. Freethinkers are scarcely wider than the orthodox in
this matter, — they all want to see themselves and their own opinions
held up as the true and the lovely."[3] Lord David Cecil will have it
that George Eliot was "not religious"; I cannot agree with him — or
rather, I cannot agree that that is the least misleading way of saying
what he means. "Religious" seems to me to be just what she was, and
many others of whom she is the type; the whole predicament she
represents was that of the religious temperament cut off by the
Zeitgeist from the traditional objects of veneration, and the traditional intellectual formulations.[4] She was not, of course, a "practising
Christian," but in her estrangement from the "religion about Jesus"
she was none the further from the "religion of Jesus." She knew the
hunger and thirst after righteousness, and the need for renunciation
— the need to lose one's life in order to gain it. And, though her
religious consciousness was pre-eminently moral, it was not exclusively so; she also had the faculty of reverence, the capacity to acknowledge the reality of the unseen. When reading Darwin's Origin
of Species she writes: "to me the Development Theory, and all other
explanations of processes by which things came to be, produce a
feeble impression compared with the mystery that lies under the
processes."[5] Hers was in fact the middle position of conservatism-
liberalism; it is a position not easy to sustain, and I do not think that
George Eliot ever — at least not for any long period — recovered
lasting heart's-ease. There could only be, for her, effort, striving, endurance, and that "terrible earnestness" recorded by F. W. H. Myers.
"I have faith in the working out of higher possibilities than the
Catholic or any other Church has presented," she writes in Comtist
language, 'and those who have strength to wait and endure are bound
to accept no formula which their whole souls — their intellect as well
as their emotions — do not embrace with entire reverence." — and then
follows the phrase about doing without opium.[6] One of the clearest
statements is this, taken from another letter to Mme Bodichon
(written during the composition of Romola):

2 Cross, I, 432 (Feb. 24, 1857).
3 Cross, II, 118.
4 Was Carlyle "not religious"?
5 Cross, II, 148 (letter to Mme Bodichon, Dec 5, 1859).
6 Cross, II, 283.

Pray don't ever ask me again not to rob a man of his religious belief, as if you thought my mind tended to such robbery. I have too profound a conviction of the efficacy that lies in all sincere faith, and the spiritual blight that comes with no-faith, to have any negative propagandism in me. In fact, I have very little sympathy with Freethinkers as a class, and have lost all interest in mere antagonism to religious doctrines. I care only to know, if possible, the lasting meaning that lies in all religious doctrine from the beginning till now.[7]

It is a sentiment which would have been echoed by Coleridge, Carlyle, Maurice, Arnold, Sidgwick and many others. Her technique for retaining what she considered this "lasting meaning," while rejecting what her intellect found unacceptable, was that of Strauss and the German "higher criticism," and of Matthew Arnold and later modernists. Writing of Renan's *Vie de Jésus* she says: "It seems to me the soul of Christianity lies not at all in the facts of an individual life, but in the ideas of which that life was the meeting-point and the new starting-point. We can never have a satisfactory basis for the history of the man Jesus, but that negation does not affect the Idea of the Christ either in its historical influence or its great symbolic meanings."[8] Or again: "The divine will is simply so much as we have ascertained of the facts of existence which compel obedience at our peril."[9] Thirty years after the letter to Sara Hennell about religious conformity [9 October 1843] her position is virtually unaltered: she would go to church constantly, she says, for the sake of fellowship in worshipping "the highest good," were there no reasons against following this inclination. For those without definite religious convictions, church-going will be better than mere negation. My last extracts on this theme are from letters written to Mrs Ponsonby in 1874 and 1875:

My books have for their main bearing a conclusion . . . without which I could not have cared to write any representation of human life — namely, that the fellowship between man and man which has been the principle of development, social and moral, is not dependent on conceptions of what is not man: and that the idea of God, so far as it has been a high spiritual influence, is the ideal of a goodness entirely human (i.e. an exaltation of the human).

Loss of belief in a future life, she goes on, does not rob us of our moral sense, our sense of duty, our sympathy; we retain our "sense

[7] Cross, II, 343 (November 26, 1862).
[8] Cross, II, 359–60 (to Mrs Peter Taylor, July 30, 1863).
[9] Cross, III, 48.

of quality in actions," just as we continue to appreciate colour even after becoming aware of the laws of the spectrum. We should consider our early religious experience as "a portion of valid knowledge," and "cherish its emotional results in relation to objects which are either substitutes or metamorphoses of the earlier. . . . And I think we must not take every great physicist — or other 'ist' — for an apostle, but be ready to suspect him of some crudity concerning relations that lie outside his special studies, if his exposition strands us on results that seem to stultify the most ardent, massive experience of mankind, and hem up the best part of our feelings in stagnation."[1]

This instinct for the understanding of all forms of thought and feeling, this quest for that which is essentially human in all varieties of belief, can of course be illustrated to any extent from the novels. "Pity and fairness," she once wrote, "embrace the utmost delicacies of the moral life," and this delicacy, together with her balanced regard for improvement and for old imperfect things, appears clearly in her treatment of contrasted types of churchmanship. Mr Gilfil's sermons (of which he kept a large heap, "rather yellow and worn at the edges") certainly belonged to the class of the old and imperfect, but when his congregation, having dozed through the sermon's "agreeable monotony," "made their way back through the miry lanes," they were "perhaps as much the better for this simple weekly tribute to what they knew of good and right, as many a more wakeful and critical congregation of the present day."[2] The same attitude appears in her treatment of Mr Irwine in *Adam Bede*, and in the contrast between him and Mr Ryde: "Mrs Poyser used to say . . . Mr Irwine was like a good meal o' victual, you were the better for him without thinking on it, and Mr Ryde was like a dose o' physic, he gripped you and worreted you, and after all he left you much the same."[3] The contrast reappears, in *Middlemarch*, in Mr Farebrother and Mr Tyke: Mr Farebrother, the man of the world who plays for money, yet who has pity and fairness, fine human tact and ripe wisdom, and knows the secret of renunciation; Mr Tyke, protégé of Bulstrode, who is doctrinal and evangelical but non-human. It was George Eliot's constant objection to evangelicalism, that in its emphasis upon the will and acts of an implacable Deity it extinguished human love and service. She extended this objection to all general ethical maxims if followed without regard to their human results: "There is no general doctrine," she says in *Middlemarch*, "which is not capable of eating out our morality if unchecked by the deep-seated habit of direct

---

1 Cross, III, 245 and 253 (Dec. 10, 1874 and Jan. 30, 1875).
2 *Scenes of Clerical Life*, pp. 94–5 (World's Classics ed.).
3 [Ch. 17], p. 200 (World's Classics ed.).

fellow-feeling with individual fellow-men."[4] Fred Vincy feels no remorse for his careless borrowings until he sees their actual effect upon the Garth family: "Indeed we are most of us brought up in the notion that the highest motive for not doing a wrong is something irrespective of the beings who would suffer the wrong."[5] "We cannot be utterly blind to the results of duty, since that cannot be duty which is not already judged to be for human good."[6] The whole analysis of Mr Bulstrode's self-justifications is meant to illustrate these principles.

On the other hand, George Eliot admires the evangelical awakener if his gospel is really constructive, if it is informed with the spirit of love: it is enough to mention Mr Tryan in "Janet's Repentance." She laughs at him indeed, or rather at some of the effects he produces in Milby — e.g. Miss Pratt's literary effort, which was "Six Stanzas, addressed to the Rev. Edgar Tryan, printed on glazed paper with a neat border, and beginning 'Forward, young wrestler for the truth!' " — nevertheless,

> Evangelicalism had brought into palpable existence and operation in Milby society that idea of duty, that recognition of something to be lived for beyond the mere satisfaction of self, which is to the moral life what the addition of a great central ganglion is to animal life. . . . Whatever might be the weaknesses of the ladies who pruned the luxuriance of their lace and ribbons, cut out garments for the poor, distributed tracts, quoted Scripture, and defined the true Gospel, they had learned this — that there was a divine work to be done in life, a rule of goodness higher than the opinion of their neighbours; and if the notion of a heaven in reserve for themselves was a little too prominent, yet the theory of fitness for that heaven consisted in purity of heart, in Christ-like compassion, in the subduing of selfish desires. . . . The first condition of human goodness is something to love; the second, something to reverence. And this latter precious gift was brought to Milby by Mr Tryan and Evangelicalism.[7]

Or there is her attitude to Methodism in *Adam Bede:* "It is too possible that to some of my readers Methodism may mean nothing more than low-pitched gables up dingy streets, sleek grocers, sponging preachers, and hypocritical jargon — elements which are regarded as

4 *Middlemarch*, Ch. 61. (New Cabinet ed., 1913, III, 133).
5 *Middlemarch*, Ch. 24. I, 379.
6 Cross, III, 48.
7 *Scenes*, pp. 319–20.

an exhaustive analysis of Methodism in many fashionable quarters."
But the picture she would have us form of it is

> an amphitheatre of green hills, or the deep shade of broad-leaved
> sycamores, where a crowd of rough men and weary-hearted women
> drank in a faith which was a rudimentary culture, which linked
> their thoughts with the past, lifted their imagination above the
> sordid details of their own narrow lives, and suffused their souls
> with the sense of a pitying, loving, infinite Presence, sweet as sum-
> mer to the houseless needy.[8]

Romola's attitude to Savonarola may here be recalled; it is George
Eliot's own attitude to dogmatic religion. In so far as he stands for
the prophetic will and insight, for the determination to bring Florence
back to God, and to die if need be in the attempt, Savonarola is grand
and heroic in her eyes; such absolute devotion to the highest aims and
standards awes and humbles her; she forgets his superstitious beliefs
and sees only the saint; she returns to Tito at his command. But when
Savonarola refuses to speak the word that will save her godfather's
life, all is changed:

> "Do you, then, know so well what will further the coming of
> God's Kingdom, father, that you will dare to despise the plea of
> mercy — of justice — of faithfulness to your own teaching? . . .
> Take care, father, lest your enemies have some reason when they
> say, that in your visions of what will further God's Kingdom you
> see only what will strengthen your own party."
> "And that is true!" said Savonarola, with flashing eyes. Romola's
> voice had seemed to him in that moment the voice of his enemies.
> "The cause of my party *is* the cause of God's Kingdom."
> "I do not believe it!" said Romola, her whole frame shaken with
> passionate repugnance. "God's Kingdom is something wider — else,
> let me stand outside it with the beings that I love."[9]

In her grief and rage at finding him insensible to human appeal, she
loses all that admiration which had made her hitherto "unmindful of
his aberrations, and attentive only to the grand curve of his orbit."
It is interesting, however, that George Eliot's passion for impartiality
leads her, in a comment on the foregoing dialogue, to by-pass Romola
and partially rejustify Savonarola:

> It was inevitable that she should judge the Frate unfairly on a
> question of individual suffering, at which *she* looked with the eyes

8 *Adam Bede*, p. 38 [Ch. 3].
9 *Romola*, p. 508 (World's Classics ed.) [Ch. 59].

of personal tenderness, and *he* with the eyes of theoretic conviction. In that declaration of his, that the cause of his party was the cause of God's Kingdom, she heard only the ring of egoism. Perhaps such words have rarely been uttered without that meaner ring in them; yet they are the implicit formula of all energetic belief. And if such energetic belief, pursuing a grand and remote end, is often in danger of becoming a demon-worship, in which the votary lets his son and daughter pass through the fire with a readiness that hardly looks like sacrifice; tender fellow-feeling for the nearest has its danger too, and is apt to be timid and sceptical towards the larger aims without which life cannot rise into religion.[1]

Her typical view on the conflict between "theoretic conviction" and human tenderness (already indicated in the extract from *Middlemarch* about "general doctrine") is to be seen in a letter to Charles Bray: "I dislike extremely a passage [in his book, *The Philosophy of Necessity*] in which you appear to consider the disregard of individuals as a lofty condition of mind. My own experience and development deepen every day my conviction that our moral progress may be measured by the degree in which we sympathize with individual suffering and individual joy."[2]

To further this kind of "moral progress" was her most consciously held aim as a novelist, just as it was Wordsworth's aim to widen his readers' sensibility, and make them more "actively and securely virtuous." Indeed, George Eliot carries on the Wordsworthian tradition in more ways than one.

If art does not enlarge men's sympathies, it does nothing morally. I have had heart-cutting experience that *opinions* are a poor cement between human souls: and the only effect I ardently long to produce by my writings is, that those who read them should be better able to *imagine* and to *feel* the pains and the joys of those who differ from themselves in everything but the broad fact of being struggling, erring, human creatures.[3]

Artistic power she defined as "an instinctive perception of the varied states of which the human mind is susceptible, with ability to give them out anew in intensified expression."[4] Connected with this outlook is her deliberate renunciation of the stock themes of traditional fiction and the stage-properties of "romance," in favour of

1 *Romola*, p. 517 [Ch. 61].
2 Cross, I, 472 (Nov. 15, 1857).
3 Cross, II, 118 (July 5, 1859).
4 Cross, I, 174 (beginning of 1848).

that imaginative penetration of the commonplace which she often
achieves, and too often also rather embarrassingly *discusses* in the
novels themselves. "My artistic bent," she says (and this, in a letter
to Blackwood, will make no reader wince) — "is directed not at all
to the presentation of eminently irreproachable characters, but to
the presentation of mixed human beings in such a way as to call
forth tolerant judgment, pity and sympathy."5 It is when she breaks
off her own narratives to justify her methods that, in spite of the
interest and truth of the matter, the manner and tone make one
writhe — as when, in "Amos Barton," she archly rallies an imaginary
lady reader (who thinks Mr Barton uninteresting). . . . In her
positive creative achievement, however, she abundantly shows the
power attributed to Wordsworth by Coleridge, that of spreading
the depth, height and atmosphere of the ideal world around situations,
forms and incidents "of which, for the common view, custom had
bedimmed all the lustre, had dried up the sparkle and the dew-
drops." It was by confirming in her this conception of the novelist's
aim, namely, the enlargement of sympathy by the imaginative
heightening of the real, that G. H. Lewes probably rendered his
most valuable service to her. "You must try and write a story" —
full credit has been allowed him for that piece of wise encouragement, but what is less widely known is that Lewes had already,
before their intimacy, written an essay on "The Lady Novelists" in
the *Westminster* (July 1852), in which he outlined the theory that
became hers — that fiction should be based on real experience, and
that it should enable readers to share a profounder realization of the
feelings and the plight of common humanity. He had even, in advance
of his time, propounded a psycho-analytic theory of artistic creation,
that it is a resolution of, and compensation for, the artist's inward
conflicts and dissatisfactions, and that feminine art is the transposition
on to the aesthetic plane of the specifically feminine forms of suffering.
Lewes even anticipates the illustration of the oyster's secretion, since
popularized by Housman: the poem is the pearl which insulates
and glorifies the pain. In a second essay, "Realism in Art" (*Westminster*, Oct. 1858), published while *Adam Bede* was in preparation,
he says that "realism" should be considered as opposed, not to
"idealism" but to "falsism"; the true business of art is intensification,
not distortion or falsification of the real. The common appearances
of daily life will furnish all we ought to ask.6 No doubt Lewes was
himself influenced here by Comte's views on the social function of
the arts.

5 Cross, I, 431 (Feb. 18, 1857).
6 For these references I am indebted to P. Bourl'honne, *George Eliot*,
Paris, 1933.

The tension in George Eliot's mind between ideal and actual, action and reaction, ambition and renunciation, appears in her preoccupation with the theme of the "egotistical sublime," her recurrent treatment of efforts after sanctity, great and signal service, or self-realization — efforts which are thwarted by circumstance, "the gradual action of ordinary causes," the blight of the commonplace. We have noted the spiritual ambitiousness of her own evangelical youth — her emulation of Hannah More and St Paul, her anxiety "to be doing some little [i.e. a very great deal] toward the regeneration of this groaning, travailing creation." The content of this ambition was changed after her "conversion" (or perversion) to the Religion of Humanity, but it never left her; it remained in the form of that "terrible earnestness" we have spoken of, that sense of the peremptoriness of Duty — of duty whose claims were all the more absolute because its "divine" sanction had been destroyed. It remained, after she had found that her service must be rendered through fiction, in her haunting sense of responsibility to mankind in all that she wrote ("the high responsibilities of literature that undertakes to represent life"[7]). Of a spring trip to Italy in 1861 she writes: "We must be for ever ashamed of ourselves if we don't work the better for it." True, this was written to her publisher, but it illustrates the workings of her ever-accusing conscience: time must not be wasted, an account must be rendered, pleasure must be justified by its fruits. And soon after she adds: "I will never write anything to which my whole heart, mind and conscience don't consent, so that I may feel that it was something — however small — which wanted to be done in this world, and that I am just the organ for that small bit of work."[8] After her provincial salad days were over, the thwarting, the frustration of which she was ever conscious, came not from outward circumstances but from her unconquerable self-distrust: "Shall I ever write another book as true as *Adam Bede?* The weight of the future presses on me. . . ."[9]

Bourl'honne is right, I think, when he says that "the inspiration of her work is clearly optimistic, the intention which animates it being to show the possibility of good and the power of the will; the work as it was achieved is no less clearly pessimistic, the general impression which emerges from it being the powerlessness of man against circumstances and the checkmate of the will." The keenness of her unsatisfied yearnings was tempered in her later years, but the clear-eyed endurance had strained her to excess, and the final calm seems in part to be that of exhaustion.

7 Cross, II, 293 (to Blackwood, March 30, 1861).
8 Cross, II, 303.
9 Cross, II, 101.

Mark Schorer

Fiction and the "Matrix of Analogy"

If the novel, as R. P. Blackmur recently proposed, is now to enjoy the kind of attention from criticism that for the past twenty years has been the privilege of poetry, criticism must begin with the simplest assertion: fiction is a literary art. It must begin with the base of language, with the word, with figurative structures, with rhetoric as skeleton and style as body of meaning. A beginning as simple as this must overcome corrupted reading habits of long standing; for the novel, written in prose, bears an apparently closer resemblance to discursive forms than it does to poetry, thus easily opening itself to first questions about philosophy or politics, and, traditionally a middle-class vehicle with a reflective social function, it bears an apparently more immediate relation to life than it does to art, thus easily opening itself to first questions about conduct. Yet a novel, like a poem, is not life, it is an image of life; and the critical problem is first of all to analyse the structure of the image. Thus criticism must approach the vast and endlessly ornamented house of fiction with a willingness to do a little at a time and none of it finally, in order to suggest experiences of meaning and of feeling that may be involved in novels, and responsibilities for their style which novelists themselves may forget.

To choose, more or less at random and without premeditated end, one novel by each of only three novelists, and to examine in each only one element in the language, the dominant metaphorical quality – this, positively, is to work piecemeal, and merely to suggest. I emphasize not *metaphor* but *quality*, intending not only the explicit but the buried and the dead metaphors, and some related traits of diction generally, that whole habit of value association suggested in Scott Buchanan's phrase, the "matrix of analogy." The novels are *Persuasion, Wuthering Heights,* and *Middlemarch....*

Middlemarch is a novel written on a much grander scale than either of those others, with many points of narrative interest, a much more complex structural pattern, and an important difference in its metaphorical language. Jane Austen's metaphors are generally

Reprinted by permission from the *Kenyon Review*, 11 (Autumn 1949), 539–559.

of the "buried" kind, submerged, woven deep in the ordinary, idiomatic fabric of the language; Emily Brontë's are generally epithetical. George Eliot's tend always to be, or to become, explicit symbols of psychological or moral conditions, and they actually function in such a way as to give symbolical value to much action, as Dorothea's pleasure in planning buildings ("a kind of work which she delighted in") and Casaubon's desire to construct a "Key to all Mythologies." Their significance lies, then, not so much in the choice of area (as, "commerce," or "natural elements" and "animals") as in the choice of function, and one tests them not by their field, their content, but by their conceptual portent. I should like to suggest a set of metaphorical qualities in *Middlemarch* which actually represents a series apparent in the thinking that underlies the dramatic structure. First of all, there are metaphors of unification; then, of antithesis; next, there are metaphors of shaping and making, of structure and creative purpose; finally, there are metaphors of what I should call a "muted" apocalypse.

George Eliot's metaphors of unification pivot on her most characteristic verbs — these are of conciliation and reconciliation, of unification, of course, and of inclusion, of mingling, of associating, of merging and mixing, of embracing and comprehending, of connecting, allying, binding together, and making room for. The elements to be brought together are as various as the universe — they may be merely "mingled pleasures" or "associated facts which . . . show a mysterious electricity if you touched them," or the relation of urban and rural areas, which "made fresh threads of connection"; again, they may be attitudes — "criticism" and "awe" *mixing*, or qualities *uniting*, as, presumably, "the glories of doctor and saint" in dreary Casaubon, or men themselves making more *energetic alliances* "with impartial nature"; or they may be those yearnings of one individual for another which find completion in love, the institution of marriage, and the literal embrace; or, most important, they may be "lofty conceptions" which embrace multitudinousness — for example, the daily life of Tipton parish and Dorothea Brooke's own "rule of conduct." If only we knew more and felt more, these metaphors insist; for there *is*, we are told, "a knowledge which . . . traces out the suppressed transitions which unite all contrasts." This is religious yearning, and it finds occasional pseudo-religious fulfilment, as after Lydgate's successful cogitations on morphology: he finds himself "in that agreeable after-glow of excitement when thought lapses from examination of a specific object into a suffusive sense of its connections with all the rest of our existence," and one can "float with the repose of unexhausted strength."

The metaphors of unification imply the metaphors of antithesis;

the first represent yearnings, the second a recognition of fact. Thus we have metaphors of reality *vs.* appearance, as: "the large vistas and wide fresh air which she dreamed of finding in her husband's mind were replaced by anterooms and winding passages which seemed to lead no-wither"; or of chaos *vs.* order (humorously dramatized by Mr. Brooke's "documents," which need arranging but get mixed up in pigeon-holes) as Mary Garth's "red fire," which "seemed like a solemn existence calmly independent of petty passions, the imbecile desires, the straining after worthless uncertainties, which were daily moving her contempt"; or of shapelessness *vs.* shape, as "a kind Providence furnishes the limpest personality with a little gum or starch in the form of tradition." There are other kinds, of outer *vs.* inner, for example: "so much subtler is a human mind than the outside tissues which make a sort of blazonry or clock-face for it." It is this, the outer-inner antithesis, which underscores one of George Eliot's favorite words — "inward" or "inwardly," a usage which is frequently annoying because it is tautological, applied to states which can *only* be inward under the circumstances of the fiction, but, for that reason, all the more symptomatic. There are metaphorical antitheses of fact to wish, imbalance to balance, restlessness to repose, and many other opposites. Most important, and perhaps most frequent, are the figures which oppose freedom to various forms of restraint — burdens, ties, bonds, and so on: "he replies by calling himself Pegasus, and every form of prescribed work 'harness,' " to which the answer is, "I shall let him be *tried* by the *test* of freedom." Another example of the restraint-freedom opposition illustrates the way that reported action, which conjoined with these metaphors, pushes both on to explicit symbolism: near the end, Dorothea observes on the road outside her window "a man with a bundle on his back and a woman carrying her baby," and, still nearer the end, when Lydgate has "accepted his narrowed lot," that is, the values of his child-bride, he thinks, "He had chosen this fragile creature, and had taken the burden of her life upon his arms. He must walk as he could, carrying that burden pitifully."

The oppositions in these metaphors of antithesis are the classic oppositions between Things as They Are and Things as They Should Be, between the daily realities of a community like Middlemarch and the "higher" realities of that "New Jerusalem" toward which Dorothea and others are "on the road."

Everyone and everything in this novel is moving on a "way." Life is a *progress*, and it is variously and inevitably described as road, stream, channel, avenue, way, journey, voyage, ride (either on horse or by carriage), vista, chain, line, course, path, and process. To these terms one should add the terms of *growth*, usually biological growth, which carry much the same value. There must be at least a thousand and possibly there are more metaphorical variations on the general idea of life as progress, and this progress is illimitable. At the end of the novel we are told, in words somewhat suggestive of a more orthodox religious spirit than George Eliot, that "Every limit is a beginning as well as an ending."

Everything strains forward. Consciousness is a stream. "In Dorothea's mind there was a current into which all thought and feeling were apt sooner or later to flow — the reaching forward of the whole consciousness toward the fullest truth, the least partial good." "Character, too," we are told, "is a process," and it is a process which we recognize by achievement — "the niceties of inward balance, by which man swims and makes his point or else is carried headlong." Like Leopold Bloom, George Eliot's characters think of their existence as "the stream of life in which the stream of life we trace," but with a difference: the personal life finally flows into the "gulf of death," but the general stream flows on, through vistas of endlessly unfolding good, and that good consists of individual achievements of "the fullest truth, the least partial good," of Lydgate's individually *made points*. This is a progressive, in no sense a cyclical view of human history.

These metaphors of progress, like the restraint-freedom antithesis, involve George Eliot in her many complementary metaphors of hindrance to progress. The individual purpose is sometimes confused by "a social life which seemed nothing but a labyrinth of petty courses, a walled-in maze"; sometimes by the inadequacy of the purpose itself, as Casaubon, who "was lost among small closets and winding stairs"; experience and circumstance over and over become "yokes," which slow the progress, for there are those always "who carry a weight of trials"; one may *toil* "under the fetters of a promise" or move, like Lydgate, more haltingly than one had hoped under the *burden* of a responsibility.

These hindrances are, generally speaking, social, not moral. One submits to them in the interests of the whole procession, and when one does not submit — as Dorothea, refusing to devote herself to Casaubon's scholarship after his death — it is because one has discovered that they are not in the interests of the whole procession. The particular interests of the procession are indicated by the extended metaphors drawn from nearly every known field of physical and medical science. It is by the "serene light of science" that we glimpse "a presentiment of endless processes filling the vast spaces planked out of" our "sight by that wordy ignorance which," in the

past, we "had supposed to be knowledge." It is by the same light
that we are able to recognize our social obligations, according to
the Religion of Humanity.

Thus, quite smoothly, we come to that fourth group of prevailing
metaphors, those having to do with purpose. They are of shaping,
of forming, of making, of framing; they pivot on notions of pattern
or rule, measure or structure. They are all words used in metaphors
which, explicitly or by implication, reveal the individual directing
his destiny by conscious, creative purpose toward the end of
absolute human order. Opposed to them are the many metaphors
of derogation of the unorganized, notably the human mind, which,
at worst, like Mr. Brooke's, availing nothing perceptible in the body
politic, is a *mass*.

At the end of this grand vista are the metaphors of what I have
called the "muted" apocalypse. The frequency with which George
Eliot uses the words *up*, *high*, and *higher* in metaphorical contexts
is equalled only, perhaps, by her use of the word *light*, until one
feels a special significance in "giving *up*" and in all the faces that
beam, all the ideas that *flash* across the mind, and all the things that
are all the time being "taken" in *that light* or *this light*. Fire plays
a perhaps predictably important metaphorical role, and, together
with light, or alternating with it, usually accompanies or is implied
by those frequent metaphors in which things are *gloriously* transformed, transfused, or transfigured. Treating this complex of figures
as I do, as a kind of apocalyptic drama which of course does not
exist in the novel as such, but surely does in the imagination of
George Eliot, we have, now, at the moment before climax, all those
metaphors involving ideas of veneration and adoration, or worshipful
awe; these, in my factitious series, are immediately followed by the
climax itself, which is contained in endless use of the word "revelation" and figurative developments from it. Perception, in this novel,
is indeed thought of as revelation, and minds and souls are always
"opening" to the influx. Things are many times "manifested" or
"made manifest," as if life were a perpetual epiphany. If perception
is not a "revelation," it is a "divination," and for the ordinary verb,
"to recognize," George Eliot usually prefers to use "to divine." It
is here that we come upon her unquestionably favorite word, and
the center of her most persistent metaphors. For the word "sight" or
"feeling" she almost always substitutes the more portentous word
"vision." Visions are of every possible kind, from *dim* to *bright* to
blinding, from *testing* to *guiding*. The simplest sight of the physical
detail may be a vision; every insight is of course a vision, usually an
inward vision.

The experience now subsides. If perception is revelation, then it is, secondarily, nourishment, and the recurrence of metaphors in which perception is conceived as spiritual food and drink, and of all the metaphors of *fullness, filling,* and *fulfilment,* is perhaps predictable. It is likewise energizing, in various figurative ways, and in moments of climactic understanding, significantly, a charge of electricity flows through the human organism.

Illumination, revelation, fulfilment. One step remains in this pattern of a classic religious experience; that is expectation. Metaphors of expectation are everywhere; I will represent them in their most frequent form, a phrase so rubbed by usage that it hardly seems metaphorical at all. It is "to look forward," and it appears on nearly every page of *Middlemarch,* a commonplace there too, yet more than that: it is the clue to the whole system of metaphor I have sketched out; it is the clue to a novel, the clue to a mind.

I have separated into a series a metaphorical habit which of course always appears in conflux, and it is only because these metaphors do constantly associate themselves in the novel, that one may justifiably hit upon them as representing George Eliot's selectivity. One of many such elaborate confluences is as follows:

> Mr. Casaubon's talk about his great book was *full* of *new vistas;* and this sense of *revelation,* this *surprise of a nearer introduction* to Stoics and Alexandrians, as people who had ideas not totally unlike her own, kept in abeyance for the time her usual eagerness for a *binding theory* which could bring her own life and doctrine into *strict connection* with that amazing past, and give the remotest *sources* of knowledge some *bearing* on her actions. . . . she was *looking forward* to *higher initiation* in ideas, as she was *looking forward* to marriage, and *blending* her *dim* conceptions of both. . . . All her eagerness for acquirement lay within that *full current of sympathetic* motive in which her ideas and impulses were habitually *swept along.* She did not want to deck herself with knowledge — to wear it loose from the *nerves and blood that fed her action:* and if she had written a book she must have done it as St. Theresa did, under the *command of an authority that constrained her conscience.* But something she yearned for by which her *life might be filled* with action at once rational and ardent; and since the time was gone by *for guiding visions* and spiritual directors, since prayer *heightened* yearning, but not instruction, *what lamp* was there but knowledge? [Ch. 10.]

Here are nearly all of them: metaphors of unification, of antithesis (restraint-freedom), of progress, of the apocalypse: height, light, revelation, vision, nourishment, and, of course, the forward look. The passage is not in the least exceptional. In my analytical sketch of such persistent confluences, I separated the elements into a series to demonstrate how completely, step by step, they embody a pseudo-religious philosophy, how absolutely expressive is metaphor, even in fiction, and how systematic it can become. This is a novel of religious yearning without religious object. The unification it desires is the unification of human knowledge in the service of social ends; the antitheses that trouble it (and I observe in this otherwise classic series no antitheses either of Permanence and Change, or of Sin and Grace) are the antitheses between man as he is and man as he could be in this world; the hindrances to life as progress are man's social not his moral flaws; the purposive dedication of individuals will overcome those flaws; we see the fulfilment of all truly intellectual passions, for the greater glory of Man.

Our first observation on the function of metaphor in this novel should, then, be of its *absolutely* expressive character. The second is perhaps less evident, and we may call it the interpretive function of metaphor, the extent to which metaphor comments on subject. The subject of this novel may be Middlemarch, a community, but as even the title metaphorically suggests, the theme is the nature of progress in what is probably meant to be the typical British community in the 19th Century. (Observe, too, these names: Brooke, a running course, and Lydgate, his progress blocked by his wife, twice-blocked by his name.) Or we can select subjects within the subject, as the clerical subject interpreted by the pseudo-religious theme: the true "religious" dedication of a Dorothea Brooke, and the characters around her falling into various "religious" postures: Casaubon as the false prophet, Bulstrode as the parody-prophet, Lydgate as the nearly true prophet — a "scientific Phoenix," he is called — somehow deflected from his prophecy; and Ladislaw as the true prophet. Indeed, given the metaphorical texture, one cannot escape the nearly systematic Christ analogy which George Eliot weaves around Ladislaw, omitting from her figure only the supremely important element of Christ's sacrifice, and the reason for which He made it. This is to be expected in a novel which is about progress without guilt. Here, even the heroic characters cannot be said to have inner struggles, for all their "inward visions." Here there is much illumination and nearly no self-doubt; much science, and never a sin. One recognizes from the metaphorical structure that this novel represents a decay of the full religious experience into that part of it which aspires alone: Christian optimism divorced from the basic human tragedy.

The metaphorical complex provides a third, and a more interesting function: a structural function. *Middlemarch* is concerned with nearly every important activity in community life — political, clerical, agricultural, industrial, professional, domestic, of course, even scholarly. It involves many different characters and groups of characters. The relations between some of these characters and even between some of these groups are often extremely tenuous, often merely accidental. The dramatic structure, in short, is not very taut, yet one feels, on finishing the book, that this is a superbly constructed work, that, indeed, as foolish Mr. Brooke observes, "We're all one family, you know — it's all one cupboard." What makes it so is thematic rather than dramatic unity.

The measure of *Middlemarch* is Dorothea's *sublimity*, the interpretive height from which she judges. From her sublimity, everything shades off, all the way down to garrulous Mrs. Cadwallader and villainous Mr. Bulstrode. The metaphors of unification which George Eliot enjoyed to use, those images of intermingling and embracing, are important in a double sense: they express Dorothea's ethical sentiments, and, actually, they and the others, bind the material together. They tell us *how to take* each Middlemarcher, *in what light.* They do this chiefly through the creation of symbolic echoes of the major situation in the minor ones, echoes often ironic, sometimes parodies.

Thus, in the imagery of vision, Dorothea's remark, made so early as in Chapter 3, has a special ring: "I am rather shortsighted." In the imagery of human progress, Mr. Garth's question about Bulstrode, the pious fraud, — "whether he shall settle somewhere else, as a lasting thing" — has such symbolic value. Mr. Garth's own attitude toward agriculture is a thematic parody of the exaltation of Dorothea, Lydgate, and Ladislaw: "the peculiar tone of fervid veneration, of religious regard in which he wrapped it, as a consecrated symbol is wrapped in its gold-fringed linen." In the imagery of structure, a special meaning seems to attach to the word "dwell," when it refers to characters experiencing some state of mind. Lydgate's morphological research is another such symbolic extension of the metaphors of structure. Dorothea's avenue of limes outside her window, leading toward the sunset, becomes, finally, a representation in the landscape of the idea of progress. The political newspapers, notably unenlightened, are called *The Pioneer* and *The Trumpet*, and these are surely parodies, one of the progress metaphors, the other of the apocalyptic. Even that humble rural tavern, the *Weights and Scales*, reminds us of more exalted concern, in this novel, with justice and with metaphors of balance. And so that wretched farm called Freeman's End, which has nearly destroyed its tenant and his family, is an eloquent little drama of the freedom-restraint metaphors.

"We all of us," says George Eliot, "grave or light, get our thoughts

entangled in metaphors, and act fatally on the strength of them."
If the writing of a novel is a deed, as Conrad liked to think, she
spoke truer than she knew.

John Holloway

George Eliot

George Eliot is quite plainly a novelist who is also a sage. . . .
The didactic intention is perfectly clear from the novels alone.

In *Adam Bede*, for example — and it is George Eliot's first full-
length work — she says that so far from inventing ideal characters,
her "strongest effort is . . . to give a faithful account of men and
things as they have mirrored themselves in my mind". Realistic
pictures of obscure mediocrity serve a didactic purpose: "these fellow-
mortals, every one, must be accepted as they are . . . these people
. . . it is needful you should tolerate, pity and love: it is these more
or less ugly, stupid, inconsistent people whose movements of goodness
you should be able to admire". Finally, she gives the lesson an
autobiographical import: "The way in which I have come to the
conclusion that human nature is lovable — . . . its deep pathos, its
sublime mysteries — has been by living a great deal among people
more or less commonplace and vulgar" (*Adam Bede*, Ch. 17).

But George Eliot is not interested only in people and in their good
and bad qualities; she wishes, beyond this, to impart a vision of the
world that reveals its whole design and value. Her teaching may
be partly ethical, but it is ethics presented as a system and grounded
on a wider metaphysical doctrine. Her early novels emphasize how
an integrated scheme of values is a help to man — "No man can begin
to mould himself on a faith or an idea without rising to a higher
order of experience" ("Janet's Repentance," Ch. 10) — and she vividly
indicates the forces in her own time that impelled men to seek such
a scheme. For one class to be cultured and sophisticated another must
be

Reprinted from John Holloway, *The Victorian Sage*, London, Macmillan
& Co. Ltd., 1953, pp. 111–128, by permission of the Shoe String Press.

in unfragrant deafening factories, cramping itself in mines, sweat-
ing at furnaces . . . or else, spread over sheepwalks, and scattered
in lonely houses and huts . . . where the rainy days look dreary.
This wide national life is based entirely on . . . the emphasis of
want. . . . Under such circumstances there are many . . . *who
have absolutely needed an emphatic belief:* life in this unpleasurable
shape demanding some *solution* even to unspeculative minds . . .
something that good society calls "enthusiasm", something that
will present motives in an entire absence of high prizes . . . that
includes resignation for ourselves and active love for what is not
ourselves (*The Mill on the Floss*, Bk. iv, Ch. 3).

This is an interesting passage for the social historian, and for the
critic of nineteenth-century capitalism too; but its present importance
lies in showing what was of concern to George Eliot as she wrote,
and how we are justified in searching her novels for philosophy as
well as ethics. . . .

IV. THE ETHICS

First of all, in this complex world, duty is not always easy to
recognize. We might expect not. But sometimes it *is* easy. As
Mrs. Farebrother is made to say, "Keep hold of a few plain truths,
and make everything square with them. When I was young, Mr.
Lydgate, there never was any question about right and wrong"
(*Middlemarch*, Ch. 17). This proud, kindly, distinguished old lady
is a reliable authority. George Eliot is fairly clear about what leads
in moral questions to definite answers. Objectively, duty is settled
by fixed and unalterable circumstances — by the constants in the
system of Nature. We require "that knowledge of the irreversible
laws within and without . . . which, governing the habits, becomes
morality" (*The Mill on the Floss*, Bk. iv, Ch. 3). Sometimes the
relevant circumstance is an established human tie or bond. "She had
rent the ties that had given meaning to duty" (*The Mill on the
Floss*, Bk. vi, Ch. 14). . . . But duty is determined in the sense of
recognized, less by ingenuity or logical acumen than by deep true
feeling. "That signifies nothing — what other men would think,"
says honest Caleb Garth in *Middlemarch*, "I've got a clear feeling
inside me, and that I shall follow" (Ch. 56). In *Theophrastus Such*
comes the formal — and as it is called, "persuasive" — definition:
"*Let our habitual talk give morals their full meaning* as that conduct
which . . . would follow from the fullest knowledge and the fullest
sympathy" (my italics; "Moral Swindlers"). Knowledge itself, if
we may judge from an observation in *Middlemarch*, is in these
matters a kind of feeling; and the passage quoted from *Theophrastus*

Such goes on immediately to relate duty to the natural system, for
it says that this "meaning" is "perpetually corrected and enriched
by a more thorough appreciation of dependence in things, and a
finer sensibility to both physical and spiritual fact." The word
"sensibility" is significant. According to George Eliot, we cannot
fully unravel the system of "dependence"; we must know it by the
partly non-logical comprehension appropriate to it.

So much for what factors determine duty and what processes of
thought discover it. In both, George Eliot's view follows from her
whole metaphysics. This is true also of what she says about the
behaviour that constitutes duty. To her, dutiful behavior is renouncing pleasures in excess of our obscurity and unimportance, and
resigning ourselves to the privations of a system of nature where
personal happiness is subordinate and accidental. Resignation is a
duty because Nature is as it is. "Our life is determined for us,"
says Maggie, "and it makes the mind very free when we give up
wishing and only think of bearing what is laid upon us" (Bk. v,
Ch. 1). . . . Renunciation, for George Eliot, is the essential part of
virtue; and it is the chief moral reality implied by her whole outlook.

Vice and virtue contrast with each other point by point. Wrong
actions, like right ones, are determined by all the slow complexity
of events: this determines them, however, not in the sense of making
them wrong, but in the plainer sense of bringing them about. Lydgate
sees himself "sliding into that pleasureless yielding to the small solici-
tations of circumstance, which is a commoner history of perdition
than any single momentous bargain" (Ch. 79). This too is how the
thought of a sinful course of action grows in the mind. There is
no need to reflect; sin proffers itself freely as what is most attractive.
But according to George Eliot, what makes it possible for the sinful
thought to dawn and to influence is the converse of what enables us
to see the path of righteousness. It is not deep feeling but a lack of
feeling, it is an insensibility blinding us to feelings and sufferings in
others, and causing us to face life with excessive demands. . . .
Bulstrode, in *Middlemarch*, could combine wrong-doing with evangelicalism because "he had argued himself into not feeling it incompatible . . . the years had been perpetually spinning . . . intricate
thickness, like masses of spider's web, padding the moral sensibility."
And it is emphasized that his aptitude for wrong followed from a
combination of excessive demand and defective emotion: "age made
egoism more eager but less enjoying" (Ch. 61). Every word of
that phrase directs us to something in the outlook of the author.

The consequences of virtue and of vice are the one point in
George Eliot's view that remains to be stated. Here the case of vice
is clearer. Righteousness may be rewarded, or may have to be its

own reward (See *Romola*, Epilogue), but the ultimate consequences of wickedness are never in doubt. No one in George Eliot's novels ever sins and escapes; even though punishment may be long delayed and its local source quite unexpected. Tito Melema, Mrs. Transome, Bulstrode, in a sense Lydgate, Grandcourt — however tardily or unpredictably, Fate ultimately chastises them all. The fate of other sinners is of course less circuitous. And clearly enough, the general action of her stories is largely modified to bring this about. At the close of "Brother Jacob" she says plainly that this is something to make a story worth telling: "Here ends the story of Mr. David Faux . . . and we see in it, I think, an admirable instance of the unexpected forms in which the great Nemesis hides itself."

Thus George Eliot has a detailed theory of human morality, and a detailed account of how it follows from what the world is like. It may seem as though in summarizing this outlook we have first surreptitiously wandered quite away from the methods of presenting it, and then, in the final quotation from "Brother Jacob," wandered surreptitiously back. But a fuller survey of the confirmatory passages quoted throughout the discussion disproves this: for the great majority of those passages are not isolated reflections, but embedded in the texture of the novels. They commented upon a concrete situation, were uttered by a distinctive character, or appeared in a fictitious argument with a definite pattern of its own. Their significance was always controlled by methods of suggestion that are George Eliot's because she is a novelist. . . .

Dorothy Van Ghent

On *Adam Bede*

Technique is that which selects among the multitude of possible qualities, organizes them in the finite world of the novel, and holds them in a shape that can catch the light of our own awareness,

Reprinted from Dorothy Van Ghent, *The English Novel: Form and Function*, Rinehart & Co., New York, [1953], pp. 172–181, by permission of Holt, Rinehart and Winston, Inc., publishers. Copyright © 1953 by Dorothy Van Ghent.

which, without shapes to fall upon, is ignorant. Technique is like
the concave or convex surface of the spoon, and the different
turnings and inclinations to which it is liable; technique elongates
or foreshortens, and while the rudimentary relationships of common
experience remain still recognizable, it reveals astonishing bulges of
significance, magnifies certain parts of the anatomy of life, of whose
potentialities we had perhaps not been aware, humbles others. The
massively slow movement of *Adam Bede* is one such shape-making
technique. It is true that we are generally persuaded of the *actual*
slow movement of rural life, and it is rural life — the life of villagers,
tenant farmers, and peasantry — that George Eliot describes. . . .
The movement is one of a massive leisureliness that gathers up as
it goes a dense body of physical and moral detail, adding particle to
particle and building layer upon layer with sea-depth patience. . . .

We enter the description of the Hall Farm in Chapter 6 at "the
drowsiest time of the year, just before hay-harvest," and at "the
drowsiest time of the day, too, for it is close upon three by the sun,
and it is half-past three by Mrs. Poyser's handsome eight-day clock."
. . . old Martin watches its hands, not through engagement with
time but through disengagement from it; he pleases himself with
"detecting a rhythm in the tick" as he does with watching the sungleams on the wall and counting the quarries on the floor. And again,
in the passage describing the Poysers on their way to church, we
are told of "the excellent habit which Mrs. Poyser's clock had of
taking time by the forelock," so that, despite interruptions in their
walk, they arrive at the village "while it was still a quarter to two."
The mechanism of the eight-day clock works in sympathy with the
week, with the rhythm of workdays and Sabbath, and we are reminded in the same passage of that other scheduling of man's time
which holds him to Sabbath observance no matter if the hay wants
turning, for, as Mrs. Poyser says, "as for the weather, there's One
above makes it, and we must put up wi't." . . .

The kitchen at the Hall Farm shines in the sun, the dairy is clean
and fragrant, Lisbeth's grief is alleviated by the funeral, and Bartle
Massey's pupils make their toilsome efforts "to learn how they might
become human," because of a moral development that has been made
possible only by slow and difficult centuries of accreted recognitions,
limitations, modulations, techniques.

Therefore the eight-day clock, with its minute rhythms for an
old man's ear, with its rhythm for the daily work that starts at
half past four, when the mowers' bottles have to be filled and the
baking started, and with its weekly rhythm for the Sabbath. The
clock is a monument not to time merely as time, but to the assured
and saving values stored up through ages of experience. In one of

her books George Eliot says, "There is no private life which has not been determined by a wider public life." In *Adam Bede*, this is the mute recognition by which the community lives: as imaginatively realized here, it is a recognition that personal good has communal determinations, that it is contingent upon the preservation of common values. But the statement bears also its converse, which might be phrased thus: "There is no public life which has not been determined by the narrower private life"; for the story of *Adam Bede* is a story of the irreparable damage wrought on the community by a private moment's frivolity.

Mrs. Poyser's clock at the Hall Farm, the clock which has sublimated all time into good, is set for daylight saving (it has the "excellent habit" of "taking time by the forelock"). Not so the clocks of the gentlefolk at the Chase. Throughout that Thursday when Arthur twice meets Hetty in the wood, the clock is watched irritably. It is "about ten o'clock" when Arthur, time irritable and bored on his hands, goes to the stables; the "twelve o'clock sun" sees him galloping toward Norburne to see a friend; but Hetty is on his mind, and "the hand of the dial in the courtyard had scarcely cleared the last stroke of three" when he is again home; so that "it was scarcely four o'clock" when he is waiting at the gate of the wood. Hetty comes daily to learn lace mending of Mrs. Pomfret, the maid at the Chase, at four o'clock, and she tells Arthur that she always sets out for the farm "by eight o'clock." They exchange a look: "What a space of time those three moments were, while their eyes met and his arms touched her!" Arthur meditates irresolutely "more than an hour" on the false impression he feels he has created in the girl; but "the time must be filled up," and he dresses for dinner, "for his grandfather's dinner-hour was six"; meanwhile Hetty too is watching the clock, and at last "the minute-hand of the old-fashioned brazen-faced timepiece was on the last quarter of eight." In the shadows of the wood he kisses her. Then he pulls out his watch: "I wonder how late it is . . . twenty minutes past eight — but my watch is too fast." Back at the farm, Mrs. Poyser exclaims,

> "What a time o' night time this is to come home, Hetty . . . Look at the clock, do; why, it's going on for half-past nine, and I've sent the gells to bed this half-hour, and late enough too. . . ."
>
> "I did set out before eight, aunt," said Hetty, in a pettish tone, with a slight toss of her head. "But this clock's so much before the clock at the Chase, there's no telling what time it'll be when I get here."
>
> "What! you'd be wanting the clock set by gentle-folks's time, would you? an' sit up burnin' candle, an' lie a-bed wi' the sun

a-bakin' you like a cowcumber i' the frame? The clock hasn't
been put forrard for the first time to-day, I reckon."

The pace of *Adam Bede* is set to Mrs. Poyser's clock, to all that slow
toil and patient discipline that have made daylight — and living —
valuable. Slower, organically, invisibly slow, are the months of
Hetty's pregnancy; the Poysers' clock, the clock at the Chase, do not
keep this time, with their eights and nines and half past nines. This
other, deep, hidden, animal time drags the whole pace down to that
of poor Hetty's "journey in despair," a blind automatism of animal
night where the ticking of the human clock cannot be heard.

Hetty's very fragility is her claim to the saving disciplines of a
traditional way of life. It is by her mediocrity that their value is
tested, for without them she is abandoned to chaos. There is probably
no other work that explores human suffering at the organic level
with such deep authority as the chapter describing Hetty's journey
from Windsor to Stonyshire. It is a suffering that has no issue in
"illumination," no spiritual value for the sufferer, for Hetty is not
the kind of character that sustains "illumination" through suffering.
If she were, we should not have had the particular insight that *Adam
Bede* affords into the moral meaning of time and tradition in the lives
of simple people. Hetty is lost because she is more fragile than the
others and therefore more dependent on the community disciplines
(far more fragile, because of her class, than "Chad's Bess" of the
village, for instance, who, with her looseness and silliness and —
like Hetty — with false garnets in her ears, has a secure and accustomed
place in the village life); lost from the only values that can support
her mediocrity, she sinks into the chaos of animal fear, which, in the
human being, is insanity. Other novelists have explored other kinds
of suffering; one might draw up a chart or a dissertation, of no
mean interest, that would show the hierarchies of human suffering
as represented in literature and their psychological, ethical, and
spiritual significance; surely Hetty's would be at the bottom of the
scale (even lower, one would think, than that of some of the least
human characters in Faulkner's novels, for Faulkner is interested in
the "illumination" of which even idiots are capable). But its lowness
and blindness in the scale of human suffering is its moving power.
For Hetty is very human, very real, and if knowledge of suffering
did not include hers, it would not include the broadest and commonest layer of human existence.

It is improbable that any but an English novelist would have interested himself in Hetty as a figure of tragic pathos. Flaubert would
have despised her: the luxury fantasies of Emma Bovary (a French
Hetty) have a richness and complexity of cultural experience, and a

play of sensibility, that make Hetty's dreams of standing beside Arthur Donnithorne as a bride look thin indeed; and the fatality of Hetty's pregnancy would not have occurred to the author of *Madame Bovary*, nor all the mess of child murder, for these are quite English habits of interest. . . . Dostoevski could not have used Hetty, for she has less of God in her, a more meager spiritual capacity, than his imbeciles and whores; she is not capable even of that kind of "recognition" which leads the abused child in *The Possessed* and the carpenter in *Crime and Punishment* to hang themselves.

But the massy line of the book is deflected toward the end. ("The mirror," George Eliot says, "is doubtless defective; the outlines will sometimes be disturbed, the reflection faint or confused.") By Mrs. Poyser's clock, Hetty's last-minute reprieve cannot really be timed with a time integral to the rest of the novel, nor can Adam's marriage with Dinah. . . . We should add Arthur Donnithorne's return in his interesting and picturesque ill-health. Hetty's reprieve, the marriage of Dinah and Adam, Arthur's reconstruction through such suffering as Arthur is able to suffer — these are no compensation for and no real "illumination" of the tragedy of Hetty. They are the artificial illumination which so many Victorian novels indulged in, in the effort to justify to man God's ways or society's ways or nature's ways. But still there is left the ticking of the oak-cased clock, rubbed by human "elbow-polish," that paces the book through its greater part: the realization of value, clean as the clock-tick, radiant as the kitchen of the Hall Farm, fragrant as the diary; and the tragic realization of the loss of however simple human values, in Hetty's abandoned foot-steps as she seeks the dark pool and caresses her own arms in the desire for life.

Martin J. Svaglic

Religion in the Novels of George Eliot

Of English novelists of the first rank, George Eliot is easily the most paradoxical. She appreciates the importance of religion in

Reprinted by permission from the *Journal of English and Germanic Philology*, 53 (April 1954), 145–159.

human life and writes novels to enforce it; but she does not believe
in God. She espouses the determinism of Bray and Mackay; yet she
makes duty, with its implication of free will, the chief word of her
creed. She does not consider herself bound in her private life by the
traditional laws of marriage; yet her journals and her novels maintain
the sanctity of the marital union and the importance of the family
bond. She is intensely intellectual, with an eager and receptive mind;
yet there is in much of her work a deep scepticism about the value
of the intellect in what she considers the most important area of life:
that of moral judgments. She is a "meliorist" who thinks the world
slowly advancing to a better life; but she finds increasing comfort
in what has been called that most melancholy of beatitudes, "Blessed
are the dead."

It may well be that there are genuine inconsistencies here, for
George Eliot likes to remind us that human beings do behave in-
consistently. But it may also be that some of these inconsistencies
are more apparent than real, and are the natural result of a vision
both comprehensive and discriminating and of a conscience determined to report experiences with scrupulous fidelity to its vision.
Such is the case in her treatment of religion and particularly of Dissent.
How does it happen that anyone who could write of Evangelical
clergymen what she wrote of Dr Cumming, the famous preacher,
and could refer to "perverted moral judgment" as inseparable from
the dogmatic system of "all Evangelical believers"[1] — how does it
happen that such a person, in little more than a year after this indictment, could present one of the most attractive pictures in literature
of an Evangelical minister: The Reverend Edgar Tryan in "Janet's
Repentance"? How does it happen that a woman who could write:
"No one can have talked to the more enthusiastic Methodists and
listened to their stories of miracles without perceiving that they require no other passport to a statement than that it accords with their
wishes and their general conception of God's dealings" (*Essays*, p. 157)
could soon thereafter pay that incomparable tribute to zealous Methodism which is the portrait of Dinah Morris in *Adam Bede?*

To understand these and other questions about George Eliot's
treatment of religion, we have to remind ourselves of a fact that should
never be forgotten in any consideration of the subsequent influences
on her development: namely, that the basic inspiration which gave
direction to all her works and led her to make of her novels a plea
for human solidarity was Christianity. Even though she came to reject
historical Christianity long before the appearance of *Scenes of Clerical
Life* in 1857, she maintained to the end the ethical idealism it had

---

[1] "Evangelical Teaching: Dr Cumming," in *Essays and Leaves from a
Note-Book* [Edinburgh and London, 1884], pp. 145, 188–9.

taught her in her Anglican home at Griff, at the Evangelical school
of Mrs. Wallington, and at the strongly Calvinistic institution of the
Misses Franklin. As much as Matthew Arnold, she thus epitomizes
in her life and works the spiritual history of the nineteenth century,
of which there is hardly a more graphic symbol than the image of
this intensely serious young intellectual lifting her eyes in sorrow
from her careful translation of Strauss's creed-wrecking *Leben Jesu*
and fixing them intently on the crucifix she kept before her.

Of an affectionate and ardent disposition, she responded eagerly to
the view that good works were the sign of a vivid faith. . . . Her
zeal was all for works, and though she might for a time profess justification by faith, she had little or no share in the specifically religious
emotions which faith usually arouses: in St. Augustine's restless heart
or in the soul afire of the great mystics. She could admire the Theresa
of Avila who founded a religious order; but the Theresa of the
ecstasy, whose writings are one of the glories of Spanish literature,
she cared nothing for. In spite of her admiration and sympathy, she
can give us in *Romola* only a partial portrait of Savonarola, whose
interior spiritual life is a closed book to her. "M. A. Evans était
fermée à la vie religieuse proprement dite, inaccessible à l'émotion
mystique. Sa foi était toute de tête . . . elle finit par devenir une
affaire de conduite et de philosophie."[2] That is one reason why most
of her good characters, though filled with charity, have no devotional life; why Maggie and Dorothea, in their moments of greatest
crisis, do not pray.[3] The other is, of course, that by the time of
The Mill on the Floss and *Middlemarch*, the creator and original of
these heroines had ceased to believe there was anyone to pray to.

George Eliot was concerned for a time with the doctrinal aspects
of religion because she thought there was a necessary connection
between them and her moral code. But during the Coventry period
she came to believe not only that there was no necessary connection
between Christian doctrine and her concept of duty but that it was
precisely Christian doctrine, with its emphasis on the glory of God
and the goal of personal salvation, which so often encouraged egoism
and ignored the social virtues. . . . The tendency to regard all metaphysical and theological discussion as vain was permanently solidified
when she accepted the thesis of Feuerbach that the God of man's hopes
was simply a projection of human consciousness, a shadow on the wall
of the universe. . . .

The kind of doctrine George Eliot particularly reacted against was

[2] P. Bourl'honne, *George Eliot: Essai de Biographie Intellectuelle et Mo-
rale, 1819–1854*, Paris, 1933, pp. 29–30. "*De coeur*" would be more exact than
"*de tête.*"
[3] This is not true of Maggie. — Ed.

Calvinism in its strictest form, the kind we may presume she was taught at the Franklin school since the proprietors were of the Particular Baptist creed. This, of course, teaches that God selects certain few — the elect — for eternal salvation and abandons the rest — the mass of mankind — to eternal damnation. God does this not for any good He foresees in the elect nor for any evil deeds in the reprobate (man is fallen, utterly devoid of goodness, and without free will[4]) but simply because it pleases Him. In the Calvinist tradition, furthermore, material prosperity has long been interpreted as one of the signs of election. This harrowing doctrine, which dominated English theology between the Reformation and the time of Laud, had by George Eliot's day been severely modified or glossed over by most Evangelicals and ordinary Anglicans, and flatly rejected by the Wesleyan Methodists. It is clear that it would logically make the concept of moral responsibility and of the value of good deeds as meaningless as any other strict determinism must do. It easily led to egoism and to clannishness: to the notion of an elect against an evil world.

Such theology must ultimately have proved abhorrent to a mind like George Eliot's, as indeed it was to the great mass of the Christian body. Nevertheless, it was still taught in some circles, and Evangelicalism and much of Dissent remained tainted with it. In George Eliot's view it was "the natural crop of a human mind where the soul is chiefly made up of egoistic passions and dogmatic beliefs" (*Essays*, p. 192). She well knew that Christianity did not have to be thus tainted and often was not so. "The best minds that accept Christianity as a divinely inspired system, believe that the great end of the Gospel is not merely the saving but the educating of men's souls, the creating within them of holy dispositions, the subduing of egoistical pretensions, and the perpetual enhancing of the desire that the will of God — a will synonymous with goodness and truth — may be done on earth" (*Essays*, p. 183). Still there was always the danger and often the fact of perversion, of the appeal to base motives of spiritual exclusiveness, an appeal which could hardly be made when one realized that this was the only world and that all men had the same destiny. Thus she could say in the 'forties, and she would have considered the remark applicable to the rest of her life: "I say it now, and I say it once for all, that I am influenced in my own conduct at the present time by far higher considerations, and by a

---

4 Is it possible to say whether George Eliot ever believed in freedom of the will, and if so, to what extent? There is much talk of inexorable laws and resignation to the inevitable in her work. Yet if men are not free, why write books proposing virtue as the way of life? Undoubtedly no simple answer is possible, but the question is important.

nobler idea of duty, than I ever was while I held the evangelical beliefs." Or as she put it succinctly in 1853: "Heaven help us! said the old religion; the new one, from its very lack of that faith, will teach us all the more to help one another" (Cross, I, 159, 302).

Nevertheless, though in her letters and essays, her strictures on the failures of Christianity are often keen, the treatment in her novels of all forms of religion is usually respectful and often, especially with Dissent (in the popular sense of the term: Evangelicalism as well as Methodism, Congregationalism, and so forth), warm and affectionate, since Dissent was more actively benevolent than the Established Church of her childhood. One reason for this apparent inconsistency we have seen: she owed her own ethics to Christianity and she knew that she did (Cross, I, 161). Consequently she would present in a favorable light every manifestation of Christianity which concentrated on the ethics, reserving her irony for indifferent Anglicans like Mr. Crewe of Milby and for concentration on doctrine, whether for selfish reasons, as with Mr. Bulstrode, or merely through the inno- cent ignorance of a Reverend Amos Barton, who preached against the Socinians to the utterly bewildered parishioners of Shepperton Church. . . .

In addition to her ethical sympathy, a second reason is suggested by the quotation above. George Eliot had a marked tendency to cherish the past and hallow it in memory, as witness the loving pictures of childhood in *The Mill on the Floss* and of farm life in *Adam Bede*. She believed that "the historian guides us rightly in urging us to dwell on the virtues of our ancestors with emulation,"[5] and this tendency was elevated to a principle by the gradual applica- tion of the theory of development or evolution to all forms of human activity. In this view, perhaps suggested to her by Mackay's *Progress of the Intellect*, which she reviewed for the *Westminster* in 1851, all our past creeds are necessary stages on the road to a higher religion than any yet conceived. They have something to teach us, but only by a willingness to understand them can we learn their lesson.

With these ideas in mind, let us look rather closely at the treatment of religion in *Middlemarch* . . . and then briefly at two other works in which religion plays a prominent part: *Adam Bede* and *Scenes of Clerical Life*.

It is true, as R. H. Hutton has pointed out, that *Middlemarch* is a deeply sceptical novel, implying George Eliot's belief that no Provi- dence guides human destinies, and that consequently formal religion is treated less favorably than in the earlier works. Nevertheless, the treatment follows the principles we have seen. The characters who

[5] George Eliot, *Impressions of Theophrastus Such* (Edinburgh and Lon- don, 1879), p. 320.

are held up for our admiration are all engaged — or trying to engage — in some form of activity that has its origin in the commandment of charity or love of neighbor. This needs no dwelling upon. It is significant, however, that all the principal good people are devoid of interest in the doctrinal or devotional aspects of religion and that one might apply to them a remark of Mary Garth about herself: They have a "dreadfully secular mind," though of a high type indeed. Dorothea, Caleb, Lydgate, Mary Garth, Ladislaw, and even Mr. Farebrother — none of them can reasonably be called devout; in fact, the idea of God scarcely crosses the mind of Ladislaw and appears to be rejected for a God of science by Lydgate. Compare Shaw's recent Postscript to *Back to Methuselah* (New York and London, 1947, p. 260) for the extreme view that in *Middlemarch* "there is not a ray of hope" and that the author herself "was broken by the fatalism that ensued when she discarded God."

The treatment of the clergy is typical. Consider the list of clergymen in the novel: Mr. Casaubon, Mr. Cadwallader, Mr. Tyke, Mr. Thesiger, Mr. Farebrother — not a very distinguished list, surely, though no worse than one might expect to find in the early nineteenth century in a community like Middlemarch. Mr. Casaubon, a Christian with certain private "reservations," is the intellect divorced from any but selfish feelings: a symbol of utter futility and desiccation who almost quenches the ardor of Dorothea, the modern Theresa of Avila. He, too, is likened to a famous saint — to the Angelic Doctor himself, Thomas Aquinas; and even though the whole thing is part of a game designed to flatter Mr. Casaubon, it is hard to avoid the feeling that George Eliot is offering a comment on the worthlessness of scholarly Christianity by coupling with his the name of the saint whom the Age of Enlightenment had set down as the unassailable proof of scholastic folly: the butt of the jokes of Laurence Sterne and even of Charles Lamb.

Mr. Cadwallader is in the line, slightly modified, of the clergymen of Fielding and Smollett. There is much evidence that he was only too typical of the clergy at the nadir of the Anglican Church — the eighteenth and early nineteenth centuries. He is a fisherman — but not of souls. "His conscience was large and easy, like the rest of him; it did only what it could do without any trouble" (Ch. 8). And since to concern himself with the affairs of Dorothea in order to be sure that she was fully aware of the nature of her contemplated marriage would, of course, be troublesome, he spares himself the pains.

Without ever stressing the fine parallelism, George Eliot gives the other two clergymen who actually appear in the novel (Mr. Tyke is only an occasion for action and a symbol . . .) an opportunity similar to Mr. Cadwallader's for moral guidance. Mr. Thesiger, moderate Evangelical and supporter of Tyke, is no more of the Good Samaritan than Cadwallader. He is rector of Mr. Bulstrode's parish, and Mr. Bulstrode is his most zealous parishioner. Yet, in a brilliant stroke of irony, at the moment when Bulstrode's little empire is crashing around him and the agonized, distracted man is almost completely alone, Mr. Thesiger can only suggest that he quit the room and later the town. There is more than a little justice in the painfully uttered indictment of the victim: "I protest before you, sir, as a Christian minister, against the sanction of proceedings towards me which are dictated by virulent hatred" (Ch. 71).

It is left to the apparent misfit among the clergy, who would rather study insect wings than theology, to be the one true pastor in all the community: to be the shepherd who not only looks out for his sheep, as he looks out for Lydgate, but lays down his life for them, as in a very real sense he does for Fred Vincy when he becomes the advocate of a marriage that will mean the death of his own hopes. George Eliot indicates her reaction by putting his praises into the mouths of her principal idealists. As Lydgate puts it, "I don't pretend to say that Farebrother is apostolic . . . he is only a parson among parishioners whose lives he has to try and make better" (Ch. 50). To which Dorothea, who is looking for someone to appoint as the new vicar of Lowick, responds:

"I have been looking into a volume of sermons by Mr. Tyke: such sermons would be of no use at Lowick — I mean, about imputed righteousness and the prophecies in the Apocalypse. I have always been thinking of the different ways in which Christianity is taught, and whenever I find one way that makes it a wider blessing than any other, I cling to that as the truest — I mean that which takes in the most good of all kinds and brings in the most people as sharers in it. It is surely better to pardon too much, than to condemn too much."

Of course Mr. Farebrother gets the appointment.

For our purpose, the most interesting character is Nicholas Bulstrode, whose story is a vivid exposition of many of George Eliot's principal ideas about religion. Before he became the Master of Middlemarch — banker, business partner in shady manufacturing enterprises, and chief doer of good works — he was a member of a Dissenting church at Highbury and "fond of theological definition" (Ch. 61). The Church was, significantly, Calvinist. In Middlemarch he had followed the custom of most newly rich in a provincial society to which all Dissenters were objects of scorn or distrust: he had joined the Established Church — not Mr. Farebrother's kind of church, however, but an Evangelical (and so possibly a Calvinist) church where doctrine was preached and which many of his neighbors regarded as a canting, hypocritical affair, words they reserved for anything which made of religion a rather serious matter or savored of what they understood by Methodism.

Is Mr. Bulstrode to be construed, therefore, as an attack on Calvinism, which after her spiritual emancipation George Eliot had referred to as a "wretched giant's bed of dogmas"? She says that it is not:

> This implicit reasoning [of Mr. Bulstrode in "adjusting" his motives] is essentially no more peculiar to Evangelical belief than the use of wide phrases for narrow motives is peculiar to Englishmen. There is no general doctrine which is not capable of eating out our morality if unchecked by the deep-seated habit of direct fellow-feeling with individual men (Ch. 61).

Yet . . . in discussing the Evangelical Dr. Cumming, with his teaching of election and damnation, of distrust of the motives of unbelievers, and so on, she had attacked such doctrine and charged it with being "the natural crop of a human mind chiefly made up of egoistic passion and dogmatic beliefs." Mr. Bulstrode could hardly have been a Wesleyan, for instance, since such a religion offers insufficient gratification to his kind of nature.

And what is that nature? It is one made up of "egoistic passions" which the "dogmatic beliefs" are employed to canonize. George Eliot believed that God was created in man's own image; and Mr. Bulstrode's God, who has placed his servant at the head of a gallant little band doing battle against an evil generation, who has manifested his blessing in true Calvinist fashion by making Bulstrode a brilliant financial success — Mr. Bulstrode's God is the image of Mr. Bulstrode. Mr. Bulstrode worships his God in all sincerity. He is no cheap hypocrite, no sable-dyed villain of the canting Methodist school in fiction, but a living, complex human being whom only a great artist could have created.

Mr. Bulstrode, too, has an ideal. He called it the glory of God, but it is in fact a selfish and egotistical one: he has "an immense need of being something important and predominating," and his neighbors are aware of it. . . . Mr. Bulstrode's Calvinism enables him to reason selfishness into a virtue. He helps only those who help himself and not those who, like Lydgate before the Raffles episode, are of no peculiar use to him; or those who, like Ladislaw's parents, might be in a position to diminish his own power — people whose very need was evidence that they seemed "to lie outside the path of remarkable providences" (Ch. 61). . . .

The remarkable example George Eliot offers us in detail of the adjustment of beliefs for the sake of gratifying personal desires is Bulstrode's treatment of the stricken Raffles, particularly on the night before his death, from the time he goes to his room until he gives Mrs. Abel the key to the wine-cellar. We cannot follow it here in detail, but it should be read carefully again as one of the author's most brilliant studies of the labyrinthine human mind at work. Three things about it might be noticed, however: first, it is an example of George Eliot's belief in the primacy of the emotions in moral judgments. We are told again and again that Mr. Bulstrode used "reasonings" and "mental exercises," that he did not follow "the order of his emotions" but "argued himself into not feeling a given deed incompatible with his religious profession." Intellect and doctrine are put in opposition to "fellow-feeling." (The development of Tito in *Romola* offers another example of a similar kind of opposition.) This is one of Eliot's most significant characteristics and connects her, for all her intellectualising and realism, with her beloved Wordsworth and the Romantic Movement. When Mr. Bulstrode is in need of comfort, he gets it not from his doctrines (any more than does Silas Marner) nor even from George Eliot's own resignation to the inevitable but, in one of the most touching scenes in fiction, from his wife. And the chapter (76) is introduced by lines from William Blake:

> For Mercy has a human heart,
> Pity a human face;
> And Love, the human form divine,
> And Peace, the human dress.

Second, the greatest sin of Bulstrode, like that of Tito, is an example of another favorite doctrine of the author, one which she learned from Bray: the idea that one's behavior at a given time is determined on the basis of the circumstances including heredity, environment, and presumably (though the measure of freedom is difficult to assess and small in any event) early choices of good or evil. . . . Finally, Bulstrode's downfall is an illustration of the inexorable law of consequences which is stressed in all of her work as the Nemesis which can take the place of a punishing God. Evil multiplies itself indefinitely — there is no point in trying to make the end justify the means, as Bulstrode does, for evil begets evil and must eventually catch up with its perpetrator. . . .

In a letter to her friend Harriet Beecher Stowe, George Eliot once wrote: "I think your way of presenting the religious convictions which are not your own, except by indirect fellowship, is a triumph of insight and true tolerance. A thorough comprehension of the

mixed moral influence shed on society by dogmatic systems is rare.
..." (Cross, III, 92) Rare indeed! But to such a comprehension, at
least as regards Evangelical religion, George Eliot herself came closer
than any other artist of her time.

William J. Hyde

George Eliot and the Climate of Realism

... Among the many articles and reviews in the *Westminster* that
have been ascribed to George Eliot, one stands out for its recom-
mendation of a thoroughgoing realism akin to naturalism ("The
Natural History of German Life," 66 [July 1856], 51–79). ... In
this article, George Eliot calls for a close, direct observation to
eliminate the joyous, healthy, smartly dressed opera peasant, the artistic stereotype, and rather "represent the people as they are." In
anticipating how the peasants really are, she suggests first of all an
idea of their uniform simplicity: "many thousands of men are as like
each other in thoughts and habits as so many sheep or oysters, which
constitutes the weight of the peasantry in the social and political
scale" (pp. 57–58). ... Novelists, George Eliot again states, have
made the mistake of overlooking the simplicity of the peasant and
complicating him with emotions, joys and sorrows, of which he knows
nothing. Family ties, for example, (and one thinks here of the family
in *La Terre*), are binding upon him, "but tender affection, as it exists
amongst the refined part of mankind, is almost as foreign to him as
white hands and filbert-shaped nails" (p. 62).

Secondly, in her account of the real peasant, George Eliot implies,
without describing in detail, his fundamental sordidness. The average
English peasant appears to her to be neither jocund nor merry. "The
slow gaze, in which no sense of beauty beams, no humour twinkles,
— the slow utterance, and the heavy slouching walk," all combine to
form a character suitable for either satire or pity. A further passage,

Reprinted from *PMLA*, 72 (March 1957), 153–158, by permission of the
Modern Language Association.

anticipating Zola's scenes of haymaking and drinking, suggests the clarity with which George Eliot understood the sordidness which Zola was later to describe:

> Approach nearer, and you will certainly find that haymaking time is a time for joking, especially if there are women among the labourers; but the coarse laugh that bursts out every now and then, and expresses the triumphant taunt, is as far as possible from your conception of idyllic merriment. That delicious effervescence of the mind which we call fun, has no equivalent for the northern peasant, except tipsy revelry; the only realm of fancy and imagination for the English clown exists at the bottom of the third quart pot (p. 53). . . .

To present "the peasant in all his coarse apathy" (p. 55) was, undoubtedly, for George Eliot not a pleasure but a duty owed to her realistic creed. Her summing up of a whole class of humanity as quite uniformly coarse, interesting externally but usually containing little beyond the appetite and stupidity of an animal within, and hence unsuitable for any extensive portrait involving inward analysis, suggests a generalized observation applied with a measure of stereotyped predisposition, for though a keen observer, George Eliot was in no sense ever a comrade of the peasant class. What appearances of the lowest orders are to be found in her rural novels will then be but brief glimpses, in which a tone of vulgar animality can be suggested. More than this was unnecessary, for an external glimpse was thought all that was needed to record the simple peasant character, and a prolonged look at this much might involve overstepping the bounds between the homely and offensive.

Numerous sketches in her earliest works illustrate George Eliot's point of view. There is the inmates' bleak unresponsiveness to Amos Barton's sermon in the poor house, where the vacant mind of Mrs. Brick, hopelessly unspiritual, cannot reach out beyond thoughts of snuff. In *Adam Bede* old Lisbeth Bede, unmistakably labeled an "aged peasant-woman" even though her social position as wife of a village carpenter is above that of rural laborers, proves more suitable for an extended portrait than do lower members of the peasant class. George Eliot derives some amusement from displaying her characteristic ignorance and querulousness but at the same time reveals the pain that Lisbeth's behavior causes her sons (Chs. 10, 11). Among the minor characters of *Adam Bede*, Chad's Bess, one whose connections with a more sophisticated life have corrupted with a shallow passion for fine clothes, shows concern for her spiritual welfare only, like an obedient animal, in Dinah's presence. Wiry Ben displays skillful

suppleness in his dance before the gentry, but his contortions together with his senseless seriousness only make him the butt of
laughter. Among the rustics whom Hetty meets on her flight are a
wagoner, generous but certainly dull; and a surly, suspicious shepherd
who finds her in a hovel in the sheep pasture and looks in upon her
"with a slow bovine gaze" (Ch. 37). The cottage woman, too, where
Dinah lives, is "slow of speech and apprehension" (Ch. 38), as in
general are the "bovine" laborers at the Poysers' harvest supper
(Ch. 53). Tom Saft, the half-wit, displays a ridiculous gravity following an uncontrollable "haw, haw!" when his second plate of roast
beef appears, but otherwise his wit is too blunt, perhaps too obscene,
to be quoted. Other rustics, more gifted mentally than Tom, simply
channel their mental energies into thievery or into grudges against
their fellow men. From the roast beef to the rowdy singing, a release
of inhibition provoked by quantities of ale rather than by any merry
disposition, the scene at the Poysers' seems to fulfill much of George
Eliot's earlier generalization about the "real" peasantry.

The literary critic, unlike the historian, often makes the mistake
of labeling as peasants the whole mass of rural people beneath the
gentry. To do so is to fail to distinguish the particular class of people
of which George Eliot was speaking in her article on Riehl, to fail
to distinguish the low from the commonplace. . . . In the latter
category belong the quite well-to-do tenant farmers, the Poysers, as
well as the village tradesmen (sometimes compared with Hardy's
"peasants") who assemble at the Rainbow in Silas Marner. It is
notable that these characters, stationed beneath the serious people in
the drama, are frequently treated with a sense of humor that verges
on satire. At the same time, they are distinguished from those beneath them. One critic [H. C. Minchin, Fortnightly Review, 112
(Dec. 1919), 899] has done well to observe that the men at the
Poysers' dinner, unlike those at the Malthouse in Hardy's Far from
the Madding Crowd, are not developed and tied to the story but
are merely lifted up to create a scene. It may be stated then that
such men, belonging not merely to the commonplace but to the low,
usually have not the inner importance to George Eliot to justify a
position in her plot. Insofar as she incorporates a low character in
her story, such as Bob Jakin in The Mill on the Floss, she is inclined
to ply him with a sense of humor that tends to brand him as comic
on his every appearance. Yet Bob Jakin, like his superiors, the
Poysers, or like Mrs. Hackit in "Amos Barton" or Dolly Winthrop in
Silas Marner, is credited with a keen wit, together with an eloquently
good heart, that raises him above the bovine shepherds and laborers
of his area. The real peasants of The Mill on the Floss are those who
are drawn to "Dickison's":

> A large low room with a sanded floor, a cold scent of tobacco, modified by undetected beer-dregs, Mr. Dickison leaning against the doorpost with a melancholy pimpled face, looking as irrelevant to the daylight as a last night's guttered candle — all this may not seem a very seductive form of temptation; but the majority of men in Basset found it fatally alluring when encountered on their road towards four o'clock on a wintry afternoon (Bk. I, Ch. 8).

This setting remains unused — the peasants do not appear — but its potentialities are clearly sordid.

The *real* peasant, then, whenever glimpses of him are unfolded, appears with underdeveloped suggestions of a naturalistic treatment. He is, like the laborers who attack the railway surveyors in *Middlemarch*, ignorant as well as surly and suspicious. He is usually slow and clumsy of speech, for his head is vacant of thought. The men at the Poysers' dinner hold no conversation because they have nothing on their minds to express. When their minds are absorbed with an idea, it is usually either of a material want, a second platter of roast beef, or of an envious grudge against one another or their master, a passion with the complexity of the growl of an animal. The animality of the peasant is suggested by George Eliot's emphasis on his dullness, his vacuous seriousness relieved only with strong drink, and by her frequent application of the word "bovine" to his facial expression. An animal's existence is the peasant's lot. When Mr. Moss undergoes social eclipse because of the debts and the ceaseless labor of his run-down farm, he, too, shows "the depressed, unexpectant air of a machine-horse" (*Mill on the Floss*, Bk I, Ch. 8).

With George Eliot's tendency to display a literally realistic peasant whose elements of sordidness are explicit though often undetailed, it may be wondered why the rustic characters of Hardy and George Eliot so often, ever since the publication of *Far from the Madding Crowd*, have struck critics as comparable. It should be understood, though, that it is not the latter's isolated and briefly revealed bovine figures that suggest a comparison, for Hardy had no sympathy with a portrayal merely of the external Hodge, stereotyped as vulgar, nor was he willing to stress realism as the basis of fiction. . . . It is in the treatment of the congenial commonplace, the middle ground of George Eliot which was most important to her, that the two authors meet. Hardy frequently selects his rustics from among the aristocracy of the peasant class. If they are not elevated socially and economically above the peasantry, appearing as tenants and village tradesmen, such as fill the scene in *Under the Greenwood Tree* and occupy a social position similar to that of the rustics at the Rainbow, they are at least morally refined and given a measure of wit or common sense which wins the reader's interest. The character of Hardy's peasants

in their gatherings on Rainbarrow, in Warren's Malthouse, or around
the base of St. Cleeve's tower is akin to that of the Poysers, the men
at the Rainbow, or the village gossips in "Amos Barton," emphasis
being never upon vulgarity of scene but upon cleverness of personality. If we could open the door of Dickison's, Joseph Poorgrass or
Grandfer Cantle might be inside, but emphasis on the ugliness of the
scene deters us from expecting to find him there. Hardy's peasants,
like George Eliot's commonplace rural people, are seldom markedly
dissipated, and even then never dull, not even at the Peter's Finger
in Mixen Lane or the low tavern in Christminster. Thus in their
treatment of the rural scene, the two novelists provide grounds for
comparison, though in their theories of the "lowest orders" they
stand widely apart. Seeing the animality of the typical peasant, George
Eliot could not in good taste select a "real" peasant as the subject
for an extensive portrait. More important, believing in the simplicity,
the essential emptiness, of the peasant character, she had neither the
need nor the means of creating an extensive portrait. There is no
peasant in her novels of the rank of Christian Cantle, Haymoss Fry,
or Joseph Poorgrass who is given that attention Hardy gives to him.

W. J. Harvey

The Treatment of Time in *Adam Bede*

. . . The larger issues involved in George Eliot's handling of the
omniscient author convention are beyond the scope of this essay, but
one aspect of her treatment is relevant to our particular interest and
is generally important for a right approach to her work. George
Eliot is very careful to establish her status within her novel and
through her we, too, are firmly and clearly related to the fictional
world of the book. She does this in that extreme instance of the intrusive omniscient author, Chapter 17, "In Which the Story Pauses
a Little." There she imagines herself as providing an audience for
the now aged and reminiscent Adam Bede, and we are meant to infer
that she has heard the story we are reading from him or from others
of his generation. This of course corresponds with the biographical

Reprinted from *Anglia*, 75 (1957), 429–440, by permission of the author.

facts as we know them; *Adam Bede* originates in an anecdote of one of George Eliot's aunts. But reference to an actual historical background is not relevant to our present purpose; what we should notice is that Chapter 17 is highly important to George Eliot's purposes, both aesthetic and moral, and also to the way in which we read the novel. We are, so to speak, doubly removed in time from the story; George Eliot tells us a tale which was told to her a long time ago and which actually happened a long time before it was told to her. Why should this be so important?

One reason concerns the nature of George Eliot's talent. Critics have often noticed that her novels are generally weakest when she fails in objectivity and allows a wrong kind of personal emotion to invade her work. The novels then become a form of therapy, an outlet for the tensions of her own life without the transmuting intervention of the creative artist. The result is either an idealization of a character (e.g. Maggie Tulliver, Will Ladislaw, Daniel Deronda) or the presence in the work of an unjustified hostility (e.g. the treatment of Hetty Sorrel in the first two-thirds of *Adam Bede*). In brief, George Eliot sometimes fails to achieve an adequate distancing of her experience; the woman who suffers, to adapt Mr. Eliot's formulation, is not sufficiently separate from the artist who creates. Were there not this removal in time, I believe she would have failed much more in that steadiness and clarity of vision so necessary to the success of her art.

The second reason concerns our approach to the novels. I believe we come close to the central moral purpose of George Eliot's art in a passage like this, from one of her reviews ["The Natural History of German Life," *Westminster Review*, 66 (July 1856), 54]:

> The greatest benefit we owe to the artist, whether painter, poet, or novelist, is the extension of our sympathies. Appeals founded on generalizations and statistics require a sympathy ready-made, a moral sentiment already in activity; but a picture of human life such as a great artist can give, surprises even the trivial and the selfish into that attention to what is apart from themselves, which may be called the raw material of moral sentiment.

Such a moral aim has clear aesthetic concomitants. If art is, as George Eliot says in the same review, "a mode of amplifying and extending our contact with our fellow-men beyond the bounds of our personal lot," it must be so contrived that it demands of the reader that kind of sympathy which is based on his deepest, most mature understanding. This George Eliot achieves by controlling our vision of the fictional world so that we see it gradually through a series of interconnected but ever-enlarging perspectives, contexts which demand greater and greater knowledge, sympathy and insight. By this means each of her characters is seen in a number of interacting relationships — Man in relation to himself, his family, trade, local community and to the whole of his historical society. (This last is muted and infrequent in *Adam Bede*, although the Napoleonic Wars, for example, do impinge in a number of ways on the sheltered community of Hayslope.) The largest of these relationships, the most inclusive of contexts, is of course the reader's deepest comprehension of the whole novel. He is granted an omniscience akin to that of the author. A character will know so much of himself and his fellow men, but the reader, by virtue of the wider perspectives given him, will know more and understand more than any character. Standing outside the novel, he will be able to connect and compare in a way that the inhabitants of the fictional world, of their very nature, cannot. From his vantage point he will perceive, let us say, a relationship between Bessy Cranage and Hetty Sorrel of which both these characters must be unaware, namely, that Bessy is a kind of comic parody of Hetty. The reader's perception of this relationship — and I have deliberately chosen a minor instance — will increase slightly his understanding of the whole fictional world of which they are a part. This increase of understanding, multiplied many times, is what George Eliot wishes to achieve; it is thus that the book will achieve its moral aim of extending our sympathies.

What has this to do with the author's control of time? Three relevant points need to be made. Firstly, the interacting sets of relationships through which each character is established or defined are not static or fixed, but evolve in time — this is all part of the Wordsworthian sense of growth and progress so often noticed by critics of her novels. Secondly, we must notice a point that is often overlooked because it is so obvious; namely, that George Eliot's control of the whole novel is temporal; the relationship of part to whole is governed by its sequential position so that what the story means is largely determined by the way in which it unfolds in time. Finally, the double remove in time I have already mentioned not only helps George Eliot to achieve objectivity but also aids the reader in achieving a stable relationship to the novel. It plays an important part in establishing this widest of perspectives; indeed, the reader must be able to count upon a stable point of view if he is to encompass the manifold, complex and changing experience presented to him. It is precisely because of this need for a stable relationship between reader and novel that the most infuriating lapse in George Eliot's handling of the omniscient author convention is precisely her juggling with time, . . . her disconcerting switch into the historic present at climactic moments in the novel. This annoys because it is unnecessary; George Eliot can render her subject sufficiently vivid without the help of a trick like this. But more fundamentally it is a flaw because it disturbs the reader-novel relationship which the double remove in time has so firmly established; for a moment our vision of the novel shifts and wobbles as we are distracted from our proper task by the need to adjust ourselves to a sudden alteration in the author's technique. This technique is not the proper object of our contemplation; it is a means to an end and should not usurp our attention.

Generally, however, George Eliot's technique, insofar as it concerns the control of time, is successfully unobtrusive, which may be the reason why one of the most interesting and important aspects of time in *Adam Bede* has . . . gone completely unnoticed. This is the part George Eliot's control of time plays in the structure — moral and aesthetic — of the novel. The theme of the novel, with its sense of nemesis, its emphasis on consequences rather than motives, clearly demands the heavy stress on temporal evolution that is reflected in the precision of the book's chronology. But a study of that chronology soon shows that the art of the novel, as well as its distinctive moral concern, is fundamentally concerned with temporal processes.

The art of narrative, at its lowest, implies a simple sequential interest; this happened and then that and then that. George Eliot's moral emphasis infuses sequential interest with a strong element of causality; this happened because of that, this results in that. Moreover, as soon as the art of the narrative advances beyond mere temporal sequence, a new kind of interest is set up, a narrative pattern based on juxtaposition, parallelism, contrast, anticipation, and recollection. George Eliot's typical method of interweaving concurrent stories lends itself readily to the establishing of a pattern of interest in which the author's control of time obviously plays an important part.

Consider, for example, the relationship of Hetty and Dinah, one of the main sources in the novel of this kind of narrative pattern. The parallels and contrasts between the two are enforced in a number of ways, sometimes indirectly (both, for instance are orphans), sometimes fairly obviously (compare, for example, their reactions to the news of old Bede's death) and sometimes quite explicitly, the clearest case of this being Chapter 15, "The Two Bedchambers." (This chapter, incidentally, by its juxtaposition with its immediate successor enforces another parallel: Dinah, at this point, is to Hetty what Irwine is to Arthur. This interlocking of parallels which creates the narrative pattern is intimately related to the effect of interconnected but ever-widening perspectives, already mentioned). In this network of connections between the two girls, time is important. For example,

Dinah leaves the Bedes' cottage, returning from her errand of mercy
(Ch. 14), at exactly the same time as Hetty parts from Arthur on
the first stage of her downfall (Ch. 13). Hetty's good angel Dinah
leaves for Snowfield (Ch. 11) at about the same time as her bad angel
Arthur leaves for Eagledale (Ch. 16). It is in November that Adam
becomes betrothed to Hetty; it is in the following[1] November that
he marries Dinah. Dinah leaves Snowfield for Leeds on the same day
as Hetty, pretending to visit her at Snowfield, sets out to find Arthur
at Windsor. And so on.

   One of the main emotional effects of this kind of pattern is clearly
that of irony; the reader perceives what the characters do not, precisely because he can make connections of this kind of which they
are necessarily unaware. This wider knowledge throws a sombre,
ironical light on the action of the novel. The most interesting example
of this is in that section which is least straightforward in its chronology, Book v. As we read this part, we encounter first Adam's
unavailing search for Hetty (which is caused by and which balances
Hetty's unavailing search for Arthur), we hear of her arrest and
witness her trial. It is only through the evidence given at the trial
and through Hetty's subsequent confession to Dinah that we learn
what happened to Hetty after her return from Windsor. Meanwhile
Arthur, hearing of the old Squire's death, has been journeying home-
wards, pleasantly anticipating the future and little knowing what the
future holds in store for him. Apart from the irony directed at
Arthur, one other ironical stroke of fate emerges with appalling
clarity from the disordered chronology; in Chapter 39 Adam, not
knowing of Hetty's arrest, tells Irwine: "You was t' ha' married
me and Hetty Sorrel, you know, sir, o' the 15th o' this month." The
15th of March is, in fact, the date fixed for Hetty's execution. Adam
spends the previous night with Bartle Massey:

   Sometimes he would burst out into vehement speech.
   "If I could ha' done anything to save her — if my bearing anything would ha' done any good . . . but t' have to sit still, and
   know it, and do nothing . . . it's hard for a man to bear . . . and
   to think o' what might ha' been now, if it hadn't been for *him*. . . .
   O God, it's the very day we should ha' been married."

This is surely emphatic enough. What I wish to stress are the submerged parallels and the unemphatic ironies. I insert, for convenience
here, a diagrammatic outline of the novel's action at the one point
where the technique of straightforward narration is complicated.

   [1] Adam was betrothed to Hetty in 1799 and married Dinah in 1801. — Ed.

BOOK V.

Chapter	Time	Day	Date	Event
43	Evening-Night	Sunday	27 February	Hetty sleeps at Stoniton on her way back from Windsor. A baby is born during the night. (Sarah Stone's evidence)
38	Morning	Sunday	28 February	Adam goes to Snowfield in search of Hetty.
43	8.30 p.m.	Sunday	28 February	Hetty leaves the lodging with her baby.
38	Evening	Sunday	28 February	Adam returns to Oakbourne.
38	11 a.m.	Monday	1 March	Adam goes to Stoniton to search for Hetty.
43	1 p.m.	Monday	1 March	John Olding sees Hetty; hears the baby crying.
43	2 p.m.	Monday	1 March	Olding finds the dead baby. He and the constables search for Hetty.
38	Night	Monday	1 March	Adam sees the coachman who drove Hetty to Stoniton on the 12 February.
43	Morning	Tuesday	2 March	Hetty is arrested.
38	Morning	Tuesday	2 March	Adam searches for Hetty at Stoniton; gives up and starts to go home.

Reshuffling the events in this way reveals what the arrangement of the narrative conceals; reveals, for example, how nearly the paths of Adam and Hetty cross, how nearly he saves her from her fate, since on Monday, March 1st, when Hetty abandons her child just outside Stoniton, Adam comes to Stoniton from Oakbourne in search of her. Brought to light in this way the facts pose an interesting critical problem. I assume that an ordinary, non-analytical reading of the novel does not make the reader aware of these facts. I also assume that George Eliot herself was very well aware of them; the unique detail and precision of time and the careful construction of the narrative must force us to that conclusion. Why, then, did she conceal this crossing of Adam's path with Hetty's, or rather, why did she not choose to draw the reader's attention to it? We can imagine what Hardy would have done with such a situation, the bitter irony he would have extracted from a contemplation of these two frustrated searchers almost, but not quite meeting, the tragedy nearly, but not quite being averted.

In fact, the reference to Hardy may help us towards answering the question why George Eliot did not exploit the possibilities latent in the situation. The sense we derive from say, *Tess of the D'Urbervilles*, which Hardy sums up in his famous final paragraph about the President of the Immortals at his sport, is precisely the sense that George Eliot wishes to avoid in her novels. Her work does, it is true, exhibit a variety of determinism, does rigorously show the workings of Nemesis, but these workings are rarely made so explicit by her as they are by Hardy; they are not obtruded or advanced as a philosophy of life but are thoroughly submerged beneath the surface of the novel's action. To draw attention to the fact which I have, by rearranging the chronology, elicited, would be to convert the novel into another, and possibly lower, form of art. These coincidences, these criss-crossings of individual destinies are more potent if left unremarked, working beneath the level of conscious attention and only indirectly contributing to our sense of a remorseless destiny inexorably working itself out in consequence of man's moral blindness and his egoistic refusal to face the facts of his day. These consequences, this destiny, represent perhaps the deepest, most intimate connection of the basic themes of the novel with the temporal processes through which they must, of necessity, work themselves out. The working out makes in itself a sufficiently powerful impact on the reader; there is no need for the author to call these processes to our attention by an over-conscious manipulation of the novel's chronology.

In one sense, of course, every aspect of time in the novel is functional. Thus George Eliot's stress on the natural background and on the rhythm of the seasons — so much emphasized by other critics — is a basic part of her vision of life and the most important way of establishing her narrative in a larger temporal context. Beginning and end in the strict Aristotelian sense, *Adam Bede* does not possess; rather we feel that the story has been taken from a larger continuum of time which envelops it and to which it looks both backwards and forwards. This is achieved in a number of ways; memory, especially the memory of old men like Martin Poyser, is an important agent here. Or again, we have at the outset of the novel the sense of other lives and other stories which impinge only briefly and tangentially on this life, this story. The history of the Bede family, and especially Adam's relationship with his father, is one instance. Here, for a moment, a shaft of light is thrown back in time on a set of human relationships that we never actually see in the novel, except obliquely in their effect on the character of Adam. Moreover the particular stories with which we are concerned are already under way when the novel opens; Dinah, for instance, has not just arrived in Hayslope — in fact, she is shortly to depart; the affair between Arthur and Hetty has already started, though as yet so imperceptibly that they are not really aware of it. Many more cases could be cited; all through the book we are similarly made aware of contiguous and contingent lives — such awareness is, indeed, a necessary part of George Eliot's naturalistic technique. Many tributaries flow into the mainstream of the novel; there are many quiet and enticing backwaters, but we are not allowed to stop and explore them, even in conjecture, so firmly does George Eliot guide us on our journey. All that she asks of us is that we should be aware of these tributaries and backwaters; this is part of the characteristic solidity and density of the life portrayed in her novels and part, too, of that technique of ever-widening perspective I have already tried to describe.

It should be stressed that *Adam Bede* differs from the rest of George Eliot's fiction only in degree, not in kind. None of the other novels exhibits the same astonishing chronological detail but all of them are equally rewarding when subjected to the kind of analysis attempted here. I will quote only two examples of functional time by way of justifying this generalisation. In *Daniel Deronda* we have not only the characteristic interweaving of different narrative strands but also a complicated temporal pattern which begins in a dramatic present and then makes a series of excursions into the past histories of Gwendolen and Deronda, always returning to the same present. Clearly such a pattern is a fruitful source of those temporal contrasts and parallels I have mentioned; the one I would isolate occurs if we compare Chapter 10 with Chapter 17; Gwendolen meets Grandcourt at about the same time (July) as Deronda saves Mirah from committing suicide. The interacting destinies of these two couples, if we charted them on a graph, would share the same starting-point in time; this cannot be coincidence.

My second example is taken from *Silas Marner*; the symbolic connection between the miser's loss of his gold and his discovery of the golden-haired Eppie has frequently been remarked. What has not been generally noticed is that this symbolic balance is reinforced by a careful temporal symmetry. In Chapter 1 we are told that it is fifteen years since Silas appeared in Raveloe; in Chapter 16 (the opening chapter of Part II), we jump forward sixteen years in time. Allowing for the time taken up by the narrative action of Part I, this jump forward in time almost exactly equals the initial flashback;

in other words, the period of Silas's miserdom and exile from society
is neatly balanced by the period of his redemption and gradual re-
integration into the community.

Many more examples could be cited, but these should suffice to
show that the method of *Adam Bede* is typical of George Eliot's
novels. There are only two exceptions; *Romola*, being a historical
novel, poses special problems, while the action of the short tale,
"The Lifted Veil," based as it is upon the prevision of the future,
clearly demands an abnormal tampering with temporal processes.
But these are exceptions; George Eliot's distinctive talent is intimately
linked with a full sense of time in all its complexities, some of which
I have here tried to disentangle. It is no accident that George Eliot
looks back in so many ways to Wordsworth, nor is it a coincidence
that Proust should have found her so great a novelist.

Jerome Beaty

History by Indirection:
The Era of Reform in *Middlemarch*

Few readers notice how many details from the political history of
a period forty years prior to the time of composition are present
throughout *Middlemarch*. I wish here to give some idea of the nature
and pervasiveness of those details — though indeed there are so many
I cannot include them all — and to indicate how George Eliot
managed to keep them, numerous as they are, from obtruding upon
the fiction.

The events in *Middlemarch* are supposed to take place between
30 September 1829 and the end of May 1832. Most of the historical
references in the novel therefore concern events and personalities
involved in the struggle for political reform which culminated in
the passage of the First Reform Bill in June 1832. For roughly the
first half of this period the Tories — under Wellington, Peel, and
George IV — are in control, and though they are forced to give
ground grudgingly on some issues — Catholic Emancipation, for in-

Reprinted by permission from *Victorian Studies*, 1 (December 1957),
173–179.

stance — they manage to hold out against the forces of reform, even against such moderate reform as that urged by men like Huskisson. With the death of George IV in June 1830 and the assumption of power by the Whigs under Lord Grey in November reform of some kind is inevitable; interest centers on the parliamentary election of 1831 and the controversy, particularly in the House of Lords, over Lord Russell's Reform Bill.

In *Middlemarch* political events manifest themselves early, though at first only as background. In Chapter 3 Mr. Brooke is already showing Casaubon "documents" on machine-breaking and rick-burning, signs of the political discontent of the period. A few pages later, George Eliot, in one of the few historical utterances made directly to the reader in this novel, speaks of "those ante-reform times." Beginning with the very next scene political references become more specific: Mr. Brooke conjectures that Casaubon may be made a bishop "if Peel stays in," for, we later learn, Casaubon has written "a very good pamphlet for Peel" on the Catholic question. These references to Peel and Catholic Emancipation, here lumped together, are worked into the text of *Middlemarch* with the greatest of circumspection: the fact that Casaubon may hope to profit by Peel appears in Chapter 4; that he has written a pamphlet on the Catholic question appears near the end of Chapter 7; that it is this pamphlet which should put him in Peel's favor appears in Chapter 30. In none of these chapters is a date mentioned; indeed, the year 1829 is specified only once in the novel, and that not until Chapter 15. The novel thus refers to Peel's tenure (1829–30) in the Wellington, not in the earlier Liverpool Cabinet, and to his favoring Catholic Emancipation — first publicly announced on 5 March 1829 — not to his earlier bitter opposition to Emancipation.

Peel is mentioned several more times. On one occasion during Peter Featherstone's last illness Borthrop Trumbull notes that Peel has just inherited his father's title (Ch. 32), an event which actually took place on 3 May 1830. Two chapters later the chronology is confirmed; we are told that "It was on a morning of May that Peter Featherstone was buried." A last mention of Peel, in Chapter 37, links his name with that of Wellington — "Wellington and Peel generally depreciated." After the first reference to Wellington as Prime Minister in Chapter 19 he is mentioned on three occasions and on all three is in disfavor. The first of these links him to Peel, as I have just noted; the second occurs at the auction, when Trumbull is trying to sell "an engraving of the Duke of Wellington surrounded by his staff on the field of Waterloo . . . notwithstanding recent events which have . . . enveloped our great Hero in a cloud . . ." (Ch. 60); the last is a remark by Mr. Limp, one of the company at

Dollop's, who has read in the *Trumpet* a statement made by the Duke "when he turned his coat and went over to the Romans" (Ch. 71).

Already we can see certain of George Eliot's techniques for handling political history: she introduces it largely through references to historical personages; she mentions but never explains issues; she scatters references to the same person or issue through the novel rather than lumping them in a single paragraph or chapter; she separates the event from specific dates. In other words, she presents history dramatically, within the story, as part of the lives of the characters; she rarely offers it directly to the reader as history.

About the time Peel's name disappears from the novel a new one, that of Huskisson, is introduced. A Canningite, Huskisson lost his place in the Wellington Cabinet by trying to transfer two disenfranchised seats to growing towns, a kind of moderate reform. As a private member, in March 1830 he again supported such a move. During the summer of that year Huskisson's name and views appear in *Middlemarch*: Hackbutt and Hawley are discussing reform, Rights of Man, the non-representation of large towns, and pocketboroughs. Hackbutt says,

> "I myself should never favour immoderate views – in fact I take my stand with Huskisson – but I cannot blind myself to the consideration that the non-representation of large towns –"
> "Large towns be damned!" said Mr. Hawley. . . . "Let 'em quash every pocket-borough to-morrow, and bring in every mushroom town in the kingdom – they'll only increase the expense of getting into Parliament" (Ch. 37).

This is more direct and extensive than previous political references; politics is beginning to move closer to the foreground of *Middlemarch*: Mr. Brooke has bought a newspaper, has hired Will Ladislaw to edit it, and is obviously preparing to stand for Parliament. Nevertheless, this too is presented in dialogue, dramatically, and there is no identification and little explanation of Huskisson.[1]

The coming to the fore of politics in the novel actually depends

---

[1] Huskisson is mentioned again in *Middlemarch*, his death, like Peel's peerage, being casually mentioned at the right time in the novel. Huskisson was killed in an accident at the opening of the Liverpool and Manchester Railway on 15 Sept. 1830. Raffles, boarding a train on one of his departures from Middlemarch, remarks that the train is "pretty well seasoned now it had done for Huskisson" (Ch. 41). Since the last chronological reference in the novel was to "August lights" (Ch. 40) and some unspecified time has passed since then, the historical date of the event is not only consistent with the fiction, but indeed dates it more accurately than does any internal reference.

to some extent on the most important historical event of the years 1829–30, the death of George IV, which seems to mark the real end of the "ante-reform" era and the beginning of the most heated period of the reform movement, leading to the passage of the First Reform Bill on 7 June 1832. George Eliot's handling of this important event is an excellent example of "history by indirection." George IV is first mentioned in 1829, the year in which the novel opens, in an overt, author-to-reader historical reference to those "good old days," when "George the Fourth was still reigning over the privacies of Windsor, when the Duke of Wellington was Prime Minister, and Mr. Vincy was mayor of the old corporation in Middlemarch" (Ch. 19). In December of that year there is a picture of the monarch hanging in the inn at Houndsley (Ch. 23). In May 1830, "some months before Lord Grey came into office," Peter Featherstone dies, and everyone at the time is concerned about "the last bulletin concerning the King" (Ch. 35). The actual death of the King, however, is not introduced into the novel as news, even though its effects are felt. Indeed, Mr. Vincy is not certain that the world is not coming to an end: "The doubt hinted by Mr. Vincy whether it were only the general election or the end of the world that was coming on, now that George the Fourth was dead, Parliament dissolved, Wellington and Peel generally depreciated, and the new King apologetic, was a feeble type of the uncertainties in provincial opinion at that time" (Ch. 37). Thus one of the most important historical events of the time, and one that is important as a turning point in the novel, the death of George IV, is not reported directly or immediately in the text of the novel itself. We hear of his last illness; we learn that he is dead through the effect of his death on the political (and fictional) situation; but no one rushes in with the news, no one refers to it as news.

Political history, which has pushed almost into the foreground in Chapter 37 with the events surrounding the death of George IV, quickly subsides, and does not come forward again[2] until the opening of Chapter 46:

> While Lydgate, safely married and with the Hospital under his command, felt himself struggling for Medical Reform against

[2] There is reference to the July Revolution in France: Brooke says to Chettam, "Well, what do you think of things? — going on a little fast! It was true enough what Laffitte said — 'Since yesterday, a century has passed away'; — they're in the next century, you know, on the other side of the water" (Ch. 38). Laffitte's remark, made on 29 July 1830, fixes the time of the conversation. The only other references to time in this portion of the novel are in Ch. 37 — "the summer had gradually advanced" — and in Ch. 40 — a reference to "August lights."

Middlemarch, Middlemarch was becoming more and more conscious of the national struggle for another kind of Reform.

By the time that Lord John Russell's measure was being debated in the House of Commons,[3] there was a new political animation in Middlemarch, and a new definition of parties which might show a decided change of balance if a new election came. And there were some who already predicted this event, declaring that a Reform Bill would never be carried by the actual Parliament. This was what Will Ladislaw dwelt on to Mr. Brooke as a reason for congratulation that he had not yet tried his strength at the hustings.

The dissolution of Parliament "predicted" in this passage — which actually took place on 22 April 1831 — is an important event, both in the history of the Reform Bill and in the plot of *Middlemarch:* historically it marks the end of the last Parliament successful in blocking reform; in the novel it marks the occasion for Brooke's standing for Parliament. As in the case of the King's death, however, the historical event is heralded — "dissolution might happen any day" (Ch. 49); "certain dissolution forthwith" (Ch. 50) — and its having occurred is assumed — by Brooke's candidacy — but the event itself is not specifically mentioned on or immediately after the day it occurred.

It is surely the subtlety and indirectness with which George Eliot introduces and uses historical dates, issues, and events which largely accounts for the average reader's impression that there are only a few minor references to political history in *Middlemarch* and his feeling that this is not in any sense a "historical novel." The major political events are forecast and have effects with no surrounding air of "momentous occasion"; they assume their natural place in the lives and actions of the characters, yet they do not distract the reader from the fiction. The death of Casaubon does not have to compete for the reader's attention with the death of George IV, for surely the fictional event would shrink in its significance should history force us to recall our willing suspension of disbelief of the fiction. Even Chapter 51, which includes Brooke's memorable speech at the hustings, the most directly political chapter in the novel, contains little or no contemporary history.

Politics and political history, which have again briefly approached the foreground of the novel, disappear almost entirely, this time for sixteen chapters, more than half a volume. When history reappears, it is already the spring of 1832 and Lord Russell's Bill has gone to

[3] The Bill was introduced on 1 March. Several pages later in Ch. 46 there is reference to "an evening in March." Thus the chronology, as usual, is consistent.

the House of Lords. This is a suitable example with which to end the study of George Eliot's handling of history in *Middlemarch*, for though in part she uses some of the techniques of history by indirection, she reverses her practice, makes history obtrusive (though dramatic) and heightens the intensity of the fiction.

In Chapter 67 there is reference to "early March," and in Chapter 71 to "gleaming April lights." Twice between these references the question of the House of Lords' disposition of Lord Russell's Reform Bill is discussed in the novel: Lydgate and Bulstrode, riding back to Middlemarch after the death of Raffles, talk "of many things — chiefly cholera and the chances of the Reform Bill in the House of Lords, and the firm resolve of the political Unions" (Ch. 70); a few days later, after Bambridge has repeated Raffles' story to the Middlemarchers, the Green Dragon and Dollop's are the scenes of more discussion of the Raffles-Bulstrode-Lydgate affair than of "the question whether the Lords would throw out the Reform" (Ch. 70). This resembles the scattered, indirect references we have previously noted, but there is a new element: in the latter instance the fictional event is magnified by indicating the extent to which it overshadowed an important historical debate (or, to put it another way, it shows that the provincial mind is more concerned with the scandalous event under its nose than with the more important but remote event in London). In this case, as in that of the King's death or of the dissolution of Parliament in 1831, the political action itself does not enter the story, but here the more or less immediate reaction of characters to the event is suggested — though again with the effect of intensifying the fiction — for Chapter 84 begins: "It was just after the Lords had thrown out the Reform Bill [7 May 1832]: that explains how Mr. Cadwallader came to be walking on the slopes of the lawn . . . at Freshitt Hall, holding a 'Times' in his hand behind him, while he talked . . . about the prospects of the country to Sir James Chettam. . . ." This sets the stage for Brooke's entry with a long face. Cadwallader, knowing Brooke's pro-Reform views, attributes the melancholy look to the political news:

> "Don't take the throwing out of the Bill so much to heart, Brooke; you've got all the riff-raff of the country on your side."
> "The Bill, eh? ah!" said Mr. Brooke, with a mild distractedness of manner. "Thrown out, you know, eh? The Lords are going too far, though. They'll have to pull up. Sad news, you know, I mean here at home — sad news. But you mustn't blame me, Chettam."

The news Mr. Brooke has is of Dorothea's decision to marry Will, an announcement of such import to the gathering and to the reader, that it is no wonder the political news, important as it is, is forgotten. Thus the political event is foreshadowed and has its effect, but does not appear on stage in the novel. Here there is an interesting switch in George Eliot's use of history, however. The political event seems to be reported directly in the novel either as fresh news or as an event of historical importance; it obtrudes. Yet here it is so closely followed by the momentous fictional "news," that the reality itself is overshadowed. History is a counter in the dramatic irony: the group on the lawn is trying to console Mr. Brooke for the political news that is "good" to them though "bad" to him — they are gloating, in fact — but it is not that bad news that he is concerned with at all, but the news of Dorothea's decision to marry Will, which, if bad to him, is nearly catastrophic to Sir James and the Cadwalladers. The reader and the gathering on the lawn brush aside the political event impatiently.

After all, the Lords' rejection of the Bill is not of great historical importance. It is only the dying gasp of ante-reform England. Within a few weeks, the First Reform Bill will be finally passed. That is the great political event of the period. And, characteristically, it too occurs off the Middlemarch stage, taking place in fact after the action of the novel is finished. Indeed, there is a parallel in the fiction. The old world of Middlemarch makes a final effort to resist Dorothea's marrying an unsuitable foreigner: Casaubon's codicil to his will cuts her off; Sir James fumes and sputters; Brooke will not attend the wedding and threatens more drastic action; Celia visits Dorothea in a last effort to make her change her plans. All is in vain. Dorothea will marry Ladislaw. But the wedding, the most important fictional event of the novel, takes place off stage, after the action in the novel ends, too: it is scheduled for three weeks after the scene at Freshitt, very close to the June seventh date of the passage of the Reform Bill. This coincidence lends an air of finality or completeness to the story that began nearly three years earlier by bringing to a close a historical as well as a fictional series of events.

In *Middlemarch*, then, George Eliot uses details from the political history of the years 1829–32 accurately and extensively. On those rare occasions when she introduces relatively important political events as news directly into the novel she so surrounds them with momentous fictional events that the history is brushed aside. Most often, however, she introduces history indirectly; she rarely addresses historical information directly to the reader, preferring to introduce it as part of the everyday affairs of the fictional characters, rarely overshadowing personal affairs, often overshadowed by them; she disperses references to a single historical person or event rather than

lumping or explaining them in a single paragraph or chapter; she
never mentions the historical event and the date in the same or even
in adjacent passages; she does not show or immediately report the
most important political events of the period (including the passage
of the First Reform Bill itself) in the text of the novel. Because
she skilfully uses indirection, few readers realize they are reading
a novel full of documented, accurate historical information; none
feels history obtrudes inorganically upon the fiction.

Quentin Anderson

George Eliot in *Middlemarch*

In *The Prelude* Wordsworth notes that while he was taken up
with Godwinian rationalism he had discovered that rationalism had
a special danger: it denied the existence of the passions which actually
informed it. The briefest possible answer to the question, What is
the greatness of George Eliot? is to say that she knew and could
show that every idea is attended by a passion; that thought is a
passional act. Of course it is on the showing, the accomplishment
of the artist, that the emphasis must finally rest, but it seems politic
to begin this account by suggesting to a somewhat unreceptive age
how much she has to tell her readers. Widely read and highly respected during the last four decades of her century, George Eliot
became schoolroom fare in ours; but the assumption that she is
once more coming into the light is current, it may be the misleading
consequence of the appearance of Professor Gordon Haight's monumental edition of her *Letters* and F. R. Leavis's fine chapters on her
in *The Great Tradition*. There is a seeming paradox in the fact
that, although admired, she is not much read, because no novelist in
English has come closer to answering a question which is very important to us: How can a social world be felt and understood? It
appears probable that there is some resistance in us against the terms
in which George Eliot answers this question; we may well want

Reprinted with permission of Penguin Books, Inc., from *From Dickens to
Hardy* (Volume 6 of *The Pelican Guide to English Literature*), 1958, pp.
274–293.

a chance for vicarious or imagined mastery over the social order—
a chance to judge and discriminate with sureness -- but most of us
find something remote, something truly "Victorian," in a world so
fully humanized as the world of *Middlemarch;* perhaps this is because
it requires more love than we can give, more assurance than we
can muster. . . .

To find George Eliot at her best one turns to the three books which
follow *Romola.* Among these, *Felix Holt, the Radical,* is much the
weakest, though it contains superlative passages. *Daniel Deronda*
is about the most splendid failure among English novels, and the
reader who responds to *Middlemarch* may be assured that it is well
worth his time. But *Middlemarch* is unquestionably the best of the
three.

This novel is subtitled "A Study of Provincial Life," and the
climax in the national life which it partly chronicles, the period in
which the Reform Bill of 1832 was moving towards adoption, was
selected with the apparent intention of giving the novel the representative quality which we associate with Flaubert's *Sentimental
Education* and Tolstoy's *War and Peace.* But one of the first things
we must note about the novel is that this particular intention masks
a more general one. Flaubert's choice of the revolution of 1848 or
Tolstoy's of Napoleon's invasion of Russia as events which bring
together various strands of the national experience was motivated
in part by a desire to put that experience before us. George Eliot's
notebook for the novel shows that she looked up such matters as the
stages in the passage of the Reform Bill, the medical horizons of the
1830s, the industrial uses of manganese, and various other details.
But the uses to which she puts these things are not terminal; she is
not concerned as Flaubert is to lodge firmly in the reader's sensibility
a mass of impressions deliberately selected to inform us of the
political, industrial, and social life of the time. She is, in fact, incapable of suggesting the tone of a given period or historical moment.
In the Middlemarch world, as in George Eliot generally, change is
something intrusive, an irruption from without. The more general
intention of which I have spoken is the attempt to render in a
novel her sense of the "primitive tissue" of a community.

This term is employed by Tertius Lydgate, a surgeon with excellent training, who buys a Middlemarch practice and hopes to
combine medical work with research in physiology. His studies in
Paris have persuaded him that a promising line of inquiry lies in the
attempt to find the primal tissue which is the basis of all those
adapted to special bodily functions. The master image of the book
precisely parallels Lydgate's physiological inquiry; this is the image
of human relationships as a web. Each of us stands at what seems

to us a centre, our own consciousness, though it is in fact but one of numerous nodes or junction points. This is further illustrated in George Eliot's figure of the metal mirror bearing many scratches, which when illuminated at any given point produces the illusion of concentric circles ranged about that point. This figure enriches the suggestion of the recurrent web image and those associated with it by enforcing the fact that in dealing with a particular person we must consider: his appearance in the eyes of each of the other persons whom he encounters; the way he appears among various social groups to which he is known or which know of him; and his own complex of feelings which leads him to offer the world a version (or various versions) of himself. This does not at first seem an epoch-making kind of viewpoint for a novelist, since all novelists must somehow convey the quality of each character's self-regard and the opinions that others have of him. But George Eliot's special success in *Middlemarch* is the consequence of making the reciprocal workings of self-regard and opinion primary — in effect an extraordinary economy of means, and not simply of means, for it appears when we look closely that the matter of the book is people's opinions about one another, and that its particular method consists in contriving scenes in which the disparity between the intentions of agents and the opinions of observers is dramatically exhibited. This consistency of method accounts for our sense of the unity of a book which embraces a whole social order and four, or by another reckoning, five principal stories.

Of course these stories are intertwined by the plot as well as by our developing sense of Middlemarch as a community. The first of these stories is that of Dorothea Brooke, which was begun as an independent tale and later worked into the plan of the larger novel. Dorothea is somewhat externally characterized in a brief "Prelude." She belongs to a group of great spirits who remain unknown and unsung: "With dim lights and tangled circumstance they tried to shape their thought and deed in noble agreement; but after all, to common eyes their struggles seemed mere inconsistency and formlessness; for these later-born Theresas were helped by no coherent social faith and order which could perform the function of knowledge for the ardently willing soul." The account concludes: "Here and there is born a Saint Theresa, foundress of nothing, whose loving heart-beats and sobs after an unattained goodness tremble off and are dispersed among hindrances, instead of centering in some long-recognisable deed." F. R. Leavis discerns a tendency on the part of George Eliot to make rather too personal investments in her heroines, and the tone of this "Prelude" bears him out. The reader ought to be assured that the Dorothea he meets in the opening scenes of the novel is not this portentous figure, but a young lady whose foible in marrying an elderly pedant has the consequences – comic, pathetic, and even, in a minor and domestic key, tragic – that we might expect it to have in life. As the novel goes forward, however, Dorothea's demand that the world afford chances for heroic achievement does begin to seem much too categorical. We must return to the question of her role in the imaginative economy of the novel at a later point.

Lydgate, the principal figure of the second intrigue, is closer to the working centre of the book than Dorothea, since his fate turns not simply on his marriage to Rosamond Vincy, but upon the sum of his actions and reactions in response to Middlemarch. His story is linked with the third in the group of four, the story of Bulstrode, the banker guilty of moral defalcations, whose self-arraignment is one of the finest episodes in the book (although the whole Bulstrode strand in the novel is less impressive than the others because his past is somewhat stagily rendered and the agents out of that past who hunt him down seem melodramatic conveniences). The fourth strand, closer in tone to the earlier Midland novels, functions in part to provide a standard by which the others may be placed and judged. It involves the Garth family, Mary, her father, Caleb, her successful suitor, Fred Vincy, and the Reverend Mr Farebrother, who also aspires to Mary. Here also belong the provincial humours of the book, which centre about old Peter Featherstone's disposition of his property.

Middlemarch is carefully (contemporary readers tend to say exhaustively) plotted. One or more of the characters in each of the four stories plays an important part in each of the other three. The Victorian reader was offered a multiplicity of occasions for sympathetic concern. One of the things about George Eliot and her readers which it is hardest for us to recapture is the artless and unashamed emotionalism of the latter over the fate of her characters, and the benign acceptance of this situation on the part of the writer. The century which wrenched Hamlet out of *Hamlet* had not the least scruple about lobbying for its favourite character while the novel was in the course of publication in parts – while it was in fact still being written. One may imagine that if the modern objection to such innocence about the fashion in which a work is made an artistic whole had been stated it would have been met with the response that the whole was really constituted by the assurance of moral conformity – George Eliot could be trusted. Blackwood, George Eliot's publisher, wrote her in this vein while *Middlemarch* was appearing; he sets down his hopes and fears for the characters, and tells her in effect that her interposition in their lives has been both touching and morally impeccable. The novelist and her fellows were of course affected by this atmosphere: they wrote with a consciousness of the awakened and palpitant sensibilities of the readers who were speculating about what would happen in the next part; they watched the sale of each part with anxiety, and made anxious inquiry about a falling-off. Some of the occasions for sympathetic concern in this novel may be listed: How will Dorothea awake to a consciousness of the meaning of her marriage to the pedant, Casaubon? Will Fred Vincy inherit old Featherstone's money? Failing that, will he reclaim himself and marry Mary Garth, or will Farebrother cut him out? Will Rosamond's "torpedo contact" paralyse her vigorous husband, Lydgate? Can he succeed in medical practice in the face of the bigotry of Middlemarch? Can he extricate himself from his debts? How will Bulstrode be found out, and what will thereupon happen to him and his devoted wife? There is a cognate familiarity about many of the motifs of the story: the idealism of Dorothea, the earnest and rather wry Christianity of Farebrother, the weakling reclaimed in Fred Vincy, the dryness, harsh fun, and moral beauty of the plain Mary Garth. Neither plot nor traits of character taken alone are sufficiently distinctive to set this novel apart from others. I have found that youthful readers nowadays are restive when confronted by such careful plotting and such familiar traits of character; they shy away and quite miss the light which illuminates all these things in their mutual relations, the voice of the wise woman. That voice is often heard speaking directly with an authority which makes use of the Victorian reader's involvement with the characters to make him look up and look about, to see how human relations are established within the world of the story – to see the whole of what the wise woman surveys.

What she surveys may be called a landscape of opinion, for it is not the natural landscape that is dominant here. In fact, there are only two fully realized natural landscapes, Lowick Manor and Stone Court, and in these cases the landscape is realized by an individual whose situation and interests make him aware of an external world at that particular moment. For the most part we may characterize the book's use of the physical world by referring to George Eliot's own sense of Warwickshire as a physical locale which has been wholly humanized, and to the Reverend Mr Cadwallader's half-serious remark that it is a very good quality in a man to have a trout stream. This transposition of the natural into the moral and psychological is further illustrated by the novelist's use of snatches of poetry – Dorothea Brooke's hope for social betterment "haunted her like a passion" – and we may say that the affectionate sense of nature and the objects that man makes and handles which suffuses *Adam Bede* has been deliberately subdued here. Nothing comparable to the description of Hetty Sorrel in Mrs Poyser's dairy can enter into *Middlemarch,* not because it is a more "intellectual" book, but because its immediacies are not things seen but things felt and believed. It is striking that we know almost nothing of the appearance of Middlemarch itself, although our sense of the life of the town as a community is very full indeed, ranging as it does from a pot-house to the Green Dragon, the town's best inn, from horse-dealers, auctioneers, and grocers to the lawyers, physicians, merchants, clergymen, and landowners who stand at the head of the scale. Although we see little of the activities of all these people we hear their voices, each pitched to the tone of its own desire, each capable of dropping suggestively or rising assertively on grounds which George Eliot shows to be wholly inadequate when related to the facts of the particular case. Chapter 45 is a good instance of the masterly way in which she can demonstrate the drifts and swirls of opinion through the town. In this account of various responses to Lydgate's principled refusal to dispense drugs himself, each of the voices establishes a character so fully and with such economy that it is hard to believe that Mawmsey, the grocer, and Mrs Dollop of the Tankard have not always been known to us. Yet this single chapter does much more. In it we learn that the clouds of mis-apprehension and selfishness gathering about Lydgate cannot possibly be dispelled, that he is more than likely to get into debt, and that his wife's awful insularity will resist his earnest and even his desperate attempts to penetrate it. George Eliot had much earlier (Ch. 15) used her author's privilege to warn the reader of all these possibilities. "For surely all must admit that a man may be puffed and belauded, envied, ridiculed, counted upon as a tool and fallen in love with, or at least selected as a future husband, and yet remain virtually unknown — known merely as a cluster of signs for his neighbours' false suppositions." The novelist, writing of *Middle-march,* says: "I wanted to give a panoramic view of provincial life . . ."; but what she does give is something far more active, far more in accord with the image of the web — or perhaps a vast switch-board in which every signal is interpreted differently by each receiver, and each receiver is in its turn capable of propagating in response a signal of its own with equally dissonant consequences. Yet in the end, roughly but surely, the dissonances die out and a consensus of sorts emerges, for as George Eliot remarks at one point, not everyone is an originator, and there is a limit to the varieties of error people can fall into.

The characters move in a landscape of opinion, but those who concern us have an inner life; they can look within as well as without, and measure their sense of themselves against the world's demands and expectations. The economy of means and materials I have referred to consists in the use of the landscape of opinion as the scene of action. It does not exclude, it rather informs and gives depth to the conventional motifs and the conventional attributes of character mentioned above. A long quotation extracted from the description of Casaubon illustrates the method: [Ch. 10]. We have come a long way from Fielding's interposed addresses to the reader in *Tom Jones*, a long way from Dickens and Thackeray as well — Thackeray cannot step on his stage without shaking it or dwarfing it; the effect is always of diminution, a voice which condescends to or coos about the pettiness or charm of the creatures displayed, while Dickens's effects in this kind involve facing about, leaving the characters to fend for themselves while he carries on his special pleading. George Eliot, however, speaks to the issues of her own work, and addresses the reader in terms which set her above it but never to one side. In her "I protest against any absolute conclusion . . ." we find a gentle schoolmistress's irony which places her between the book and our apprehension of it. In this instance she is saying that we are guilty, not because we are all egocentrics by definition, but because these notations about Casaubon have indeed composed our picture of him. She goes on to indicate what she is about to do with the figure: we shall end by finding him pathetic; we are to be converted — to be forced to abandon the stereotyped social gesture which leads us to "refer him [Casaubon] to the Divine regard" and refer him instead to our own failures to get the world to concede our majesty. Her own rhetoric, the somewhat heavy verbal play of "solitary superlative," the clinical remoteness and buried scientific analogy of "what deeper fixity of self-delusion the years are marking off within him," the carefully indicated central image of the mutually mirroring selves, the fact that she is playing prologue to her own action — for each of her generalities is a forecast of a part of Casaubon's fate — are all elements of that voice which frames the whole book.

Within this frame the dialogue presents dramatically the same interplay between opinion and self-regard, mirror and mirrored self. . . . Each leading character has a serious delusion: Dorothea's belief that she can do good through learning; Lydgate's that the demands of science are compatible with those that Middlemarch makes of its physicians; Mr Casaubon's idea that marriage with a beautiful and passionate young girl will bring him pleasure and repose; Bulstrode's belief that he can make an inward moral restitution for the act of misappropriating his original fortune. . . .

Some of George Eliot's devices to enforce her view of the land-scape of opinion are transparently such. Young Fred Vincy has long held expectations based on old Peter Featherstone's will. Peter, who lives to torment his relatives, teases him about a story that he has been trying to borrow money on post-obits. Fred is instructed to get a letter from the stiff-necked Bulstrode to the effect that this is not true. . . . Old Featherstone is here made to demand of Fred Vincy more than Bulstrode's testimony as to the *facts;* had he limited himself to this Fred would be less uncomfortable — but what has actually been demanded is an account of the way in which Fred is envisioned by another man — an account of one facet of his social being. The imaginative coherence of *Middlemarch* is ob-servable on many levels; in this instance old Featherstone's demand is the counterpart of what chiefly obsesses his last months: the effect that another document, his will, will have on those who survive him. *His* opinion will emerge when his last will is read, and it will comfort no one on the Middlemarch scene. Fred, meanwhile, is buoyed up by an opinion generally held that he will inherit from old Featherstone: "In fact, tacit expectations of what would be done for him by Uncle Featherstone determined the angle at which most people viewed Fred Vincy in Middlemarch; and in his own con-sciousness, what Uncle Featherstone would do for him in an emergency, or what he would do simply as an incorporated luck, formed always an immeasurable depth of aerial perspective." . . .

Fred's own sense of the way in which the world ought to respond to the desires of a young man in his position in life has been fostered by the father who rejects him. He has long been fond of Mary Garth; this affection and the more effectual fatherhood of Caleb Garth rescue him from the family delusion that the world will cater to their handsome children. Caleb Garth is strongly reminiscent of the novelist's father, Robert Evans. He is wholly committed to the religion of "business," by which he means the actual performance of work. In Middlemarch he stands very much alone. It is not the least important of George Eliot's observations about this community that it lacks the instinct of workmanship and the pleasure in a job well done. We hear of shoddy cloth, inferior dyestuffs, oppressed weavers, ill-housed tenants, and all these things are comments on the adequacy of the landscape of opinion; it is very badly and weakly rooted in nature.

Moreover, it can show few explicit principles. Most of those who advance moral or political convictions are shown to be riding a hobby or exhibiting a personal foible. . . . There is shrewdness on many levels, but respect for accuracy, dispassionate judgement, are confined to the Garths and Farebrother, persons who are of little consequence on the Middlemarch scene. The other character whose judgement and information are offered as authoritative is Casaubon's cousin, Will Ladislaw, who marries Dorothea after her husband's death. He, however, is so alien to Middlemarch that he cannot act on it directly: the principles, ideas, and standards which prevail in the wider world outside Middlemarch cannot be articulated within it. The medium is too dense; it is not permeable from without. . . .

George Eliot has created a common medium which completely immerses most of the characters. It is hard to conceive how an individual can on this scene really originate anything. Dorothea's wide charity finds no direct expression; Lydgate's scientific interest in the town's health meets blank incomprehension and effectual resistance, not only from all ranks in the medical hierarchy but from almost every element in the town. Indeed, the reader may by now feel (partly because I have played down the humour of the book) that Middlemarch is as oppressive as that provincial town inhabited by Emma Bovary in another study of the *mœurs de province*. In Flaubert's book there are at least the passionate impulses of Emma to combat her stifling world. What is there here? . . .

Professor Haight, in his introduction to a recent edition of *Middlemarch*,[1] repudiates the figure of the Wise Woman, which he finds rampant in John Walter Cross's biography. However, George Eliot herself is partly responsible for the dissemination of this image . . . , and the Wise Woman, or whatever we wish to call her, is an indispensable figure in discussing her work. In fact, the only thing which can possibly balance, can possibly support *Middlemarch*, is this image of the writer which the novel creates in the reader. Were she not there we should not be attending. George Eliot is present as the only fully realized individual in her book. This sounds like a harsh saying, but it may not be quite so harsh as it sounds. When one is reading *Middlemarch* there are many moments when one looks up and says, "How intelligent, how penetrating this woman is!" And, of course, one is speaking of George Eliot. . . . Those who like *Middlemarch* take pleasure in the writer's judiciousness. They are far more tempted to invest themselves with her sensibility than they are to identify themselves with that of any of her characters. It is notable that analytic passages . . . predominate among those chosen for quotation from Leslie Stephen's day to our own. The description of Caleb Garth, of Rosamond Vincy's terrible self-absorption, of Dorothea's aspirations and her blindness to his sister Celia's world, of Bulstrode's casuistical inner life, of Casaubon's tortured consciousness of inadequacy — all these are analytic though all are matched by passages of dialogue in which their substance is

[1] In *George Eliot and John Chapman*, New Haven, 1940, p. viii. — Ed.

exemplified. Certain dramatic scenes — that between Dorothea and
Rosamond in particular — are also favourites, but again the most
familiar passage about Rosamond seems to be that which describes
her reaction to the awful, the inconceivable fact that there is another
self in the world, one which Ladislaw cherishes far more than hers.
These fine and satisfying analytic passages are not additions or
decorations, nor do they represent a division within George Eliot,
rather they exhibit her sense of process at work within the frame of
actuality; it is her life *in* the novel which lies at its heart; this is
what we rejoice in. Admittedly this means that no character is
freed to exist as Don Quixote or Julien Sorel are enfranchised; the
very firmness and clarity of George Eliot's vision, extending to the
edges of her canvas, quite preclude her granting to any one of
her creatures the authority of existence. Like a goddess she suffers
them to exist in so far as they may be known through sympathy
and comprehension. No more life than this can emerge — any further
measure would make her characters novelists. Those who are her
surrogates, her delegated voices, are in a sense independent of her,
but they are wholly caught up within a system of morally and
aesthetically stable responses — as is Mary Garth — and correspond
rather to Mary Anne Evans, who had once lived within a provincial
society, than to George Eliot, the novelist. . . .

Middlemarch, the scene of this novel, is wholly dominated by
the finely tempered mind which envisions it. But how is this scene
framed and judged from without? What are the effectual boundaries
of the landscape of opinion? The town — though it is a middling
place from the point of view of one considering a group of provincial
towns — lies on the marches, it is on the periphery of the great
world, not simply the world of London or even Rome, but the world
of science, the arts, and of history; realized human greatness does
not enter it. We must inquire how the writer who herself moved
in the great world acknowledged that world in *Middlemarch*.

There is a finely scaled scene in *Daniel Deronda* in which
Gwendolen Harleth asks the musician, Klesmer, to help her to
launch a musical career on nothing more than a feeble talent and
her social pretensions. Klesmer confronts Gwendolen with the
audacity and the ignorance of her claim. The scene has a wonderfully tonic effect — it is as if George Eliot had managed a dramatic
confrontation of the austerities of art with the blind abundant energies
of youth and beauty. Klesmer's treatment of Gwendolen is exquisitely modulated; it is at once a denunciation and a tribute to
her as a woman. But she must be told that social lies and politeness
have nothing to do with being an artist. In the world of art you must
tell the truth; self-regard and the world's opinion must give way

before realized mastery. There is an analogous scene in *Middlemarch*, though the standard invoked is not impersonal. Rosamond's flirtation with Ladislaw is abruptly ended when she discovers that Dorothea is all-important to him. She had found in Ladislaw a representative of the world outside Middlemarch to which she had ignorantly aspired, and Ladislaw thinks her of no account. She is momentarily awed into a generosity which brings Ladislaw and Dorothea together. Throughout the book Ladislaw speaks authoritatively about the world outside the town's awareness. It is he who tells Dorothea that Casaubon's work is useless because he has not read the German scholars; it is he who demands fidelity to a standard of artistic accomplishment; he alone has some sense of national politics.

Yet Ladislaw does not have the authority of Klesmer; he is the weakest of the major characters, not merely because he is made to behave like a dilettante, but because George Eliot's judiciousness does not extend to him; he is not understood. In fact, he is rather like a character in an ordinary novel. F. R. Leavis sees this as a consequence of the weakness of the figure of Dorothea. Since she is in part a self-indulgent fantasy of George Eliot's and not wholly disciplined by the demands of the novel, we may think of Ladislaw as an accessory required by the fantasy. Certainly the scenes they share are full of high-flown nonsense. But there is a good deal of evidence that Dorothea and Ladislaw represent something more than the unresolved longings of Mary Anne Evans. The leading characters in *Romola, Felix Holt, Middlemarch,* and *Daniel Deronda* all escape the circle of the author's judgement. It is claimed for each of them that they aspire to or escape into the great world. Dorothea is the partial exception. When confronted by her uncle, Casaubon, her sister Celia, or the Chettams, she is fully controlled, fully understood. But Romola, Felix Holt, and Deronda are all extravagantly moral or extravagantly spiritual or both. And Dorothea and Ladislaw in their scenes together have the same defect.

Instead of thinking of *Middlemarch* as showing two strains, an artistically responsible element and a neurotically compelled one, we must, I believe, adopt a fresh version of the traditional assertion that George Eliot's conception of her fiction is internally divided. Leavis has pointed to the meaninglessness of the form this assertion of a split took in the criticism of Henry James and Leslie Stephen. The disjunction between an "intellectual" George Eliot and a George Eliot who has the novelist's sympathetic comprehension of human beings is, as we have seen, a clear-cut contradiction. It is the voice heard within the frame of her best fiction which has high intellectual distinction.

But there is an internal division in her conception of *Middlemarch* which corresponds to the far more serious split in *Daniel Deronda*, in which Deronda's mystical religiosity is given precedence over the fictionally superior story of Gwendolen Harleth. (The argument may also be applied to *Romola* and *Felix Holt*.) This split in the writer's conception of fiction appears to have a biographical root. The novels of George Eliot's maturity re-enact her own emancipation; the values which the Garths and Farebrother assert within the little world of Middlemarch are reasserted from the viewpoint of liberated intelligence by the voice of the narrator; her loss of faith, her translation to the metropolis, her defiance of propriety in living with Lewes, are all justified by the activity of the novelist who surveys Middlemarch. The right opinion of the Garths and Farebrother gives way before the knowledge of the novelist. But for George Eliot the re-enactment brought with it an irresistible impulse to include a character who could function as knower, an *embodied* voice.

She was unable, even in the years of her maturest art, to conceive of fiction as a truly independent form. It would seem to have been enough to bring that fine intelligence to bear on the enclosed world of Middlemarch, but she is never content with this. She must bring forward some instance of principled nonconformity, as if to feed an appetite for self-justification. We must conclude, I think, that the fairy-tale triumph of Romola over the physical and moral ills of a fever-stricken village, and the fantastic errand which takes Deronda to Jerusalem — he is, in effect, to build a culture! — are not merely tributes to a Victorian taste for moral exaltation. They are attempts on the part of the writer to give herself a recognizable moral status.

The English novel is so much the richer for George Eliot's contribution that one may be tempted into scolding her for not doing what no English novelist of the century did: for not taking possession of the great world. Her sense of community, her finely modulated articulation of passion and idea, the clarity and firmness of her characterization — these things alone justify Virginia Woolf's remark that *Middlemarch* was one of the few English novels written for grown-up people. Since the grown-up perspective includes Flaubert and Tolstoy, we are of course conscious that George Eliot did not share their power to incarnate the great world in the lesser one, to make the novel an instrument which can register the fate of a society in the perspective of history and heroic achievement. To exercise this power she would have had to take her own splendid powers for granted, and this she could not do.

Barbara Hardy

Possibilities

Although George Eliot's use of coincidence shows her occupied with personal destiny as something fixed and determined, she has . . . a certain interest in the "external" social or accidental causes of action. She follows the quotation from Novalis — "Character is destiny" — with an instance of the delicate poise of destiny:

> Hamlet, Prince of Denmark, was speculative and irresolute, and we have a great tragedy in consequence. But if his father had lived to a good old age, and his uncle had died an early death, we can conceive Hamlet's having married Ophelia, and got through life with a reputation of sanity notwithstanding many soliloquies, and some moody sarcasms towards the fair daughter of Polonius, to say nothing of the frankest incivility to his father-in-law (*The Mill on the Floss*, Bk vi, ch. 6).

I am going to suggest that George Eliot would have written *Hamlet* with this alternative life in mind, having a ghostly presence within the actuality of event, and playing some part in final impression. Professor Haight's edition of the letters has some revealing details of George Eliot's workmanship. There seems to have been a stage in the imagining, or even in the writing, of the novels, in which her imagination played with possibility. After this preliminary period, which she describes as the "simmering," the imaginative decision passed into the "irrevocable" stage. At one time, for instance, as we can see from the letters she wrote asking Frederic Harrison for legal advice about the plot of *Daniel Deronda* (Haight, VI, 100), she was playing with the possibility of giving Gwendolen a son. The kind of change which would have been made in *Daniel Deronda* if this possibility had become a fact is extensive: Gwendolen's relation to Grandcourt might conceivably have been shown as much the same, though surely without Gwendolen's final isolation, but her dependence on Deronda, on which the final irony of structure seems to turn, must have been cancelled or modified in some radical way.

Reprinted from Barbara Hardy, *The Novels of George Eliot: A Study in Form*, London, 1959, pp. 135–154, with the permission of the Athlone Press of the University of London and the Oxford University Press of New York.

There is nothing very startling in this method of trial and rejection in the inventive process, but it has a special interest in George Eliot because it draws attention to an interesting characteristic of her imaginative method. There is something very like the actual appearance of alternative destiny within the "irrevocable" and finished book. There is a strong and deliberate suggestion of the possible lives her characters might have lived.

Sometimes the hinted possible world is there to give the sense of immediacy in crisis, as it is in Gwendolen Harleth's "alternate dip of counterbalancing thoughts begotten of counterbalancing desires" before she accepts Grandcourt. Sometimes it seems to be there to underline the fragility of destiny, or its opposite, the fixity of moral tradition. At all times it results in a tremendous increase in realism, and the constant sense of alternatives and possibilities is a rare and difficult thing to combine with the unity and definiteness of this kind of moral novel. Her characters are sometimes haunted — or their author is haunted on their behalf — by the vision of possibilities from which they are redeemed, or seduced, or diverted, and the strength of the possibility is usually in contrast with their apparently determined process. The characters often walk on a razor-edge of action which has the appearance of a moral necessity achieved at great and rare peril. Both the necessary action and the possible one are a part of the purpose of the novels.

In a sense, all her novels overlap with each other in a way which shows them to be explorations of what she calls "the sameness of the human lot." The recurrence of the moral situation is less striking than its versatility, and yet we can see a constant process of attempted and rejected variants bearing some resemblance to each other. Arthur Donnithorne's degeneration takes the same course of self-persuasion and determining action as Tito's, but one has a kind of redemption, the other none. Dorothea is a more complicated Esther, Gwendolen a less successful Esther, and so on, though with the proviso that each version is clothed in a new personality, and it is only a new trial when we are considering the moral implications and not the individuality in which they are clothed. But it is because the moral is constant that the story of "Miss Brooke" could be fused with *Middlemarch*, and it is because the moral is constant that we find this process of rewriting one novel in the next eventually catching up with itself and resulting in her special use of double plot within the novel. William Empson suggests in *Some Versions of Pastoral* that the double plot of *Wuthering Heights* is a device for telling the same story twice, with different endings, and this is exactly the sort of thing achieved by George Eliot.

Perhaps the best example comes in *Felix Holt*, where Mrs Transome and Esther are carefully drawn in parallel, not merely for the usual purposes of generalization and thematic precision, but for the purposes of a curious causal relation. To begin with, there are carefully underlined resemblances in their presentation. Mrs Transome has "a high-born imperious air" and Esther "had too many airs and graces, and held her head much too high." Mr Transome "shrank like a timid animal" when his wife appeared and Mr Lyon found himself "in timorous subjection" to Esther's wishes. Both women are fastidious, accomplished, clever. Mrs Transome "had secretly picked out for private reading the lighter parts of dangerous French authors — and in company had been able to talk of Mr Burke's style, or of Chateaubriand's eloquence — had laughed at the *Lyrical Ballads* and admired Mr Southey's *Thalaba*." Esther makes her first appearance to defend Byron: "I have a great admiration for Byron," she says, when Felix has knocked the book down and picked it up to abuse it. Felix's denunciation of the Byronic heroes as "the most paltry puppets that were ever pulled by the strings of lust and pride" echoes Mrs Transome's reading list: "She was interested in stories of illicit passion." The insistent details make a kind of fluidity in the novel — the relationship of the characters challenges us to see them temporarily as doubles. But it is there for a decided moral emphasis: Esther escapes the temptation of her romantic dreams of love and this decomposition of character underlines the narrowness of her escape. There, but for the angry pedagogy of Felix, went another Mrs Transome. There is also the human generalization and change: life repeats itself but with a difference. Where there was tragedy there is redemption, and the second chance is shown in another generation, rather as it is in *The Winter's Tale*. This gives a kind of human optimism rising above any one individual failure. We do not have to make this deduction from the formal parallel alone. The characters make it for themselves. Mrs Transome has a generalization which brackets her life with Esther's:

> "I wish it were true, Denner," said Mrs Transome, energetically. "I wish he were in love with her, so that she could master him, and make him do what she pleased."
>
> "Then it is not true — what they say?"
>
> "Not true that she will ever master him. No woman ever will. He will make her fond of him, and afraid of him. That's one of the things you have never gone through, Denner. A woman's love is always freezing into fear. She wants everything, she is secure of nothing. This girl has a fine spirit — plenty of fire and pride and wit. Men like such captives, as they like horses that champ the bit

and paw the ground: they feel more triumph in their mastery"
(Ch. 39).

This is actually more than a generalization. Harold, who might have
made Esther's love "freeze into fear," is the son of Jermyn — the
man who mastered Mrs Transome — and heredity becomes an agent
in the action. Esther's own consciousness of the parallel hastens her
renunciation of what Mrs Transome chose. . . .

There are many other instances of this use of the parallels of character. There is the coincidence of Gwendolen's ambition and Mirah's
achievement, partly visible to Gwendolen as she goes to hear Mirah
sing:

> While turning her glance towards Mirah she did not neglect to
> exchange a bow and smile with Klesmer as she passed. The smile
> seemed to each a lightning-flash back on that morning when it
> had been her ambition to stand as the "little Jewess" was standing,
> and survey a grand audience from the higher rank of her talent —
> instead of which she was one of the ordinary crowd in silks and
> gems, whose utmost performance it must be to admire or find
> fault (Ch. 45).

Gwendolen and Klesmer's recognition of the smaller irony encour-
ages the reader to see it in full. Mirah and Gwendolen each sing,
one a professional, the other an ill-taught amateur. Each has the
opportunity to sell herself, but Mirah flees from her Count, who,
accidentally or deliberately, seems to bear some resemblance to
Grandcourt not only in his title, but in appearance, for he "was
neither very young nor very old: his hair and eyes were pale; and
he was tall and walked heavily and his face was heavy and grave."
There is the rather different social possibility in the parallel of
Dorothea and Lydgate, so alike in mind and ardour, but — significantly — a woman without a vocation and a man with one. Here the
moral is underlined further by the likeness in their lots; each chooses
badly in marriage, and there is even a close repetition of scenes which
echoes from one life to the other. The words "chill" and "yoke" are
used of both marriages.

This is not the only way of suggesting the possible and plausible
life that might have been lived but was not. There is also George
Eliot's special treatment of crisis and decision. She somehow manages
to give an impression of inevitability which is not rigid and not artificial. Her characters "make a moral tradition" for themselves, and
their deeds determine them, but since the characters are morally
"iridescent" there is a certain stage when the determination is held

in suspense. She obviously needs a strong suggestion of plausible alternatives at these moral crossroads where redemption and damnation are equally — or almost equally — likely. There are many examples, but perhaps the most striking are Maggie's, Tito's, Will Ladislaw's, and Gwendolen's.

Maggie's vision of possibility is conveyed in the imagery of the river: its enchantment, its power, its isolation, its languor. When she listens to Stephen singing, she is "borne by a wave too strong for her" and the metaphor comes true when she is really borne on the river with Stephen in the chapter "Borne Along by the Tide" (Bk. VI, Ch. 13). . . . This part of Maggie's fantasy-life is presented strongly, and it comes back twice, with the pressure of a possibility, after she has left Stephen. It is a vision which is strictly in character. it develops all the qualities we have been shown in the earlier parts of the book — her romantic dreaming, her need of love, even her absentmindedness. But the strength of the vision is needed to show the conflict, and perhaps also to be echoed ironically at the end when her dreamy vision of effortless gliding with the stream turns out to be true, though in a different sense. Once more she is carried by the river, but does more than drift, and "more and more strongly the energies seemed to come and put themselves forth."

Tito's crisis of decision is the opposite of Maggie's. There is again not really any strong likelihood that Tito will free himself from the "moral tradition" — he has already betrayed Baldassarre. But there is a point where possibility suggests itself: the possibility of undoing what he has done. His subsequent failure reinforces the theme of the deeds that determine us:

> A new possibility had risen before him, which might dissolve at once the wretched conditions of fear and suppression that were marring his life. Destiny had brought within his reach an opportunity of retrieving that moment on the steps of the Duomo, when the past had grasped him with living quivering hands, and he had disowned it. A few steps, and he might be face to face with his father, with no witness by; he might seek forgiveness and reconciliation.

The moral scheme does not permit a change of heart, and one vision of possibility, based on expediency alone, is succeeded by another:

> But with this possibility of relief, by an easy spring, from present evil, there rose the other possibility, that the fierce-hearted man might refuse to be propitiated. Well — and if he did, things would only be as they had been before; for there would be *no witness by* (Ch. 34).

Where the vision of possibility – like Maggie's or Tito's – is the imaginative trial of something out of keeping with the moral tradition of the character it has of course the obvious effect of insisting on the irrevocability of that tradition. But I think it also adds a dimension to the reader's imaginative experience of the character's complexity. This is particularly true of Gwendolen's moment of choice, where she waits for Grandcourt's offer of marriage, determined to refuse. Here there is, at first reading, no sense of moral inevitability: Gwendolen's first symbolic gamble, and the subsequent exposition of her character, have remained open. It is a genuine moment of indecision which is so strong that even when one has read the book many times there remains within the wisdom which knows the event the innocence of the first reading.

The tension is introduced by the chapter-motto of Chapter 26, which reads as irony only when we move on to the next chapter:

> He brings white asses laden with the freight
> Of Tyrian vessels, purple, gold, and balm,
> To bribe my will: I'll bid them chase him forth,
> Nor let him breathe the taint of his surmise
> On my secure resolve.

It is a slightly deceptive use of the motto, unlike the usual function of moral summary or forecast. The moment of choice is preceded and accompanied by George Eliot's close tracking of Gwendolen's oscillating reflection, and there are one or two hints that her earlier decision is weakening. But until Grandcourt begins to speak her mind is apparently made up. She is going to refuse him. . . . That vision of possibility is gradually dissipated: Grandcourt asks her questions she cannot answer, because she is beginning, significantly, to be impossibly literal-minded and reflects that she cannot say "yes" or "no" when he asks if she is "reckless about him." After the next question "Is there any man who stands between us?" she feels herself "against a net." This feeling of helplessness is the shifting-point. Suddenly comes another possibility. He speaks of riding away, and her reaction surprises her: "Almost to her own astonishment, Gwendolen felt a sudden alarm at the image of Grandcourt finally riding away. What would be left her then? Nothing but the former dreariness. She liked him to be there. She snatched at the subject that would defer any decisive answer" (Ch. 27). The deferred answer – the evasive reference to her mother's losses – is the beginning of her capitulation. And as the veiled motto to this chapter has explained:

> Desire has trimmed the sails, and Circumstance
> Brings but the breeze to fill them.

It is a scene which manages to convince by its immediacy that this is indecision, "the alternate dip of counterbalancing thoughts begotten of counterbalancing desires." In George Eliot's moral scheme Gwendolen has to commit herself and choose.

This kind of possibility must be present whenever a novelist succeeds in dramatizing the tension of conflict and choice. But George Eliot also presents us with a rarer vision of possible worlds. In *Middlemarch*, for instance, we feel the pressure of an enormous number of human beings, similar and dissimilar, modifying the doctrines of the novelist as well as contributing to them. George Eliot has a simple and not very varied moral scheme, but her novels are never schematic or rigid in their generalizations about human beings. The human examples are always variations of the theme rather than examples which fit it perfectly. The result is an impression of expansiveness which gives new life to the old cliché of the novelist's imagined "world": this is like a world because of its flux and its size. This sense of expansion and movement — life going on beyond this particular selection of life, implied in all the characters, in their convincing shadows which establish them all as human centres — this depends to some extent on actuality blurring into unacted possibility.

A simple example of this pressure of possibility is found in the relations of Dorothea and Lydgate. Some readers — encouraged no doubt by the serial habit of guessing what is to follow — found some hint of a lovers' ending for these two. The reviewer in the *Edinburgh Review* for January, 1873, expected the "real hero" to marry the "real heroine." The guess may have been encouraged by the initial pointed exclusion of Dorothea from Lydgate's desires:

> "She is a good creature — that fine girl — but a little too earnest," he thought. "It is troublesome to talk to such women. They are always wanting reasons, yet they are too ignorant to understand the merits of any question, and usually fall back on their own moral sense to settle things after their own taste" (Ch. 10).

This possibility, if it is felt at all, is there as a faint stirring of irony asserting itself whenever Lydgate is made to reassess his first intellectual rejection of Dorothea or to make the contrast between the woman he wanted and the woman he did not want. It is certainly not felt at all on Dorothea's side. Both Dorothea and Lydgate are committed by their disastrous desires before they meet, but Dorothea plays a larger part in his reflections than he does in hers.

The romantic possibility for Dorothea might be expected to arise in her early relation with Will, but in fact there is instead a marked

and sometimes irritatingly innocent absence of the kind of speculative
fantasy which might well mark such a relationship. Will, it is true,
has "dreamy visions of possibilities" but these are left vague, and
George Eliot emphasizes that the precise fantasy about the future
is Casaubon's, while Will takes a romantic delight in the very hope-
lessness of his love. . . . Dorothea, in spite of her short-sighted
abstraction from the present in dreams of "things as they had been
and were going to be," has "no visions of their ever coming into
closer union." The innocence of this relation may be exaggerated by
the sexless glamour George Eliot often casts over love, but it is
presented in striking contrast to Rosamond's vulgar little dreams of
uncommitted adultery. Will has certainly no room in his dreamy
visions for Rosamond, but the reader's knowledge of her fantasy-life
supplies an ironical supplement to their relationship. And when he
is cut off from Dorothea Will moves into a curious imagined relation
with Rosamond. It is perhaps one of the best examples of what
George Eliot said she wanted to show in *Middlemarch* as the slow
movement of ordinary causes.

She often shows temptation as a casual almost undesired drift
towards the strongest current. Fred's drift back to gambling is like
this, and so in a sense, though it is also characteristic of the man, is
Lydgate's drift towards the engulfing Rosamond. At one stage in
Middlemarch both Lydgate and Ladislaw are held in moral suspense,
and it is then that they come for the first time into a formally
emphatic relation. Lydgate is poised between two ways, the way of
redemption which means staying in Middlemarch, and the other way
of capitulation, which means Rosamond's victory and departure from
Middlemarch. Ladislaw, though with less prominent urgency, since
his presence in the book is considerably less concentrated and sustained than Lydgate's, is also torn between staying and going. His
departure is brought into direct contact with Lydgate's.

This pressure of possibility begins in the scene with Rosamond, after
Dorothea's departure, when for the first time her egoism is bitten
into by Will's "I would rather touch her hand if it were dead, than
I would touch any other woman's living." Then Will's anger goes
beyond his fear of what may have happened to Dorothea's faith in
him, and this is where the vision of possibility comes in:

The vindictive fire was still burning in him, and he could utter
no word of retraction; but it was still in his mind that having come
back to his hearth where he had enjoyed a caressing friendship
he had found calamity seated there — he had had suddenly revealed
to him a trouble that lay outside the home as well as within it.
And what seemed a foreboding was pressing upon him with slow

pincers[1]: — that his life might come to be enslaved by this helpless woman who had thrown herself upon him in the dreary sadness of her heart. But he was in gloomy rebellion against the fact that his quick apprehensiveness foreshadowed to him (Ch. 78).

This crisis is complicated because it is Lydgate's crisis too. In an earlier scene with Rosamond he has failed in his effort to "bring her to feel with some solemnity that here was a slander which must be met and not run away from" and he has also said to Dorothea "I have not taken a bribe yet. But there is a pale shade of bribery which is sometimes called prosperity." And there is the additional irony that Dorothea's discovery of Will and Rosamond is brought about by her promise to help Lydgate.

The next step brings the possibility of a linked future for the two men:

> When Lydgate spoke with desperate resignation of going to settle in London, and said with a faint smile, "We shall have you again, old fellow," Will felt inexpressibly mournful, and said nothing. Rosamond had that morning entreated him to urge this step on Lydgate; and it seemed to Will as if he were beholding in a magic panorama a future where he himself was sliding into that pleasureless yielding to the small solicitations of circumstance, which is a commoner history of perdition than any single momentous bargain.
>
> We are on a perilous margin when we begin to look passively at our future selves, and see our own figures led with dull consent into insipid misdoing and shabby achievement. Poor Lydgate was inwardly groaning on that margin, and Will was arriving at it (Ch. 79).

The possibilities cross. But it is only Lydgate who is led into the shabby achievement. The crisis gives Will's character a measure of realistic toughening which counteracts the glamour and innocence with which the imagery endows him. Once more fate is seen as fragile, success as variable. The rigid moral process is there, but so is the precariousness of chance. The elaborate pattern of reflecting mirrors is given a further recession. The real event is not only mirrored and modified in other real events but in the flickering reflection of possibilities. . . .

The unplayed possibilities emerge everywhere in *Middlemarch*. There are the possibilities which Featherstone dangled before his prospective heirs, which certainly played a large part in Fred's life. There is Dorothea's decision to accept Casaubon's blank cheque for

[1] Another echo in imagery: the "pincers" are used of Rosamond's power over Lydgate (Chs. 65, 78).

the future – it is cancelled only because she finds Casaubon is dead before she can accept. And there is the backward glance cast by Bulstrode, whose "imagined otherwise" was having his time again – "And yet – if he could be back in that far-off spot with his youthful poverty – why, then he would choose to be a missionary" (Ch. 61). This persistent vision of possibilities plays an extensive part because it becomes part of the theme. Like the image of the mirror, it is one of George Eliot's ways of showing the nature of illusion and the colliding multiplicity of human points of view.

The world of unrealized possibility is most prominent in *Daniel Deronda*. It first shows itself in a new way, in the actual repetition of choice. In *The Mill on the Floss* and *Romola* the heroine's choice is repeated, the decision is repeated with the opportunity, and the result is a reiteration of the moral purpose. Gwendolen, unlike Maggie and Romola, is a very uncertain character, and indeed the very shape of the novel emphasizes the uncertainty. The novel turns back on itself after first showing us Gwendolen – Gwendolen in her egoism, Gwendolen gambling, and Gwendolen raising the questions in Daniel's mind: "Was she beautiful or not beautiful? . . . Was the good or the evil genius dominant . . . ?" This means that her first act of renunciation comes in flashback after the reckless and uncertain mood of the first scene has been established, and there is no surprise when the second temptation, or what is really the second presentation of the same temptation, made in the changed circumstances of poverty and disenchantment and humiliation, brings the new result. But the contradiction between the two moral decisions introduces the variety of possibility in Gwendolen's progress.

The central unacted possibility lies in the relation of Gwendolen and Daniel. This is another consequence of the turn in the novel. We are first presented to Gwendolen and Daniel in a promising romantic situation: he sees her gamble and asks his questions, then steps into her life by sending back the necklace she has pawned. Then the novel turns back in time and shows their separate worlds, and their firmly committed lives in those separate worlds. But the first encounter acts as a stimulus to expectation, and it is not only the reader who feels the pressure of possibility. The possible relations of Gwendolen and Daniel discussed with varying degrees of serious-ness by Sir Hugo and Hans Meyrick, and also in a way which recalls Will's sharp vision of a future altered by Rosamond, by Daniel himself. The part the vision plays in Gwendolen's mind is even more prominent, and makes a special irony emerge from the double action.

The ambiguity of Daniel's place in her life begins perhaps when Gwendolen asks Mr Vandernoodt – a useful functional character who

turns up later in Sir Hugo's house-party and gives Daniel some necessary information about Grandcourt's past — to introduce Daniel to her.
The first flicker of other possibilities comes — though not till the
second reading — when we read: "But Gwendolen did not make
Deronda's acquaintance on this occasion. Mr Vandernoodt did not
succeed in bringing him up to her that evening, and when she re-
entered her own room she found a letter recalling her home" (Ch. 1).

She is not yet committed, but after fourteen chapters in which we
go back to the beginning of Gwendolen's acquaintance with Grandcourt, we turn to Daniel. The double plot, as in *Middlemarch*, can
hold characters in convenient suspension, and here the reader is put
in the same position as Gwendolen: interest is aroused and information is withheld. But after the fourteen chapters the reader's position
shifts to something approaching the omniscient author's. We share
the direct impact of her ambiguous interest but then receive our fuller
knowledge, from which Gwendolen herself is excluded:

> "You won't run after the pretty gambler, then?" said Sir Hugo,
> putting down his glasses.
> "Decidedly not."
> This answer was perfectly truthful; nevertheless it had passed
> through Deronda's mind that under other circumstances he should
> have given way to the interest this girl had raised in him, and tried
> to know more of her. But his history had given him a strong bias
> in another direction. He felt himself in no sense free (Ch. 15).

With an easy transition the two actions then begin their movement
in counterpoint. Having followed Gwendolen for fourteen chapters,
we return to Leubronn and Deronda, accompanying Grandcourt as
he follows Gwendolen. Daniel's flashback emerges as the parallel of
Gwendolen's and with the parallel comes the slowly growing irony.
It is another way of giving full expression to the theme of isolation
which she had expressed in *Middlemarch*, and it is also the emphatic
expression of Daniel's destined vocation. The pull which the two
actions exercise on each other intensifies the fantasy with which
George Eliot presents, in images and premonition, the destiny of
Daniel Deronda.

The misinterpretation of Daniel's interest in Gwendolen runs like
a thread through the book, sometimes there as a piece of comic
ignorance on the part of Sir Hugo or Hans, sometimes making the
further ironies of Mirah's and Grandcourt's jealousy. It is not until
Grandcourt's death that Gwendolen's vision of Daniel's relation to
her becomes tragically prominent. It is not Gwendolen alone who
has this vision at this point in the story. The crudest reaction is Sir

Hugo's — he has earlier warned Daniel against "playing with fire," and he comes to hope that "the lofty and inscrutable Dan" should have no scheme "in his head, which would prove to be dearer to him than the lovely Mrs Grandcourt. . . . To him it was as pretty a story as need be that this fine creature and his favourite Dan should have turned out to be formed for each other, and that the unsuitable husband should have made his exit in such excellent time" (Ch. 64). Then there is Daniel's sense of commitment. . . . He goes to her when she asks for him and says, "Think that a severe angel, seeing you along the road of error, grasped you by the wrist, and showed you the horror of the life you must avoid," and Gwendolen, like Maggie or Romola or even Fred Vincy, has the sensation of a new beginning. Her vision of Daniel's place in her future is managed with extraordinary tact. . . . With the end of the novel the two actions come together in collision, and Gwendolen for the first time shares the reader's view of Daniel's separate world.

There are many ironies confirmed and brought together by Gwendolen's final exclusion. There is first George Eliot's rejection of the ending she had used in the two preceding novels — the combination of a happy ending and a moral victory. Esther and Fred Vincy confirm their moral progress by marrying their mentors. Gwendolen is left alone, and for her the loneliness seems to be the only appropriate state. It is rather like the storm for Lear — we are conscious of the tragic reversal of power, warmth, ceremony, illusion, and love. For Gwendolen the final loneliness is not only an extension of suffering when she feels she has already suffered and recovered, but a suggestion that her tragic nurture is still incomplete. It is expressed in terms of her egoism, in terms of her innocence in the world of action and great causes (to which Daniel belongs), and in terms of her superstitious fear, which has been kept in our minds throughout the book. There is even the backward glance at her early casual anti-Semitism, when she dismisses the Jew dealers as unscrupulous. Her discovery is made slowly: "I hope there is nothing to make you mind. *You* are just the same as if you were not a Jew." Then he tells her that he is glad of the discovery, and his words inspire her "with a dreadful presentiment of mountainous travel for her mind before it could reach Deronda's." When he explains his political mission, she undergoes the equivalent of Rosamond's experience when forced by Will's anger to see the world outside herself. Gwendolen thinks that she has suffered in her marriage, and she thinks she has learnt a tragic lesson, but her egoism is to meet another violent shock. It has been prepared for not only by our knowledge of Daniel's commitment but our knowledge of her careless ignorance of "the great movements of the world":

. . . She was for the first time feeling the pressure of a vast
mysterious movement, for the first time being dislodged from her
supremacy in her own world, and getting a sense that her horizon
was but a dipping onwards of an existence with which her own
was revolving. All the troubles of her wifehood and widowhood
had still left her with the implicit impression which had accompanied her from childhood, that whatever surrounded her was
somehow specially for her, and it was because of this that no
personal jealousy had been roused in her in relation to Deronda:
she could not spontaneously think of him as rightfully belonging
to others more than to her (Ch. 69).

This is still before she knows that Daniel is going to marry Mirah.
Her reaction to "I am going to marry" is done entirely from the
outside, from Daniel's point of view and from the tense dialogue.
There is no return to Gwendolen's consciousness — in fact the only
return to her in any way is in her short letter to Daniel on his
marriage. Her shock is presented partly by the long elaborate exposition describing her reaction to Daniel's vocation, and by the con-
trasting absence of any commentary on her reaction to his love and
marriage. We are abruptly shut off from her responses.

The novel has an open ending, in very marked contrast to the closed
conclusions of death and marriage in the earlier books, and in particularly marked contrast to the end of *Middlemarch*, where the moral
direction of each set of characters is established, and their future lives
briefly and definitely surveyed. In this way *Daniel Deronda*, for all
its flaws, is an experiment in realism.

This openness must not be exaggerated. As far as Daniel Deronda's
Zionist mission is concerned, silence is plainly as necessary as it is at
the end of *The Family Reunion*. But as far as Gwendolen's future is
concerned, the novel is as functionally non-committal as the end of
The Portrait of a Lady. It is true that there is a moral conclusion:
Gwendolen is "redeemed" — as George Eliot had promised Blackwood
when he began to read the book — and her letter to Daniel has a
moral finality. It is also true that there is a very faint and tactful
and almost unobtrusive suggestion of a possibility that appeared at
the beginning of the novel. When George Eliot first presents Rex
and Gwendolen in the imagery of youth and nature with the pathetic
wish that they could pledge themselves "then and there" she makes
some preparation for Hans Meyrick's suggestion. This is only a hint
(one taken, by the way, by Henry James's Theodora), and it is carefully placed in the prejudiced speech of a character. Hans says:
"I understand now why Gascoigne talks of making the law his mistress
and remaining a bachelor. But these are green resolves. Since the
duke did not get himself drowned for your sake, it may turn out

to be for my friend Rex's sake. Who knows?" (Ch. 60). Speculation is checked by Daniel, whose reaction (a well-observed mixture of guilt and disapproval) reminds the reader that "Hans's success in constructing her fortunes hitherto had not been enough to warrant a new attempt," and by Rex himself, who suppresses his first reaction — the "egoistic escapes of the imagination" — to the news of Grand-court's death by saying to himself "She would not have me on any terms, and I would not ask her. It is a meanness to be thinking about it now — no better than lurking about the battle-field to strip the dead" (Ch. 58). But the question has at least arisen, and Rex is brought back into our interest, briefly but sharply after a long absence. It remains as almost less than a possibility, and George Eliot's own voice says nothing. The novel expands through its open ending, an ending rare in its century though common enough in ours, where the openness is sometimes organic or sometimes an inconclusive play-ing at slice-of-life realism. A striking illustration of the rareness of this kind of ending is found in the objection, made by the reviewer in the *Westminster Review* of April 1859, that even the ending of *Adam Bede* was "abrupt": "The reader longs to know somewhat of the fate of Hetty during those dreary years of transportation, as well as the circumstances of her death. It would also be a satisfaction to him to be informed of the chief events of Arthur Donnithorne's life after his return to Hayslope." For Gwendolen and for Isabel Archer the unfinished ending has genuine thematic significance. Dr. Leavis does not mention this resemblance, but it strengthens his comparison of the two novels. For both Gwendolen and Isabel the blank future has its moral import, but in *The Portrait of a Lady* Isabel returns to the world she has left, while Gwendolen's is the isolation of a new beginning. Isabel is left without her other possible worlds, all of which she rejects in favour of the undesired return to Gilbert and her promise to Pansy. Gwendolen is free from her imprisoning mar-riage, but she is now without Daniel, and the ending gives us the imaginative equivalent of the shock of space confronting a narrow and protected vision for the first time. There is perhaps the slight invitation to speculate, but it is vague. The very openness checks speculation by its lack of cues. Blackwood wrote to her on 12 July 1876 after finishing the book: "There will I know be disappointment at not hearing more of the failure of Gwendolen and the mysterious destiny of Deronda, but I am sure you are right to leave all grand and vague" (*The George Eliot Letters*, VI, 272).

Gordon S. Haight

The Mill on the Floss

The flood that ends *The Mill on the Floss* was not an afterthought
to extricate the author from an impossible situation, but the part of
the story that George Eliot planned first. At the British Museum in
January 1859 she copied into her commonplace book accounts of
inundations from the *Annual Register* with details of ships driven
onto flooded fields, bridges washed away, and a family rescued from
the upper story of their house, all of which appear in the final pages
of the novel. She had nearly finished Volume I (Ch. 20) before
she went to Dorsetshire in September to look at mills near Weymouth
and along the Frome, none of which quite satisfied her. Three weeks
later in Lincolnshire, where the Idle joins the Trent River near
Gainsborough, she found a locale suitable for the flood. In some
ways, however, it was ill adapted as the site of the Dorlcote Mill she
had been describing, for the flat country along the Trent lacks the
picturesque wooded lanes that Maggie haunted and the Red Deeps
with their grand fir trees: a too-literal reader trying to map the
geography of the novel will be baffled by certain inconsistencies. If
the scenery of the early part sticks more vividly in the mind than
the much vaguer landscape through which Maggie and Stephen drift
down the Floss it is because Dorlcote Mill with its great heaps of
grain for little children to slide on and its family of fat, flour-dusted
spiders was drawn from memories of Arbury Mill, close by George
Eliot's birthplace in Warwickshire. Knowing that a catastrophic flood
was impossible there, she transferred the scene to Lincolnshire, which
she hardly knew. This probably accounts for the revision in Chapter
23 that removed Mrs. Glegg's nephews from the "Fens" to the re-
moter "Wolds." It certainly explains why Maggie, who is supposed
to have lived all her life at the confluence of two rivers, should be
nineteen before she first learned to row a boat.

The characters in *The Mill on the Floss* also belong to Warwickshire. The Dodson sisters were quickly recognized about Nuneaton
as George Eliot's aunts, the Pearsons, "a very respectable family

Reprinted from the Riverside edition of *The Mill on the Floss*, Houghton
Mifflin Company, Boston, [1961], pp. v–xix.

indeed." Unlike the "originals" sometimes dragged into novels for variety or comic relief, the Dodsons are an integral part of the carefully studied background of provincial middle-class society against which Maggie's tragedy is acted. Conventional, conservative, unimaginative, they make the accumulation of property their principal concern in life. . . . Their religion is of "a simple, semi-pagan kind," consisting in "revering whatever was customary and respectable: it was necessary to be baptized, else one could not be buried in the churchyard, and to take the sacrament before death as a security against more dimly understood perils; but it was of equal necessity to have the proper pall-bearers and well-cured hams at one's funeral, and to leave an unimpeachable will" (Ch. 30). George Eliot was troubled when a reviewer in *The Times* suggested that she had made the Dodsons appear "mean and uninteresting," for, in spite of their absurdity, she was fond of them. As she told Emily Davies, "we owe much to them for keeping up the sense of respectability, which was the only religion possible to the mass of the English people." A careful reader will not mistake her solid realism for satire.

George Eliot's parents bore no resemblance to the Tullivers. . . . But readers can hardly help feeling that the childhood experiences of Tom and Maggie Tulliver must have been autobiographical. The episodes of the doll, the dead rabbits, the fishing, the jealous impulse to push innocent little Lucy into the mud seem too convincing to have been invented. . . . What Victorian novel gives a more truthful picture of childhood than that in the first two books of *The Mill on the Floss?* Oliver Twist's defiance of Mr. Bumble catches our sympathy so completely at the start that we forget the unlikelihood of the workhouse and Fagin's developing the sterling virtues he shows later. Paul and Florence Dombey are never naughty, never quarrelsome, never real. David Copperfield, oppressed by the cruel Murdstones, and Pip, brought up by hand, both live in worlds of self-pitying fantasy. But in *The Mill on the Floss* the reader sees in two dimensions, a mature view of life placing the child's view in perfect perspective. . . .

Every characteristic portrayed in her childhood reappears in the grown-up Maggie. Her flight to the gypsies is recalled in the days before Thomas à Kempis taught her renunciation — in those sad days when "her brain would be busy with wild romances of a flight from home in search of something less sordid and dreary: she would go to some great man — Walter Scott, perhaps — and tell him how wretched and how clever she was, and he would surely do something for her" (Ch. 32). The "dreamy state" into which she often fell while gazing at the glassy water of the Round Pool till she forgot all about fishing (Ch. 5) recurs when she sits in the boat opposite Stephen Guest, enveloped in the same sort of enchanted haze and "borne along by the tide" (Ch. 52).

Maggie's extraordinary susceptibility to music is another recurrent trait that George Eliot stresses carefully. On Christmas Eve the singing of the waits, recognized at once by the prosaic Tom as "old Patch, the parish clerk, and the rest of the church choir," seemed to Maggie supernatural music from angels resting on the parted clouds. Even the simple little tune played by Uncle Pullet's snuff-box transports her, stirring an affectionate impulse to run and put her arm round Tom's neck, spilling half his cowslip wine. In adolescence the "inexorable power of sound" still sways her in the same way. After Mr. Tulliver's bankruptcy the privation she feels most sadly is the lack of music — "no piano, no harmonised voices, no delicious stringed instruments, with their passionate cries of imprisoned spirits sending a strange vibration through her frame" (Ch. 32). And love of music is one of the strong bonds in her friendship with Philip Wakem.

On first meeting him at Mr. Stelling's Maggie thought Philip just a clever schoolmate of Tom's, who knew many marvellous stories. His hump-back interested her, for she had "rather a tenderness for deformed things . . ." (Ch. 18). In Tom's anxiety over his cut foot Philip's thoughtfulness was enough to quicken Maggie's love; she kissed him like a brother. When they meet again in the Red Deeps, Philip is twenty-one and fully aware of what he wants; but Maggie at seventeen is sexually still quite naive. To her their meetings offer a chance to vary the grim monotony of her life with talk of books and music. The idea that Philip might become her lover in more than a fraternal sense occurs to her only unconsciously as a "sweet music," which in spite of her awareness that family loyalty made it wrong, "would swell out again like chimes borne onward by a recurrent breeze" (Ch. 33). A whole year later, when pressed by Philip to admit that she loves him, she replies quite truthfully, "I had not thought of it." But his direct question repeated "seemed not easy to answer." This was one of those "dangerous moments when speech is at once sincere and deceptive — when feeling, rising high above its average depth, leaves flood-marks which are never reached again." . . . But her affection for him always comprises more pity than love. . . .

With her appealing childhood in mind and her ascetic life in "The Valley of Humiliation," many readers fail to notice the hints of strong sensuality in the Maggie of Book vi, "The Great Temptation." Physically, she looked older than she was. Even at seventeen her tall, "broad-chested figure has the mould of early womanhood"; her arms

recall the Demeter group of the Parthenon marbles; her "coronet" of
hair is jet black, her brown cheek firm and rounded; her eyes are
liquid, her lips full and red. Both in build and complexion she resembles her Aunt Gritty Moss, that "patient, prolific, loving-hearted
woman," who though she has eight children can't overcome a regret
that the twins hadn't lived. At nineteen Maggie's dusky vigor is
accented by the pretty slimness of Lucy Deane, who inherited the
fair skin and curls of the true Dodsons as well as their habit of doing
what is expected of them. Before Maggie meets Stephen Guest, Lucy
has made it clear that she is not engaged to him: "I would rather not
be engaged. When people are engaged, they begin to think of being
married soon, . . . and I should like everything to go on for a long
while just as it is. Sometimes I am quite frightened lest Stephen
should say that he has spoken to papa" (Ch. 41). At the end of
Chapter 45 George Eliot blurs the impression by making Stephen
in his inner monologue reflect: "It was all madness: he was in love,
thoroughly attached to Lucy, and engaged — engaged as strongly as
an honourable man need be." His detractors, denying him immunity
from self-incrimination, fall on such unspoken thoughts to condemn
Stephen's evasiveness. Yet his wavering uncertainty as to what he
feels about either girl does not alter the fact that, so far as Lucy is
concerned, she is not yet engaged. Though more mature than David
Copperfield's Dora, she is still not ready for marriage. There is a
sound instinct behind Stephen's delay.

He has been harshly treated by critics from the beginning, when
the *Westminster Review* in 1860 referred to "his dishonourable abduction of Maggie." Swinburne calls him "a cur . . . beneath the
chance of promotion to the notice of [any man's] horsewhip, or
elevation to the level of his boot." Sir Leslie Stephen dismisses him
as "a typical provincial coxcomb," "a mere hair-dresser's block." Joan
Bennett finds him "a disagreeable vulgarian," "an insensitive egotist,"
"far from being physically charming to the reader." And W. R.
Steinhoff is troubled by his "open contempt of the Tullivers" and his
"evasive behavior with Lucy." From the charge of evasiveness Lucy's
own statement may help to exonerate Stephen; and, as for contempt,
nothing he knew of the paranoid miller or his addle-pated widow
could be expected to inculcate a favorable opinion of the Tullivers.
Bulwer-Lytton, who knew the dandy of 1830 well, took no personal
exception to Stephen, not even mentioning the details that dilate the
nostrils of modern readers: the "diamond ring, attar of roses, and air
of *nonchalant* leisure at twelve o'clock" — which, it would be fair to
add, George Eliot herself undercuts instantly as "the graceful and
odoriferous result of the largest oil-mill and the most extensive wharf
in St. Ogg's." Of course Stephen is provincial; to make him an Evan

Harrington would violate George Eliot's canon of realism: "the faithful representation of commonplace things" (*Adam Bede*, Ch. 17). Maggie is provincial, too, with a meager experience of society limited to a third-rate schoolroom. Readers who feel that she is too good for Stephen, that she ought to be disgusted by him, are making the same identification with her that Dr. Leavis so unjustly accuses George Eliot of making.

The opening books of *The Mill on the Floss* contain many references to domestic animals and those proper to a country setting. There are also bits of natural history such as the rock-boring molluscs or the seeds with hooks to cling to unreceptive surfaces (Ch. 30) that George Eliot had picked up from G. H. Lewes while he was working on his *Sea-side Studies* (1858) and *The Physiology of Common Life* (1859); she was writing Chapter 27 when he was beginning his *Studies in Animal Life*, serialized in the initial volume of the *Cornhill Magazine* in 1860. To their friend Richard Owen's lecture on the gorilla we may trace Bob Jakin's thumb, "a singularly broad specimen of that difference between the man and the monkey" (Ch. 32), and the picture of Maggie, abandoned by Tom, sitting on a bough with "that superior power of misery which distinguishes the human being and places him at a proud distance from the most melancholy chimpanzee" (Ch. 6).

George Eliot was familiar with the theory of evolution (or the development hypothesis, as it was then called) as early as 1851, when she used to discuss it with her friend Herbert Spencer, who wrote some pioneer articles on the subject for the *Leader* and the *Westminster Review*, of which she was then sub-editor. She was almost at the middle of *The Mill on the Floss* when Darwin's *The Origin of Species* appeared in November 1859. She read it immediately and a few days later wrote to a friend that

> it makes an epoch, as the expression of his thorough adhesion, after long years of study, to the Doctrine of Development — and not the adhesion of an anonym like the author of the "Vestiges" [Robert Chambers], but of a long-celebrated naturalist. . . . it will have a great effect in the scientific world, causing a thorough and open discussion of a question about which people have hitherto felt timid. So the world gets on step by step towards brave clearness and honesty! But to me the Development theory and all other explanations of processes by which things came to be, produce a feeble impression compared with the mystery that lies under the processes.

While there are no direct allusions to *The Origin of Species* in *The Mill on the Floss*, in the latter half of the novel an occasional note of

melancholy is heard that may echo Darwin's Struggle for Existence.
The dismal villages along the Rhone at the opening of Chapter 30,
"dead-tinted, hollow-eyed, angular skeletons of villages," George
Eliot says,

> oppress me with the feeling that human life — very much of it —
> is a narrow, ugly, grovelling existence, which even calamity does
> not elevate, but rather tends to exhibit in all its bare vulgarity of
> conception; and I have a cruel conviction that the lives these ruins
> are the traces of, were part of a gross sum of obscure vitality, that
> will be swept into the same oblivion with the generations of ants
> and beavers.

Looking up at the old fir trees in the Red Deeps, Maggie "thought
that those broken ends of branches were the records of past storms,
which had only made the red stems soar higher" (Ch. 33). . . .
Perhaps in the contrasted attractions that Philip and Stephen offer
Maggie it is not too fanciful to see "the struggle between the males"
that Darwin calls sexual selection.

In simple biological terms Stephen is a better mate for her than
the sickly Philip or the silly red-headed young Torry with his preposterous eye-glass, the only other males that the environment of
St. Ogg's can offer. (George Eliot eliminated Bob Jakin from the
contest during revision by providing him with a wife.) Compared
with the studious Philip, Stephen seems rather flippant in his intellectual interests, though he has good taste in music and like Maggie
has done some serious reading. When they are alone together they
have surprisingly little conversation; the bantering chatter is heard
only when Lucy or Philip is with them. The attraction they feel for
each other is almost entirely instinctive, conveyed by long, mute looks
rather than words. Stephen too is tall. He has long legs, strong, firm
hands, a large head "with a square forehead, short dark-brown hair
standing erect with a slight wave at the end like a thick crop of
corn, and a half-ardent, half-sarcastic glance from under his well-
marked horizontal eyebrows." His first glance at Maggie produces
the wholly normal masculine inference, "An alarming amount of devil
there," an observation we recall when, after her disgrace, the gossips
of St. Ogg's declare that "there had always been something in Miss
Tulliver's very *physique* that a refined instinct felt to be prophetic
of harm." George Eliot conveys Stephen's effect on Maggie by the
old susceptibility of sound. When Philip sings "Ah! perchè non
posso odiarti?" in the "fine tenor voice" she had often heard in the
Red Deeps, Maggie is "touched, not thrilled." But Stephen's full-
toned bass, rolling out "Shall I, wasting in despair?" seemed to "make
all the air in the room alive with a new influence, . . . and Maggie,

in spite of her resistance to the spirit of the song and to the singer, was taken hold of and shaken by the invisible influence — was borne along by a wave too strong for her." Against her will the music draws her to Stephen by what Wordsworth (in "The Power of Sound," st. 6) calls "the cozenage of sense."

Stephen is certainly more honest about his love than Maggie, who is deeply committed to Philip and far less candid with herself and others in acknowledging it. There is no premeditation in his first offense at the ball (Ch. 49). Instead of waltzing he walks with Maggie into the conservatory, gazing at her, but silent. "The hovering thought that they must and would renounce each other made this moment of mute confession more intense in its rapture." As she reached for a flower, Stephen in "a mad impulse" kissed her arm. The violence of her resentment is an index to the depth of her passion for him; for regret came, not from the affront to herself, but from "the sin of allowing a moment's happiness that was treachery to Lucy, to Philip — to her own better soul." Her mild interview with Philip the next morning, looking down into his gray eyes, comforts her with a deluding sense that her "better soul" has regained its mastery. Yet four days later in the lane at Basset, when she could have freed herself at once from Stephen's importunity by saying "that her whole heart was Philip's, her lips would not utter that, and she was silent." In putting "pity and faithfulness and memory" before love, she can only — illogically — beg Stephen to "help me, *because* I love you." . . . The evidence, fairly weighed, makes it clear that Maggie was compromised, not by any dishonorable deception of Stephen's, but by her own divided nature. She was defeated by a power too strong for argument. As Thomas Hardy put it a generation later in *Tess of the d'Urbervilles* (Ch. 30): "that tremendous force which sways all humanity to its purpose as the tide sways the helpless weed, was not to be controlled by vague lucubrations over the social rubric." The difficulty lies, not in believing that Maggie was "borne along by the tide," but that she could have turned back when she did.

No part of the novel provoked such violent denunciation as Maggie's relation with Stephen — "forgetting themselves in a boat," as Ruskin vulgarly put it in 1880, before he had ever read the "vile book." Swinburne denounced it as "the flagrant blemish" defacing George Eliot's most noble work, . . . Bulwer-Lytton, a more temperate judge of the moral issue, objects to Maggie's conduct as a violation of the Ideal: "It may be quite natural that she should take a liking to [Stephen], but it is a position at variance with all that had before been Heroic about her." Bulwer was more concerned with Maggie's breach of decorum: "The *indulgence* of such a sentiment for the affianced of a friend under whose roof she was, was a treachery and

a meanness according to the Ethics of Art, and nothing can afterwards lift the character into the same hold on us. The refusal to
marry Stephen fails to do so." This may well have reminded George
Eliot of Lady Macbeth's exclamation on being told of the King's
murder: "What, in our house?" But when Blackwood sent her the
letter she replied:

> Maggie's position towards Stephen is too vital a part of my whole
> conception and purpose for me to be converted to the condemna-
> tion of it. If I am wrong there — if I did not really know what
> my heroine would feel and do under the circumstances in which
> I deliberately placed her, I ought not to have written this book at
> all, but quite a different book, if any. If the ethics of art do not
> admit the truthful presentation of a character essentially noble
> but liable to great error — error that is anguish to its own nobleness
> — then, it seems to me, the ethics of art are too narrow, and must be
> widened to correspond with a widening psychology (III, 317–318).

The reminiscence of Aristotle in her dismissal of Bulwer's old-
fashioned conception of the "Heroic" and the "Ethics of Art" indicates that George Eliot conceived of Maggie as the protagonist of
a genuine tragedy of modern life. . . . England had not had a more
successful tragic novel since Richardson's Clarissa (1747–48), which
offers some interesting parallels to The Mill on the Floss. In each
of them the heroine is a beautiful young girl, living in the country,
intelligent, religious, but thrown into conflict with unreasonable
family authority exercised by her father and brother. Through an
impulsive mistake she is compromised by running away from home
and becomes an outcast from family and respectable society. She
persists to the end in rejecting the offers of marriage, which would
have required a surrender of the high principles on which, after the
initial error, she acted, and dies.

Ironically, it is Lucy and Philip who unwittingly send Maggie and
Stephen off in the boat alone. No "abduction" ever required less
force. Maggie was persuaded merely by looking into his eyes, and
she went without a word. Neither of them had the least notion of
an elopement; the idea did not occur to Stephen till after they had
passed Luckreth. His most serious offense lay in not rousing her
then from her dreamy absent-mindedness. Though he is truly contrite, his plan of marriage seems the most practical course. By any
standard it would have been more honorable than for them to return
and marry Lucy and Philip, whom they have admitted they do not
love. When they are picked up by the small Dutch vessel, Maggie
(again like Clarissa) hears herself introduced as Stephen's wife and
does not protest. But when she woke in the morning after her

highly symbolic dream, "the whole terrible truth urged itself upon her . . . ; she had rent the ties that had given meaning to duty, and had made herself an outlawed soul, with no guide but the wayward choice of her own passion." Yet (again like Clarissa's) "her soul, though betrayed, beguiled, ensnared, could never deliberately consent to a choice of the lower," and she tells Stephen that she must leave him. While Stephen's motives in combating her decision are less noble than Maggie's, there is no trace of the Lovelace in his character. He is deeply enamoured, wholeheartedly intent on persuading her to be his wife. If that be egotism, it is very natural. He insists that they have failed to keep their resolutions because "the feeling which draws us to each other is too strong to be overcome; that natural law surmounts every other." But Maggie will have none of this appeal to instinct: "If the past is not to bind us," she asks, "where can duty lie? We should have no law but the inclination of the moment." From this lofty stand Stephen's vehement arguments cannot budge her. . . .

The last three chapters deal with the principal figures in Maggie's tragedy. In Chapter 56 Philip's letter assures her of his belief that the strong attraction which drew her and Stephen together "proceeded only from one side of your characters, and belonged to that partial, divided action of our nature which makes half the tragedy of the human lot." He confesses his jealousy, which sent Stephen to take his place in the boat. His brief dream of becoming Maggie's husband is over: "I have no just claim on you for more than affectionate remembrance," he writes. In Chapter 57 Lucy bestows her forgiveness: "It is a trouble that has come on us all: – and you gave him up when . . . . you did what it must have been very hard to do." Maggie insists that Stephen struggled too, and urges Lucy to "Forgive him – he will be happy then." In Chapter 58 Stephen writes to Maggie, reiterating all his former arguments, appealing against her useless sacrifice of them both, and denouncing the "perverted notion of right which led her to crush all his hopes for the sake of a mere idea." Though the stress on *his* hopes and *his* pain is meant to emphasize his egotism, Stephen's sincere letter, of which only two paragraphs are quoted, is more natural than Philip's rather rhetorical epistle; it was the "tone of misery" in it that made the balance tremble during Maggie's "last conflict." When Stephen said, "Call me back to life and goodness! Write me one word – say 'Come!' " she started from her seat to reach for pen and paper. But she did not do it. It was her worst temptation; and when it was over she burned Stephen's letter. Again she turned back. Why?

The most serious objection, her engagement, has been dissolved by Philip's letter, though, if she were to yield now, both his belief that

"There is something stronger in you than your love for [Stephen]" and her plea to Lucy to take him back would be stultified. On the other hand, Dr. Kenn, when he first heard Maggie's story, had thought that ultimate marriage to Stephen would be the least evil, though he was sensitive enough to respect the delicacy of conscience that made the prospect seem to Maggie "a desecration." That word recalls again the Clarissa of the last volumes, whom every one was pressing to marry Lovelace. Stephen's fault (if he must assume all the blame for Maggie's absent-mindedness) is trifling in comparison with Lovelace's monstrous crime; why is it not within reach of the forgiveness that Maggie was always begging for her own mistakes? Professor Steinhoff sees her after each failure turning "naturally back to a period of relative happiness and security, her childhood, in which her father and brother are sources of comfort and authority." But other motives may be involved than "a fatal timidity toward life." Certainly in Book VII she has not taken the easiest way, nor has her brother, her strongest tie to the past, supplied any comfort. It is true, however, that she gave the past as the reason for parting with Philip: "I desire no future that will break the ties of the past." And she rejected Stephen at Mudport because to marry him would "rend me away from all that my past life has made dear and holy to me." She also refused to leave St. Ogg's as Dr. Kenn urged because she would feel "cut off from the past." And in her last temptation victory was won by "memories that no passion could long quench: the long past came back to her, and with it the fountains of self-renouncing pity and affection, of faithfulness and resolve." . . .

I wonder whether a new light might be thrown on Maggie's divided character by the heated discussion of Darwin's *The Origin of Species* that raged while *The Mill on the Floss* was being written? In rejecting Stephen's appeal to "that natural law" Maggie set herself in opposition to the crude early interpretations of evolution that sought to base all human behavior on the law of the jungle. Darwin's careful observations confirmed the theory that George Eliot had accepted in principle years before. But her keen intelligence questioned the optimistic assumption that the course of evolution was always towards the best. "Natural selection," she remarked, "is not always good, and depends (see Darwin) on many caprices of very foolish animals." She saw at once what Huxley admitted years later, that the survival of the fittest is not always the survival of the best, and that moral factors — faithfulness, generosity, renunciation of present pleasure, duty rooted in the past — also play their part in evolution. . . .

George Levine

Determinism and Responsibility

The nature and degree of George Eliot's commitment to a deterministic world view have been the source of considerable difficulty in the criticism of her work. Critics who concern themselves with the subject take, for the most part, the view either that her belief in determinism seriously marred her art or, on the other hand, that despite appearances she was not a consistent determinist. In both cases, however, determinism evokes extraordinary intensity of feeling, almost everyone agreeing that a commitment to it tends to be detrimental to the artist because it forces a distortion of the facts of existence (or at least a depressing interpretation of them) and leads to an underestimating of man's capacity for action and of his potential dignity.

I shall argue, however, that in one important and widely acceptable use of the term, George Eliot was a consistent determinist, and that this sense is in no way incongruous with her continuous emphasis on moral responsibility and duty. Her novels, letters, and essays suggest that her position — never, so far as I know, fully articulated in print — was very close to John Stuart Mill's, and if she was inconsistent she was no more so than Mill. Mill's views on determinism, moreover, though they have never pleased absolutists, have considerable philosophical support, belonging as they do to a tradition which stems back at least as far as Hume's *Inquiry* and extending forward to one of the most powerful contemporary schools of academic philosophy — that of linguistic analysis. With the philosophical tools at their disposal neither Mill nor George Eliot could have carried analysis as far as contemporary analysts do; but the position is not an easily discredited one, either philosophically or, as it is embodied in George Eliot's works, artistically: it does at least as much justice to the facts of existence as any indeterminist position or any less flexible determinist one.

The danger in a detailed discussion of this position, of course, is to treat George Eliot as a philosopher rather than an artist. For although she was widely read in philosophy and translated Spinoza's

Reprinted by permission from *PMLA*, 77 (June 1962), 268–279.

Ethics, Feuerbach's *Essence of Christianity,* and Strauss's *Life of Jesus,*
the fact that she never felt impelled to set down her own thoroughly
worked out system or to state finally her views on the problem of
determinism should suggest that at best she was an amateur philosopher
using her wide reading for purposes essentially unphilosophical. Her
novels and essays are full of protests against the rigidity of systems,
but refusal to work out an all-embracing philosophical system is
not necessarily incompatible with consistency. And her determinism
was flexible enough, she thought, to be applicable without distortion
to the life she tried to represent with scrupulous fidelity. Determinism
informed her artistic vision; she not only believed in it as an abstract
truth but saw it working even in the routine actions of ordinary
life. To be sure, in her novels she does not use it as an abstract
argument, but it is persistently there; and for this reason it is important
that it be understood by her critics and, where necessary (though
abstractions are regarded by critics with a kind of horror), even
discussed in the abstract.

There are three basic stances taken by philosophers on the matter
of determinism: (1) that the world is rigidly determined and that,
in fact, there is no such thing as human responsibility; (2) that
though almost everything is determined, the relation of cause and
effect is broken in matters of human choice: thus man is free and
therefore responsible; (3) that the world is rigidly determined, even
in cases of human choice, but that man remains responsible for his
actions. The last position of course causes most of the logical
difficulties, and it is this position which, I believe, George Eliot
shared with Mill.

If one can accept it (as most contemporary analytic philosophers
do), one not only avoids the underestimation of man's capacity to
learn and to act with dignity and responsibility which many writers
feel is an inevitable conjunct of determinism; one sees it also as it
was for George Eliot, an indispensable means of rationally defending
the possibility of just those qualities. She found, one might infer
from available materials, that the only valid interpretation of her
vision was deterministic, for it was the only one that could adequately
account, among other things, for her sense of man's dependence on
man, his ability to learn and grow, and his obligation always to
follow the promptings of duty. The key to her determinism lies in
her refusal to discount the human will. Thus, an investigation of
what her deterministic position was and of why she made so full a
commitment to it, may make it possible to move a little closer to
understanding how determinism actually works in her novels and in
what important ways it affected, whether to distort and darken or
to enrich, her particular artistic perception of the world. . . .

Despite her emphasis on the claims of duty and the power of the will, the world which George Eliot describes in her novels is meant to be consistently deterministic. And I should like here to look briefly at some of the most important philosophical and moral implications for her of the deterministic idea — simple at bottom but leading to enormous complications — that every event has its causal antecedents.

(1) George Eliot saw a deterministic universe as a marvelously complex unit in which all parts are intricately related to each other, where nothing is really isolable, and where past and future are both implicit in the present. Nothing in such a universe is explicable without reference to the time and place in which it occurs or exists. This suggested that one can never make a clear-cut break with the society in which one has been brought up, with one's friends and relations, with one's past. Any such break diminishes a man's wholeness and is the result of his failure to recognize his ultimate dependence on others, their claims on him, and the consequent need for human solidarity. For George Eliot, every man's life is at the center of a vast and complex web of causes, a good many of which exert pressure on him from the outside and come into direct conflict with his own desires and motives.

It is obvious that George Eliot's extraordinary insight into the workings of society is closely related to this view, probably both as cause and effect. The full scale portrayals of small town society which we get in *The Mill on the Floss* and pre-eminently in *Middlemarch* depend on a rich and vital sense of the way in which every man's life impinges on many others. A refusal to accept responsibility for the claims that society puts upon one leads to destruction or dehumanization. . . . The persistent theme of egoism which isolates man from his natural ties is also related to the notion of a complex deterministic universe. This theme is worked out almost in paradigm in the story of Hetty Sorrel in *Adam Bede*. . . .

In her review of Riehl's *Natural History of German Life* George Eliot emphasizes the importance of continuity. . . . This view accounts in part for her insistence on the importance of early life in the formation of character in, for instance, the portraits of Maggie and Gwendolen. It accounts, moreover, for what seems her almost melodramatic concern with people cut off from their real parents. . . . Thus, we find her "radical" novel, *Felix Holt*, to be firmly anti-revolutionary, and her radical hero actually forced to battle with the proletariat whose interests he in theory protects. Since real change can only come about through the slow increment of myriad causes working through history, revolution is doomed to failure.

The insistence on unity, harmony, duty, and slow growth, which we see in George Eliot's broad social analyses and in her minute psychological investigations of egoism and division within a single human soul, obviously has its roots in a moral bias. But the bias, for George Eliot, has its rational justification in determinism.

(2) A deterministic universe, as George Eliot understood it, is a democratic one. . . . The occurrence of large heroic action is unlikely though not by any means impossible. Since, as John Holloway says, George Eliot believed that "Man is a part of Nature, and Nature is a vast and complex system of which the parts are subordinate to impersonal forces governing the whole," she felt as well that "the individuals that belong to such a system cannot be heroes."

Determinism, of course, need not necessarily be anti-heroic. . . . But even in [Marxism and Hegelianism] the hero is a rare figure behind whom the great masses of people struggle helplessly in the grip of historical processes.

The heroic, as we shall see, is not entirely excluded from George Eliot's novels, but even the strongest figures in the novels — with the possible exception of Savonarola, Deronda, and Mordecai — could be better described as ordinary than heroic. . . . Moreover, the heroic — even the nobly heroic — is inevitably combined with egoism and a consequent tendency to disregard the necessary but ordinary ties which bind man to his friends, relatives, and society. No man is entitled to expect much personal gratification from so complex a universe running according to invariable laws which apply indifferently to all men. The external pressure of these laws (or, as they manifest themselves in the novels, the external pressure of society) is too great for any single man completely to overcome. "There is no creature," she warns, "whose inward being is so strong that it is not greatly determined by what lies outside it." Thus, in all the novels but *Daniel Deronda*, heroism takes the shape of resignation exclusively, a willingness to renounce not only personal satisfactions but the possibility of great achievement for good causes. The brilliant hovering irony of the portrait of Dorothea in the early part of *Middlemarch* suggests how, even for the characters with whom she tended to sympathize excessively, George Eliot was aware of the important and debilitating role egoism plays in the shaping of heroic objectives.

The one significant exception to this tendency deserves more extended treatment than it can be given here. But in Daniel Deronda and Mordecai George Eliot creates characters who are meant to have heroic stature. Their activities are to help create a new nation. It is not surprising that they are two of the weakest (if still the most interesting) characters George Eliot ever created. Their kind of heroism was what she aspired to, but it was also incompatible with her particular vision; it suggested the possibility of great and rapid changes, of significant and conscious tampering with the course of history, where, as a determinist, she instinctively felt that such tampering had become almost impossible. To create such characters she had to go outside the limits of the ordinary life of England which her novels (except *Romola*, of course) had hitherto described, into a world which, however wide her reading, she did not really understand.

It is important to note, on the other hand, that George Eliot did not believe, as Holloway argues, that individuals, if they can't be heroic, must then be obscure and petty. . . . Since, that is, every act is related in some way to every other, the most apparently unimportant act may have important ramifications, and the most apparently unimportant person must be accorded considerable respect. "We insignificant people," she says in the famous "Finale" of *Middlemarch*, "with our daily words and acts are preparing the lives of many Dorotheas, some of which may present a far sadder sacrifice than that of the Dorothea whose story we know. . . . The growing good of the world is partly dependent on unhistoric acts."

(3) Deterministic theory translated into the practice of her fiction became grounds according to which one might abjure coincidence and condemn chance. Nothing, she argued, happens accidentally, and a belief in the possibility of some kind of occurrence not usually produced by the normal workings of the laws of nature became to her one of the positive signs of moral weakness. . . . For example, Gwendolen expects triumph from her marriage with Grandcourt, Arthur expects nothing to come of his liaison with Hetty, Lydgate imagines he can break his vow of temporary celibacy without hurting his scientific work: in each case the more likely upshot helps destroy the character who would rather hope for the unlikely. When "chance" does occur, to be sure, George Eliot is not suggesting that it is outside the normal laws of nature, but only that the elaborate and complex system of causes has been working beyond the knowledge of her characters. . . .

(4) Finally, and most important for George Eliot, a deterministic world such as she envisioned is one in which duty becomes primary (as it does, of course, in Comte's positivistic system). Since, as we have already remarked, every act, no matter how trivial, has a vast number of consequences, not all of them traceable, she felt that it behooves every human being to exercise the greatest care in his actions to avoid causing misery to others. To F. W. H. Myers she made a remark which has since become notorious: that although God

was "inconceivable," and immortality "unbelievable," Duty was
"peremptory and absolute." In a letter written to Mrs. H. F. Ponsonby
in 1874 she explained this severe and tough-minded view:

> I suppose that there is not a single man, or woman, who has not
> more or less need of that stoical resignation which is often a
> hidden heroism, or who, in considering his or her past history, is
> not aware that it has been cruelly affected by the ignorant or
> selfish action of some fellow-being in a more or less close relation
> of life. And to my mind there can be no stronger motive, than
> this perception, to energetic effort that the lives nearest to us shall
> not suffer in like manner from *us* (*The George Eliot Letters*, VI,
> 99).

This idea is so fundamental to the novels that examples here would
be superfluous.

It would seem that at least a fifth implication should follow from
the belief that every event has its causal antecedents, and this, perhaps, the most important of all: that what man is, what he wills,
what he becomes, is necessarily determined in such a way that he
is incapable of anything but acquiescence in the pull of his unconscious
desires and the push of external forces. But this is precisely the
view the George Eliot despised as morally enervating and vicious,
and which she tended to call necessitarianism. Along with John Stuart
Mill, she insisted that this position did not follow. . . . Any one
wishing to find a more systematic and full exposition of the position
would do well to read the Sixth Book of Mill's *System of Logic*,
"On the Logic of the Moral Sciences," especially Chapters 2, 10,
and 11.

George Eliot worked her way out of the dilemma of determinism
because of her deep moral bias. Aware of the philosophical commonplace that no one can be obliged to do something unless he is capable
of doing it, yet feeling with equal strength the call of duty, she
asserted the common sense point that nothing will get done unless
we make the effort and that experience tells us we can make it:
"Every fresh morning is an opportunity that one can look forward
to for exerting one's will. I shall not be satisfied with your philosophy
till you have conciliated necessitarianism — I hate the ugly word —
with the practice of willing strongly, of willing to will strongly,
and so on, that being what you certainly can do and have done about
a great many things in life." (*The George Eliot Letters*, VI, 166).
This is clearly not yet a sufficient justification of the position, but it
is an important first step toward what might very well be the
solution of the modern school of linguistic analysis (an immediate

descendant of positivism). What it amounts to, however, is that in matters of choice determinism is "ethically irrelevant."

It is important to see, however, on what grounds Mill and, one might safely infer, George Eliot were able satisfactorily for themselves to reconcile determinism with responsibility. . . . What I wish to do is outline the way Mill and George Eliot made the reconciliation and to suggest that if their answer is not *the* answer, it is *an* answer which must be accorded respect; if this is the vision embodied in George Eliot's works, one cannot dismiss her determinism out of hand. . . .

The three major aspects of George Eliot's reconciliation of determinism with responsibility seem to correspond to those of Mill: (1) her sense of the great and bewildering complexity of the causes which form human behavior; (2) her recognition of the difference between cause and compulsion; (3) her belief that each man's character plays an important role in determining what he becomes. . . .

(1) *Complexity.* . . . Here is Mill's statement: "the agencies which determine human character are so numerous and diversified . . . that in the aggregate they are never in any two cases exactly similar. Hence, even if our science of human nature were theoretically perfect, . . . still as the data are never all given, nor ever precisely alike in different cases, we could neither make positive predictions, nor lay down universal propositions." Accordingly, the argument from complexity merely suggests that man is too ignorant to know *how* he is determined, and that whatever laws apply to character, they are more complex than physical laws. Complexity may account for the "mystery" in human behavior and even for man's natural feeling that he is a morally free agent, but it cannot logically justify that feeling.

(2) *Cause and Compulsion.* On this point, George Eliot has very little explicitly to say, but in her treatment of character the idea is often implicit. . . . The point is that although every action is caused, few causes are uncontrollable in the sense that no effort to alter them can succeed. (I recognize the circularity of this reasoning. To say that a cause is controllable by other causes is simply to push the question back, not to resolve it. The act of controlling a cause is itself caused, and one might go on infinitely asking what causes the cause which causes the cause, etc. This is precisely the kind of difficulty the analytic philosophers would object to. One must recognize, for example, the difference between robbing a bank because one wants the money and robbing it because one is forced at gunpoint to do so.) As long as the cause is not a compulsion, that is, as long as it is not physically impossible or excessively dangerous to will

differently and as long as one is not so mentally ill that one cannot will differently even if one wants to, one is responsible for his actions. To take an example: in *Adam Bede*, Arthur Donnithorne was free to avoid the circumstances which drew him into sexual relations with Hetty Sorrel. He was aware that he should have told Mr. Irwine about his feelings, but he chose not to. And even though he was helped in avoiding confession by Irwine's overly decorous refusal to make him talk, Arthur was under no compulsion to be silent. At one point in the conversation between Arthur and Irwine, Irwine figuratively and implicitly makes the distinction between cause and compulsion. Arthur says to him:

> "Well, but one may be betrayed into doing things by a combination of circumstances, which one might never have done otherwise."
> "Why, yes," [Irwine replies], "a man can't very well steal a bank-note unless the bank-note lies within convenient reach; but he won't make us think him an honest man because he begins to howl at the bank-note for falling in his way" (Ch. 16).

The bank-note's presence, that is to say, is one of the causes of the theft, but there is nothing in its presence serving as a compulsion to make a man steal it. The thief could have avoided stealing it had he wanted to strongly enough, and he was therefore responsible for his action. . . . And in the novels there are no occasions I can think of in which a character is *compelled* to make an important choice. Many of the moments of choice do, however, give the impression that the main character is coerced into the action by some internal compulsion. One thinks of Tito, suddenly confronted by the escaped Baldassarre at the Duomo in Florence. His rejection of his foster father escapes from him almost instinctively. But what George Eliot is suggesting in this incident and in many others in her novels is that we frequently make our decisions long before we are required to make them public. Thus Tito, through his elaborate course of deceit about Baldassarre before the encounter at the Duomo, had in fact already chosen to reject him. . . .

For the most part, it is true, George Eliot concerns herself in her novels with external pressures or internal desires which give the appearance at least at some point of being remediable. She does not press back to ask what were the causes which shaped the susceptibility or what were the causes which shaped the causes which shaped the susceptibility. Her concern is with the immediate and the practical (but this we see is true of Mill as well). The typical George Eliot story shows how a character (Lydgate, for example) under the influence of strong social pressures reveals certain flaws in his character which, in combination with the social pressures, cause his moral failure. But it is important to see that George Eliot holds him responsible for his own character and his own motives.

Moreover, she doesn't suggest that Adam Bede, for example, because he is strong, is less fully determined in his actions by external and internal causes than Arthur, who is weak. For George Eliot strong will is a sign rather of a man who, aware of the power of causes to shape him (as Tito, for example, was not aware), is educated by this awareness. . . .

(3) *Character*. This brings us to what Mill regarded as the strongest argument against necessitarianism: a man is himself one of the causes of what he becomes. . . . Man is on this account no longer a merely passive figure compelled by the power of innumerable causes, but an active force with some power to choose among a number of possible alternatives. According to this argument, it is true, a man's action can never be uncaused. If, however, we put the idea in different terminology — "He can never act without a motive, conscious or otherwise" — it loses its depressing effect. And his character, shaped in the past by experience of right and wrong, pain and pleasure, can act on what the experience taught, if it will. . . . When her characters come to a point at which they must make a crucial decision, she does not mean the decision to be a mere formality. Arthur really has an opportunity to confess to Mr. Irwine, just as Romola has the opportunity *not* to return to Tito at Savonarola's prompting, and Gwendolen not to marry Grandcourt. The difference lies in the characters' consciousness of their own motives. Arthur yields to the habits of his nature without fully understanding them. Romola, on the other hand, behaves in a way counter to her usual proud nature, and humbles herself before Tito. A character, for George Eliot, becomes what he makes himself: he can, in some limited degree, move counter to the push of external circumstance, and, by allowing himself to become aware of his own motives, can even at times overcome them by changing them. In "Janet's Repentance," for example, Janet Dempster, an alcoholic and therefore almost compelled, not merely caused, to drink, is saved from moral destruction by her own powerful desire to overcome her habit — (and by Mr. Tryan).

There is nevertheless no indication in George Eliot's writings that, as Ernest Baker wishfully remarks, for her "Ultimately, the will is free."[1] She did not believe that the will had to be "free" in the sense of "uncaused" (the sense to which, unless specifically stated otherwise, I am attempting to restrict it in this paper) in order that every

[1] *History of the English Novel*, 10 vols. (London, 1930), VIII, 235.

man be responsible for his actions. . . . Her insistence that every man should exercise his will did not commit her to the view that every man is capable of any choice. As Irwine says to Donnithorne, "A man can never do anything at variance with his own nature" (Ch. 16). But within the limits of his nature, man is capable of altering his character by willing to alter it. Only people who surrender hopelessly to their impulses or to the pressures of external circumstances — people like the young Arthur Donnithorne — appear wholly determined in their actions by forces external to themselves. And even they, since they almost deliberately refuse to be more than passive and unaware of the forces that are driving them, are contributing to the external causes of their moral decline. . . .

It might seem that for a moralist, belief in a universe wholly governed by the laws of cause and effect is the starting point for little more than a series of subtle wranglings about the possibility of any moral act whatever. On the contrary, however, according to George Eliot and to most determinist moral philosophers, a deterministic universe is the *only* kind of universe in which moral acts are possible. In a wholly or even partially undetermined universe, every act would be capricious because it need not be the result of one's own past thinking and experience or of one's consciousness of its possible effects. . . .

It is therefore, George Eliot says, the presence of "undeviating law" which "alone can give value to experience and render education in the true sense possible." Experience is valuable only in so far as it can teach, and it can teach only in so far as it is consistent. . . . Thus for George Eliot morality and responsibility are wholly bound up in determinism, and they are not achievable, as libertarians would have it, by denying the universality of cause and effect. A man is only good in so far as he has trained himself to exercise his will for what past experience has taught him is the good. George Eliot believed that the only way one can transcend circumstance is by recognizing clearly that the "law of consequence" is irrevocable and invariable — "human duty is comprised in the earnest study of this law and patient obedience to its teaching" — that the past is a permanent part of one's character, and one's society is, and should be, a very powerful influence on one's actions. In other words, one overcomes the depressing effects of determinism by understanding it. This can be viewed, of course, as just another version of the vicious Hegelian-Marxist paradox that freedom is the recognition of necessity. But a theory has its value, in good part, in the context which it fills. For Hegel and Marx the paradox was intended to shift responsibility from the individual to the state and to make the individual a passive creature of the state. And it is to the credit of George Eliot that she indulges this paradox in its most acceptable form — not to diminish man's responsibility or to submit him to some higher power, but to increase it and to give meaning and direction to his activity for good.

Moreover, the determinist-freedom paradox, as George Eliot resolves it, is not paradoxical at all. The difficulty, according to her implicit analysis, is essentially linguistic. If we mean by free "uncaused," then our actions are never free and the paradox is meaningless. But if we are willing to shift the meaning of "free" to "capable of reasonable choice in accordance with our motives" (which is all the novels or letters allow), then there is no conflict between determinism and "freedom." This kind of semantic shift is unlikely to satisfy those who argue that man is wholly the master of his fate, and who mean something quite different by the word. But such "freedom" has its attractions: it is the condition of a man who knows why he does what he does, who knows the probable effects of his actions, who understands the forces of habit, emotion, and circumstance working upon him, and who is therefore able to avoid succumbing irrationally to their influence. . . .

Determinism, then, manifests itself in Gorge Eliot's works, not only in her analysis of how her weak characters degenerate, but equally in her description of the growth to maturity of her heroes and heroines. Determinism, for her, is at the root of education, and it therefore pervades her novels: in the constant interplay between the individual and society and the consequent elaborate portraits of, for example, the towns of St. Ogg's, Florence, and Middlemarch; in the instinctive and traditional shrewdness of Mrs. Poyser in *Adam Bede*, the Dodsons in *The Mill on the Floss*, and the Garths in *Middlemarch;* in the ineluctable reactions of their deeds upon the virtuous and villainous alike, in the traditionalism and fundamental conservatism of the strong-willed, powerful Adam Bede and Felix Holt, in her analysis of the debilitating effects of egoism and of the moral power of external goodness (as exemplified by Maggie's edition of *The Imitation of Christ* or the homiletic and tedious Daniel Deronda). And the insights and limitations of these specifically deterministic aspects of her work are linked — whether as cause or effect is not clear — to her vivid sense of introspective psychology, and social relations in a universe undirected by any supernatural being and therefore indifferent (as any later naturalist would have seen it) to the problems of humanity.

Whatever her philosophical conclusions might have been, George Eliot's handling of the problem was artistic rather than theoretical. Determinism was for her not a rigid and depressing system but an aspect of the world which she saw and dramatized. She was concerned with the practical rather than the philosophical consequences of her views. She knew that somehow evil was to be avoided and her interest was not in finding someone to blame for it — in discovering whether or not she had a philosophical right to blame anyone — but in averting it. For her, the man who excuses himself from responsibility because he was caused to do wrong is arguing beside the point. In *Adam Bede*, when Arthur Donnithorne suggests that a man is excusable if he succumbs to a severe temptation, Mr. Irwine replies with what must be George Eliot's own answer: "Our deeds carry their terrible consequences, quite apart from any fluctuation that went before — consequences that are hardly ever confined to ourselves. And it is best to fix our mind on that certainty, instead of considering what may be the elements of excuse for us" (Ch. 16). And Adam Bede takes a similar common sense position: "I see plain enough we shall never do it without a resolution, and that's enough for me" (Ch. 17).

Index

Titles of works by George Eliot are in capitals. Names of characters and places in George Eliot's works are indexed under the title of the work in which they appear.